LAND FICTIONS

A volume in the series
Cornell Series on Land: New Perspectives on Territory,
Development, and Environment
Edited by Wendy Wolford, Nancy Lee Peluso, and Michael Goldman

A list of titles in this series is available at
cornellpress.cornell.edu.

LAND FICTIONS

The Commodification of Land in City and Country

Edited by D. Asher Ghertner and Robert W. Lake

CORNELL UNIVERSITY PRESS   ITHACA AND LONDON

Copyright © 2021 by Cornell University

All rights reserved. Except for brief quotations in a review, this book, or parts thereof, must not be reproduced in any form without permission in writing from the publisher. For information, address Cornell University Press, Sage House, 512 East State Street, Ithaca, New York 14850. Visit our website at cornellpress.cornell.edu.

First published 2021 by Cornell University Press

Library of Congress Cataloging-in-Publication Data

Names: Ghertner, D. Asher, editor. | Lake, Robert W., 1946– editor.
Title: Land fictions : the commodification of land in city and country / edited by D. Asher Ghertner, Robert W. Lake.
Description: Ithaca [New York] : Cornell University Press, 2021. | Series: Cornell series on land : new perspectives on territory, development, and environment | Includes bibliographical references and index.
Identifiers: LCCN 2020021490 (print) | LCCN 2020021491 (ebook) | ISBN 9781501753732 (hardcover) | ISBN 9781501753961 (paperback) | ISBN 9781501753749 (ebook) | ISBN 9781501753756 (pdf)
Subjects: LCSH: Land use—Economic aspects. | Land use, Urban—Economic aspects. | Land use, Rural—Economic aspects.
Classification: LCC HD156 .L277 2021 (print) | LCC HD156 (ebook) | DDC 333.73—dc23
LC record available at https://lccn.loc.gov/2020021490
LC ebook record available at https://lccn.loc.gov/2020021491

Contents

Acknowledgments	vii
Introduction: Land Fictions and the Politics of Commodification in City and Country *D. Asher Ghertner and Robert W. Lake*	1
1. Fictitious but Not Utopian: Land Commodification and Dispossession in Rural India *Michael Levien*	26
2. Fictions of Surplus: Commodifying Public Land in Canada and the United Kingdom *Brett Christophers and Heather Whiteside*	44
3. Fictions of Safety: Defensive Storylines in Global Property Investment *Sarah Knuth*	62
4. Ground Fictions: Soil, Property, and Markets in the Colombian Conflict *Meghan L. Morris*	86
5. Narratives of Waste: The Fictions and Frictions of Land Commodification in Liberalizing India *Sai Balakrishnan*	104
6. Rental Fictions: Speculating in Rent-Regulated Housing in New York City *Benjamin F. Teresa*	124
7. The Fiction of Formalization: Titles, Concessions, and the Politics of Landownership in Cambodia *Michael B. Dwyer*	144
8. Regularization and the Fictions of Planning "Unauthorized Delhi" *D. Asher Ghertner*	161
9. The Sanctuary of the Collective: Contesting the Fictions of State-Led Land Commodification in Peri-Urban Guangzhou *Mi Shih*	180

10. Rights Gone Wrong on the City's Edge: The Fictions
and Fetishes of Land Documents in Ho Chi Minh City 200
Erik Harms

11. Where Materiality Meets Subjectivity: Locating the
Political in the Contested Fiction of Urban Land
in Camden, New Jersey 224
Robert W. Lake

12. The State of Land Grabs: Regulatory Fictions in
Ghana's "Small-Scale" Gold Mining Sector 243
Heidi Hausermann and David Ferring

Afterword: Land Fictions in the *Longue Durée* 257
Michael John Watts

Notes 271
References 283
Contributors 315
Index 319

Acknowledgments

This book began as the Eighth Biennial MaGrann Conference held in the Department of Geography at Rutgers University, New Brunswick, in May 2015. The contributors to the book first presented working papers there with the collective aim of exploring the geography and politics of land commodification from a comparative perspective. The original concept motivating the conference stemmed from the observation that urban and rural processes of dispossession were becoming increasingly intertwined, and that understanding land commodification—what Karl Polanyi famously called "the weirdest of all undertakings"—required bringing the agrarian question to town (see Chari 2004) and the urban question to the countryside. Recognizing the extent to which financial models, land marketization schemes, and development policy themselves were moving between city and country—such as the intersecting developmentalist calls to close agricultural yield gaps and capture urban rent gaps—our claim was that critical development studies and the respective urban and agrarian fields needed to take bolder steps to learn from each other's rich but stubbornly nonconversant traditions. Assembling a mix of urbanists and agrarianists with deep familiarity with land and environmental politics in diverse national contexts spanning the global North and South proved highly generative in identifying shared storylines driving the intensifying patterns of land commodification so many of us had been observing over years of fieldwork. By focusing on the powers of persuasion that go into narrating land as first-and-foremost an object of commodifiable potential, we played with Polanyi's concept of commodity fiction, operationalizing it not as an empirical condition—a "crude fiction," as Polanyi put it, *given* by or inherent within market society—but rather an active process of storytelling.

Jia-Ching Chen, Jo Guldi, Don Mitchell, Tania Murray Li, Malini Ranganathan, Melanie Somerville, and Wendy Wolford presented research at the initial Land Fictions conference. Although they were unable to contribute chapters to the book in the end, we would like to think that they remain part of the conversation. Michael Watts generously joined that conversation at a later date. We are grateful to Priti Narayan and Sangeeta Banerji, doctoral students in Rutgers Geography at the time, for helping select and invite participants, organize the conference sessions, and discuss the individual papers. We thank the Department of Geography at Rutgers for supporting the conference and especially the late Mark MaGrann for most generously creating the endowment that made that support possible. Mark attended the first day of the conference, and we have full faith that he would have found all kinds of ways to read the storylines explored in the present book into the New Jersey environments he knew so well. We also thank Rutgers Global, especially Rick Lee, for cosponsoring the event.

We are grateful to Wendy Wolford, Nancy Peluso, and Michael Goldman for endorsing the book and inviting it into the Land Series they coedit at Cornell University Press. We also thank Jim Lance and his editorial team at Cornell for masterfully shepherding the book forward. Preetha Mani provided cutting insights into the power of narrative, and Rick Schroeder helped encourage our thinking about rural and urban connections.

INTRODUCTION
Land Fictions and the Politics of Commodification in City and Country

D. Asher Ghertner and Robert W. Lake

> **What we call land is an element of nature inextricably interwoven with man's institutions. To isolate it and form a market for it was perhaps the weirdest of all the undertakings of our ancestors.**
> —Karl Polanyi, *The Great Transformation*

Just days after the 2016 US presidential election, president-elect Donald J. Trump met with three Indian real estate executives in Trump Tower, New York. In one of the first in what would be a long string of incidents raising ethical concerns about Trump's unwillingness to separate his real estate business from his political duties, commentators questioned why the engagement with the three property moguls preceded Trump meeting Indian prime minister Narendra Modi or indeed any other world leader, with the exception of Japanese prime minister Shinzo Abe.[1] Two of the executives who met Trump—Sagar and Atul Chordia—were building the first Trump Tower in India, located in Pune, Maharashtra, a booming city 150 kilometers from Mumbai.

The New York meeting was read in India as a sign that Trump's business in the country—already the Trump Organization's largest international market—would only grow in the wake of his electoral triumph (see Babar 2016). Unlike in other countries where the Trump brand has been less successful—reflected in canceled projects in Argentina, Azerbaijan, Brazil, and Georgia—Trump's Indian partners reported units selling approximately 30 percent per square foot above market rates (Venkataraman 2016). Kalpesh Mehta, the third executive at the November 2016 Trump Tower meeting and Trump's chief marketer in India, explained this trend by calling the Trump brand "a lead generator," providing wealthy Indians with the opportunity to become "members of the Trump family" (Abi-Habib and Lipton 2018).

Trump's international projects typically require that he neither make a capital contribution nor play a role in project design, planning, or delivery. The Trump name is the sole form of value addition he brings, ostensibly allowing luxury developers—who bear all the investment risk—to upcharge properties under the appearance of delivering a superior, globally recognizable product. The Trump Organization receives a cut of sales in exchange. Here, then, is a fiction of brand, of the creation of real estate value through the power of the name. In India, latent consumer desire for iconic status (see Brosius 2009) is coupled via Trump projects to a dogged pursuit of control and timeliness, qualities central to Trump-the-man's self-styling. In an opaque real estate market where multiyear delays and project cancelations are the norm, who better to "finish the deal"?

And yet "the deal"—itself built on the fictions of real estate brand as something more than mere citational embellishment and of a real-estate-tycoon-as-president divorcing his private business from international affairs—is underpinned by a still more fundamental set of land fictions. The Trump Tower in Pune, run by the Chordias, has been under investigation since 2011 on charges that the land on which it is located was fraudulently acquired. The story goes that a public charitable trust entered into a dispute in 1951 with the Pune collector—a senior bureaucrat responsible for land administration and tax collection (Khetan 2011). The trust subsequently petitioned the Bombay High Court to claim 3.26 acres of village land in Pune district, but the claim was rejected in 1964 (*The Hindu* 2011). While the case was still pending in 1988, the Pune collector stepped in to "settle" the dispute by offering the trust not merely 3.26 but 326 acres of land as a "soil grant entitlement." This rural–urban frontier, like other transitional spaces, operated as a zone of unmapping (Roy 2004; Tsing 2005) in which the transfer—and slipped decimal place—was facilitated by classifying the land as "vacant" despite the presence of a government jail and mental hospital and allocations for a future school, community center, and park (*Hindustan Times* 2014).

The fictions of vacant land and of land growing from 3.26 to 326 acres were facilitated by a further institutional fiction. Evidence suggests that the trust was actually a partnership between two real estate companies connected to powerful sugar families—the dominant agrarian bloc in western Maharashtra—that were seeking inroads into urban land markets at the time. Panchshil Realty, the Chordias' company, is one of these groups. The trust's fictional status as a charitable organization enabled the village land to be rezoned for commercial use, clearing the way for the Chordias to eventually build luxury hotels, corporate parks, and elite residential complexes—the most iconic example of which is the Trump Tower Pune (Khetan 2011; Joshi 2014).

The agrarian roots of this urban land grab begin with the Chordias' father, who was born into a family of wealthy sugar traders and became college friends with Sharad Pawar, one of the most influential politicians in Maharashtra whose career has been driven by his deep ties to the state's powerful "sugar constituency"

(Joshi 2014). Pawar is the long-time president of the Nationalist Congress Party (NCP) and was the chief minister of Maharashtra in 1988, the year the land transfer took place. The Pune collector who mutated the 3.26 acres into a 326-acre urban estate was later made a leader in Pawar's NCP, winning a seat in parliament before becoming the governor of the state of Sikkim in 2013 (Jaleel 2014). Pawar's daughter, now a leading NCP politician herself, was given an ownership stake in Panchshil at the time of the land transfer (Joshi 2014), exemplifying an "entangled agrarian–urban land system" (Balakrishnan 2018) wherein state politicians and those favorable to them capture windfall land increments through their oversight of land acquisition, allocation, and use (Baviskar 1980). As Balakrishnan (2018, 58–59) explains regarding the shifting political economy of land in contemporary Maharashtra, "Land is the new sugar," leading state politicians to "forge new pathways for the entry of their agrarian propertied constituents into booming real estate" markets.

The saga of an elite sugar family in Maharashtra leveraging agrarian political power to capture urban land and then linking up with an American real estate tycoon to construct a triumphant symbol of contemporary land fraud may seem like an exceptional story. Yet consider a strikingly similar episode situated 7,500 miles away in the bleak postindustrial landscape of Camden, New Jersey, a city beleaguered by massive deindustrialization and disinvestment that for decades has ranked among the poorest cities in the United States (Lake et al. 2007). This story, too, involves multiple intersections of state power, individual guile, and market-making technique in constructing distinct fictions facilitating land commodification.

In 2002, the New Jersey state legislature passed the Municipal Rehabilitation and Economic Recovery Act (MRERA), which placed Camden's municipal government under state control by creating the position of chief operating officer (COO) with administrative and budgetary authority over the locally elected mayor and city council. MRERA also established an Economic Recovery Board (ERB) armed with a $175 million fund to support a "strategic revitalization plan ... encouraging strategic land assembly, site preparation, and infill development." In addition, the statute authorized the Camden Redevelopment Agency (CRA) to employ eminent domain to acquire private property in the city for land redevelopment.

Within two years of MRERA's adoption, the entire land area within Camden's municipal boundaries was included under proposed redevelopment plans worth a combined $8 billion.[2] The redevelopment plans contained long lists of land parcels, many still occupied, slated to be acquired through eminent domain, raising the prospect of displacing more than 10 percent of Camden's resident population. Yet despite the specter of large-scale displacement, proponents presented the land redevelopment strategy as a public boon and source of hope, a means of making this "weak market city" into a site for a new type of (tax-paying) community. Elected officials privy to the full redevelopment vision spun this tale of real estate magic through repeated public statements, infusing public conversations with an optimism that positive change might finally have come to Camden. A local newspaper announced that a "Dramatic Era of Rebirth Energizes Hope-Filled City" (*Courier-Post*, quoted in Gillette 2005, xiii), articulating the hope that MRERA's takeover represented "the greatest potential for the long-awaited renaissance of [the] city that began life more than three centuries ago" (Riordan 2005). Here was the fiction of a city reborn, where a shot of financial stimulus, mixed with a dose of neighborhood demolition, and chased with corporate tax breaks would rejuvenate the slumping urban body.

The sponsor of the MRERA statute in the state legislature was State Senator Wayne R. Bryant, representing Camden in the Fifth Legislative District covering south Jersey. Bryant had served continuously in the New Jersey General Assembly and then the State Senate from 1982 to 2008. While chairman of the Senate Budget and Appropriations Committee in the later years, he wielded vast power over state expenditures, which he used both to spin the promise of real estate driven regeneration and to steer public money to himself and his family. In 2005, for example, the CRA issued a $270,000 no-bid contract to Bryant's law firm to represent the city in displacing residents through eminent domain proceedings. When the sole dissenting member of the city council challenged the contract, the council obtained a letter from the city attorney, Lewis Wilson—himself with close financial ties to Bryant family business—dismissing the complaint (*Courier-Post* 2005d). When the CRA issued an $11 million contract for housing construction to a local builder for the redevelopment of Camden's Cramer Hill neighborhood, it was discovered that the company's vice president in charge of the project had previously worked as an attorney in Bryant's firm (*Philadelphia Inquirer* 2005; *Courier-Post* 2005c). A year later, in September 2006, Bryant cast the deciding vote in the New Jersey senate to allocate $1 million to the city of Camden "as a reserve for expenses," which included payments to Bryant's firm for defending the CRA from lawsuits filed by residents protesting the Cramer Hill redevelopment plan that threatened to displace more than a thousand families from the predominantly Hispanic neighborhood (*Courier-Post* 2006b; *Star-Ledger* 2006). Despite increasingly strident neighborhood opposition, Governor James McGreevey credited the Cramer Hill project with placing Camden "on the verge of an explosive, dynamic renewal" that would more than double the city's annual property tax revenues (Lyne 2004). The fiction of hidden housing demand—and the implicit claim that mass displacement served the public interest—had become almost unquestionable.

Following a two-year federal investigation, Bryant was charged in March 2007 with a twenty-count indictment alleging a pattern of bribery and fraud associated with the allocation of public funds over which Bryant exerted control (*Philadelphia Inquirer* 2007; *New York Times* 2007). The indictment alleged that Bryant had held several no-show jobs—for which he received a salary but did little or no actual work—in Camden-based institutions that subsequently received substantial allocations of public funds under Bryant's control (US Department of Justice 2008). Among other charges, the indictment held that Bryant was paid $38,000 annually "to lobby himself" by the University of Medicine and Dentistry, which then received $12.8 million in state funds over three years. He also earned $134,000 as an adjunct lecturer at the Rutgers University School of Law, which garnered $11 million from the ERB to expand its Camden campus. The indictment calculated that, including his $49,000 salary as state senator, Bryant's annual income averaged $643,000 between 2003 and 2006, which also produced a three-fold increase in his public pension eligibility on his retirement.

Bryant was convicted on all counts in November 2008, stripped of his public pension, and sentenced to a four-year prison term, "a fall of Shakespearean proportions" (*Star-Ledger* 2008). While still serving his prison sentence, Bryant was indicted a second time on charges stemming from city contracts issued for the $1.2 billion Cramer Hill redevelopment project, and neither that project nor any of the land redevelopment plans proposed under MRERA in Camden ever came to fruition.

The Commodity Fiction of Land

Donald Trump's luxury development in Pune was aggressively global, in contrast to the local scale of Wayne Bryant's land deals in Camden. Pune, a booming metropolis on the leading edge of India's urban revolution (Ghertner 2014), differs markedly from Camden's eighty thousand population and marginal identity at the outer fringe of metropolitan New Jersey. And yet, common to both stories are hyperintense and destabilizing transformations of land's economic, political, legal, cultural, and social status—rapidly developing in the case of Pune and rapidly de- and redeveloping in Camden. Both stories contain many of the ingredients found in global narratives of what has variously been called land grabbing (Perry 2013; Wolford et al. 2013; Steel et al. 2017), the new enclosures (White et al. 2013; Christophers 2018), speculative urbanism (Goldman 2011; Shin and Kim 2016; Watson 2014), or simply land commodification—what Karl Polanyi (2001 [1944], 187) described as "separating land from man [sic] . . . to satisfy the requirements of the real-estate market."[3] The story of local elites manipulating regulatory frameworks, capturing state institutions, and partnering with development outfits to create internationally legible real estate portfolios, often via violent processes of dispossession, is indeed a defining political-economic trend of our times (Harvey 2003; Hall 2011; Shatkin 2017). Modify some of the legal fictions deployed, change a character type here or there, rewrite the script to focus, perhaps, on resource extraction or coastal access or public land concessions, as the case may be, then shake and stir, and you have the master recipe for the cocktail of land commodification being applied across much of the so-called emerging market world—whether located in newly urbanizing agrarian peripheries or in disinvested and recently rediscovered urban centers straddling the far side of the rent gap (Smith et al. 2001).

This book explores the "land fictions" underpinning this variable land commodification recipe, without presuming that the cocktail of commodified outcomes it produces follows a single storyline or shares a fixed cast of characters. Refusing the presumption that land commodification is inevitable or that marketization or neoliberalization are inexorable forces, the contributors to this volume emphasize the continuous work of legal, regulatory, and narrative fictions that go into the making of land as a commodity and that enact and sustain the property relations that underpin linked value projects. This involves following the stories spun by land aggregators, developers, financiers, and marketers in all their guises about the transformational powers of land as real estate; it involves rooting these situated narratives in wider institutionalized storylines about the social function and organization of property; and it involves tying these storylines into globally circulating market discourses that treat land as an element of industry, a financial asset, or a potential resource.

To open up the narratives, storylines, and discourses that govern the commodity world of land, we take as our starting point Karl Polanyi's classic argument about the commodity fiction underpinning what he termed market society, by which he meant a political-economic order in which social life is organized to meet the pecuniary, ideological, and administrative needs of a so-called self-regulating market. Writing in the waning days of World War II (with an eye toward influencing the Bretton Woods Conference where world leaders would assemble to organize a postwar global financial architecture), Polanyi (2001 [1944], 76) was deeply concerned about the still-pervasive influence of economic liberalism, stubborn adherence to which, he argued, had dragged the world into two great wars and, he warned, threatened nothing less than "the demolition of society." His book, *The Great Transformation*, sought to deliver a death knell to "the utopian premise" of the self-regulating market. At the heart of this utopianism, he argued, is the commodity fiction, which, simply put, is the presumption in market society that land, labor, and money—what Polanyi (2001 [1944], 75) called "essential elements of industry"—constitute "fictitious commodities" that, while not in their original form produced for purposes of production and exchange, are transmuted into commodity form in order to be bought and sold under the control of nothing more than the price mechanism.[4] As Polanyi explained,

> Labor is only another name for a human activity which goes with life itself, which in its turn is not produced for sale but for entirely different reasons, nor can that activity be detached from the rest of life, be stored or mobilized; land is only another name for nature, which is not produced by man; actual money, finally, is merely a token of purchasing power which, as a rule, is not produced at all. (Polanyi 2001 [1944], 75)

While the commodity description of land, labor, and money is hence entirely fictitious, Polanyi tells us,

> It is with the help of this fiction that the actual markets for labor, land, and money are organized; these are being actually bought and sold on the market.... The commodity fiction, therefore, supplies a vital organizing principle in regard to the whole of society affecting almost all its institutions in the most varied way, namely, the principle according to which no arrangement or behavior should be allowed to exist that might prevent the actual functioning of the market mechanism on the lines of the commodity fiction. (ibid.)

The commodity fiction, Polanyi held, underpins both market liberalism's seductive ideological durability—what he called "the marketing mind," defined by an "ingrained habit of thought peculiar" to market forms of economy—as well as its destructive social and environmental effects (Polanyi 1977, 9; see also Polanyi 2002 [1947]). A key contribution of Polanyi's thinking is thus to disabuse us—those of a "marketing mind"—of the economism that narrowly equates all economy with the market or presumes that all economic activities follow the supposed "law" of supply and demand.[5]

The commodity fiction, in this sense, is an example of what Haraway (1991, 135) calls a regulatory fiction, or a set of idealized and reified norms governing social conventions and ways of being. Less a story with questionable or unverifiable truth conditions or a compelling narrative whose social effectiveness is based on its ability to capture an audience, fiction here refers to the terms through which categories of being and codes of conduct become internalized as the routinized basis for social action. As Butler (1990, 33) puts it, regulatory fictions operate as "a set of repeated acts within a highly rigid regulatory frame that congeal over time to produce the appearance of substance, of a natural sort of being." While often established through historical acts of violence (Mitchell 2002;

Thompson 1975; Watts 1983), their routinization gives these fictions the appearance of necessity and permanence, morphing variable and contextual social history into ontological inevitability, as when submission to the wage relation is perceived not as submission at all but simply and "naturally" the way a modern subject earns a living (or doesn't) or when land commodification is treated as a simple expression of economic reason rather than, as Polanyi (2001 [1944], 178) put it, as "the weirdest of all the undertakings of our ancestors."

Recognition of the commodity fiction thus impels us to reveal and explain the constitutive fictions by which various nonmarket functions of land, labor, and money become imaginatively and practically stripped away, reducing complex social and natural systems to "elements of industry" or mere objects of exchange. It forces us to ask how "land" is reduced to a discrete, measurable, and marketable object: a delimited and bounded acreage with biophysical, agroclimatic, and locational characteristics that can be benchmarked, compared with other land objects, priced, alienated, and transferred from one user to another. Polanyi insists that what we call land in market society assumes its character—as property, as object to be possessed and exchanged, as source of profit, or as a discrete set of resource characteristics or ecosystem functions (Robertson 2012)—through historically and geographically specific processes. As Campanile (2016, 365) explains it, land, once commodified, "is not an inert thing of independent material existence, but a conceptual and social relation produced through the *appropriation* of material existence. Land is, therefore, an historical and geographical invention fundamentally tied to economy and power."

The Trump Pune and Camden land stories help elucidate the historical and geographical specificity of the social relation that is "land." In the case of rural Maharashtra, the Land Ceiling Act of 1961 empowered the state to redistribute surplus land so as to maximize its "full and efficient use for agriculture." Wastage in Maharashtra, as in India as a whole, was defined in the developmentalist phase in which the Land Ceiling Act was implemented in terms of agricultural yield. The narrative of land development at the time was one of minimizing lost agricultural potential through transferring vacant or underutilized land to productive agriculture.[6] Moderately successful land reform efforts combined with the influence of a powerful bloc of agrarian elites to produce a postcolonial land dispensation in which urban economic surpluses from the state's advanced industrial sector were used to subsidize rural development—that is, to put land to agricultural use (Baviskar 1980). An expensive irrigation infrastructure, subsidized inputs, and price supports led the western part of the state, where Pune is located, to attain some of the highest crop yields in India, driving Maharashtra to become the highest sugar-producing state, which in turn drove India to become the world's second-largest sugar producer (after Brazil) (Balasaheb 2013, 5). The promise of land-as-agricultural-yield-maximizing was clearly being advanced. Maharashtra's sugar fields were valuable, sucking up 60 percent of the state's irrigation supply (ibid.), and highly valued, as reflected in relatively high rural land prices and sustained state investment in crop capitalism.

However, these indicators of value—and the agrarian-urban relations they sustained—have been largely swept away as past land uses have been actively devalued and as urban expansion and infrastructure-driven growth have turned attention toward newly emerging urban rent gaps forming as peri-urban, exurban, and even outright rural land has been targeted for special economic zones, infrastructure corridors, smart cities, and private townships (Balakrishnan, this volume; Levien, this volume; Parikh 2015), making Trump's entrance just one recent example of the urbanization of land rent nationally (Chakravorty 2013, 26). The narrative of land as source of agricultural production has now given way to land as a financial instrument for rent generation, a pattern of "declining rurality, booming peripheries" (Anwar 2018) now globally ascendant.[7] Land today, in other words, is not what it used to be: yesterday's value is today's waste; yesterday's "highest and best use" is today's "vacant" or "underutilized;" yesterday's public land is today's surplus; yesterday's agriculture is today's "not-yet-urban."

Camden's recent land fictions reflect a postindustrial rather than an agrarian transition. For half a century through World War II, Camden served as a leading US manufacturing hub. The Campbell Soup company located there in 1869 to gain access to south Jersey's rich agricultural produce (Sidorick 2009). RCA Victor, established in 1901, chose Camden as the site of its electronics assembly plant to exploit the surplus female agricultural labor in the region (Cowie 1999). With a population that peaked at 125,000 in 1950, Camden touted itself as "the city that works" (Gillette 2005), and local economic vigor became synonymous with the growth of manufacturing employment supported by public services and infrastructure provision. But Camden lost 157,000 manufacturing jobs between 1950 and 1970 as industry fled in search of low-cost, nonunion labor (Gillette 2005), plunging the city into economic decline. The city's inability to fund municipal operations through local property tax revenues was labeled a "structural deficit" requiring annual state appropriations of more than $35 million to balance the budget (The Annie E. Casey Foundation 2001). Under these circumstances, Camden's land became redefined from a site for industrial commodity production to a marketable commodity in its own right, a commodity that promised to solve the mounting structural deficit through increased property taxes. The resident population was similarly reimagined as a parasitic drain on public resources rather than an entitled citizenry or productive labor force. The solution, according to MRERA, was clear: "In order to ensure the long-term economic viability (of Camden), it is critical that the Legislature encourage . . .

the production of market-rate housing ... so as to expand the local tax base. ..... It is incumbent upon the State to take exceptional measures ... to strategically invest those sums of money necessary in order to assure ... long-term financial viability." In Camden, as in Pune, land is defined based on the rent it can generate—its capacity to realize value through real estate—and not on alternative social valuations such as might be pursued through agrarian developmentalism in India or spatial Keynesianism in the United States.[8]

Reading Land's Fictions

As Raymond Williams (1973) explains in his magisterial *The Country and the City*, the idea of producing value in land was invented, not found. With regard to the English feudal estate, he shows how, through the sixteenth and seventeen centuries, it "passed from being regarded as an inheritance, carrying such and such income, to being calculated as an opportunity for investment, carrying greatly increased returns. In this development," Williams observes, "an ideology of improvement—of a transformed and regulated land—became significant and directive." But not without its social costs, he concludes, because "social relations which stood in the way of this kind of modernization were then steadily and at times ruthlessly broken down" (Williams 1973, 60–61). Williams's use of contemporaneous literary fiction to illustrate the transformations of city and country offers a way to think about the narrative conventions (e.g., the pastoral and counterpastoral, the new metropolis), images and characters (e.g., the yeoman, the rural idyll, the avaricious estate-owner), and plotlines (e.g., cities of darkness [as in Dickens] or the creation of pleasing agrarian prospects [as in Austen]) through which such transformations are imagined, enacted, justified, and contested.

Land Fictions similarly attends to the social stories used to narrate the commodified reinventions of land and the implicit forms of land valuation such stories help secure. The literary and social imaginary of England as a "small-holder republic," in which the cultural stability of the nation rests on the economic security of a society of land owners (Williams 1973, 44), is but one example of how story and myth undergird historic property relations. Unlike Williams, whose epochal project was necessarily historical through its reconstruction of the lived experience—the "structures of feeling"—of a community that lived through rural–urban change, our project is contemporary and far more modest. The fictions explored in the chapters that follow are not those of high literature. They are hence not yet canonized, making them more open to contestation, not having been fully "socially ratified," to use Williams's language for ideological formations, into popular consciousness. The land fictions examined in this book are thus less reflections of past country–city relations than (re)enactments of contemporary ones. They are contested stories in the making. Studying how land markets are made as stories, we suggest, is instructive for understanding their social effectiveness as well as their vulnerability. Building a less-commodified world, defending a politics of the commons, or contesting mass displacement and the environmental degradation associated with planetary urbanization and global land grabbing require telling better stories, but also being able to tell what makes stories travel and stick. This is our collective task.

The fictions we examine in this volume might be thought in relation to the now substantial body of work on economization, which focuses on the rules and instruments of market making (Çalışkan and Callon 2009, 2010) or what Li 2014a) calls the techniques of "rendering land investable." By treating land as "a provisional assemblage of heterogeneous elements including material substances, technologies, discourses and practices" (Li 2014a, 589), this approach understands land as commodity to be made up through expert techniques of abstraction, simplification, and standardization (Richardson and Weszkalnys 2014) that allow land's "lumpy" material specificities to be reduced to a form of fungible "resourceness" governable by market signals. While all processes of commodification operate through such market-making tools, these tools are uniquely significant in the case of land since it cannot move as other commodities can. As Harvey (2007 [1982]: 367) writes, "What is bought and sold is not the land, but title to the ground-rent yielded by it. . . . The buyer acquires a claim upon anticipated future revenues," which is represented as shares or other securities. Land hence must be figured into paper or electronic documents that can be transferred through the legal and regulatory frameworks governing ownership. Economization, in this sense, is a directly inscriptive process oriented toward producing a market of representations that facilitate the generation of liquidity—"the mobility of the property of securities" (Corpataux et al. 2009, 318)—from a solid, immovable surface.

The influential science-studies approach to studying these techniques focuses on the "dominant role of materialities and economic knowledges in processes of market-making" (Çalışkan and Callon 2009, 369; Callon 1998). With a trained "attentiveness to things and materialities" (Çalışkan and Callon 2009, 384), this approach emphasizes market technics over market rhetorics, though, focusing on the material technologies—boundary markers, land surveys, tax ledgers, deeds of ownership—that perform markets through their deployment and use. As Visse (2017, 188) puts it, this work "pays more attention to how material changes of the object itself . . . and wider economic and technological change affect the value of resources." Li (2014a, 592), for example, focuses on "technologies to make land productive, metrics to adjudicate between more and less 'efficient' uses, and inscription devices that make land into a resource for different actors." Technique, or what Callon (1998) calls "economization activities," is hence seen as a series of rational procedures of rule setting, standardization, calculation, and benchmarking that produce a coherent field of scientific thought (Mitchell 2005)—economics—to which rhetorical flourish, tales of social betterment, and marketing hype are often treated as a residual addendum.

While there is a rhetorical or "persuasive element" (Li 2014a; Blomley 2007) to these material practices, rhetoric as such is often left as the overdetermined remainder or speculative void that fills the gap between market-making techniques and actual consumer and market behavior. The inventiveness and captivating powers of a compelling story, in other words, too often are missed in the focus on material technique. In expanding and developing this approach, this book dwells on the powers of rhetoric and discourse as narrative techniques of "inventing" land as commodity. Among these techniques are the arts of projecting visions of a future, narrating a story, drawing the interest of an audience, constituting appropriate subjects, and establishing the institutional means to translate stories into social realities. As Searle (2018, 528) points out, to appropriate future rents, capitalists must not just devise means of trading land but also conjure the possibility of those rents; they must create not just an asset class (e.g., luxury housing or surplus government land) but also construct a plausible story of a future revenue stream from it. This involves delivering PowerPoint presentations, reciting tales of great land deals and eager buyers, designing glossy brochures, and whispering inside scoops about getting rich quick or finding a dream home.

The land fictions thus produced are not epiphenomenal or simply cultural expressions of somehow more fundamental political-economic processes, nor are they merely the rhetorical flourishes added to market-making techniques such as valuation estimates, price indexes, yield curves, cost-benefit analyses, profit projections, or other expert technical operations. Yield curves, as representations of future interest rates and borrowing risk, are of course stories (Zaloom 2009), just as valuation estimates narrate conditions under which profit can be extracted. All commodity objects are a mix of materiality and semiotic meaning, invoking a range of both potential uses and potential exchange values, and the diverse discourses that attach to them work on these potentials to form value projects (see Agha 2011). Yet, other kinds of stories—superficially more "cultural" to the extent that they intertextually engage local histories, signifiers of value, and indexes of social differentiation—also figure in commodity worlds, working on, with, or against techniques of economization. As Watts (2014) reminds us, a view of new frontiers of accumulation is incomplete without consideration of its representational constitution, or formation through a distinct repertoire of cultural productions, stories, and often spectacularized images.

Land fictions, in other words, cannot be reduced to market technics; such technics, rather, work through and are productive of their own rhetorics of the future. As Rose (1994, 27) argues, any given "property regime needs the rhetorical mode of narrative and storytelling." De Boeck (2011, 278), for example, describing "the spectral fantasy" animating popular longing for a better Kinshasa, explains how a strong story can escape "standard forms of classification and accumulation, if only because it conjures up the marvelous through its appeal to the imagination." We thus maintain that these fictions—whether small and localized, such as the story of a fraudulent "soil grant entitlement," or large and expansive, such as the promise of a global brand—are productive and even performative of so-called "fundamental" political-economic processes. As Searle (2016, 81) puts it, "Coordination among landowners and developers producing new landscapes for capital accumulation comes not from land markets—since those are being transformed—but from shared stories.... Stories provide signals for the production of land and property markets." Campbell (2015, 96–97) describes the "conjuring of property" on Amazonia's capitalist frontier as a narrative process driven by "often-repeated fables of founding settlements, establishing towns, or taming the wilderness." The rent gaps emerging on newly urbanizing lands—whether in peri-urban Pune or redeveloping Camden—are similarly premised on speculative fictions about who will potentially occupy these previously peripheral territories and what developers, investors, and state agents can do to enact the spatial transformations and conjured futures necessary to secure higher rents.

In speculative real estate projects the world over, luxury estates are built without luxury occupants already in place (De Boeck 2011; Shatkin 2017; Woodworth and Wallace 2017), and private townships are approved before water access or environmental clearance is granted (Gururani 2013; Watson 2015). As Searle (2016, 51) again notes, "High land prices precede discernable economic activities and demand; colorful brochures describe buildings which, in present form, are muddy lots; and predictions of India's glorious globally integrated future coincide with its impoverished present." The displacement of thousands of households from Camden's Cramer Hill neighborhood was rendered legitimate by the proffered vision of a luxury housing estate, marina, and golf course to be populated by an as-yet unidentified but eagerly imagined reservoir of pent-up demand. Without a cast of characters imagined as ready and able to purchase the properties being developed, and without a narrative of a rising class of potential homeowners who can (and are willing to) pay for the transformation of so-called "underused" land into urban real estate, the story of endogenous growth collapses, and the speculative projection of a future consumer society paying elevated urban rents to live in dense apartment buildings—"the global flat"—is undermined (Ghertner 2015a). Character, sequence, plot, chronotope, image—the basic elements of narrative—come together to make markets, recruiting audiences, pulling them into a shared presentation of event, sequence, and role, and thereby organizing action in the here and now in seductive anticipation of the narrated future. "Follow along," the narrative commands, "the story is a good one; the future is at hand!"

While *Land Fictions* maintains the broad Polanyian focus on the social violence necessitated by liberal drives to disembed land from the social world of which it is a part, its contributing authors adopt a more performative approach to fiction than Polanyi. They do so by interrogating what it means for land to function as a fiction by attending to the special character of *land's fictions*, or the social stories through which land is narrated as a commodity to produce particular political-economic effects. This means treating fictitiousness as a social relation, a tool of invention, and an ideological project, not simply as an empirical condition or pregiven effect of land's status as a noncommodity-nonetheless-treated-as-commodity. This departure from empiricism is of course the very terrain of literary studies, which considers fiction not as a way of representing reality but rather a way of signifying a set of relations with the "real." While Polanyi is of course correct that land is not something materially given for the purpose of sale, the student of processes of signification does not dwell solely on the problem of verification/falsification and understands the challenge of transforming lived relations with land to require more than revealing a *false* conception of what land is. Fiction, like ideology, Eagleton (1979, 65) writes, is "a complex encodement of certain 'lived' relations to the real which may be neither verified nor falsified;" its power comes, in other words, not from its referentiality to the real (which may be more or less "true") but in its significatory power to invest energies, desires, or emotions in the relation to the real that it frames, creating conventions or expectations about how that relation *should be*.

The book's chapters follow this approach to the expressive or performative power of fiction by noting how land fictions often become powerful through their iterability, or their capacity to build up a citational structure in which the intermediate steps of market making—land alienation, the granting of an environmental clearance, reallocating water rights, pooling scattered properties into a shared asset class—appear inevitable in light of the expected realization of the cited conclusions. If a real estate project begins before environmental clearance is granted, then developing a narrative of environmental proceduralism—of a pro forma sequence of bureaucratic steps—can make a potentially controversial project's approval appear routine. The larger the audience of susceptible listeners and the tighter the iterative sequence of transitive presumptions that A (rural, underdeveloped, waste, low density) will become B (urban, developed, valuable, high density), the less likely disruption is to take place. In other words, when the storyline anticipates progress in the plot, any potential disruption will appear irregular, a denial of progress, an aberration to be corrected so as to get the story back on track. The very language of "emerging market" or "undercapitalized resource" or "agro-ecological potential" signals an anticipated and prefigurative transition—it tells us about a future relation to land. This is the nature of regulatory fictions, where iterability establishes a citational structure of presumed outcomes—the future, as Appadurai (2013) puts it, as cultural fact.

Legal fictions form an additional tool for constructing the commodity fiction of land. As suggested by Riles's (2011, 175) anthropological research on financial markets, legal fictions have a legitimating function similar to broad regulatory fictions but operate as "more tool than text," enacting the realities they purport to represent. A defining feature of legal fictions is that they are widely understood to be untrue—such as the fiction that a corporation is a person—and yet are adopted as operating principles that become real in their consequences. Riles explores the legal fiction of collateral in detail, showing how it operates via the presumption that the collateral taker has an unfettered right to repledge the asset to which it is given possession. What is effective about this fiction is not its truthfulness, given that there actually is no inherent ability to repledge except under the special condition of nonpayment, but rather its ability to enable actors to agree on a course of action in the future. Such fictions organize fields of action, helping disparate actors gain confidence in the stability of market-bureaucratic procedures and providing a secure platform for collaboration based on conventions of exchange. In this sense, legal fictions are nonrepresentational, lacking particular meaning or a strong narrative dimension, making them "more like machines than stories" such that "the truth or falsity of its content is really beside the point," and "what matters rather is what possibilities for action it opens up or forecloses" (ibid.).

While a legal fiction operates as a contractual instrument tying bounded parties together, the commodity fiction has a similar function, although operating in this case as a societywide regulatory arrangement. This sense of fiction as a pact organizing action through an agreed-on social convention thus helps turn our attention to the collective, social, contract–like practices in which we, as market participants, agree to act "as if" land is a commodity each time we acknowledge a boundary marker or make a rent payment (see Rose 1994), even though we know it is not. In addition to the machinelike character of legal fictions, the contributors to this book also attend to the representational and directly meaning-making land fictions that shape conditions of the future through formal elements of narrative comprising a sequence of actions—the content of the story—and the discursive presentation of those actions (see Culler 2001, 189). The relative truthfulness—or at least the appearance of fidelity to reality—of the land fictions in question hence matters even if it is not the only thing that matters. The fiction that a 3.26 acre "soil grant entitlement" could become a 326-acre speculative real estate zone, for example, depended precisely on the presumed truthfulness of the developer's legal claim to ownership. That ownership of apartments in the Trump Tower may make one a "member of the Trump family" or imbue that owner with a prestigious social persona is a major part of an investor's willingness to pay for brand iconicity. New Jersey voters' willingness to accept mass displacement in Camden was informed by a faith that private land development would indeed fill public coffers.

The focus on regulatory, legal, and narrative fictions adopted in this book differs from critical political-economic analyses that disregard the fictions of market makers as mere rationalizations or fetishizations of market power. Dismissing the stories told by the "masters of finance," for example, Harvey (2013, 146) writes that "the bankers and financiers are, in some ways, the very last people to trust, not because they are fraudsters and liars (even though some of them patently are), but because they are likely prisoners of their own mystifications and fetishistic understandings." Harvey's remark builds on Marx's (1981 [1894], 969) observation in volume 3 of *Capital* that "it is an enchanted, perverted, topsy-turvy world, in which Monsieur le Capital and Madame la Terre do their ghost-walking as social characters and at the same time directly as mere things." Aligned with the broader revelatory impulse of critical political economy that aims to avoid the mystifying narratives of capital, Harvey is of course right that it is only in a mystified (i.e., commodified) world that capital and land occupy the role of social characters in a drama and are not recognized as mere objects directed by the social (class) interests behind the stage. Given that such a perverted world is the one in which we live, however, we insist that tracing these objects' scripting as characters is essential for understanding how their commodity form *appears* as the product of "overwhelming natural laws that irresistibly enforce their will" (Marx 1981 [1894], 969).

Just as it is imperative, as Marx pointed out, to explain not just how value is generated in production but also how value is realized in the social play of the market (Harvey 2014, 78), so, too, is it useful to understand how the commodity form of land is realized in the ongoing social drama of market making. Value realization in land projects, we argue, depends precisely on the stimulation of wants and desires via carefully scripted narratives of land's fictional powers—be they of prestige zip codes or a vineyard's *terroir*. Accounting for narrative is thus particularly urgent precisely because of how productive capital's "mystifying powers" can be in, for example, sustaining the fiction that privatization of state land saves the tax-paying public from an undue debt burden (Christophers and

Whiteside, this volume), the story that land is a "safe asset" because of its material fixity (Knuth, this volume), or the logic that driving residents of informal settlements into market housing will ensure their emergence as modern, rights-bearing subjects (Harms, this volume; Shih, this volume). The approach of this book, therefore, represents a shift from an abstract focus on the creation of value in production to the prior requirement for performing the commodity fictions that enable production in a market economy and the subsequent need to realize that value through the stimulation of demand.

What holds together the multiple regulatory, legal, and narrative land fictions we explore, then, is their function as value projects that evoke and emphasize particular commodity registers of land and draw in willing subjects seeking to remake the world through the modified relationships and roles they promise to enact. Land fictions hence invent not just land qua commodity but land as a particularly socially indexed commodity, one that promises to transform its uses and hence its users in ways that align with desirable social imaginaries of value. So, speculative urban real estate projects operate through a fiction of forever rising rents (see Teresa, this volume) but also by narrating a set of transformed social roles: luxury housing promises to generate a class of luxury consumers or "world-class citizens" willing and able to pay for and properly occupy globally recognizable commodity housing; those buyers are narratively linked to developers and financiers in debt relations that offer predictable streams of rent and conditions of obligation; and these buyer-seller-lender relations further narrate a reformulated social condition wherein speculative real estate investment reshapes the nation from "developing" to "developed" or transforms the declining, postindustrial city into a middle-class mecca (see Lake, this volume). Fictions of closing agricultural yield gaps, a major developmental aim of World Bank land projects, similarly mobilize commodity registers of land to index improved social roles and relationships. In this scenario, "underproducing" farms and their associated underproducing farmers located in underproducing countries are narrated as available through land deals for technological input and financial assistance (see Dwyer, this volume), as a result of which yields are narrated as set to improve, poorer nations as primed to feed their hungry, and investors as sure to profit. Deininger and Byerlee (2011, 83) explain in their influential World Bank report, *Rising Global Interest in Farmland*, for example, that "adopting a commodity perspective" helps "identify how private investment in agriculture—badly needed in many circumstances—can improve smallholder productivity as a central pillar of a pro-poor development strategy." Land deals related to mineral extraction similarly rest on implicit stories of modernization's power to transform subjects and remake society, as Hausermann and Ferring (this volume) show of the presumed skills transfer associated with foreign investment in Ghana's gold reserves.

As value projects, land fictions invite forms of uptake but because they are but projects, they may or may not be effective in securing the forms of uptake they offer. Their fictitiousness hence lies in their narration of certainty when the promised transformations are anything but sure. While the fiction of Camden's property-driven revitalization generated windfall profits for Bryant and his associates, the resistance to displacement by neighborhood residents led the Cramer Hill scheme to flop, making visible the castle in the sky it could only be, but also leaving New Jersey taxpayers to foot the bill. While Trump Tower Pune is up and running, Trump's earlier attempted foray into India—a proposed Trump Tower Mumbai—failed due to a lack of consumer willingness to pay above Mumbai's already inflated luxury housing prices. Land fictions thus often fail, as the social powers ascribed to land commodification—closing the urban rent or agricultural yield gap, becoming a member of the Trump family, feeding the hungry, or generating public revenue—depend on a transformation of social relations that the commodity form alone can never wholly deliver and at times can undermine.

The variability of the stories explored in the chapters that follow thus attest to the fragility and provisionality of even the most convincing land fictions, echoing the philosopher MacIntyre's (2007, 215) observation that "at any given point in an enacted dramatic narrative we do not know what will happen next." These stories train analytical attention on cases in which transformative fictions succeed in their objectives and others in which fictions fail, and with what costs. Polanyi's concept of the "double movement," coupling the onward march of markets with society's protective countermovements, is useful for opening up the politics of commodification to contestation and debate (Block 2016; see Lake, this volume). The form of the double movement in any particular instance, however, is both dependent on and formative of social relations rather than simply aligning with already determined class interests (Balakrishnan, this volume). In Polanyi's (2001 [1944], 163) words, "The process in question may decide about the existence of . . . class itself." The chapters that follow attend to how subjects are narrated within commodity worlds, the relative positions they adopt or reject in sustaining or challenging those worlds, and the manner in which coherent narrative projections of class interest or subject position receive variable uptake across disparate settings.

Comparative Land Fictions

When Polanyi described the great commodity fiction of "separating land from man . . . to satisfy the requirements of the real-estate market" (2001 [1944], 187), he used a comparative analogy between "the colonial situation today and that of

Western Europe a century or two ago." Whereas the process of commercializing land, ripping it out of its feudal ties, and rendering it alienable took place over centuries in the West, it required just "a few years or decades" in the colonies. While acknowledging these differences between historical epochs, metropole and colony, city and country, Polanyi noted that, across widely disparate contexts, what he called the "weird" undertaking of commodifying land required that local lifeworlds be "shattered" (2001 [1944], 188) and new forms of market rationality be imposed in their place.

Despite Polanyi's insistence that land commodification be studied comparatively over time, across North and South, and between the city and countryside, contemporary scholarship on land markets tends to reinforce these very North-South and urban-rural binaries. The vast urban literatures on gentrification and the right to the city, for example, evidence a striking silence on questions of customary use, legal pluralism, or the political economy of tenure, despite the persistence in much of the urban world of nonprivatized and "intermediate" tenure regimes such as urban villages, squatter settlements, auto-constructed and unauthorized neighborhoods, state-owned land, community land trusts, and various commons and wastelands (Benjamin and Raman 2011; Abasa et al. 2012; Ghertner 2015b; Kinder 2016). Similarly, the now substantial agrarian literature on rural land grabbing and speculation takes little from the writing on spatial relegation, informality, or spatial justice, despite the emergence in villages and peri-urban areas of new forms of exclusion produced through differential insertion into urban economies and differential access to urban rents and legal protections (Hsing 2010; Levien 2018; Ghertner, this volume; Harms, this volume). Within both critical urban studies and critical agrarian studies, comparative insights into how tools of land commodification, instruments of financialization, or forms of dispossession move between North and South are rare—although not nonexistent (e.g., Edelman and Wolford 2017; Lees et al. 2015). These gaps in the academic literature contrast with the real-world rise of Polanyian protective countermovements against commodification's most deleterious social and environmental effects, such as Occupy, Vía Campesina, Slum Dwellers International, and the Right to the City Alliance that stretch across these domains and aim to embed land within less- or nonmarketized regulatory frameworks.

Land Fictions seeks to begin a process of bridging some of these divides, treating the country and the city as relational categories that have been used popularly to establish and maintain cultural and social norms for the uses to which land is expected to be put, as well as the functional benefits it is expected to deliver through those uses (Williams 1973). It further builds on Polanyi's historical-anthropological method and, following Peck's (2013a, 1545) call for "a more engaged Polanyian economic geography," focuses on actually existing real economies while avoiding entrapment in the abstractions of conventional economic theorizing or rural–urban binaries. As Peck (2013b, 1542) observes, "Actually existing markets, in all their variety, warrant attention not as special cases, or as deviations from a pristine model, but as particular forms of economic coordination." Further, by focusing on actually existing institutional arrangements and discursive enactments across a broad variety of historical and geographic contexts, the analysis of land fictions here seeks to be relationally comparative (Hart 2016) by following an open, nonteleological conception of historico-geographic difference that refuses to presume that patterns established in one place will necessarily materialize elsewhere, even while attending to mutual, and multiple, determinations that shape broad trajectories of capitalist transformation.

Combining new empirical material from North and South America, Europe, sub-Saharan Africa, South Asia, Southeast Asia, and East Asia, this book thus contributes to a comparative study of land markets as mechanisms and representations with globally circulating but locally specific characteristics. Less oriented toward achieving global coverage, the book brings together chapters that explore contemporary land fictions that, as nodes in a global story, inform our understanding of the politics and practices of land commodification in the contemporary moment. Based on in-depth fieldwork or careful archival and documentary analysis, the chapters collectively show how attention to fiction offers a unique and necessary vantage point for discerning the political and analytical stakes in how land's social worlds are being remade today.

Peeling back the layers of dispossession that led to the eventual formation of a special economic zone in Rajasthan, India, Michael Levien in chapter 1 traces the conversion of feudal land tenures into private agricultural property in the immediate post-Independence (1947) period, a subsequent phase of agricultural corporatism, and the recent subsumption of agrarian land into the current regime of urban rent-seeking. Throughout this history, he finds, different configurations of state force were required to disembed land, first, from a feudal regime, then from the joint family, and finally from regulated agricultural developmentalism. Underlying each of these transformations were particular narratives of land's social function— as symbol of sovereign power, as grounds for productivist nation building, and ultimately as a source of foreign investment. Levien uses this historical analysis to offer a sociological reconstruction of Polanyi's concept of fictitiousness, elucidating the unique challenges of commodifying land and the crucial role of extra-economic forces in the process.

Brett Christophers and Heather Whiteside next turn to a context where land commodification is driven less by extra-economic force and more by the lure of economic efficiency. Focusing on the narrative construction in Canada and the

United Kingdom of public land as surplus, they show how in each national context a shift in accounting practices rendered public land an apparent drag on the exchequer. But market-making technique alone was not enough to "free" public land. Instead, a carefully orchestrated story of public land wastage, mismanagement, and dereliction had to be coupled to a neo-Physiocratic narrative of land's power to generate value on the market. Surplus, however, has greatly different meanings in the United Kingdom and Canada given the vastly different land resources of each country. Comparative analysis of the fictions of surplus thus illuminates how a neoliberal privatization narrative attains global reach through regionally particular stories and myths: of Britain's sacred green pastures on the one hand and Canada's underutilized assets on the other.

Sarah Knuth explores the flipside of public land disposal, turning to the financial dynamics that have led institutional investors to aggressively incorporate rural farmland, long-term commercial leases, surplus public land inventories, and other low-rent-yielding properties into their portfolios, thereby transforming land into a fungible global asset. She specifically explores how shocks in asset prices in the wake of the 2008 global financial crisis led investors to mobilize defensive understandings of land. In contrast to the more commonly studied speculative storylines of closing rent and yield gaps, Knuth shows how the narration of land as a "safe" asset is significant in shaping patterns of global land investment, banking the stability of financial markets on social presumptions of land's countercyclicality and capacity to retain value. While these performative storylines build on historical patterns and statistical pictures, the fiction of safety that they collectively enact also fuels fresh risk taking, putting land to use in ways more tightly attuned to the logics and cycles of international finance and thereby undermining the fixity of the ground itself.

Meghan L. Morris examines a context where the material fixity of land has been repeatedly called into question, examining how stories about soil's materiality become key factors in bringing new forms of property into being in post-conflict Colombia. While soil is often assumed in law to be unchanging, Morris demonstrates how its actual fluidity makes what she calls "ground fictions" central to many land claims. Building on long-term fieldwork in both rural Urabá and urban Medellín, she finds that legal moves, such as land titling and the establishment of protected land reserves, are only part of market making. Surface water flows expand and dry up seasonally, making fictions of soil's dryness via alluvial accession central to encroaching claims to "new land" on Urabá's floodplains. Similarly, fictions about land's physical instability and landslide risk first became central to squatters' ability to access peripheral, nonmarket land in Medellín but subsequently undermined their ownership claims once the state sought to protect these long-neglected urban residents from their own risky soils.

Sai Balakrishnan analyzes the contradictory regional class and caste politics of large-scale land investments in Maharashtra, India, focusing on the conversion of peri-urban agricultural land into urban real estate. Whereas dominant agrarian castes long-invested in commodity agricultural production and with the deepest ties to urban capital vociferously protested land acquisition for the formation of a special economic zone, Adivasi "tribals" along with Dalit groups historically dependent on "waste" lands embraced forced land acquisition. Following Polanyi's observation that protective countermovements are not always and only led by the subaltern class, Balakrishnan shows how historic narratives of waste that twin expectations about poor land quality to presumptions of wasteland occupants' social backwardness were leveraged by lower-class and -caste groups to portray land expropriation as a means of pursuing a place in the urban economy. Forced dispossession via compensated insertion into urban land markets thus became a means to escape the caste hierarchy and ascribed backwardness of occupying peripheral, historically devalued lands. Fictions of waste that previously excluded the most socially subordinated groups from crop capitalism thus became an instrument of urban inclusion.

Moving from the peri-urban expanse of Maharashtra to the rental fictions underpinning investments in rent-regulated housing in New York City, Benjamin Teresa shows how historically devalued lands can become new sources of profit without requiring wholesale regulatory transformation. While protective countermovements against housing market liberalization have tended to operate through an individualistic logic of consumer protection, Teresa shows how such efforts have tacitly accepted commodity housing as an inevitable future, with the result that speculative investment in rent-regulated housing has emerged as a major growth sector. Parallel fictions of "undervalued assets" focused on core, upmarket Manhattan districts and "mismanaged assets" focused on lower-income, mostly outer-borough neighborhoods have helped financial institutions engineer the facts of rising rent. In undervalued assets, speculative mortgage underwriting methods introduce expectations about future neighborhood income profiles to narrate the inevitability of rent deregulation. Future asset pricing in so-called mismanaged assets, in contrast, constructs a picture of the inevitable relationship between property improvement and tenant turnover, where the narration of tenant departure prefigures increases in rent even in what remain rent-regulated buildings.

Michael Dwyer explores the regulatory fictions of presumably fixed administrative categories in the vastly different context of rural Cambodia. In the wake of aggressive private land concessions and associated dispossessions, land titling emerged there as a development fix intended to register presumably unambiguous ownership conditions and reduce forced displacement. Through an impressive cartographic deconstruction of Cambodia's uneven geography of formalization as well as the land allocations for a private sugar plantation, Dwyer shows that this formalization fix operates more as a promise than a reality. Property, he finds, is produced, not merely inventoried or registered, via the formalization process, as past categories of "forest" versus "degraded" land are reanimated in the present to justify the removal of people seen as obstructing investment. The gap between the promise of formalization and the minimal emphasis in practice on enhancing the land rights of the marginalized is what produces formalization as a fiction: a story that continues to be narrated as possible and desirable despite evidence that it is not doing what it purports to do.

Flexible state-administrative distinctions between land types also organize the regulatory fiction of planning in D. Asher Ghertner's chapter on Delhi's "unauthorized colonies"—peripheral neighborhoods located outside the city's master-planned areas that have long been denied state services. As the population and electoral influence of unauthorized colonies have grown, the planning authorities have introduced rules for regularizing these areas, which allows them to be retroactively incorporated into the plan and subsequently supplied with state water, sewerage, and related services. Focusing on three planning spaces—the map, water infrastructure, and the illegal building—Ghertner shows how practices of mimicry build material planned-ness into the core of supposedly unplanned spaces. The fiction of a distinction between the planned and the unplanned must hence be upheld by performative acts of naming that reify a difference that has become materially difficult to sustain but that is responsible for maintaining a highly uneven land system defined by inflated ground rents and premium services in the core and planned insecurities elsewhere.

Mi Shih focuses on a village in peri-urban Guangzhou that stubbornly refused to be relocated to state commodity housing. Narratives associating land type with social backwardness are prominent in China, and Shih examines how the regulatory equation of "urban" with "state ownership" entrenches a social fiction that occupants of collective land suffer from an innate rurality ill-suited to the conditions of modern living. State land expropriation is hence constructed as necessary not only to commodify once-rural land and deliver it to a higher and better use but also to modernize a backward population clinging to rural ways. Shih's account shows how villagers, without directly challenging state policy, mobilize a quality-driven language emphasizing "the sanctuary of the collective" (*jitidebihu*) as a communal way of being that fosters a vitality (*renqi*) that villagers and other urban outcasts otherwise consider absent from the homogenized commodity world taking over the city. Refusing to become urban—despite the economic and environmental hardships associated with this refusal—reinforces the fiction that collective land holds back China's modern future but also enacts a critique of the glass towers now symbolically dominating the urbanizing landscape.

In contrast to the urban villages in Guangzhou, China, the village residents Erik Harms describes as being displaced for a new urban zone in Ho Chi Minh City, Vietnam, very much participated in the vision of an aesthetically upgraded city. Using state resettlement policies to examine the fiction that liberal property automatically delivers liberal political rights, Harms shows how residents adopted the expectation that improvements to the land they occupied would improve their standing as urban citizens. They did so by investing in a document-based rights framework aimed at maximizing their legal compensation and asserting a distinctly urban form of citizenship. This had the unintended effect, Harms shows, of reducing their historical land claims to monetary terms, thereby minimizing the political potency of their demand for a place in the city at the very moment they achieved legal property rights. The new rights emerging on the edges of Vietnamese cities, he argues, hence cannot be disentangled from the very process of land commodification fueling dispossession. By studying the work that documents do, as well as the fetish objects they become, Harms further uses insights from actor-network theory and Marx's critique of the commodity form to show the work of nonhuman actors in staging and maintaining the commodity fiction.

Robert Lake examines two interrelated practices integral to the construction of urban land as a fictitious commodity in the redevelopment of Camden, New Jersey. First, a process of rule making establishes an institutional structure that makes Camden's land available for middle-class investment while displacing existing residents who are constructed as a deterrent to a resurgent land market. Simultaneously, the successful performance of the urban land market necessitates the alignment of actors' subjectivities such that they are willing and capable of performing the roles required for the redevelopment process to achieve its objectives. These interrelated practices locate the urban political in the highly contested domain in which the materiality of urban land meets urban subjectivity in the performance of the land market. Political contestation takes place through three distinct but interrelated narratives enacting this domain: in the construction of land as an investable commodity; in the countermovement against displacement attendant on proposed redevelopment; and in constructing the subjects whose self-governance enacts the land market in Camden.

Heidi Hausermann and David Ferring explore the regulatory fictions underpinning foreign investment in "small-scale" gold mining in Ghana. While Ghanaian mineral law requires mining concessions to be domestically owned and operated, the reality is that most mines are run by foreign, largely Chinese, operators. Detailing the shifting performances and practices facilitating foreign gold mining, they show how unremediated mining landscapes and associated environmental impacts are enabled by fictions of mining's developmental benefits and of rational environmental regulation. Focusing on how agents of foreign capital help foreign investors procure official paperwork and concessions, they show how key state and nonstate intermediaries maintain both the appearance of legality as well as the fictional neutrality of the state as public servant, reproducing the historic and problematic narrative that farmers and traditional authorities "giving away land" are ignorant of existing laws.

Michael Watts offers closing remarks by way of an Afterword, which places the largely contemporary land fictions explored in the preceding chapters in a longer historical context: specifically, Marxian reflections on the commodity fetish, the historical challenge of peasant production to agroindustry (the agrarian question), and the biological underpinnings and specificities of agriculture. Watts also indicates ways in which the study of land fictions might be productively expanded from viewing land as a horizontal domain of property into closer consideration of land's vertical properties, including both the subterranean and the aerial.

1

FICTITIOUS BUT NOT UTOPIAN

Land Commodification and Dispossession in Rural India

Michael Levien

Contemporary protests over "land grabs" have renewed interest in the relationship between land dispossession and capitalism. Searching for theoretical foundations, scholars of almost every persuasion have found inspiration—and a reservoir of good quotes—in Karl Polanyi's (2001 [1944]) classic account of land commodification in *The Great Transformation*. Polanyi argued that land—like labor and money—is a "fictitious commodity"; that its transformation into a commodity generates profound social dislocations; and that these dislocations generate countermovements for social protection. Polanyi thus saw the long stretch of history between the English enclosures and World War II as defined by a "double movement" in which, "the extension of the market organization in respect to genuine commodities was accompanied by its restriction in respect to fictitious ones" (Polanyi 2001 [1944], 79). While Polanyi took midcentury state capitalisms as evidence for such restriction, his concept of the double movement resonates again amid the intensifying land commodification of the neoliberal era and the land struggles this has produced.

Despite such resonance, Polanyi's treatment of land is arguably the most cursory of his "fictitious commodities"; there is significant disagreement among scholars about what "fictitiousness" actually means; and some have recently argued that the concept hinders rather than helps our ability to grasp the very "real" political economy of land (Christophers 2016). The purpose of this chapter is to clarify the meaning and defend the utility of Polanyi's conception of land as a fictitious commodity. Drawing on historical and ethnographic research into processes of land commodification and dispossession in rural northwest

India, I argue that Polanyi's conception of land as a fictitious commodity helps to explain why state action—including but not limited to dispossession—is an important mechanism for transforming land into a commodity. Land is a fictitious commodity, I will suggest, not because commodifying it is utopian (Block 2001; Block and Somers 2014) or unethical (Li 1991, 220); nor is it because commodifying land necessarily destroys its use value (Burawoy 2015, 19) or undermines capitalism's ecological conditions of possibility (O'Connor 1988, 12; Fraser 2014, 547). Rather, land is a fictitious commodity because it is enmeshed in nonmarket institutions and value practices that must be overcome if it is to be governed by markets.

This interpretation of fictitiousness depends neither on a romanticized defense of precapitalist institutions nor a claim that land is unique in creating obstacles to commodification—the basis of two important critiques of the concept (Fraser 2014; Christophers 2016). Rather, it rests on the simple observation that land was not—like most other commodities—created to be sold on the market and that, therefore, attempts to turn it into a commodity must overcome the diverse and historically sedimented institutions and social values in which it is embedded. The sociological significance of Polanyi's conception of land as a fictitious commodity, thus interpreted, is that it helps us to understand why land's social integument poses obstacles to capitalist accumulation; and why dispossession—and state action more generally—are necessary for its transformation into a commodity. The concept thus fills a troubling gap in Marxian theories of dispossession, such as Harvey's (2003, 2005) accumulation by dispossession, which do not explain why *dispossession* becomes an important mechanism of commodification in particular times and places. Polanyi himself did not grasp, however, that it is dispossession not commodification that generates countermovements over land; that such countermovements can fail to emerge or succeed; and that the relentless march of commodification is therefore far from utopian, social and ecological havoc notwithstanding.

In what follows, I will first review and critique recent prominent interpretations of the meaning of fictitiousness and then advance my own reading of Polanyi's concept. I will then try to show how this reading of land as a fictitious commodity helps to explain the role of states in transforming rural land into a commodity. I do so by drawing on the case of Rajpura, a rain-fed farming village in the Indian state of Rajasthan that I studied intensively between 2009 and 2011, with four further revisits between 2012 and 2017. As late as 1950, Rajpura was a feudal demesne with no private property or land market; in 2005, it housed one of India's largest private special economic zones (SEZ)—essentially a privately run city for multinational corporations and high-end real estate. With deep class, caste, and gender inequalities, at no point was Rajpura idyllic. But using the insight that land is a fictitious commodity does not require an ahistorical or romantic depiction of Rajpura's precapitalist institutions. Rather, the concept methodologically directs our attention to different phases in the transformation of Rajpura's land from noncommodity to commodity. These phases include post-Independence land reforms that abolished feudal tenures and created small-holding private property; post-1990s deregulation that lifted many constraints on land markets while intensifying demand; and the coercive use of eminent domain by the Rajasthan government to dispossess the village for a private SEZ. State-orchestrated dispossession, in this and similar cases across India, was the coup de grâce that overcame the remaining obstacles that even deregulated rural land markets pose to large-scale land commodification.

Yet, while widespread land dispossession of this kind has provoked militant farmer protests elsewhere in India, I show how the Rajasthan state government was able to absorb Rajpura's dispossessed farmers into the process of commodification itself, thus undermining the second leg of Polanyi's double movement. While the dispossession and commodification of Rajpura's land has produced dramatic ecological and social consequences, as Polanyi would predict, it has not produced a countermovement, much less decommodification. Rajpura's land is now a commodity integrated into a global real estate market.

Land as Fictitious Commodity

The Fuzziness of Fictitiousness

Among the fictitious commodities, Polanyi's discussion of land is arguably the least coherent. To begin with, it is scattered across the book and unevenly integrated into his larger argument. While Polanyi's account of the English enclosures begins in chapter 3, chapter 4's important discussion of precapitalist economic systems—in which Polanyi argues that economic systems were subordinated to society for most of human history—contains no discussion of land. It is only in chapter 6 that Polanyi fully introduces his "fictitious commodities," while chapter 15 focuses on land specifically. Polanyi's discussion of land commodification in these sections is empirically thin and ad hoc. While, like Marx, he focuses on the English enclosures, he also mentions the need for land for mills and worker housing (Polanyi 2001 [1944], 188), the role of the Code Napoleon in instituting private property in France (ibid., 189), and rather vaguely, colonial expropriations (ibid., 187). Most confusingly, however, Polanyi constantly conflates the commodification of *land* with the extension of trade in agricultural *products* (these markets have an empirical connection, but are not the same). His account of the nineteenth-century "double movement" thus actually focuses on protectionist movements against free trade and *not* movements against land commodification. Even when discussing agrarian protectionism, Polanyi cannot decide if the peasantry is "least contaminated by the liberal virus" or the "champions of market economy" (Polanyi 2001 [1944], 196, 197). Like the entire text, moreover, Polanyi's discussion of land suffers from his organic and functionalist conception of society, which protects *itself* against the market through the medium of classes (Burawoy 2003). Not only does Polanyi assume that reembedding is in the interests of everyone, but he simply assumes that the countermovements succeed—though there is great disagreement among scholars about what, exactly, reembedding entails (cf. Block and Somers 2014; Burawoy 2003; Lachman 2007). All of this makes for a frustrating read, which undoubtedly explains why Polanyi is so often mobilized through à la carte quotations. While Polanyi's theory of a double movement resonates at a relatively high level of abstraction—intensified marketization produces social resistance across multiple domains of life—almost everything else remains to be filled in.

Despite these deep ambiguities in his classic work, Polanyi bequeathed an important concept in fictitious commodities. But much like Polanyi's far more debated and parallel term *embeddedness* (Krippner et al. 2004), fictitiousness has been interpreted in remarkably divergent ways. For Block and Somers (2014), land—like labor and money—is a fictitious commodity because it *cannot* be fully commodified; any attempt to do so is "utopian" since the resulting social havoc calls forth countermovements and government intervention. Commodifying fictitious commodities thus "describes something that cannot actually exist" (Block and Somers 2014, 32). On this basis, they argue that Polanyi's most important insight is that markets are *always* embedded in society (see also Block 2001).

In Burawoy's reading, by contrast, the double movement rests on the idea that there are historical waves of commodification (2015). Land, in this reading, not only can be commodified; but its commodification defines the most recent "wave of marketization." What makes land a fictitious commodity, for Burawoy, is that this commodification leads to ecological destruction. Commodities are fictitious "if their unregulated commodification destroys their 'true' or 'essential' character" (ibid., 19). Thus, "when land, or more broadly nature, is subject to commodification then it can no longer support the basic necessities for human life" (ibid., 19). In this interpretation, fictitiousness is thus defined not by the impossibility of commodification but by its (negative) results. In a parallel reading, Nancy Fraser argues that fictitious commodities are those things that, if commodified, undermine the market's conditions of possibility (2014, 548). Dispatching with what she calls an "ontological" interpretation of fictitiousness, which she argues is based on an essentialist and ahistorical conception of land that overlooks "relations of domination" and thus lends itself to a reactionary project (Fraser 2014,

547), Fraser advances what she calls a structural interpretation: land is a fictitious commodity because commodifying it destroys capitalism's ecological foundations (see also O'Connor 1998, 12).

Noting the concept's ambiguities, and taking exception to the idea that land commodification is utopian, Christophers (2016) has recently argued that we should dispatch with the concept of fictitiousness altogether if we are to understand very *real* processes of land commodification under capitalism. Building on Fraser's (2014) argument above, Christophers issues a two-fold critique. First, while Polanyi "links the difficulty of marketization to the original, non-sale-oriented condition of land, labour and money," Christophers asks, "How often does society actually confront these three entities in their *original* forms, and thus also confront properties nominally militating against marketization?" (Christophers 2016, 140). Polanyi's conception of fictitiousness, Christophers concurs with Fraser, assumes an ahistorical conception of land. Second, Christophers (2016, 140) questions the uniqueness of land, labor, and money, asking whether they are really the only things not created as commodities but treated like commodities and, relatedly, whether there are any other commodities "that resist commodification and/or pose problems for market formation," generate countermovements, and/or obligate efforts at social and political reembedding? Christophers provides the examples of human organs and knowledge.[1] But, unlike Fraser, Christophers believes that we should get rid of the concept of fictitiousness altogether since "treating land as fictitious has demonstrably been hobbling, making political economists circumspect about land and its conceptual significance" whereas "a shedding of ideas of fictitiousness.... can empower them to place land at the very heart of theory, which, in an era of land grabbing, 'planetary urbanisation' and proliferating international housing crises, is clearly where it needs to be" (Christophers 2016, 143).

Christophers's call to treat the political economy of land more seriously is welcome, as is his challenge to clarify what, if anything, is useful in designating land a fictitious commodity. But I do not believe his—or Fraser's—critiques are fatal to the idea of land as a fictitious commodity, which in my reading depends neither on an ahistorical concept of precommoditized land nor on the claim that land is ontologically unique (rather than simply specific).[2] Indeed, I argue that Polanyi's conception of land as a fictitious commodity fills a real gap in our understanding of the "real" political economy of land under capitalism. Below, I take up Christophers's challenge to clarify its meaning.

The Sociological Meaning of Fictitiousness

Polanyi argues that commodities "are objects produced for sale on the market" (Polanyi 2001 [1944], 75). What makes land, labor, and money peculiar is that while they "are essential elements of industry" and "must be organized in markets" they "are obviously *not* commodities" as "none of them are produced for sale" (ibid., 75, 76). The implication is that land preexists commodification and is, therefore, deeply embedded in nonmarket institutions: "What we call land is an element of nature inextricably interwoven with man's institutions. . . . with tribe and temple, village, guild and church" (ibid., 187). Not only is land historically embedded in social institutions, but it is correspondingly valued in multiple ways that are not reducible to its economic value. Thus, Polanyi elaborates, "The economic function of land is but one of many vital functions of land. It invests man's life with stability; it is the site of his habitation; it is a condition of his physical safety; it is the landscape and the seasons. We might as well imagine his being born without hands and feet as carrying on his life without land" (ibid.). While Polanyi phrases this in typically functionalist and lyrical fashion, the point stands. Land has historically been embedded in nonmarket institutions and socially valued in ways that are irreducible to its economic value. Under European feudalism, to take Polanyi's main example, land was "*extra commercium*" (ibid., 73) and embedded in political, military, and judicial structures: "Its status and function were determined by legal and customary rules" (ibid., 72–73). A market society, however, must treat land *as if* it were a commodity like any other; as an essential factor of production, it must be responsive to price signals. For this to happen, however, land must be extracted from its social entanglements: "To separate land from man and to organize society in such a way as to satisfy the requirements of a real-estate market was a vital part of the utopian concept of a market economy" (ibid., 187). We shall return to whether this is, indeed, utopian.

Polanyi is vague about how this separation happens (Burawoy 2015, 20), though like Marx's (1990 [1867]) analysis of primitive accumulation, he emphasizes the role of the state, less forthrightly, violence.[3] In his account of the enclosures, Polanyi focuses more on the ineffectual efforts to check its progress than the political forces and administrative mechanisms that made it possible.[4] Of Europe's agrarian transition more generally, however, Polanyi observes that "some of this was achieved by individual force and violence, some by revolution from above or below, some by war and conquest, some by legislative action, some by administrative pressure, some by spontaneous small-scale action of private persons over long stretches of time" (Polanyi 2001, 189). Also like Marx, Polanyi believes that more contemporary processes of colonization illustrate the same mechanisms that were involved in the enclosures. In an even sparser account, Polanyi notes—like his precursors Marx (1990 [1867]) and Luxemburg (2003 [1913])—that colonialism involves "smashing up social structures" in order to extract both labor and resources (Polanyi 2001 [1944], 71, see also 188). The main difference between the enclosures and colonization is that the process of commodification that took centuries in the West "may be compressed into a few years" in the colonies, which also lack the political sovereignty necessary to place checks on this process (Polanyi 2001 [1944], 192).[5] While in both cases Polanyi notes the role of private persons (whether landlords or colonizers), his emphasis is on the role of the state—consistent with the *Great Transformation*'s larger argument that "the *laissez-faire* economy was the product of deliberate State action" (ibid., 147).[6]

It is certainly true that Polanyi operates with a vague conception of the "organic" precapitalist societies thus shattered. It does not follow, however, that his concept of land as a fictitious commodity implies an ahistorical conception of land unshaped by "human activity or relations of power" (Fraser 2014, 547). In fact, Polanyi is clear that producing fictitious commodities is a process that can take many centuries and run through various historical phases. Polanyi offers his own impressionistic history of such phases (having more to do with commercializing agriculture than land itself), which he calls "stages in the subjection of the surface of the planet to the needs of an industrial society" (Polany 2001 [1944], 188).[7] If land commodification is a prolonged process involving different phases—which, as his discussion of colonization suggests, may be more or less temporally compressed in different contexts—then one can examine such processes without reference to "an original condition"; one must simply pick up somewhere. And while Polanyi's Durkheimian conception of social order *does* emphasize "disintegrative effects on social communities" more than relations of power (Fraser 2014, 547), Polanyi was also not a blind romantic. Polanyi's approach to the "ultimately beneficial enclosures" (Polanyi 2001 [1944], 36) is actually quite similar to Marx's—while denouncing the brutal theft and social havoc this involved, Polanyi observes that it was nevertheless part of "the Western European trend of economic progress which aimed at eliminating an artificially maintained uniformity of agricultural technique, intermixed crops, and the primitive institution of the common" (ibid., 39). Polanyi is more concerned with the rate of change than the fact of change, emphasizing that because the Tudors and Stuarts slowed the process, "England withstood without grave damage the calamity of the enclosures" (ibid., 40). Indeed, throughout the *Great Transformation*—and again much like Marx—Polanyi does not contemplate turning back the clock but is rather concerned with how "complex societies" can ensure freedom by reembedding the market through modern democratic institutions.[8] To use the language of Tönnies (2002 [1887]), the German sociologist who Polanyi read closely and who had previously advanced the idea of fictitious commodities (see Dale 2016, 23–29)—though only with respect to labor and in a far more limited away—while the first leg of the "double movement" involves a move from *gemeinschaft* to *gesellschaft* (Dale 2016, 23–29; see Li 1991, 223), the second leg involves a modern and qualitatively different reembedding (a *gesellschaft* with *gemeinschaft* elements?)⁹ Most important, one need not romanticize agrarian social structures to use Polanyi's concept of fictitious commodity.

Polanyi is clear that commodification produces negative social and ecological dislocations, and he provides many colorful quotes to this effect. But it would be a mistake, in my view, to reduce the concept of fictitious commodities to a critique of ecological destruction (Fraser 2014; Burawoy 2015). The transformation of land into a commodity means only that it is bought and sold, not that it is destroyed. Buying and selling land may lead to changes in the land's use value, and no doubt commodification makes land available for uses that tend to be more degrading, but organic farms also sit on commodified land. Commodification and ecological destruction are causally related but should be analytically separated. So while it may be that land commodification is gradually undermining capitalism's ecological conditions of possibility (O'Connor 1988; Fraser 2014), it would be teleological to define land's fictitiousness by this eventuality. Land is a fictitious commodity because of its enmeshment in nonmarket institutions and values; this creates obstacles to commodification; these obstacles must be overcome through state power; and overcoming them does often produce grave social and ecological consequences. But commodification and its attendant consequences may go on indefinitely.

Commodifying fictitious commodities is therefore not utopian. Polanyi's argument on this score is the most puzzling of the *Great Transformation*. Polanyi (2001 [1944], 3) famously states on the first page of the book that the "self-adjusting market implied a stark utopia. Such an institution could not exist for any length of time without annihilating the human and natural substance of society. It would have physically destroyed man and transformed his surroundings into a wilderness." Block and Somers (2014) place great emphasis on such statements. But when discussing the commodification of fictitious commodities, Polanyi more circumspectly conditions this argument. Thus: "No society could stand the effects of such a system of crude fictions even for the shortest stretch of time *unless* its human and natural substance as well as its business organization was protected against the ravages of this satanic mill" (Polanyi 2001 [1944], 77, my emphasis).[10] In other words, treating land, labor, and money as commodities will destroy society, nature, and the economy *only if it is not accompanied by social protection*. This begs the important question of what Polanyi means by social protection: does it actually involve decommodification or might it simply mean more limited state regulations that leave in place land's commodity status? If the latter, commodifying fictitious commodities is not really utopian, even if a purely "self-regulating market" is, which suggests that Polanyi's arguments about fictitious commodities and embeddedness should be analytically separated rather than conflated.[11] At any rate, the argument that commodifying fictitious commodities is utopian hinges on Polanyi's assumption that countermovements always emerge and succeed.

The obvious problem is that they don't. Indeed, Polanyi himself provides no evidence of land actually becoming decommodified in *The Great Transformation*, nor even of substantial checks being placed on land markets. Not only do the English enclosures, his main example, demonstrably commodify land for good, but his only supposed example of a countermovement against land commodification is agrarian protectionism; but placing tariffs on corn does not abolish capitalist land markets.[12] At most, Polanyi provides evidence that the Tudor and Stuart monarchs slowed down land commodification via the enclosures and thus gave people more time to adjust—a strange argument since, if one is to be dispossessed of land, one would certainly hope for the *rapid* creation of alternative employment.

Leaving Polanyi's text for the empirical world, moreover, it is patently the case that land functions as a commodity in large swathes of the world today. And while there are many contemporary examples of social opposition to commodification, what Polanyi did not understand is that it is dispossession rather than commodification per se that generates countermovements. It is coercive land grabs, rather than land titling or land deregulation, that generate the land struggles that many today interpret as a Polanyian countermovement. And a cursory survey of those movements suggests that there are few cases in which they actually succeed in decommodifying land. Commodifying fictitious commodities, as Friedman (2014) argues with respect to labor, may create insurgency; but this insurgency may never achieve institutionalized social protection, much less decommodification. Indeed, as I will show for land, it is possible for states to absorb cultivators into the process of commodification itself. The last leg of Polanyi's double movement is anything but automatic.[13] And if it is not automatic, land commodification is not utopian, regardless of its social and ecological consequences. It is a very real dystopia.

In sum, when we discard the substantial chaff in Polanyi's treatment of land, what remains is the concept of land as a fictitious commodity. Polanyi's simple but useful point is that land is a fictitious commodity because it is enmeshed in nonmarket social institutions and values; and, further, that overcoming such obstacles to commodification requires concerted state action, including dispossession. That such processes *often* generate resistance—a soft version of Polanyi's argument—is also correct, with the important caveat that it is dispossession rather than commodification per se that generates this effect. But it is also possible that countermovements to dispossession never emerge or fail; and that commodification proceeds apace, social and ecological dislocations notwithstanding.

In what follows I demonstrate the utility of this limited appropriation of Polanyi to help us understand historical and contemporary processes of land commodification in a region of rural India.

Commodifying Land in Rajasthan

Land Reform and the Creation of Private Property

Until India's Independence in 1947, Rajpura was a minor fief in the princely state of Jaipur. Jaipur was one of the twenty-two princely states of "Rajputana," most of which were founded by Rajput "warrior caste" clans in the first and early second millennia. Although reduced to tributaries by the Mughal and British empires, the princely states held onto land and power until India's Independence (Rudolph and Rudolph 1984). Under the form of indirect rule known as paramountcy, the British gave the princes substantial domestic autonomy in return for their allegiance and tribute. The princes, in turn, parceled out land and local sovereignty to fellow Rajput clansmen who became the hereditary nobility of the countryside. These local notables were both the rulers and landlords of "their" villages. Under various forms of tenure that can appropriately be described as feudal—the most prominent of which was *jagirdari*—this landlord class exacted crushing rents,[14] forced labor (*begaar*), and a plethora of taxes from peasants.[15] The peasantry had only customary claims to land, which belonged to the *jagirdars* by hereditary right. While *jagirs* could theoretically be resumed by the king, land was otherwise inalienable (Singh 1964, 32). Not only was there no land market, but local land tenures within jagirdari areas were heterogeneous and deliberately opaque. Despite late prodding by the British, jagirdari land was neither mapped nor settled before India's Independence (Stern 1988; Singh 1964). Land in Rajpura, like most of rural Rajputana, was not a commodity; it was "embedded" in the far-from-idyllic political structure of princely rule.

After India's Independence, the Congress regime was clear that princely rule was incompatible with "a modern democratic state" (Government of India 1950, 46). Pushing through land reform in Rajasthan involved several legislative acts, many amendments and much political negotiation between Prime Minister Nehru and the jagirdars over the 1950s.[16] Ultimately, a series of "land to the tiller" laws abolished *jagir* intermediaries and created a direct relationship between cultivators and the state. Land ceiling laws, which sought to redistribute surplus land over a politically determined limit, were less successful (Singh 1964). The largest cultivating castes under princely rule—most notably the Jats—were the biggest winners and established themselves as dominant landholding castes, while lower castes received much less. Many former jagirdars, moreover, successfully evaded land ceiling reforms to retain very large landholdings. The main difference is that they were now *only* landholders.[17] If Rajasthan's land reforms failed to equalize landholdings, they did transform feudal jagirs into private property. Whatever was left—very significant forms of de facto grazing and forest commons—became various categories of state land (Brara 2006). While it took more than a decade after Independence, by the early 1960s the central and state governments had largely accomplished the first stage of transforming Rajasthan's rural land into a commodity: making it private and alienable (Castree 2003).

If land was largely freed from its feudal integument, there remained many checks on its full commodification: legal, administrative, and political economic. Even as it was creating a rural land market, the Indian state was also hedging it with a variety of regulations. Rajasthan's Land Revenue Act (1956)—like those elsewhere in India—placed rigid restrictions on the conversion of agricultural land to nonagricultural uses without government permission. The Rajasthan Tenancy Act (1955) capped rents, outlawed continuous tenants (to discourage landlordism), regulated mortgages, and prevented Scheduled Castes and Scheduled Tribes from selling or mortgaging their land to upper castes. The Rajasthan Tenancy (Fixation of Ceiling on Land) Rules (1963) fixed a rural land ceiling of thirty standard acres and required that surplus land be redistributed to the landless. While the effectiveness of these policies should not be overstated—their intent was often subverted by influential people in connivance with state functionaries (Singh 1964)—they did represent checks on the full commodification of land, evidenced, as we will see, by the rapid effort to remove them in the neoliberal era.

Beyond these laws and regulations, there were administrative obstacles to a well-functioning capitalist land market. Cadastral surveys and land titling not only took almost two decades after independence to complete, but a combination of corruption—especially by local land records officials (Singh 1964, 350)—and distance between a largely illiterate peasantry and the state ensured that land titles were often not updated. As a consequence, divisions between heirs—and sometimes even sales—occurred in practice but not on paper. Ambiguous titles and legal disputes made it hard for outsiders to buy rural land with confidence. Undivided and/or contested family property—the "embeddedness" of land in the joint family—thus interacted with interventionist but not always efficient state institutions to create significant obstacles to land commodification.

This was less of a problem (for capital) for most of the twentieth century because demand was limited. Not only was Rajpura's agricultural land—like much of Rajasthan's—unirrigated, but increasingly erratic rains over the second half of the twentieth century inhibited the development of fully capitalist agriculture. Most of Rajpura's farmers became petty commodity producers cultivating coarse grains and raising livestock for commercial milk production. Water scarcity limited land concentration and, along with the generational march of subdivision, forced most cultivators to diversify into nonagricultural pursuits—unskilled wage labor, off-farm businesses, or formal sector employment depending on their resources. Land in Rajpura, meanwhile, had limited-to-no value for nonagriculturalists. Although only twenty-five kilometers from Jaipur and five kilometers from what would become a national highway, outside demand for land would only emerge in the 2000s. Until then, buyers were mostly local farmers. Selling land was, moreover, a last resort for both socioeconomic and cultural reasons (which are difficult to separate). Given the centrality of agriculture to livelihoods and to social status, land was usually sold under duress to meet contingent expenditures, pay for weddings, and/or to liquidate debts (see Bailey 1957). All of this ensured that the overall volume of land sales remained low. Land was alienable but not often alienated. Demand was limited and supply was relatively inelastic.

In Harvey's terms, therefore, the rural land market was not fully capitalist: it did not provide, for the above reasons, an "open field" for the circulation of capital (Harvey 2007, 271). Creating such an open field would be central to the political project of neoliberalism.

Liberalizing Land Markets

India's adoption of neoliberal economic policies from the early 1990s onward greatly increased the demand for rural land. Although India's manufacturing sector would remain relatively sluggish, India's information technology (IT) and business process outsourcing (BPO) sectors boomed and drove relatively rapid growth over the next two decades. Requiring commercial office space not available within many cities, IT/BPO companies looked to peri-urban and rural land for their campuses, software technology parks, and "Hi-Tech Cities," and would ultimately lead the rush into India's special economic zones (SEZs) during the 2000s. Progressive liberalization of India's infrastructure sector, moreover, sought to attract private capital into roads, airports, power, and industrial infrastructure on a public-private partnership (PPP) basis, often using land giveaways as an incentive. This culminated with India's Special Economic Zone Policy (2000) and Special Economic Zone Act (2005), which incentivized private investors to develop these tax-free economic zones-cum-satellite cities. Infrastructure liberalization thus dovetailed with the liberalization of India's real estate sector (Ghertner 2015a; Searle 2016) to steer unprecedented volumes of capital into India's rural land markets. While prices in India's large cities rivaled those of Western metropolises (Chakravorty 2014), this boom radiated out from cities, small towns, transportation corridors, and large capital projects to engulf the farmland of thousands of villages. Beginning in the 1990s, but particularly in the mid-2000s, this boom transformed Rajasthan's sleepy provincial capital of Jaipur, which quickly began to swallow its peri-urban periphery.

Turning farmland into real estate, however, required significant state intervention to overcome the obstacles outlined above. As Nikita Sud (2012) has outlined for the state of Gujarat, the "liberalization" of land was central to India's neoliberal reforms at the state level. In 1999, the Rajasthan government inserted a clause in the Land Revenue Act that eased the conversion of agricultural land to nonagricultural uses. This "90B" clause would become an infamous tool for illicit rent-seeking, as government bureaucrats (and their political backers) routinely demanded huge kickbacks for granting this approval, which would automatically increase the value of land manifold. Over the following decade, the state government made such conversions progressively easier, even when they violated the city's master plan. Urban land ceilings also received the ax, allowing private individuals and companies to consolidate large chunks of farmland for conversion into urban real estate. Easing (or flouting) norms for environmental clearances further helped to facilitate industrial and extractive projects (Sud 2012). To overcome the problem of shoddy land records, the state government began—though much more slowly—to undertake land record modernization and digitation, moves that the World Bank predicted would "make available a huge amount of high-value peri-urban land for productive investment and development" (World Bank 2007a, 2).

By the early 2000s, land in Rajpura was not only alienable but substantially deregulated. But two points must be made. First, none of the processes that furthered the process of land commodification produced a countermovement. With land already divided into small private holdings, few would object to measures that removed restrictions on its alienability or increased its value. Second, Rajpura's land still did not provide an open field for the circulation of capital. Unclear titles remained a large barrier to fully functioning rural land markets. Very small holdings made it difficult to consolidate large contiguous chunks of land. And the continued centrality of agriculture to rural livelihoods—and the absence of a labor-intensive industrialization dynamic to moderate this centrality—ensured that the supply of rural land remained inelastic. Before the SEZ arrived in 2005, my informants in Rajpura made clear, owning land was still central to social status and thus to conducting good marriages. Land was still referred to as *jamin;* the English term *property*, which would come to connote the buying and selling of land as a distinct domain of business, was still unfamiliar to most. The upshot is that if private investors had wanted to consolidate a large contiguous chunk of land—say over a hundred acres or so—in Rajpura, they would have had a very difficult time. Land was still embedded in social institutions and value practices that posed obstacles to large-scale commodification. And it was for these reasons that, immediately following the commencement of neoliberal reforms in the early 1990s, the Rajasthan government also began to rapidly increase its use of eminent domain.

Dispossession

Such obstacles to consolidating large chunks of rural land have long provided the main rationale for eminent domain: the coercive appropriation of land for so-called "public purposes." In India, the principle of eminent domain was introduced by the British in the 1820s and multiply revised, culminating in the Land Acquisition Act of 1894. One of its primary uses was to acquire land for privately built railways and canals, the circulatory infrastructure of an extractive colonial capitalism (Krishnan 2014). While the post-independence state attempted to overcome colonial extractivism to build a self-sufficient national economy (Goswami 2004), accomplishing this would also require the large-scale dispossession of land, for which colonial laws proved useful. The post-independence Rajasthan state, along with its counterparts across India, would use the 1894 act to dispossess millions of farmers from their lands for public sector industry, mining, and infrastructure—especially large dams. In the postliberalization period, such state-orchestrated dispossession not only increased quantitatively but expanded qualitatively

The main problem, for state and capital, was that escalating private demand for land encountered the same old obstacles in India's rural land markets. As government officials and corporate executives repeatedly told me over the course of my research, a private company looking to consolidate a larger contiguous chunk of land would have a very difficult time acquiring it through market purchase. When negotiating with hundreds of farmers, there are sure to be holdouts given both the economic and social value of land and because some farmers will calculate that they can receive more by waiting. Moreover, the problem of undivided family holdings and ambiguous land records remained significant. While these obstacles had existed during the developmentalist period, they posed greater obstacles amid the escalating private demand generated by liberalization. If large private SEZs, factories, and real estate developments were to be built, the government would have to acquire land for them. And the government had two major incentives to do so. The first was intensifying interstate competition for investment, in which supplying land to investors quickly became a key criterion. And the second was the massive amount of rents this role made possible to government officials and politicians.

The result of this confluence of forces was that by the 1990s, the Rajasthan government had become what I call a land broker state. No longer just dispossessing land for public sector industrial and infrastructure projects, its parastatal agencies were routinely engaged in dispossessing land for private capital for any purpose that represented growth, no matter how speculative. The state's industrial promotion arm, the Rajasthan State Industrial Development and Investment Corporation (RIICO), had morphed from builder of public sector industrial estates to facilitator of hotels, waterparks, and private SEZs. The Jaipur Development Authority (JDA), meanwhile, had become an aggressive dispossessor of peri-urban farm and grazing land for private builders. In 2005, these two agencies came together to dispossess Rajpura and eight other villages for what was advertised as the largest IT SEZ in India, the Mahindra World City (MWC).

Promoted by the Mahindra & Mahindra Group, a tractor and truck manufacturer at that time capitalized at $8 billion that had diversified into real estate, the MWC would be a three-thousand-acre "integrated industrial city" featuring IT/BPO companies, four other sector-specific zones, and a lifestyle zone with upscale residential colonies, shopping malls, and the like. The Mahindra World City, a special-purpose vehicle that was majority owned by Mahindra, would be the landlord of this private city, reselling developed plots of land to companies and residents at a large markup. With the assistance of the Rajasthan government, then, it established a fully functioning urban land market for global capital inside its ten-foot high boundary walls. Disinterred from its agrarian social milieu, this land—once the fields and grazing commons of nine villages—was now an open field for domestic and global capital.

Countermovement Absorbed

This did not generate a countermovement. While SEZs were being met with "land wars" elsewhere in India, the Rajasthan government shrewdly avoided one against the MWC by absorbing farmers into the spectacular land commodification the SEZ generated. Instead of giving farmers below-market compensation, which has triggered militant resistance in many other cases, the Rajasthan government gave farmers small plots of land adjacent to the SEZ that would be zoned for commercial and residential use. The purpose, as one government official described it, was to "soften opposition." It was an attempt, in other words, to overcome potential opposition to dispossession by inclusion into land commodification.

The strategy proved effective. While these small plots had no agricultural value and were only equipped with the most rudimentary infrastructure even a decade after they were allotted, their price quickly skyrocketed. Brokers created "power of attorney" contractors that allowed farmers to sell their rights to these plots before they physically existed; and they persuaded many to do so. Through various combinations of enticement, fear, misinformation, and outright fraud, many heavily indebted lower-caste farmers were persuaded to sell their land rights relatively early and cheaply. Many upper castes, meanwhile, shrewdly calculated that these plots would soon have an astronomical exchange value, and held onto them. The result was not consent to dispossession—farmers were not consulted much less given the right of refusal—but individualized compliance. By absorbing farmers into a speculative land market that they had uneven abilities to navigate, the Rajasthan government effectively utilized preexisting agrarian inequalities to prevent collective opposition.

Other Indian states have, before and since, similarly tried to overcome resistance to land dispossession with land prices. States with strong farmers' movements—most notably Uttar Pradesh and Haryana—were the first to pass new compensation policies, though by the end of the 2000s few states' compensation policies were unchanged. In 2013, faced with escalating "land wars," the Congress government finally passed—with bipartisan support—a replacement to India's colonial-era Land Acquisition Act. The Right to Fair Compensation and Transparency in Land Acquisition and Resettlement and Rehabilitation Act (LARRA for short) sought to buy consent from farmers by, among other things, multiplying compensation levels by two to three times based on proximity to the city. While the law also created some administrative hurdles to dispossessing land, including a consent clause for private projects that could be taken as evidence for limited "reembedding," the law's overriding purpose was to facilitate commodification by giving farmers a greater stake in it. Because of aggressive corporate lobbying, this stake wound up being much lower than originally proposed and thus probably insufficient to generalize compliance to dispossession across India. It is especially unlikely to work in villages that, unlike Rajpura, have more profitable irrigated agriculture, stronger village solidarity based on lower inequalities, and long histories of peasant insurgency. This continued difficulty, in turn, has prompted efforts to further facilitate land commodification without state-orchestrated dispossession, whether by further liberalizing land conversions, modernizing land records, or by deploying what are often called "land mafias": essentially informal networks of private investors and public officials who deploy coercion and fraud to grab and develop land.

But the point is that while India's land wars may be interpreted as a Polanyian countermovement, India's central and state governments have responded not by decommodifying land but by trying to absorb farmers into the land's commodification. The case of Rajpura suggests that this is very possible. Although farmers there received a higher stake in its commodification, this did not alter or even slow down the fact of commodification. While one could certainly point to the ways in which the regional land market—like those anywhere—continued to depend on state action and regulation, the important point is that their land was now as commodified as capitalism would ever need it to be. In Rajpura, as elsewhere in rural India, deepening land commodification was the overwhelming secular trend, and fixating on minor forms of embededdness is rather beside the point. Land is very much commodifiable, and there is nothing automatic about Polanyi's double movement. The emergence of countermovements rests, rather, on the contingent and uneven ability of states to generate compliance to dispossession in specific agrarian milieu. While land is a fictitious commodity, and this is what makes dispossession an important mechanism for capital accumulation, its commodification is not utopian, whatever the social and ecological consequences.

Social and Ecological Dislocations

Those consequences are real. As Polanyi would expect, dispossessing and commodifying Rajpura's land did have serious social and ecological implications. As I have documented in more detail elsewhere (Levien 2018), loss of farmland and grazing land destroyed agriculture while the loss of fodder forced a massive selling off of livestock. The resulting lack of income and food security deepened market dependence for subsistence in a time of drastic food inflation and very slow job creation. In 2008, the SEZ was just becoming operational when the global financial crisis rippled through Rajpura, stalling the land market and slowing down related construction and commercial activity. My survey of four villages found that a majority of families, and a large majority of Dalit families, reported having less income and less food after losing their land for the SEZ. Many families also lost their homes, for which they were undercompensated. A hamlet of landless Dalits was driven from their huts on the village grazing land and received nothing in turn. Loss of wells, demolition of the village catchment pond, and a new industry of extracting ground water for sale to the SEZ further depleted village aquifers, making villagers dependent for household consumption on toxic tanker water tractored in from villages contaminated by industrial effluents—a huge health crisis in the making. Dispossession was, moreover, particularly deleterious to women who not only saw their reproductive labor become more difficult (as fodder and firewood became scarce) but lost their only relatively autonomous economic activity—livestock raising—while being almost entirely excluded from the ensuing real estate economy by virtue of a patriarchal system of landownership.

Many of these consequences did generate anger among large sections of Rajpura. But with dispossession a fait accompli and villagers sharply divided by their ability to profit from land commodification, these consequences of the SEZ largely went unchallenged. It is not that Polanyi was wrong about commodification's baneful consequences. He was just wrong that it could not continue.

Polanyi's contribution to our understanding of land commodification is ultimately limited. While the apparent upsurge of land struggles since the 2000s has renewed interest in Polanyi's theory of the double movement, on closer inspection there is very little in Polanyi that can help us explain the dynamics or future possibilities of these struggles. What Polanyi did understand, however, was the historical specificity of, and social obstacles to, treating land as a commodity. Land was not, like most commodities, brought into the world for the purpose of selling it on the market; to make it governed by markets, therefore, requires the use of state power to overcome social institutions and value practices that do not have the realization of exchange value as their purpose. This may have significant, even devastating, social and ecological consequences. And it may generate social protest. But it can be accomplished, at least to a sufficient enough extent.

Polanyi is useful today, then, not because he identified the impossibility of commodifying land, offered a novel critique of ecological destruction, or provided a particularly accurate depiction of precapitalist institutions. Rather, Polanyi helps us understand why state-orchestrated land dispossession is such an important component of contemporary capitalism. Recent attempts to theorize the relationship between dispossession and capitalism notably overlook this question, simply taking for granted the link between economic forces and dispossession. While Harvey (2003, 2005) derives his theory of accumulation by dispossession from an analysis of global circuits of capital, Polanyi helps us understand why there actually needs to be dispossession for land to be absorbed into those circuits. Overcoming social barriers to commodification is a political process undertaken by states, often involving dispossession, which may or may not succeed. Understanding the conditions for this success is a major task for a comparative sociology of dispossession. Polanyi does not provide us with that sociology, but helps us see the need for it.

2

FICTIONS OF SURPLUS

Commodifying Public Land in Canada and the United Kingdom

Brett Christophers and Heather Whiteside

In September 2017, planning officers of Cornwall Council in southwest England gave the go-ahead to the property developer Comparo to build 134 homes and four business units on forty acres of clifftop land between Perranporth and Newquay (Smallcombe 2017). The development was controversial. When the council had launched a consultation earlier in the year, twenty-two objections and no supporting comments were lodged; locals labeled the plans "absolutely outrageous." The opposition is easy to understand. Not only did the proposed development raise concerns about sewage, flooding, traffic, parking, and possible environmental and wildlife impacts, but, seven years previously, Comparo had acquired the site from the government, in the shape of the Ministry of Defence, for the princely sum of just £750,000. Planning permission now promised significant development-based gains. Why, then, had the land been sold? Because, the government had said at the time, it was *surplus*.

Meanwhile, an iconic heritage building in the heart of downtown Toronto, once the government of Canada's first customs house and later redeveloped in the 1930s for other government operations, was sold in March 2017 to the highest bidder. Public input was not solicited and city planners were not consulted—groups who might have had their own preferences for what to do with this centrally located two-acre plot. Described by the city as being "a rare and exceptional example in Canada of Beaux-Arts Classicism," the Dominion Public Building is now private property, and one more item in Larco Investments' expanding portfolio of hotels, malls, apartments, and office buildings (McGillivray 2017). The sale, which brought the Government of Canada C$275.1 million, was made possible only once the land and building were declared *surplus* to government needs—despite it bustling with fifteen hundred Canada Revenue Agency (taxation department) employees. The city, meanwhile, is experiencing an affordable housing crisis, significant property price inflation, and widespread gentrification. Larco has yet to release its redevelopment plans for this choice property, but so long as it honors the heritage designation, it is free to do as it pleases with this land zoned commercial-residential; it may even build (yet another) forty-one-story tower for condo market investors. By rooting out "surplus" in the public sector, government created scarce new private land in Canada's biggest city.

These specific cases of land privatization on either side of the Atlantic represent individual instances of much wider trends. In both countries, much public land has been commodified—rendered tradable in capitalist markets—through "surplus" identification and disposal. Like other aspects of neoliberalism, privatization unites otherwise distinct national experiences in Canada and the United Kingdom, and yet the legitimizing narratives, processes, and procedures underpinning the commodification of public land have gone underexamined.

In this chapter, focusing comparatively on the Canadian and UK experiences, we explore one particular component of the wide-ranging work involved in privatizing and commodifying public land: the discursive component. What arguments—not just about land per se but about the different types of owners it can have—have been advanced to rationalize and justify this process of commodification? We refer to such legitimizing narratives as land "fictions" (and explain why), and our objective is to identify, understand, and critique them. As we will show, the kernel of these fictions is the particular idea invoked by the state that public land is often "surplus" land, and thus free to be commodified. Further, we describe how surplus labels are readied, and land released to the private sector, through techniques of (dis)incentivization, the normalization of public land disposal practices, and the transfer of authority to different actors.

There are three main sections to the chapter. In the first, we provide some essential preparatory material. What constitutes "public land" in Canada and the United Kingdom? What types of land, or land under what types of public use, have been commodified? Who has driven this process of commodification, to whom has the privatized land been sold, and, last but not least, how much public land has been commodified? The second section unpacks the pivotal concept of "surplus," considering its distinctive articulation and coloring in each national context. Finally, in the third section, we turn to the ways in which these fictions of surplus are brought to life. Ideas about the land do their most efficacious work when they are operationalized in and through institutional structures, practices and processes that assume their veracity. We therefore consider how, in Canada and the United Kingdom, various laws, calculative techniques, modes of representation and institutional rearrangements have been mobilized to help turn the core fiction—surplus—into historical-geographical fact.

Commodifying the Land

Canada

Canada is a vast country, covering an area of nearly 10 million square kilometers, second only to Russia, but one with equally vast tracts of land undeveloped by capital and the state—nearly 85 percent of the population lives within three hundred kilometers of the American border and over half live in four urban regions clustered close to the United States. Its colonial heritage means that all land in Canada is ultimately owned by the English monarch. Land tenure rights, not absolute ownership, therefore legally underpin all land activities. Most land is public land, generally referred to as "Crown land," split between federal jurisdiction (approximately 40 percent of total land) and provincial jurisdiction (approximately 50 percent). Private land—roughly 10 percent of the entire landmass—is where rights to (but not absolute ownership of) the land have been transferred to the private sector through a system based on English common law (outside of Quebec, where French civil law informs property rights).

The constitutional division of powers in Canada (unlike in the United Kingdom) awards many economically significant sectors to provincial jurisdiction, including Crown land activities relating to mining, oil and gas, and forestry.[1] However, given that the country's single largest landholder is the federal government (making it one of the world's largest landholders as well), and that each of the ten provinces has its own distinct history and practice relating to Crown land, this chapter engages with federal jurisdiction policies and procedures only. We do so in light of space constraints, the unequal power of the federal purse and its administration of pan-Canadian programs (including relations with indigenous communities), and to allow for a simpler comparison with the United Kingdom.

Excluding the three northern territories in the high arctic where population is sparse and government activities are minimal, the federal government manages 28 million square meters of building space and 23 million hectares of land. If all this land were put in one place, it would cover about the same area as Great Britain. Prior to the 1990s, it was typical for the federal government to engage in the long-term retention of Crown land, mainly to service government departments, the activities of Crown corporations (like Canadian National Railways [CNR] and Air Canada), and to house military bases, airports, and ports.

The late 1980s and early 1990s were a time of fiscal austerity and divestiture of public assets. Between 1985 and 2004, more than thirty-five federal Crown corporations were sold for a total of C$12 billion (Padova 2005). When ranked according to sales proceeds (in nominal dollars), we see transportation-related Crown corporations top the list, including: CNR (1995, $2.1 billion); Petro-Canada (1991, $1.7 billion); Navcanada (1996, $1.5 billion); and Air Canada (1988, $474 million) (McBride 2005, 103). Two alternative fates befell the previously public land used by those corporations. On the one hand, commercially viable portions were divested alongside the corporations, becoming private property. On the other hand, contaminated or otherwise unmarketable land was retained by the state, thereby becoming "surplus" in the sense that by definition it was, at least in the short term, unused or unneeded. Examples included huge tracts of land once owned by CNR (several key parcels of which were located in or near urban centers), abandoned or damaged spur lines, and vacant or dilapidated real estate like stock and maintenance yards.[2]

The 1995 federal budget introduced the deepest spending cuts ever experienced in an effort to balance the books and pay down national debt. So significant were the cuts that 1995 can be described as a "watershed year" that "brought wholesale change" so fundamental that it "reverberated through all areas of the federal government, including the system of real property management" (McKellar 2006, 54–55). The size of public sector operations and staff reduced dramatically, and so did the need for government departments to hold public land, buildings, and equipment.

Areas of federal public land retention that escaped the early neoliberal privatization wave were targeted for more routinized surplus disposals by the mid-1990s and beyond. Notable surplus federal land sales include: rail–CN shops (Moncton); urban ports–historic properties (Halifax), Market Square (Saint John), Le Vieux Port (Montreal), Harbourfront (Toronto), Granville Island (Vancouver); commercial ports–Ridley Terminal (Prince Rupert) (ultimately nationalized); airports–Mirabel (Montreal), Pearson (Toronto); and military bases–Chilliwack (BC), Downsview (Toronto), Kapyong Barracks (Winnipeg). Military bases have been particularly targeted; between 1994 and 2000, half of all military bases in Canada were deemed "surplus" and sold, cutting the number from fifty-two to twenty-four. Nearly 60 percent of all federal office space is now leased from the private sector; two of three northern territories (Yukon and Northwest Territories) encompassing enormous tracts of land have been transferred from federal oversight to province-like status; federal airport authorities were devolved to quasi-private agencies; and several national parklands were transferred to local (private nonprofit) community groups.

Obtaining accurate statistics on federal land transfer and sale by geographical size and ownership is difficult given that the often lauded Directory of Federal Real Property does not contain time series data or privatization records. Piecing together the story using multiple sources reveals a stark decline: from approximately fifty thousand items listed in the Directory in 1995 to twenty thousand items in 2016 (Hodge et al. 1995; Treasury Board of Canada 2016). In other words, more than half the catalogue of public land, buildings, and equipment held by the Canadian federal government has disappeared through transfer or sale over the past twenty years. And who exactly is purchasing or receiving that land? Case study evidence is needed here given the paucity of official statistics. In the only extant book on the subject, the authors conclude, "What interests predominate in policy about federal property? In general, it is business" (Ircha and Young 2013, 168). While sales of federal public land within urban centers may elicit a range of competing interests—from municipal government to heritage preservation groups to local development coalitions—commercial interests dominate surplus land disposal strategies.

The United Kingdom

In the United Kingdom, public land is owned by ministerial departments, local authorities, public corporations, and various other state entities. In England, Northern Ireland, and Wales, as in Canada, the Crown is the ultimate, absolute owner of such land (just as it is of private land), with the state holding merely an "estate" (freehold or leasehold) therein; this was also the case in Scotland until 2004, when the abolition of feudal tenure ended the Crown's position as so-called "Paramount Superior." Somewhat confusingly, whereas in Canada "Crown land" *is* public land, in the United Kingdom the latter *excludes* the "Crown Estate" (where the freehold as well as absolute ownership belongs to the reigning monarch).

Although the commodification-through-privatization of UK public land predates neoliberalism, the period since the beginning of the 1980s indisputably marks the heyday of this phenomenon. Before the 1980s, sales of public land were periodic and piecemeal and were frequently offset or outweighed, particularly in the 1950s and 1960s, by land acquisitions by the state; since then, sales have been sustained and substantial. Reliable estimates are not available for the precise magnitude of UK land privatization between the beginning of the 1980s and today, but it is possible to give an indication of the approximate scale of the transformation. In the mid- to late 1970s, the public sector was estimated to own "about 19 per cent of total acreage" in Britain (Massey and Catalano 1978, 6). Christophers (2018) estimates that today only around half of that land remains in public ownership. An enormous chunk of UK real estate has passed from public to private hands.

Who has been responsible for this disposal program? All individual sales of public land parcels have been actioned by the land's immediate owners—which, as mentioned, run the gamut of public sector bodies—but those owners have often been acting according to firm guidance and under considerable pressure from central government. Land privatization has, in short, been very much a Whitehall-led initiative (Christophers 2017). Not all government administrations have been equally zealous in their pursuit of disposal, however. The original impetus came with Margaret Thatcher's accession to power in 1979; the flow of disposals ebbed somewhat, albeit without drying up altogether, during the Labour years (1997–2010); it has since regathered pace under the Conservative-led coalition (2010–15) and subsequent Conservative (2015—today) administrations. All the while, private-sector interests keen to acquire "surplus" public land have been busily lobbying in the background, seeding and reinforcing the idea that the land *is* surplus and should therefore be disposed of.

In the United Kingdom, as in Canada, a significant amount of land has disappeared from public ownership as a kind of ancillary baggage of "other" privatizations. Through the privatizations of water, electricity, coal, and rail between 1985 and 1997, "up to one million acres [or 400,000 hectares], some of it immensely valuable development land, was transferred, often without a proper evaluation, often without any disclosure as to its scale" (Cahill 2001, 138). But a much greater area of land has disappeared through the privatization and commodification of land qua land—in the region of 1.6 million hectares (Christophers 2018). This land has been shorn from both the local and central government estates. The former has seen the more severe reductions, as local authorities have disposed of everything from school playing fields to allotments. Central government disposals have been more modest. Much of the land that has been privatized has been released by the Forestry Commission and the Ministry of Defence, which, despite decades of estate shrinkage, remain the largest central government landholders.

Where land has been privatized as part of a wider enterprise privatization (e.g., of the water authorities), it is generally known to whom the land has been sold. In the case of the privatization explicitly and solely of land, however, it frequently is not. When, for instance, the secretary of state for health was asked in early 2016 about subsequent uses of land sold by the National Health Service, the answer was that "the Department has only collected data on surplus land sales since 2011" (and even since then, such data do not include "information about whether or not sites were sold on the open market, or the final sale price") (HC Deb 27 January 2016, 24634W). This paucity of information concerning what has happened to land privatized in recent decades is typical across the public sector.

Nevertheless, two important observations about the beneficiaries of land privatization can be made. The first is that, especially since the turn of the millennium, corporate buyers have become increasingly important, while sales to wealthy individuals have declined (Cahill 2010). The second is that among corporate buyers, property developers—not coincidentally the most active lobbyists of government on public land disposal—have increasingly come to the fore. As releasing land for the construction of housing by the private sector has turned into a central rationale for disposal (DCLG 2012), so housebuilders have become the preferred bidders—and their landholdings have mushroomed accordingly.

Fictions of Surplus

The large-scale privatization and commodification of public land in Canada and the United Kingdom have been animated by a dense array of powerful legitimating narratives. These narratives, which we refer to as "fictions," are our concern in this section of the chapter. What form do they take, who articulates them, and what political work do they do? In designating these narratives as "fictions," we follow the legal anthropologist Annelise Riles. Riles (2011, 175) understands a legitimating fiction as "more tool than text" and she emphasizes that "the truth or falsity of its content is really beside the point" when trying to understand its power: "What matters rather is what possibilities for action it opens up or forecloses." The fictions we examine here have opened up the privatization vista while simultaneously closing down the viability of continuing public ownership.

Generally speaking these fictions relate to two primary sets of objects and their interrelations. The first object, of course, is land per se. These are, precisely, *land* fictions; they make certain claims about the nature of land, its properties, and its potentialities. The second object is the land's owner. In the pre-commodification conjuncture that the fictions in question agitate against, that owner is the state; in the post-commodification future that such fictions champion and help bring into being, ownership becomes located within the private sector, ordinarily figured in this generic, undifferentiated form. As well as making claims about land, then, our fictions also make certain claims about the public and private sectors respectively—about the inherent qualities they do or do not possess. More important, the fictions we explore below make claims about land-and-owner *combined*. That is to say, they profess certain truths about land *when in public ownership* (essentially, bad) and about land *when in private ownership* (good).

The principal fictions to have circulated in support of public land's commodification in Canada and the United Kingdom have been first and foremost fictions about economic value: land in private ownership has positive value connotations that land in public ownership singularly lacks. Value is both a preeminent thematic and the most important ground for distinguishing public *from* private land ownership. Justifying the privatization and commodification of public land thus finds root primarily in the alleged positive value characteristics of private land ownership.

These fictions are not unique. They parallel and perhaps even implicitly trade on comparable fictions narrated and mobilized in different contexts, in different parts of the world, in times past and present, and to underwrite all manner of different types of land transfer. Fictions of surplus today clearly trace back to Lockean "Laws of Nature"—seventeenth-century commandments justifying private property and encouraging land improvement and the accumulation of stock. For Locke (1980 [1690], 21), "nothing was made by God for man to spoil or destroy" and thus productive (private, individual) activity was essential for the common good. The idea that common land is idle land, and idle land breeds waste and spoilage, would become established stock-in-trade of liberal—and especially colonial—capitalist discourse aimed at conceptually devaluing one type of land ownership and use in order to legitimate its replacement by another (favorably valued) type. Thus, our fictions variously echo, inter alia, the depiction of unimproved commons as "wastelands" by advocates of enclosure in early nineteenth-century England (Goldstein 2013) and in colonial India (Gidwani 2008); the imagery of urban "blight" and "obsolescence" invoked in calls for commercial redevelopment in the postwar United States (Weber 2002); and perhaps especially, the late nineteenth-century rendering of indigenous lands, in the same territory, as "surplus" or valu*eless* (Hanke and Dowdle 1987).

There are also clearly family resemblances between the fictions of surplus that energize land privatization today and the market-privileging ideas about land that Polanyi, calling land a "fictitious commodity," attacked in *The Great Transformation* (2001 [1944]) (on which see the Introduction and chapter 1 of the present book).[3] But there are important differences, not least in the understanding and application of the idea of fictitiousness. For Polanyi, it was the idea that land was a commodity like any other that was fictional. The ideas and arguments we document and dissect in what follows, by contrast, do not designate land a commodity so much as inform political action designed to turn it into one. They do so not by pinning the label "commodity" on it, but instead by imbuing it with differential qualities of value and valuelessness when held in different—commodified and non-commodified—ways by different political-economic actors.

The fictions we discuss in this chapter, in any event, are not entirely unique. But neither do they exactly mirror cognate fictions; they have distinctive characteristics that we can usefully flesh out. Our starting point is that since the beginning of the 1980s, federal/national governments in Canada and the United Kingdom, supported by a sundry cast of actors from the private sector, have consistently declared that public land not currently used for the delivery of public services is *surplus* land. In doing so, they have explicitly devalued that land. In Canada, for example, Erik Nielsen, the government minister in charge of a special task force on federal property management in 1985, called the previous management scheme (when surplus disposals were not common), a "system which is bloated with inventory, undermanaged and overstaffed," and recommended that "a divestiture strategy should be implemented immediately" (Nielsen 1986, 13–14). Surplus is excess, and excess must be shed.

But it is not only that public land is often stripped of value by positing it as valueless "waste." Officials have often gone further still, arguing that such land makes a *negative* value contribution. Consider, for instance, UK Conservative Party grandee Michael Heseltine's (2012, 112) influential claim that "derelict and unused [public] properties are a major drag on our local economies." Surplus public land, he suggests, not only adds no value; it pulls economies *back*. And who, of course, could argue with Heseltine's adamancy that "surplus and derelict land should not be wasted"? If it constitutes an economic drag, then releasing surplus land to the private sector to ensure it is "brought back into productive use" becomes the most natural thing in the world.

This discourse of surplus public land, while common to Canada and the United Kingdom, has inevitably been invested with distinctive inflections in each place. In Canada, for example, this discourse, at least since the early 1990s, has displayed a striking temporality. All public property is defined by its "life cycle," comprising a series of stages through which such property typically passes during the course of its "natural" life (Treasury Board of Canada 2011). Secured by the types of accounting practices that we turn to in the following section, this life cycle has a natural terminus or endpoint to which all public property—exempt as it is from the disciplinary hygiene of the market—ineluctably gravitates or decays: surplus, and hence sale.

In the United Kingdom, the surplus discourse displays a noteworthy spatiality. It is tightly bound up with recurrent concerns about land scarcity which, unsurprisingly given that country's scale, do not feature in Canadian political discourse. The central concern is that creeping urbanization will eat into Blake's "green and pleasant land," a mythical milieu long idealized within English culture in general but by those with a vested interest in "protection" of the countryside in particular. The upshot is that in the United Kingdom, land rendered conceptually "surplus" so as to catalyze its disposal is almost invariably *urban* land. "Since 1978, I have been asking successive Secretaries of State to do something to release public vacant dormant, derelict, or under-utilised land," railed one member of the rural landed class, the Conservative politician Anthony Steen, in parliament in 1990 (and note the litany of devaluing adjectives he used). "Every Secretary of State does a little more, but none has been adventurous enough to ensure that that land is used before the green field sites around our towns and cities are spoilt" (HC Deb 30 November 1990, c1139). Canadian public land deemed "surplus" has typically been urban, too, but only because that is where the greatest potential value (to the private sector) lies; there is no comparable "protection"-oriented country/city discourse.

Meanwhile, two dimensions of the discourse that devalues land in public ownership by positing it as waste or surplus call for particular attention. First, this discourse is widely predicated on a fundamental closure that is itself rarely disclosed. Specifically, certain uses of public land by the public sector are actively narrowed or closed off—without it always being publicly stated that they *are* being closed off—in such a way as to effectively *make* land surplus. In Canada, as mentioned earlier, this is most visible in the wake of Crown corporation divestiture (rail, air) and devolution (airports, parks, ports). In the United Kingdom, far and away the best example is public housing. As it has been made politically and economically harder and harder since the early 1980s for local authorities to invest in the production and ownership of public housing (Meek 2014, ch. 6), the land that many of them *would* have used for this purpose—that there exists such an appetite has never been in doubt (e.g., LGA 2016)—has consequently been rendered surplus. Surplus, in other words, is always relative; the land is surplus to requirements *that someone has defined*.

Second, the discourse is also predicated on a set of deep-seated assumptions about the public sector's deficiencies. As an owner and manager of assets in general and of land and property assets in particular, the state is deemed inherently inefficient. As such, there always *will be* surplus land to be disposed of; the existence of such surplus is guaranteed by the public sector's intrinsic inefficiency. Thus, the UK government's obligation "to manage its estate in the most efficient and effective manner . . . will often result in property or land being identified as surplus" (OGC 2005, 1). Hence Prime Minister David Cameron's 2011 request to major landholding departments to publish "land release strategies" (DCLG 2012, 7). That there *is* surplus to be released is not in question. "The public sector," by its very nature, "controls large amounts of surplus land, buildings and vacant space in buildings, which"—no less inevitably—"are not being put to good economic use" (GPU 2013, 14). "Stewardship" and "citizen focus" are two core elements of Canadian public property management that entrench the notion that public land ownership is as inefficient as government itself. These principles remove bureaucratic discretion, bind policymakers to a vision of public asset maximization through privatization, and link public land sales to "protection" from government waste.

If the fictions framing public land conceptually devalue that land *when in public use*, however, they demonstrably *re*value the same land under the coveted privatization scenario. They envision the private sector using the land more efficiently and, in the process, stimulating economic development and generating economic value for the nation. Stimulating the economy is certainly not the only rationale for privatizing public land, but it is a crucial one, as the UK Liberal Democrat peer Susan Kramer emphasized in parliamentary debate in 2014: "My Lords, maximising the release of surplus public sector land is critical to supporting the Government's ambitions to reduce the deficit, increase the number of houses being built and help to drive economic growth" (HL Deb 15 July 2014, c230). The UK government repeatedly stresses this commitment to, and confidence in, "releasing surplus assets to drive economic growth" (e.g., HM Treasury 2015, 72). And this, of course, conjures a very different type of "surplus": whereas land in public ownership allegedly often constitutes surplus in the shape of negative, valueless waste, land in private ownership helps produce positive, incremental surplus—that is, surplus (or *added*) value.

In concluding this section, we want to make two main observations about this positive figuring, one of which concerns fictions of the private sector and one of which concerns fictions of land. The first and most obvious point is that this discourse idealizes the private sector just as powerfully as it demonizes the state. It presumes that the private sector is inherently more efficient and less wasteful than the public sector in its use of land and property. Releasing public land to the private sector is a worthy enterprise in and of itself since the private sector will *not* leave it lying idle and valueless in the manner of the state. This, at least, is the assumption.

Second, and relatedly, this discourse reifies the land in value terms—as, indeed, does the converse argument that to leave "surplus" land within the public sector is to effectively handicap society. Recall Michael Heseltine's above-quoted assertion that unused public properties exert a "drag" on the economy. The flipside to this argument is the claim that privatizing such land magically generates economic growth—that to release the land to the private sector is *also* to release latent value creation potential hidden within it and restrained by the state's wasteful ownership. The term generally used to invoke such release is "unlocking," a powerful concept that evokes the public sector keeping value "locked up." In the United Kingdom, those in favor of public land disposal widely enthuse about unlocking the value harbored in such assets, as if commodification is all that is required to do the trick. In making its case for "accelerating the release of surplus public sector land," for example, the Department of Communities and Local Government (DCLG 2012, 6–8) infers that to "unlock this land" is, in turn, to "unlock homes and jobs."

Of course, the idea that land has this power—the power to create value or, alternatively, hinder its generation—is not new. And while it was influentially resuscitated by Hernando de Soto in his paean to private property ownership in *The Mystery of Capital* (2000), the idea arguably originates with the group of eighteenth-century French economists known as the Physiocrats. For them, in the words of one (Quesnay 1963 [1767], 232), "land is the unique source of wealth." Today's advocates of public land privatization may not agree with the "unique" bit, but their pronouncements otherwise concur. So when scholars dismiss Physiocracy as a mere "historical curiosity" (Cleveland 1987, 50), they are wrong; Physiocracy is very much still with us, haunting the most powerful of contemporary land fictions in Canada and the United Kingdom.

From Fiction to Fact: Realizing and Releasing "Surplus"

We now turn to the instrumentalization of the surplus fiction, identifying how the ideational is enacted through new bureaucratic procedures and pathways of institutional decision making, and illuminating how these in turn mobilize powerful calculative devices and regimes of "expertise." More often than not, practices of commodification of surplus public land are rooted in neoclassical economic thought and/or modeled after private-sector practices promoted by consultants spanning the accounting, management, and real estate fields. The public sector is reconfigured, with both perception and practice realigned to the view that public land holdings are surplus and that surplus is to be disposed of primarily through market sale.

While acknowledging some notable national differences, namely emphases on temporality (Canada) versus spatiality (UK) along with a variety of sectoral-historical discrepancies, we highlight the following similarities exhibited in Canada and the United Kingdom: (i) techniques of (dis)incentivization, (ii) routinization and normalization of public land disposal (including through the use of benchmarking to ensure public sector conformity with market ideals), (iii) the privileging of privatization as a disposal strategy after a surplus designation is rendered, and (iv) the transfer of authority to different actors. Fiction thus becomes fact through, inter alia, new laws, regulations, accountancy standards, measurement practices, and special-purpose public sector agencies.

Techniques of (Dis)incentivization

Accounting treatment determines how the footprint of government property is perceived and valued financially. Until the 1980s and 1990s, public sector departments in Canada and the United Kingdom commonly used cash accounting, measuring annual real property revenue against annual expenditures, and reporting fixed assets, like land and buildings, at a nominal value on the balance sheet. Meanwhile, the private sector used a different toolkit, accrual accounting, which reports on an overall financial position, taking an asset-by-asset perspective (building-by-building and at the portfolio level), discounted over time. Full accrual accounting considers the cost of the property, equipment, and other assets to be a long-term prepayment of an expense in advance of the use of the asset. As the economic service life of the asset expires, the cost is allocated to operations as an expense ("depreciation").

By the 1990s, with government departments seeking the "efficiencies" and "economies" of business (this being, of course, the height of early neoliberal and new public management zeal in both Canada and the United Kingdom, along with much of the rest of the world), accrual accounting was widely taken up within the public sector. Previous practices viewed public land and real property as a free good; now with depreciation and corresponding "asset rents" applied, land and real property came to be seen as a cost of program delivery—a liability to be shed. Public sector bodies now carry assets at their book value (historical value minus depreciation) or market value. Regardless of the exact numbers plugged into the formula, the ends are the same: public property becomes a cost of program delivery. The accounting switch, dry in detail though it may be, ensures that public land and buildings are seen as a cost and their depreciation becomes included in public bodies' financial statements. Holding public property now incurs financial disincentives, while financial incentives flow in the direction of market sales and leases. Accounting techniques of dis-/incentivization dovetail with wider neoliberal directives: government costs are to be minimized, efficiencies are to be found.

Linking financial accounting to property management, the use of a "portfolio management approach" is another key part of the surplus land story. Like accrual accounting, the portfolio management approach was a private sector development introduced into government through new public management reforms that imported microeconomic principles and indicators. With portfolio management, departments group public land and other property holdings into sets of strategies aimed at minimizing costs and risks, and optimizing efficiencies. Public bodies assess their real property needs in terms of present and future uses: the cost to maintain certain assets and their relevance to long-term strategic goals.

Surplus holdings are considered a potential future liability and thus disposal not only raises revenue, it also reduces liabilities. This is a "win-win" for privatization, shot entirely through the lens of a particular accounting and property management approach geared to finding surplus and selling it—granting reality to the neoliberal fiction that the future needs of government will dwindle. Once public land is sold, any expansion in government operations will require significant capital expenditures or leasing from market actors, an expensive proposition closed off by broader fiscal austerity. Surplus becomes a one-way street to privatization.

In both Canada and the United Kingdom, surplus disposal, as we discuss further below, does not *necessarily* mean market sale; in fact, the option to transfer to other government bodies must be explored first through "first look" requirements. However, if surplus property is a liability to one public body, its uptake within other areas of the public sector becomes unlikely if it is booked with depreciation and sale as a terminal stage in the life cycle of public property, and all other such bodies are also using the same asset management strategies and accounting techniques (for broader evaluation of these strategies and techniques, see Froud et al. 1998; Guthrie 1998; Olson et al. 1998).

In the Canadian context, a fiscal carrot (or disposal incentive) has also been created in the form of revenue sharing. Historically, all revenue from the sale or transfer of real property went into a consolidated revenue fund with no financial benefit seen by the body that once held that property (other than reduced maintenance and operating costs). Beginning in the 1990s, surplus-disposing departments were allowed to retain all net proceeds from their land sales, encouraging them to accelerate surplus land identification. Similar incentives, meanwhile, have been selectively introduced to the public sector in the United Kingdom.

Routinization and Normalization of Public Land Disposal

Accounting and property management techniques are but one part of larger programs in each country routinizing and normalizing the sale of public land. Companion policies include creating and publishing registers of surplus holdings that originate through ideas around property life cycle and benchmarking practices. Core public property benchmarks, whether adopted from the private sector through enthusiastic emulation or pushed by private consultants, include the facility condition index (FCI), operating and maintenance expenses, and office space utilization. These benchmarks are believed to enhance the efficiency and effectiveness of property management, the intention being to minimize the space taken up in the formulation and execution of public policy. Public sector bodies must assess and report on the functionality and utilization of their real property and develop disposal strategies accordingly. Annual performance assessment shapes plans for surplus disposal.

In the United Kingdom, surplus land registers have been a feature of government policy for more than three decades. The 1980 Local Government Planning and Land Act introduced them for local authorities and equivalent requirements for central government departments and agencies were introduced in 2003. Government watchdogs—not least the Audit Commission and National Audit Office—have consistently scrutinized different bodies' asset management performance, with the Treasury on hand to quantify the expected benefits of property rationalization "best practice" and new oversight bodies (such as the Government Property Unit, since 2010) periodically being created to enhance centralized coordination of efficient estate management.

In Canada, each federal department must keep a current record of its real property as part of the Directory of Federal Real Property. The DFRP classifies the primary use of each land parcel as well as the public property security designation, land area, building count, floor area, geographical classification, surplus site data, structure data, and contaminated site data. Departments send these reports to the Treasury Board and update the DFRP whenever there is a change to the property, including acquisition and disposal. More than a mere cataloging exercise, the information contained in these reports becomes a sales brochure of sorts, used to advertise surplus inventory. Surplus property must be shed within three years.

Privileging of Privatization as Disposal Strategy

As mentioned earlier, both Canada and the United Kingdom have guidelines in place giving other public bodies rights of "first look" when surplus public land is earmarked for disposal. So why have privatization and commodification—as opposed to retention by the public sector—actually been the typical outcome of the disposal process?

In the Canadian case it is because exchange value determinations are privileged once a surplus designation has been rendered. Decisions are explicitly justified in terms of market value as determined through "highest and best use" (HABU) appraisal. HABU assigns a price to public land by establishing what market actors would likely do with it; it does not and cannot address why public land should be retained and what government might want or need to do with it in the future. Mainstream economic assumptions inform the nuts-and-bolts of HABU analysis, and the exercise itself is underpinned by classical Ricardian economics: land is assumed to have an inherent value but "improvements" augment its exchange value.

HABU incentivizes market sale rather than transfers of surplus property *within* government because its calculations assume improvements are of highest and best use *if* commercially oriented (retail, residential, industrial). Other government bodies interested in acquiring surplus federal land before it goes to open market sale must be able and willing to match the market value as established through HABU appraisal. This is difficult, if not impossible, for public bodies subject to budget restraint. Sometimes such bodies are "assisted" with public-private partnerships underwriting municipal bids for surplus federal land. But even here, though the land itself is not fully privatized after disposal, market-oriented and commercialized activities prevail nonetheless.

In the UK case, exchange value considerations have also become more important. Prior to 1980, public sector land sellers were expected to achieve market value *unless* selling to other public bodies, but that exception has long since been buried. Privatization is also privileged over intragovernment transfer via more mundane mechanisms. Often, the first-look guidelines—public sector bodies theoretically have forty working days to express an interest in a surplus asset before it is advertised on the open market—are simply ignored. Moreover, Whitehall has been pushing for the disposal of public land to enable more homebuilding in areas of perceived housing shortages by explicitly and avowedly releasing land *to the market*. Here, the first-look maxim is nowhere to be seen.

Transfer of Authority to Different Actors

HABU appraisal in Canada not only determines the market value of public land, it activates particular disposal routes for surplus land. "Routine" disposals are those where surplus properties can be sold easily without enhancements ("as is") or where enhancements will not increase the market value of that land. "Strategic" disposals refer to properties where enhancements (e.g., subdividing, rezoning, presale development) can generate substantial increases in sale proceeds. If a property is deemed "strategic," the selling body transfers the title to Canada Lands Company (CLC), in exchange for a non-interest-bearing promissory note, and CLC handles the rest: financing enhancements, rezoning, marketing, and sale, streamlining the commodification process and paving the way for privatization (Whiteside 2017). CLC has been mandated to maximize returns from surplus sales, giving privatization a degree of institutional support not previously available. CLC can enter into financial and joint-venture arrangements not seen in the rest of the public sector, and it is staffed with private real estate experts. CLC has also been more recently empowered to handle land transfer to First Nations communities as settlement for disputes surrounding unceded land. With these transactions, "surplus" does not necessarily translate into the creation of a real estate market opportunity (as Polanyi emphasized), but HABU market appraisal techniques are the sole avenue for determining compensation.

The transfer of authority and decision making away from the selling body in the disposal process is even more pronounced in the United Kingdom, where we see both centralization and privatization. Since 2013, the Homes and Communities Agency has come to hold full responsibility for disposal of *all* developable surplus lands held by government departments and their agencies; and, on the other hand, private authority and control have developed in parallel with state agencies. "A number of public sector organizations such as the Ministry of Defence and Central Bedfordshire Council are starting to partner with the private sector to promote their surplus land holdings," one private-sector beneficiary of such outsourcing (the property company Telereal Trillium) reports on its website.[4] "The public sector retains ownership of the land whilst the private sector funds, manages and leads the planning and disposal process." This privatization of land disposal authority smooths and sustains the wider political-economic dynamics of making fiction (surplus) into fact.

The notion of "surplus" is in many ways foundational to theories and practices of political economy, from the Physiocrats and classical liberal thought, to neoclassical economics and accountancy norms today. Surplus can at once be bounty and waste, asset or liability. With respect to public landownership in the United Kingdom and Canada during the neoliberal period, negative fictions of surplus have come to dominate: "surplus" public land is deemed the ineluctable embodiment of public sector hoarding and squandering of valuable resources; selling such land to the private sector, in turn, is regarded as the rightful means to ensure that the land is used to foster rather than retard value creation.

This book, as outlined in the Introduction, "dwells on the powers of rhetoric and narrative as oft-neglected techniques of 'inventing' land as commodity," taken up in this chapter through its analysis of "surplus" land designations in the UK and Canada. The book is equally concerned with legal and regulatory frames. For "surplus" public land, fiction becomes fact through a set of interlocking, often subtle, bureaucratic processes and procedures ranging from obscure property management techniques to reconfigurations of institutional authority. Notwithstanding important national differences relating to colonial-capitalist histories, spatial and temporal emphases, and the legal construction of land agents in both the UK and Canada, commonalities include benchmarks (property life cycles, portfolio management, key performance indicators, best value appraisal), disposal and reporting rules (registers and directories, first-look requirements), and accountancy standards (accrual), the result of which, for both countries, has been massive—and ongoing—transfer of landholdings from the public to private sector.

The main claim we have sought to develop in this chapter is that fictions of surplus matter. To be sure, they have been formulated and propagated within the context of a wider neoliberal political-economic hegemony in both countries that militates more generally against state ownership of *any* kind. Even in the absence of the particular surplus fictions we have examined here, then, it is likely that public sector ownership of land—as of other assets—would have come under considerable pressure. Nevertheless, we cannot understand the particular force and scale of the land disposal program in each of the two countries, or the particular trajectory it has followed in each case, without attending to the fictions mobilized specifically vis-à-vis land and its differential "value" in, respectively, public and private hands. And if either country is to have any realistic prospect in the short or even medium term of nurturing alternative, socially valuable uses of un-/underused public land—ones not tethered to the market or its logic of value—then it is imperative that the fictions currently privileging privatization and commodification be identified and critically interrogated. This chapter has tried to take a short step in that direction.

3

FICTIONS OF SAFETY

Defensive Storylines in Global Property Investment

Sarah Knuth

In the decade since the 2008 financial collapse, a crisis triggered by failed financial experiments in American real estate produced, seemingly paradoxically, a fresh wave of land and property speculation globally. Among its other consequences, the renewed property boom in the 2010s rapidly exported and adapted US real estate–tied financial instruments to a startlingly diverse set of places and realms. Banks and fund managers in thirty-six countries across six continents are now using US-invented real estate investment trusts (REITs) or REIT-like vehicles to speculate in urban real estate. More radical financial innovators are engineering REITs around farmland and timberland in the United States and beyond, and ambitious solar and wind infrastructure developers have tried their hand at asset-backed securitization and even more exotic financial vehicles in their international expansions. Even subprime mortgages have begun to return in reskinned forms, such as US "nonprime" housing loans. Explaining this multiheaded global phenomenon is imperative: the lives of billions of people, from country and city, Global North and South, stand to be affected by its transformations in the meanings and treatment of land and real property.

In this chapter, I suggest that these diverse geographies and forms of real property financialization in urban real estate, infrastructure, and rural resource-producing land are being driven by common storylines and institutional imperatives, even as contingent politics and cultural meanings shape diverse experiences on the ground.[1] It is tempting (not least via the financial sector's own narratives) to read today's financial experiments as simply capitalism's latest move to transcend traditional boundaries in search of gain; for example, in Hernando de

Soto–style "yield gap" arguments about markets' power to unlock nascent value in the world. Conversely, I argue here that *defensive* understandings powerfully shape the new property boom, in ways highly significant for understanding evolutions in US capitalism within and beyond territorial borders. The new financialization offers an important lens into how formidable but brittle financial institutions and their neoliberal regulators are attempting to secure their power in an era of "too big to fail" and an increasingly unruly world. Major financial institutions in the United States and beyond and system regulators such as the International Monetary Fund (IMF), US Federal Reserve, and Bank of International Settlements (BIS) have been rocked by repeated shocks since 2008, made no less serious by their ability to displace this pain onto the less powerful. In response, they have promulgated influential storylines about how stability and long-term viability might be restored, especially via a new prioritization of "safe asset" holding. I argue that these fictions of safety are paradoxically fueling fresh risk-taking with land, real property more broadly, and other "alternative" assets in a structurally troubled financial system.

In exploring the financial sector's use and production of collective stories and working fictions about land, real property, and safety, I follow one thread among many performative discourses powerfully shaping financial and property markets today (see, for example, MacKenzie, Muniesa, and Siu 2007; Langley 2010; Christophers 2014; Li 2014a). Building on my own past work (Knuth 2015), in conversation with scholars such as Fairbairn (2014) and Weber (2015), I unpack deeper material transformations and trends within which these discourses and policies are embedded, and on which they are working—evolving techniques and practices, but also broader livelihood strategies, sectoral reorganizations, and systemic political-economic shifts. To piece together contemporary financial storylines, I focus particularly on a set of influential reports and industry surveys prepared between 2009 and 2016 by market-making asset managers and consultancies, the IMF, and other regulators, as well as critical discussion of these statements and policies among high-level economists and central bankers. I examine direct and indirect effects of this debate: how elements of it have been materialized in the US Dodd-Frank Wall Street Reform and Consumer Protection Act (Dodd-Frank), the Basel Committee's international regulatory framework for banks (Basel III), and other post-2008 financial reforms, but also in the mechanics of financial institutions' renewed market making at experimental land and real property frontiers.

Through this exploration, I identify multiple and sometimes conflicting understandings of safety at work in high-level financial discussions, variations that produce distinct appeals to land and real property. Crucially, in engaging these financial conversations, I aim to shed light on the financial sector not only as a key driver of global land and property transformations but one whose defensive strategies continue to shape US security in divergent ways. The worldwide ravages of the subprime crisis exposed central fictions of the American Dream as it faced the twenty-first century, amid ongoing turmoil in financialized late capitalism. Settler-colonial promises of mass land ownership are as old as the United States itself, from Jeffersonian agrarian visions to the suburban boom fostered by mid-twentieth century Keynesianism. Such sociopolitical grand plans have been projects of security as much as imagined prosperity and national greatness, for small land- and homeowners and their life chances (unevenly) and for US capitalism (crucially). Architects of such designs variously sought to buffer an early modern propertied elite from a landless mob, deradicalize an industrial proletariat, and durably bolster mass production and consumption against a descent into crisis. This "great American land grab" (Sakolski 1932) and centuries-long reimagination of real estate and debt markets premised the economic security of working Americans ever more centrally on their ownership of valuable homes and land—while waging war against indigenous peoples and other project "enemies" and violently excluding racialized Others through a host of governmental and financial practices.[2]

The turbulent period since the 2008 financial collapse has seen persistent calls to reform neoliberal property relations and rebuild US population security, through recovering such Keynesian ownership pathways (for many, building those for the first time) or embracing more radical social visions.[3] Mounting tensions in Keynesianism's marriage of biopolitical and capitalist security, which drove the turn to apparent new allies in the financial sector, had a role in precipitating the subprime crisis. As Robert Brenner (2009), Greta Krippner (2011), and other critical scholars have chronicled in depth, worsening US economic polarization and precarity for many has been both a cause and consequence of financialization in the neoliberal era: important US manufacturing regions fell in international competitiveness from the late 1960s and were abandoned by the state, and financial firms and centers, exports, and "asset-price Keynesianism" were allowed to replace them in US economic strategy. In eroding working Americans' livelihoods, such commanding heights choices undermined homeownership promises made via subprime mortgage loans and other much-touted financial innovations, over and above now-infamous financial predation and racialized wealth extraction in their application. More than a decade after the crisis, recovery in US housing markets remains skewed strongly toward relatively wealthy, "creditworthy" homebuyers, and the wealth disparity between rich and poor Americans has climbed steeply.

However, despite the threat of renewed crisis, it is far from clear that the architects of US capitalism today seek any return to the Keynesian compromise that secured it for so long (including via promised pathways to middle-class homeownership). I argue in this chapter that this departure is true even as real property in its various forms—urban real estate, rural land, physical infrastructure such as power grids—has become significant in new ways within contemporary capitalism's financialized command centers. Notably, Karl Polanyi's (2001 [1944]) sense of the security to be found in traditional forms of land tenure continues to circulate in unexpected ways today: in financial institutions' own search for safe havens, assets seen as plausibly able to escape devaluation in an economic shock and that therefore *gain* value in crises (a self-fulfilling prophecy). As I will discuss, real property has been one route to short-term safety for flight capital precisely because it is *not* entirely assimilated to modern capitalism: because it has been commodified but is not seen as a fully "financial" asset like debt, equity, and other intangible forms of property. Alternately, unusually patient investors, especially insurance companies, historically sought a different form of safety in real property's quasi-"outside" status. More concerned with cumulative threats to their accumulated capital such as gradual devaluation through inflation than acute financial shocks, they accepted the distinct risks of investing in a fixed, illiquid, often difficult form of property in the hope of securing durable value.

Today, decades of efforts to financialize real property more fully have caused investors and regulators to question *both* of these aforementioned pathways to safety, short- and long-term, as the IMF, US Fed, BIS Basel Committee on Banking Reform, and similar institutions have made the search for safe assets a major discussion point and regulatory mandate. If tools like REITs and mortgage securitization more fully assimilate real property as a true financial asset (via making it liquid, transparent, readily transferable, and so forth), can real property join money and "moneylike" assets as safe havens ne plus ultra—or, more precisely, can real property *re*acquire this classification, after US mortgage securities arguably won and lost it in the subprime bubble? The question underlying these appeals is whether real property can still work as a store of value either in a crisis or over the longer term. Conversely, has it lost its claim to safe haven status? Although debates over these questions are ongoing, many participants since 2008 have claimed that a systemic shortage of safe assets is collapsing yields and profitability as financial institutions compete for the same scarce investment opportunities. Paradoxically, that competition is driving risky new experiments, including with real property, as investors have rushed to untried assets in their scramble for returns.

Even as visions of mass private property ownership and middle-class status fire fresh development imaginaries globally (as chronicled in various ways in this volume), working Americans excluded from homeownership must increasingly turn to financial institutions and financial forms of property in their hopes for long-term economic security. At the same time, this collective investment provides the capital that pension funds and other "too big to fail" investors set to work in commodification drives within and outside US territory. The United States has so far retained important powers amid significant challenges to its hegemony: to export financial storylines and instruments worldwide, to equate its own economic stability with the health of the broader financial system, and to watch crises—even US-caused crises—swell the value of many US assets as safe havens. Yet the tensions weaving through today's real property boom suggest important limitations of post-2008 financial reforms: US financial institutions may once again be purchasing temporary safety at the cost of heightened insecurity for the many, within and beyond US borders.

Land as a Financial Asset: The Ascent of "Alternatives"

Until quite recently, major institutional investors in the United States infrequently sought land or real property as an investment—even as it became the dominant (if persistently uneven) form of wealth for everyday Americans. Investment banks rarely used land for collateral and asset managers like pension funds used it sparingly in their portfolios. Instead, institutional investors were major consumers of the long revolution in intangible financial assets such as bonds and corporate stocks (equity) that unfolded through the nineteenth and twentieth centuries (see, for example, Clark 2000; Laulajainen 2003). The financial sector sidelined real property in its various forms as an "alternative" asset, a category that included residential and commercial real estate in cities; economic and social infrastructure (transportation and power systems, hospitals, schools); and farmland, timberland, and other forms of resource-bearing rural land—even when located relatively securely within the United States. Industry literature has typically argued that intangible assets have the major advantage of liquidity—they can be rapidly moved at will, exchanged in secondary financial markets, or paid out on demand. Real property, in contrast, remains fixed in place, is inconveniently "lumpy" when large properties are purchased directly, demands time-intensive management to secure rental return or long-term value preservation and appreciation, is appraised and sold (often frustratingly slowly) in idiosyncratic local markets, and is subject to other geography-specific risks including, not insignificantly, political risks in the case of international property.

Important exceptions prove this rule. For example, during eighteenth- and nineteenth-century settler-colonial expansion, when rural land was the United States' main resource, early American land speculators (US-based and foreign) and banks often used land as collateral, sometimes in highly experimental forms (Sakolski 1932; Frehen, Goetzmann, and Rouwenhorst 2014). Amid social questioning of residential mortgage securitization and other practices that fueled the subprime collapse of the late 2000s, National Bureau of Economic Research economists examined a longer US history of real estate securitization, including its role in a 1920s investment bubble in New York and Chicago skyscrapers (Goetzmann and Newman 2010). Perhaps most significantly, US insurance companies have long bucked financial industry trends by investing heavily in real property (they were also long classified as only quasi-financial institutions; see, for example, Laulajainen 2003). According to Hanchett (2000), a handful of major life insurance companies, especially Prudential and MetLife, held more than 25 percent of all US mortgage debt in 1950. Notable investors in commercial mortgages, they were early adopters of commercial mortgage-backed securities and other long-duration assets only later taken up by pension funds (Wissoker 2013). Insurance companies also became major direct investors in commercial real estate, owning and leasing office towers in large US cities and offices and shopping centers in the suburbs (Hanchett 2000). In explaining this unusual strategy, commentators have pointed to insurance companies' atypically long time horizon as investors. Institutions only intermittently pressured to liquidate assets in a hurry (for example, in a major disaster), they have looked to real property as a store of long-term value. More recently, rising sovereign wealth funds have invested directly in real property and other alternative assets (Clark, Dixon, and Monk 2013). Finally, as I will discuss below, crises have historically prompted institutional investors to consider real property and other alternative assets in ways they would not under "normal" conditions.

The neoliberal era beginning in the 1970s saw a revolution in the financialization of real property, building on but also transforming Keynesian innovations in mortgage finance and dramatically altering established institutional investment patterns. Harvey (1982) theorized that a fully developed capitalism should treat land, both urban and rural, as a financial asset, collapsing different kinds of rentiership into one another. Recent developments are making that assertion a more accurate description of actually existing capitalism (and see Knuth 2015). Investment banks and other market makers sought to transform the very nature of real property by allowing institutions to invest in it without conventional direct ownership of properties or mortgage debt. They engineered financial vehicles like real estate investment trusts (REITs) that allowed investors to own pieces of a large commercial property in ways similar to owning stock in a public corporation. They accessed increasingly privatized infrastructure markets via project finance and secondary market-creation tools such as listed funds and asset-backed securities (ABSs). They bought into aggregated and securitized streams of residential and commercial mortgage repayments using mortgage-backed securities (RMBSs and CMBSs), increasingly repackaged and tranched as collateralized debt obligations (CDOs, and further-repackaged CDOs-squared). And they speculated using financial derivatives such as credit-default swaps (CDSs), instruments that ostensibly insured the risks of this collective sectoral experimentation. Advocates have framed this financial revolution as giving institutional investors the best of both worlds: access to the supposedly unique qualities of real property as a store of value, about which more below, coupled with unprecedented freedom to enter and exit from these investments at will, mimicking the liquidity of intangible property. These developments create possibilities for investment in many types and geographies of property. Simultaneously, they produce greater volatility in these flows, as the new instruments allow far more rapid investment and disinvestment than is possible through direct ownership. The 2000s property bubble represented a dramatic, if in many ways ill-founded, declaration of industry faith in this frontier of financial innovation. Private credit-rating agencies (Moody's, Fitch, and Standard & Poor's) gave subprime loan-backed products investment-grade ratings. Meanwhile, pension funds and banks bought and held trillions of dollars worth of them as portfolio assets and collateral, openly and off-the-books (so-called shadow banking).

The collapse of the US property bubble in 2007–8, the systemic failure of subprime loans and the financial products backed by them, resulting bank failures and massive government bailouts, and lingering US and international crises have not halted finance's experimentation with real property. As mentioned above, financial instruments created for investment in US urban real estate are rapidly being exported to new places and property types. Industry advocates are working to reshape regulatory structures and legal geographies to support the new financialization. For example, the creation and capitalization of REITs has seen a major international upswing in the years since the 2008 financial collapse. REITs were originally created by the US Congress in 1960 as a project to democratize US financial asset holding beyond the wealthy (with limited success) and to "modernize" real estate investment (Wayne 1982; Fox Gotham 2006; Knuth 2015), part of a broader midcentury frustration with the building industry's persistent failure to resemble factory-based mass production. REITs have traditionally been used to invest in various types of commercial real estate, especially downtown office towers (mostly as equity, although the United States also has several dozen mortgage REITs). American REITs saw a quick recovery and a new boom after the 2008 collapse, reaching more than $1 trillion in assets by 2019 (see figure 3.1).

The global expansion of REITs since the crisis suggests the speed and scope of contemporary property financialization. For example, evidence suggests that REITs are becoming a more dominant form of property ownership in booming

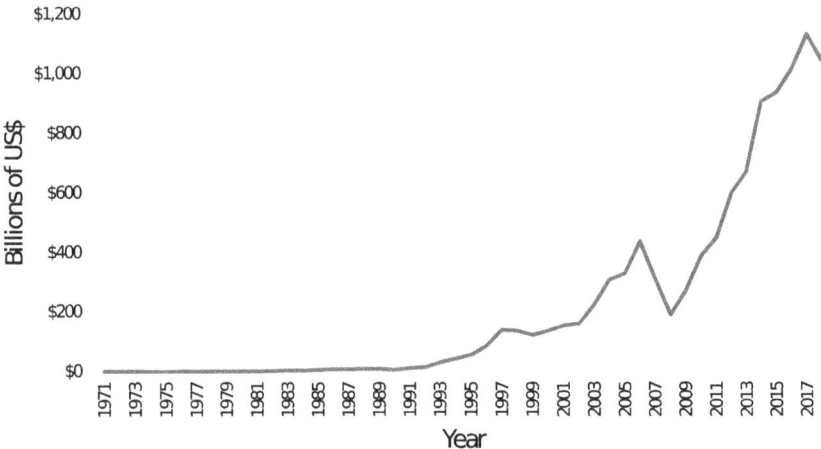

FIGURE 3.1. Market capitalization, US REIT industry 1971–2018 (billions of US$). As of end of year 2018, the United States had 226 publicly traded REITs, capitalized at $1.05 trillion.

Source: NAREIT (2019).

urban markets like the San Francisco Bay Area (Knuth 2016). At the same time, REITs have been legalized for new types of real property outside of urban areas and urban real estate, opening up investment frontiers for assets such as farmland, long considered marginal even within an alternative sector. The first timberland REIT was created in 1999 and the first farmland REIT held its initial public offering in 2013. Advocates have mounted campaigns to legalize REITs for even more forms of property, notably renewable energy infrastructure (a sector that, as mentioned above, has seen intense financial experimentation in recent years; see, for example, Knuth 2018). These investments in resource land and extensive infrastructure stand to reshape rural social relations across the United States, even as they create new property markets for financial institutions. For example, scholars have interrogated this financialization of rural land as a force for further consolidating US farmland and timberland ownership and worsening rural depopulation, including as part of a global farmland grab immediately after the 2008 collapse. They have questioned the nature of financial institutions' interest in productive land and their capacity for long-term, sustainable management, amid speculative bubbles like a dramatic run-up and slump in Midwest farmland prices in the late 2000s-2010s (Gunnoe and Gellert 2011; Fairbairn 2014; Ouma 2014; Knuth 2015). Meanwhile, financialization promises (uncertain) new capital for solar and wind infrastructure, feeding a development trend that is bringing new resources into rural economies and fueling conflicts with existing land uses (McCarthy 2015; Knuth 2018). These expanding frontiers of real property financialization do not stop at US borders: Fairbairn (2014) notes important experiments from Australia, Malaysia, and Bulgaria. Many of the thirty-six countries that now permit REITs or REIT-like investment vehicles initiated activity or saw expansions after the 2008 collapse, even if most are still minor in scale compared to REIT capitalization in the United States (PwC 2015a). Moreover, REITs, while important, are only one instrument that has seen expanding use for real property investment worldwide since 2008; they have been joined by ABSs and CMBSs, exchange-traded funds, and many other vehicles.

This ongoing financial revolution has prompted influential industry voices to proclaim a secular transformation, claiming that real property and other former "alternatives" have become increasingly mainstream financial assets. For example, in statements that have received major industry attention, BlackRock, the world's largest asset manager by a significant margin, has proclaimed "the ascent of real assets." Reporting the results of a survey of 201 institutional investors in thirty countries, BlackRock argues that "real assets—primarily real estate, infrastructure and commodities—are an increasing focus of the world's institutional investors . . . part of a broader move into alternative investments by institutions that are seeking to lessen their reliance on traditional stocks and bonds amid the challenging conditions of the post-crisis years" (BlackRock 2014, 5). The asset manager further highlighted fast-growing infrastructure investment a year later (BlackRock 2015). Almost all BlackRock's (2014) respondents invested in real estate and two-thirds had jumped into the rising infrastructure sector (although BlackRock classified timberland and farmland as still experimental). Most respondents invested in international as well as domestic real estate—some 20 percent were more truly global with more than a quarter of their investments made outside the United States—and most also reported significant interest in expanding their infrastructure investment in emerging markets as well as domestically. The quantitative results of this shift, within a broader industry turn toward alternative assets, have been dramatic. For example, BlackRock (2015) found that infrastructure funds under management rose from $1.1 billion in 2004 to $317.5 billion in 2014. Prequin (2016) reports a record $7.4 trillion in overall alternative assets under management globally in 2015. PwC (2015b) suggests that alternative assets overall could increase to between $13.6 trillion and $15.3 trillion by 2020, with about $2.5 to $2.9 trillion coming specifically from "real" assets. (Their alternatives category also includes hedge funds and private equity, which may invest in real property but may also pursue intangible assets.)

The means by which the narrative around the rise of alternative and real assets has been voiced and communicated suggests the ongoing influence of "too big to fail"–style power in the financial industry: how globally significant investment frontiers can be opened up by the advocacy of a few massive asset managers and, more broadly speaking, how a handful of key institutions continues to dominate industry storylines and storytelling. BlackRock's influential advocacy is one symptom of this condition. BlackRock, which managed $4.6 trillion in assets as of December 2015, and its closest competitor Vanguard, with a portfolio of over $3 trillion, together owned as much as 70 percent of the entire US public stock market in 2016 (both faced serious antitrust questions) (BlackRock 2016; Solomon 2016; Vanguard 2016).[4] Other market makers that have joined BlackRock in narrating and furthering the push into alternative and "real" assets include powerful industry players; for example, Deutsche Bank Research (2012), McKinsey Global Institute (2013), TIAA-CREF (2013), PricewaterhouseCoopers (PwC 2015b), and Ernst & Young (2015). As has become its common practice (Knuth 2015), McKinsey Global Institute (2013) employs a performative "financing gap" narrative to promote investment, announcing (and producing) a $57 trillion unmet need for infrastructure finance. Other influential advocates include international institutions such as the World Bank (2008) and the Organisation for Economic Co-operation and Development (OECD 2015), both now actively making markets and financial space across multiple economic and socioenvironmental realms. This financialization of land and real property is giving players at the commanding heights of the global economy increasing power to imaginatively draw together, render commensurate, and transform diverse spaces and experiences worldwide. Meanwhile, it is giving financial institutions fresh tools for creating and exploiting extractive neoperipheries across a range of geographies.

Financial Storylines: The Importance of Defensive Fictions

Understanding ongoing transformations in institutional investors' treatment of land and real property demands more than a survey of new investment vehicles under development. Although these tools open up new possibilities, particular storylines and interpretations of the current conjuncture induce institutions and investors to take them up. I argue here that defensive framings, in the form of anxieties about the contemporary moment and storylines around safety, are providing a powerful impetus toward new real property investment. If institutional investors are taking new risks on property, they are not necessarily doing so under conditions of their own choosing. As discussed, US institutional investors confront a national biopolitical tradition that has imagined land and real property as central to personal security, even while, as I will argue below, more and more of the US population loses access to property ownership and becomes dependent on pension funds, insurance companies, and similar institutions for its long-term economic welfare (Pew Research Center 2013; JCHS 2016). New defensive narratives are being circulated at the institutional level as banks and asset managers respond to the repeated shocks of today's economic climate—the lingering aftermath of the 2008 financial collapse, as well as pervasive turbulence in the neoliberal era—by seeking safe havens for investment. Storylines advanced by economists and regulators at the IMF, US Federal Reserve, Basel Committee, and other institutions charged with maintaining the stability of the international financial system are reshaping the environment within which investors operate. Notably, system regulators have set new constraints on financial institutions' collateral and safe asset holding and structured the world of safe assets available to them. In a system plagued by volatility and deeper structural problems, these security-seeking strategies have had a perverse outcome: the production of a renewed scramble for potentially risky assets by investors anxious to maintain their returns and basic long-term viability.

Imagining Security: Land and Money in a "Nation of Property Owners"

As Karl Polanyi (2001 [1944]) powerfully argued in *The Great Transformation*, embedded assumptions about the security to be found in land retained their power within advancing market economies. These assumptions constructed land as a means to traditional livelihoods, as a preserver and conveyer of familial wealth, and as a recurring refuge in times of crisis. Even as, in Polanyi's telling, the English landed elite fought a double movement against socially destabilizing free trade in agricultural commodities, they fled to their landed wealth as a refuge from the South Sea Bubble and other early financial crashes, not to mention the frequent personal financial crises of an age of aristocratic gambling (Kindleberger 1984). In the United States, capitalist crises have helped drive back-to-the-land movements, from Great Depression–era subsistence homesteads to urban farming today (Danbom 1991; Tarr 2015). Most influentially in the United States, foundational narratives of mass private property ownership equated personal security with national political stability, arguing that the growth of a "middling" population of small property owners could protect an Early Republic propertied elite from a feared "mob" of the landless and politically disenfranchised. As discussed in this chapter's introduction, this Jeffersonian vision of a republic of "independent proprietors" has since had major urban, rural, and suburban expressions (all deeply shaped by national legacies of settler colonialism and racial capitalism). The capitalist state has supported and subsidized petit-bourgeois urban shopkeepers and small business owners, small farmers—especially in the Homestead Act and other early governmental moves against both remnant feudal land practices and large-scale speculative land grabs (Sakolski 1932; Blackmar 1991)—and since World War II, a middle class of suburban homeowners.

Complicating this picture, the United States' New Deal–Keynesian welfare state appealed to both land and money as routes to biopolitical population security (Foucault 2003). Mass homeownership relied in part on a revolution in financial institutions' long-term lending, which now included multi-decadal home loans to the nonwealthy, at the time viewed as a risky proposition for both sides. Using new tools such as the thirty-year mortgage and, eventually, mortgage securitization by Fannie Mae and other government-sponsored enterprises, the US state helped create massive markets for domestic mortgage debt, providing an increasingly important way for third-party investors to bet on the value of US housing. Home equity became most Americans' primary form of wealth and a pillar of old age planning (Jackson 1985), deepening the injury of racial redlining and other systematic racial exclusions in US housing programs (Jackson 1985; Crump et al. 2008; Freund 2010). At the same time, governmental programs helped make intangible property, in the form of private financial assets and public entitlements, increasingly important to national wealth and aggregate life chances. Wealthy Americans had already thoroughly "financialized" their property holding and safety strategies alongside the growth of the stock market and rise of the private insurance industry (Kindleberger 1984; Wissoker 2013). The new biopolitics democratized access to some of these new forms for both urban and rural inhabitants through social security, agricultural insurance, and a host of other programs for socializing risk and protecting popular wealth. Notably, these ambitious experiments were enabled by Keynesian disciplining of the domestic and international financial systems as well as by the United States' unique hegemonic freedoms within the new Bretton Woods and dollar monetary order (Block 1977; Gowan 1999; Arrighi 2010).

Paradoxically, even as US pension funds and other financial institutions embrace real property investment in new ways today, small property owners are losing access to this form of national mass security. The 2000s property bubble and its exotic financial architecture—subprime MBSs, CDOs and CDOs-squared, CDSs, and so forth—highlighted the differences separating the property revolution of the United States' Keynesian "golden age" from neoliberal asset-price Keynesianism (Brenner 2009). The latter has *decreased* rather than increased US homeownership, while leaving financial power effectively unchecked. Since the 2008 collapse, US homeownership numbers have declined at a rate unprecedented in the country's modern history. By 2015, the homeownership rate stood at 63.7 percent, its lowest in almost fifty years. This aggregate number conceals even starker divides according to race and age. More and more people in the United States, especially younger Americans, are becoming renters, a trend that rising property unaffordability in major cities, climbing student debt, stagnating real wages, and other mounting forms of economic inequality and insecurity suggest may be here to stay (JCHS 2016). Moreover, the prospect of a new era for large-scale renting in (and beyond) US cities is now fueling the growth of a class of financial landlords, as private equity funds and other major institutional investors eye attractive returns from this new form of rentiership (Fields and Uffer 2016). Meanwhile, the United States' new population of renters faces diminished personal wealth and foreclosed options for long-term livelihood security.

In a further paradox, even as large financial institutions explore fresh ways to extract wealth from the US working and shrinking middle classes, these populations are now collectively relying ever more *on* financial institutions. The Pew Research Center (2013) reports that as of 2011 the percentage of US wealth held in financial assets ($23.2 trillion) significantly exceeded that held in homes and other "nonfinancial" property ($17.1 trillion). This aggregate still conceals major divides according to race and income, as financial wealth and the benefits of recent increases in financial asset values continue to be highly skewed toward the rich: "Among households with net worth of $500,000 or more, 65% of their wealth comes from financial holdings, such as stocks, bonds and 401(k) accounts, and 17% comes from their home. Among households with net worth of less than $500,000, just 33% of their wealth comes from financial assets and 50% comes from their home" (Pew Research Center 2013, 2–3). Moreover, the share of total wealth owned by the top 0.1 percent of Americans now approximately equals the share owned by the bottom 90 percent (Saez and Zucman 2014). However, notwithstanding this increasingly bitter divide, lack of access to homeownership will force more Americans to depend on pensions and other assets, even as fewer have access to assets of *either* kind. Fund holdings may certainly not make workers perceive themselves as creditors or financialized rentiers, but their life chances increasingly depend on institutions that adopt these roles (nominally) on their behalf.

What Insures Insurers? Institutional Investors Bet "Outside" and "Inside"

The stability and long-term viability of institutional investors may be an increasingly important component of US population security writ large, but these institutions have historically looked to different kinds of assets for their own insurance. Where, again, working Americans chiefly sought private property in land and homeownership, large investors far more often pursued safety in money or similar financial assets that, as discussed, have long been defined as excluding real property. This specialization in money and moneylike assets has given financial institutions unique power and freedom—but also enduring points of vulnerability. Scholars of money and the international monetary system note that within modern capitalism money is asked to perform multiple social functions at once: to store value, lubricate commodity production and circulation by bridging space and time, and serve as a unit of account (see, for example, Harvey 1982; Polanyi 2001 [1944]; Ingham 2004). These simultaneous roles typically work at cross-purposes (for example, inflationary policies facilitate circulation and aid manufacturers, while hurting bankers). This contradiction has historically pitted different social interests against each other, manufacturers, workers, and welfare states combatting banks and other players who have a vested interest in protecting money's ability to store value (Block 1977). Disastrous illusions of using a self-regulating market to resolve these conflicts without government intervention—the Gold Standard's theory if not its practice (Silver and Arrighi 2003)—provoked Polanyi (2001 [1944]) to include money among his three central fictitious commodities. These contradictions continue to generate political clashes, especially as the breakup of the Keynesian monetary regime after 1971 and gradual rollback of capital controls through the neoliberal era returned endemic volatility and frequent crises to the international monetary system (Gowan 1999). From an institutional perspective, these pressures have manifested in an ongoing search for high-quality currencies and financial assets that can escape inflation and other forms of devaluation, short- and long-term.

As we will see, precisely *why* institutional investors must hold value-bearing assets on their books, the role that these assets play in the safety of institutions and the broader financial system, and what kinds of assets are eligible for classification as value-bearing are lively topics of debate. Different institutional investors confront these questions in different ways. On the one hand, banks and other creditor institutions hold assets including, but not limited to, customer deposits as collateral against the loans they make. Since the invention of fractional reserve banking, banks circulate far more assets as interest-bearing capital than they actually hold on the books at any given moment. Bank leverage climbed dramatically in the 2000s, as banks speculated more against, and profited more from, their reserves. For example, Bear Stearns deployed $36 in loans and investments for every $1 of its equity capital (Cassidy 2014). On the other hand, asset managers such as pension funds and insurance companies work to grow their portfolio (in part to maintain its long-term value against inflation), allowing them to pay out to meet clients' demands. Insufficient or devalued assets can become a problem both in the short and the long term, whether in the face of an economic shock or catastrophic event, or due to the gradual work of inflation and stagnation. Both banks and asset management companies face collapse if they cannot meet their contracted obligations to depositors and clients, as exemplified by the phenomenon of bank runs, a traditional specter that returned in frighteningly systemic form during the 2008 collapse. An extensive public and private apparatus has been developed to protect financial institutions from individual and snowballing failures, from the Federal Reserve system to reinsurance companies (Johnson 2014). However, the revealed vulnerability of these safeguards has provoked new conversations about how institutional investors can protect themselves, and the system that increasingly depends on them, in times of economic turmoil.

Among institutional investors, performative storylines, for example, about cyclicality (Weber 2016) and "countercyclicality," have long shaped interest in real property and other alternative assets. If, before the current moment, most institutional investors avoided alternatives in "normal" conditions, these narratives justified a turn toward real property in times of crisis. Countercyclicality describes a regularized statistical observation about certain types of assets: in a "cyclical" event (i.e., an economic shock) that devalues many forms of property, certain assets have been observed to hold their value or even to *gain* in value to an unusual degree. This quality makes them attractive safe havens for capital flight. However, countercyclicality is also a contingent social construct that performative narratives and statistical picturing have helped recast as natural law. Certainly, countercyclical tendencies have a material basis situated in assets' particular characteristics and structural positioning within the global economy. Market makers deploy storylines that invoke these characteristics as fundamental qualities. However, countercyclicality ultimately works because investors *think* it will work, and because they rush enough capital into an asset to realize this assumption. These collective storylines and self-fulfilling prophecies are a classic theme in financial sector storytelling (Kindleberger 1984). At the same time, new systemic developments can readily upend historical relationships and ultimately destabilize the storylines and statistical "truths" that represent and reify them.

In crises of faith in the financial system, performative storylines that frame real property as a countercyclical refuge have often drawn on alternative assets' quasi-"outside" status in relation to that system—paradoxically, given that major financial institutions are now leaders in generating and disseminating these narratives. For example, after the 2008 collapse financial players such as Deutsche Bank (2012), TIAA-CREF (2013), and BlackRock (2014) advocated investment in "real assets" such as land and resources, promoting these assets' supposedly essential power to retain value in a crisis. This discourse rhetorically echoed—while subverting in practice—broader populist and neo-Keynesian calls for a return to a "real economy," meaning one that resubordinated the financial industry and creditor interests to manufacturers and workers.[5] Deeper skepticism about the long-term stability of the international financial (and capitalist) system manifested in more autarchic and neocolonial framings, for example, in justifications for crisis-era land grabs (White et al. 2013). These arguments for farmland, other resource-bearing land, and critical infrastructure elevate their material and political use values while downplaying their exchange value and speculative potential. Nevertheless, financial players have so far demonstrated a remarkable ability to turn even skeptical narratives to their benefit by simultaneously making their own bets on more traditional, incompletely financialized forms of wealth. Harvey's (1982, 2003) spatial or spatiotemporal fix captures elements of this strategy. Paradoxically, a major irony of today's financialization of real property is that its very success may be undermining its countercyclicality and ability to work as a spatiotemporal fix (see Knuth 2015). For example, Inderst (2010) argues that appeals to infrastructure's supposedly inherent inflation-hedging and countercyclical benefits often have an inconclusive empirical basis. Moreover, he maintains that the "infrastructure" sector actually comprises a widely diverse set of property types, ones cyclically correlated with the broader classes of financial instruments used to invest in them. In other words, to the extent that novel investment vehicles normalize land and real property as "true" financial assets, their value is likely to rise and fall along with financial markets in *general*—losing (at least some of) their ability to hold and gain value in times of crisis. Indeed, although many of today's industry statements on alternative assets continue to reference their ostensible countercyclicality (see, for example, Deutsche Bank 2012; Vanguard 2014), BlackRock (2014) similarly reports that traditional countercyclical motivations of diversification and protection from inflation had actually become far less important to investors than simply using alternative assets to increase their returns—as we will see, a different kind of defensive strategy in a period of lingering crisis.

Appeals to systemic outsides, alternative assets, and incompletely financialized forms of property are only one form of countercyclical strategy. Conversely, financial institutions also look "inside" to financial centers as a hedge against crisis. (Gold, still the classic safe haven asset a century after the effective demise of the Gold Standard, displays elements of both types of strategy—archaic commodity metal and nondenominated, universally accepted money.) Gowan's (1999) concept of the Dollar Wall Street Regime (DWSR) powerfully describes how economic shocks can generate capital flight to assets at the center, especially US dollars, US Treasury bonds and other government debt, and the New York Stock Exchange. Investors bet that in times of trouble, financial centers will retain more security than the margins through structural protections such as lower risk of default or write-downs on government debt, currencies protected for creditors, and deeper and more liquid financial markets. Fundamentally, this strategy bets on the power of financial centers to secure their own stability, if necessary at the expense of other places and the broader system—even when they are largely to blame for a localized or systemic crisis. (Again, it is also a self-fulfilling prophecy, a gamble on what other investors might be thinking.) As neoliberal deregulation returned volatility to the international financial system, it made turns to DWSR assets more frequent. Via this process, foreign investors subsidized US national debt and ongoing borrowing even as the United States ran an increasing trade deficit with China (in particular).[6] The United States' experience since 2008 demonstrates this remarkably stubborn hegemonic privilege, albeit partly because other hegemonic contenders like the European Union experienced their own crises: in a period of stagnation and recurrent shocks, international investors flocked to DWSR assets.

Safe assets sought at the center of the financial system saw a revolution in the 2000s and a major collapse after 2008, prompting a rush of explanations from influential economists and regulators at the IMF, US Federal Reserve, BIS, NBER, and other institutions (see, for example, Bernanke et al. 2011; Gorton, Lewellen, and Metrick 2012; Gourinchas and Jeanne 2012; Caballero and Farhi 2014; SEC 2014; Gorton 2016; and especially IMF 2012). It is this high-level discourse that popularized the term *safe assets* (Portes 2013, taking a contrarian view, decried this rush of concern as a "meme"). The discussion demonstrated the confusions and disagreements in a field unaccustomed to acknowledging disequilibrium, asset bubbles, and the potential for systemic crises, one deeply discomfited by too-open exposure of the financial industry's most necessary fictions. Some commentators primarily took "safe" to mean short-term safe havens "outside" as well as "inside," while others included the kind of longer-term secure investments sought by US insurance companies. For example, Portes (2013) surveyed then-circulating definitions that included conventional intangible assets such as sovereign debt and bonds, but also infrastructure and real estate. Still other commentators simply chose to equate safe assets with more traditional short-term safe havens comprising conventional financial assets with the highest levels of liquidity. These last commentators typically suggested money, "moneylike" assets (Gorton 2016), or other variations on this theme. For example, Gorton, Lewellen, and Metrick (2012, 102) considered as "safe" a range of assets that might act in "information-insensitive fashion; i.e., as money . . . bank deposits, money market mutual fund shares, commercial paper, federal funds and repurchase agreements ('repo'), short-term interbank loans, Treasuries, agency debt, municipal bonds, securitized debt, and high-grade financial-sector corporate debt." (A relatively generous appraisal given the turmoil that afflicted some of these assets in the subprime crisis.)

Like DWSR assets, more traditional havens have also claimed the implicit protection of particular national governments: strong economies that are nevertheless willing in their fiscal and monetary policies to prioritize creditors over domestic manufacturers and workers. In its 2012 *Global Financial Stability Report* (GFSR), the IMF (2012) treated high-quality currencies and highly rated sovereign debt (e.g., US Treasury bonds) as natural safe assets for this reason. What, then, is a "synthetic" safe asset? The IMF (2012, 112) has classified it as a form of property *made* safe by the power of financial engineering: subject to an architecture of financial derivatives and other tools that structure away its inherent risks. The IMF also has used the term "private-label" safe asset to describe this process. The rise of derivatives in the neoliberal era has been facilitated by this kind of security claim, that the ability to hedge risk in financial markets represents a revolution in insurance and insurability (see, for example, Bryan and Rafferty 2006; Johnson 2014). The IMF provides no guarantee that the trend will be a lasting one. For example, in the GFSR (2012), it surveyed this private-label production before and after the 2008 financial collapse, including ABSs, residential and commercial MBSs, CDOs, and CDOs-squared in this category. The IMF highlighted a rapid run-up in this private-label production in the 2000s, and a deep collapse and stagnation—particularly in the US context—in the years thereafter: according to its calculations, total US and European issuance shrunk from $3 trillion in 2007 to less than $750 billion in 2010. This representation and ones like it saw wide circulation in the financial crisis, conveying the IMF's urgency about the scale of safe assets lost (even though much of this asset value was speculative paper wealth).

Real property-backed instruments were the quintessential private-label safe asset; they drew investors via an unusual combination of supposed safety and high returns, contradicting finance's traditional risk-return pricing assumption that higher profits come at the cost of higher risks. Instead, financial discourses promoted "the perception that the instruments were nearly risk-free while offering yields above those of the safest sovereigns" (IMF 2012, 109). The IMF's rise and fall of private-label safe asset production closely tracks the specific instruments (MBSs, CDOs, and so forth) and trajectory of the subprime boom and bust, making the subsector's troubles since 2008 hardly surprising. It also included a smaller fraction of commercial MBSs, a nonresidential form of debt-mediated bet on the 2000s property bubble. Investment-grade ratings cleared the path for pension funds and other institutions that are legally required to invest conservatively, while high returns attracted them. The motivation of increased gain from subprime lending was especially salient because, like today, profitable investment options were systemically scarce because of a recent crisis—in that case the collapse of the dot.com bubble in 2001—and low interest rate strategies deployed by the US Federal Reserve to manage and mitigate the effects of that crisis (Brenner 2009).

One important storyline legitimizing subprime mortgages' unusual combination of safety and profitability was a narrative of "first-mover" advantage. The first-mover story argues that sophisticated players can reap unusually high returns simply by experimenting in new frontiers, sectors that only *seem* risky because their track record has not been fully established for the less expert. This storyline was successful enough for subprimes that it captured ratings agencies and a flood of investors, so that would-be first movers had to seek ever-riskier debt tranches to maintain returns (Brenner 2009). It is also notable that US private-label safe assets were so significant (although not exclusive) in the pool: investors in US mortgage products bet on Gowan's DWSR in a novel form, and with a greatly expanded pool of potential assets. They counted on the established power (and supposed "natural" strength) of the US housing market and the government's ongoing willingness to protect it, all the while overlooking racialized predatory lending, mounting population insecurity, and other fissures widening beneath this apparent security. Finally, the IMF, at least, has not given up on a renaissance in private-label safe asset production, arguing that "the production of safe assets by the private sector is an important source of supply and should not be unnecessarily impeded" (IMF 2012, 115).

Securing the System: A Paradoxical Search for Safe Assets

A major reason that the IMF (2012) supports ongoing experiments with private-label safe assets, and that it has joined other regulators and economists in questioning just what assets might be truly safe today, is that it has charged safe assets with a central role in stabilizing "too big to fail" financial institutions and the broader financial system. The IMF, BIS Basel Committee, US Federal Reserve, and other regulators empowered with surveillance of the financial system experienced major embarrassments in 2008 and after, catastrophically overconfident about their ability to eliminate systemic crisis in the 2000s and failing to prevent repeated economic shocks since. In response, the IMF has embarked on reforms to the GFSR and its other surveillance tools, while reoccupying itself with European crisis management for the first time in decades (Eichengreen and Woods 2016; although see Verengo and Ford 2014 on the limits to these reforms). All of the aforementioned pieces of reform legislation demanded that major financial institutions hold more safe assets as an individual and systemic security measure. Basel III, initiated in 2011 in the midst of these conversations, required banks to hold more safe assets, decrease their leverage, and hold certain *kinds* of safe assets: more liquid, more countercyclical, and so forth. In the United States, Dodd-Frank financial reform legislation, signed into law in 2010, reflected a similar philosophy. Instead of breaking up "too big to fail" financial institutions and an industry that grew even more concentrated following the collapse, or more fundamentally resubordinating finance to the state—the New Deal–Keynesian response to banks' power after the Great Depression—it argued that requiring financial institutions to hold more capital on the books could prevent crisis in the future (e.g., Cassidy 2014).

Although safe asset holding has been a centerpiece of post-2008 reforms, it is not the only form that the new regulations have taken. For example, the Financial Stability Board (new circa 2009, a successor to the BIS Financial Stability Forum) has worked to identify "global systemically important financial institutions" (G-SIFIs). The designation codified "too big to fail" institutions and provided a pathway for more stringent regulation and stress-testing of them under Basel III and Dodd-Frank (even if capital-holding requirements continue to be a major form that that regulation is taking). Moreover, this labeling-based regulation has inadvertently produced some deconcentration. For example, in the mid-2010s, AIG and Prudential both fell under rolling-out Dodd-Frank requirements as SIFI institutions. MetLife mounted a major court battle to escape this classification and avoided regulation by spinning off a major part of its business as a separate company, effectively making itself "small enough to fail." Beyond SIFI regulation, another centerpiece of financial regulation after the crisis was years of quantitative easing and very low, even negative, interest rate policies by the US Federal Reserve and other central banks. As governments used these policies to try to stabilize home lending and promote new economic growth, they contributed to decreasing yields for US Treasuries and other high-quality government debt—a classic safe asset for bank collateral and investment portfolios.

Ultimately, regulators' preoccupation with safe assets, and its codification in financial reforms, reflects the partialities of mainstream political explanations for the late 2000s financial crisis as well as lingering blind spots and evasions. First, safe asset storylines display an unsurprising preoccupation with the failures of surveillance that allowed institutions like banks and pension funds to invest heavily in ostensibly low-risk assets like subprime mortgages. Second, they focus on "overleveraging," the very high debt-to-collateral ratios that banks took on in the 2000s. Regulators argue that holding more safe assets on the books as a buffer is a key way to help banks withstand shocks, even if more conservative, lower-yield assets weigh down their profits. These narratives sidestep the more structural dangers of concentration in the US financial industry and beyond reflected in the ongoing systemic dominance of a handful of "too big to fail" players. Today's reforms have been less-than-structural in other ways. For example, as Portes (2013) points out, the IMF (2012) and other commentators acknowledge the major limitations and conflicts of interest in relying on private ratings from Moody's, Standard & Poor's and the like to formally define safety, especially in light of their complicity in the 2000s bubble. Nevertheless, the IMF and others continue to use the rating agencies and encode their judgments in regulatory frameworks. Critically, as the discussion here has indicated, regulators have also permitted fresh rounds of financial engineering, including around land and real property.

Crucially—if, yet again, paradoxically—this state-mandated search for safe assets is a major cause of today's boom in international property investment, despite the fact that many of these frontiers in land and real property financialization are new and speculative. A major reason why the IMF (2012) continued to advocate for private-label safe asset production, despite its catastrophic past failures, was via a fatalistic shrug at its necessity and recognition that there were simply few alternatives available within the existing financial system. Indeed, today's discursive framing of safe assets has near-universally coupled an emphasis on their *importance* and a warning about their *scarcity*. The argument is that the collapse of private-label safe assets has left a critical gap, that high-quality sovereign debt can only partly make up this shortfall, and that developing economies are not yet able to produce sufficiently "creditworthy" debt (for a dissenting opinion, see Portes 2013).[7] Driven by their own risk-management strategies and by new regulatory imperatives, institutional investors rushed into established safe havens such as US Treasury bonds and other high-quality sovereign debt. Collectively, they have now held these assets for years despite their infamously low—for government bonds, often *negative*—yields since 2008. Indeed, this sectoral rush on bonds is a crucial factor in these safe assets' low returns today. Institutions have been left holding more assets that are nominally safe—but at the cost of profits.

Over the longer term, these low returns may themselves threaten institutions' health via slow devaluation of their capital base. This dilemma especially applies to asset managers like pension funds that have traditionally relied on holding large amounts of low-risk, low-but-stable-return assets like US government bonds on the books, but that now compete for these assets with many other interested parties, domestically and internationally—in the case of bonds, converting modest yields to nonexistent or negative ones. Given these pressures, the institutional investment industry has mounted an ongoing search for new sources of return, including real property (although not limited to it, e.g., Johnson 2014). Industry statements acknowledge these macroeconomic pressures as a significant driver of new interest in real property and formerly alternative assets,[8] especially as diminished returns have lingered amid ongoing stagnation and recurrent shocks (e.g., Vanguard 2014; BlackRock 2015; Ernst & Young 2015). BlackRock (2014, 5) particularly highlights the connection between near-zero interest rates and investors' turn to real assets for return (although it maintains that these tactics do not capture the entirety of investor motivations, which it argues are producing a more secular shift): "There is an important caveat resulting from the same unusual financial conditions that have been a tailwind for this asset class. A majority of respondents say that a significant rise in interest rates would cause them to rethink some of their allocations to real assets."

Emerging storylines about real property as a source of returns echo many narratives that were used to inflate the subprime bubble. This resemblance is significant for the financial system and for those caught up in new financial frontiers, since either the success or failure of these aspirations stands to shape land and property relations, and broader life chances, in the United States and beyond. Material similarities—experimental financial instruments being deployed to financialize real property and turn it over to institutional investors, financial institutions like pension funds facing a systemic scarcity of profitable assets, cheap capital available for potential asset bubbles—are highlighted by corresponding similarities in narratives justifying this investment. Real property assets in the United States, for example, have again been framed as an especially safe investment. Novel DWSR extensions include not only Manhattan or San Francisco skyscrapers but also property like farmland, forestland, and infrastructure (see, for example, Fairbairn 2014; Knuth 2016; Fernandez, Hofman, and Aalbers 2016). Likewise, first-mover storylines are being deployed to rhetorically minimize the risks of new, higher-return frontiers today (Daniel 2013; Li 2014a). Fairbairn (2014) reports storylines that describe farmland in the US Midwest as "like gold with yield." This narrative argues, yet again, that the "natural" strengths of an asset can be unlocked by sophisticated investors: for farmland, timberland, and infrastructure like solar panels, the notion of reaping harvests and production as a passive investor has been a major selling point, one less dependent than residential mortgage markets on everyday Americans' economic security and "creditworthiness." Furthermore, this narrative maintains that financial innovation can overturn the conventional industry wisdom that all safety is bought at a price. Risks, as ever, are unruly. Even by the mid-2010s, industry reports (e.g., BlackRock 2014, 2015) began to suggest that first-mover advantages for conventional infrastructure investment—safer brownfield investments in major cities, for example—had been tapped out and that investors must seek still-riskier "alternatives" in search of returns.

In the contemporary moment, lingering economic turbulence has provoked uncertainty at the highest levels of the international financial system. "Too big to fail" institutional investors are seeking new ways to secure their returns and safety over the short and long term. Meanwhile, national and international regulators search for ways to stabilize a system made increasingly volatile by decades of deregulation, speculative asset bubbles and their aftermath, and broader political-economic transformation—while stopping far short of fundamental financial reforms and reorganizations, neo-Keynesian or radical. Particular explanations for the 2008 financial collapse, and regulatory enactments of these logics, have made the search for safe assets a major feature of financial reforms. Paradoxically, they have provided an impetus and justification for fresh financial experiments with land and real property, as established safe assets like high-quality sovereign debt have seen a glut of investment and diminished profitability. Meanwhile, the pathways to safety imagined by financial institutions today continue to overturn traditional narratives and storylines about the economic and social role of money, "moneylike" financial instruments, land, real property, and the increasingly blurry realm between conventional and so-called alternative financial assets.

These debates at the commanding heights of the global economy have powerful implications for land and real property transformations in the United States and worldwide. Evolving frontiers of property financialization today include but are hardly limited to the diverse forms and geographies that I have surveyed here—from a surge in REITs and REIT legalization for commercial property to the development of experimental investment vehicles for farmland, timberland, and renewable energy infrastructure to the entry of major financial landlords into urban rental housing markets. Sometimes-arcane system-level logics and mandates are structuring institutional investors' more immediate market-making stories and practices today. In turn, these investment programs are shaping many places' and peoples' experiences on the ground, from farmers to renewable energy developers to urban renters. Some are seeing new, if uncertain, capital for development projects; others face speculative land and real estate price run-ups, large-scale acquisitions, and displacements; still others confront new forms of financial extraction and rentiership.

Simultaneously, in the US context these developments deceptively—yet increasingly—frame everyday Americans as creditors whose life chances, failed more and more by traditional narratives and programs of middle-class property ownership and security, are ever more bound up in the very financial apparatus that has excluded them from this historical promise. Ostensibly, this more or less involuntary buy-in means that Americans must accede to the strategies that financial institutions and financial system regulators deploy to protect their own narrowly defined versions of security and stability, at whatever cost to the landscapes and livelihoods of the many. In reality, storylines of safe assets perpetuate deeper, more collective fictions. The safety found in US small property ownership has always been contingent and bound up in broad yet exclusionary political programs for biopolitical security. Similarly, the multiple forms of dependence framed in storylines emerging today—working Americans depend on institutional investors; institutional investors depend on safe assets; the health of the financial system depends on both safe assets and the continued security of a handful of giant institutions—are fictitious. All avoid the central structural question: can any quantity of safe assets secure a system dependent on "too big to fail" financial institutions if its regulators balk at more painful and far-reaching reforms and reorganization? At root, population security is essentially, inescapably a *political* project and responsibility, not one that can be relinquished to the "natural" safety found in any form of property: land, money, or both.

4

GROUND FICTIONS

Soil, Property, and Markets in the Colombian Conflict

Meghan L. Morris

Elvia sat down next to me in the community meeting, as we gathered into small groups to discuss the current needs of the neighborhoods in the upper *comuna* (urban district) of Medellín where she lived.[1] Residents rattled off to community organizers a long list of needs: titling of homes, soil studies, garbage pickup, and especially, more information about which residents might soon be removed from their homes by the city government. Medellín had recently initiated a large infrastructure project called the Cinturón Verde (Green Belt), a series of green spaces and walking and bike paths that would eventually circle much of the perimeter of the city. As of this meeting in 2014, construction for the Green Belt had begun in several neighborhoods in the upper comuna, including Elvia's. As construction progressed, more and more residents had received notice from the city that they would need to leave their homes.

Elvia's home, like many in the upper comuna, was a small wooden shack perched precariously on one of the mountainsides surrounding Medellín's urban center in the Aburrá valley. The vast majority of the upper comuna's residents had come to Medellín from rural areas, displaced during Colombia's long-running armed conflict. As of the end of 2016, it was estimated that there were over 7 million people internally displaced in Colombia—the highest total number in the world, representing nearly 15 percent of the country's population (IMDC 2016). The city of Medellín had received the second highest number of these displaced people, after Bogotá. Arriving with little to nothing, these new residents of Medellín built shacks in informal urban settlements across the upper reaches of the mountainsides, which were often the only places they could find a plot of land. Some residents had secured plots for free, taking down trees from municipal land to build homes, while others had purchased them from former residents or from local paramilitaries, who ran a business in the sale of plots in some neighborhoods in the upper comuna.

Along with several others at the community meeting, Elvia had recently received notice from the city that she would have to leave her home. Tears streamed down her wrinkled cheeks as she told me the news. Her children had abandoned her, she said, and she lived alone. Her shack was located next to the local *quebrada* (stream), which she said had essentially become a sewage pipe; people living above her on the mountain used the stream as a bathroom and as a dump, and the waste flowed down past her home. There was no public sewage system or garbage collection in this part of the upper comuna, leaving people with few options. And now, to make matters worse, the city was trying to kick her out. Where would she go, and who would help her?

Residents complained that the city had long turned a blind eye to the settlements and their needs, leaving significant portions of the upper comuna without public utilities or services. The Green Belt had brought more city investment to the upper comuna, some of which was welcome. This investment, however, was accompanied by increased attention to informal property arrangements and zoning violations in the poor neighborhoods the Green Belt would cross. These problems provided part of the rationale for the removal of residents from their homes to make way for the Green Belt's paths and park areas.

One of the issues the city had begun to focus on was the construction of homes in close proximity to streams, which were considered to be *zonas de alto riesgo*, areas that were at risk of landslide, flooding, or other natural disasters.[2] Both national environmental law and municipal decrees established limits on construction and private property ownership within a certain number of meters of a stream—a rule that had been widely ignored by the city for years in informal settlements but was now being enforced with more frequency, particularly around the construction of the Green Belt. The removal notice Elvia had received was part of this enforcement effort.

Even as the city distributed removal notices to residents, there was confusion in the upper comuna around precisely what the construction limits were near streams. In one community meeting, a resident expressed frustration that "the issue with the banks of the stream—yes, we have communities that are occupying these banks, but we also need to know what the space of the bank is!" Some understood the "bank" as a space of thirty meters, others as a space of fifteen meters, and still others as three meters. The diverse interpretations of the "bank" placed people in a state of uncertainty around whose homes were in violation of the rule, and thus who might be asked to leave.

There was also significant debate around what, precisely, constituted a stream. In another community meeting, a resident expressed with frustration that it was "practically a fact that they are going to kick us out." A community organizer responded, saying "but we know that this is not, in fact, *una quebrada* (a stream). It's *una escorrentía* (surface runoff). Meaning, when it rains it's there, but it's not there all the time." The organizer recognized that there were construction limits on the banks of streams but contested the notion that the area where people had been cited for removal was near a stream at all.

The debate over what constituted a stream was not simply a question of semantics or a play on legal categories but also a question of the material quality of the land in question. Was there water running over the ground in sufficient quantities and with sufficient frequency to constitute a stream? What about the many months out of the year when the land was dry? Was it still a stream then? If the land in question did not constitute a stream, residents with homes there would be more likely to be able to stay. If it did, the city would likely enforce the removal of residents and reclaim the land as municipal property.

As Colombia attempted to bring its decades-long conflict to a close, the state promoted projects like the Green Belt as part of a broader effort to bring about a new "post-conflict" era. Part of the preparation for the post-conflict involved the reordering of property, which provided the legal groundwork for the rearrangement of both land and people in the anticipatory shadow of an aspirational peace.[3] The removal of people from their homes in the upper comuna thus became part of rearrangements for a future peace in which streams receive environmental protection, people are relocated to places away from streams that might damage their homes, and the state possesses both knowledge and control over formerly peripheral areas long marked by both guerrilla and paramilitary violence, such as the upper comuna.

It is perhaps not a surprise that such an effort to create stability would rely in part on something understood to be both fixed and certain: the ground beneath one's feet. Even as social drama played out incessantly above ground, city planners took the material quality of the soil beneath as a constant, one of the few stable factors in the process of reordering for peace. But in these processes of reordering, it is often precisely those things that are taken for granted that get put in motion, emerging as fluid and shifting even as state plans presume their fixity. What appears as a stream on a city map of the comuna is nowhere to be found on a hot August morning, rendering the material quality of the ground—specifically, its wetness or dryness—the most fluid aspect of the debate over the city's reordering plans, rather than the most fixed.

As Michel Serres (1995) notes in *The Natural Contract*, soil—along with other elements in the "world of things" and the world of law—thus becomes a crucial player in war and peace, even as the fury of other struggles obscures its role (Serres 1995, 12). It becomes such a crucial player precisely because of—and not in spite of—its fluid materiality and the divergent interpretations of its qualities.

In this chapter, I argue that the centrality of the soil to matters of war and peace, combined with its shapeshifting qualities, have rendered the ground itself a subject of fictions. Rather than revolving around the *commodity* form of land, as Karl Polanyi argued (2001 [1944]), these fictions often center around the *material* form of land—its wetness or dryness, stability or instability. These fictions—which might best be called ground fictions, rather than land fictions—are stories told by state bureaucrats, local residents, scientists, businessmen, and paramilitaries about the material form of the soil.

Soil has become the recent center of a rich set of interventions in anthropology and political ecology, in which it has passed from relative obscurity—simply the ground beneath one's feet—to a focal point for conceptualizing human-nonhuman relations and forms of ecological knowledge (Puig de la Bellacasa 2014; Lyons 2020). This work is explicitly attentive to divergent stories about the soil told by different social actors, and the ways these narrate the relationships between humans and the material world.

Kristina Lyons (2014; 2020) explores these questions in Colombia, illustrating how the soil is often treated by Colombian state scientists as a natural body with a given "vocation," something that is classifiable and used to undergird territorial ordering and maps representing specific national interests. At the same time, she discusses how this same soil is often treated by local farmers as something that is living, relational, and constantly changing. She emphasizes that this does not represent "different perspectives on a common world," but rather the enacting of different worlds related to the soil (Lyons 2014, 214–15). I find that these disjunctures in the ways that soil is enacted—which often come to the fore in encounters between state actors, displaced people, and paramilitaries—are precisely where ground fictions tend to proliferate. In this chapter, I focus ethnographically on several such encounters to illustrate these fictions.

These stories lie somewhere between fact and fiction, in the sense that Donna Haraway attributes generally to fictions. In *Primate Visions*, Haraway (1989) breaks down the opposition between fact and fiction, reminding us of the origin of both fact and fiction in human action and experience. She argues that "fiction is inescapably implicated in a dialectic of the true (natural) and the counterfeit (artifactual). But in all its meanings, fiction is about human action. So, too, are all the narratives of science—fiction and fact—about human action" (Haraway 1989, 3–4). She discusses primatology as an art of storytelling, through which narratives are produced about the relationships between animals and humans, nature and culture. She devotes her analysis to what she calls "the narratives of scientific fact—those potent fictions of science" (Haraway 1989, 4–5).

In this chapter, I consider the narratives of fact—scientific, but also legal fact—that emerge around the material form of the soil in sites of conflict. These narratives of fact become what I call ground fictions. They are animated by the fact that the qualities of the soil, like the stream in Medellín, do actually change. At the same time, the stories told about those changes also employ counterfeits— ground that is variously wet or dry, stable or unstable—as required for particular legal ends. Ground fictions thus emerge through a dialectical play between truth and counterfeit.

In my analysis, I follow Lyons and Puig de la Bellacasa in foregrounding divergent narratives around the soil. I pay particular attention to the ways these narratives intersect with and are oriented toward property and land markets.[4] I examine ground fictions as they are crafted and mobilized to make certain kinds of property in land possible or impossible, rendering these fictions part of stories about property that allow land to be included in or excluded from different land markets, ranging from informal purchases and sales between small farmers and displaced people to markets run by paramilitaries. These inclusions and exclusions are facilitated by legal moves such as the redefinition of land as public or private, the use of titling to create land markets, or the establishment of protected areas or communal lands with prohibitions on sale. In this sense, these fictions return to the question of the commodity that Polanyi raises. That said, rather than the fiction appearing as an intrinsic quality of land as commodity, as Polanyi suggests, ground fictions emerge in this discussion as necessary precursors to the legal rules that permit the commodity's entry into or removal from specific markets.

The stories about the soil that I explore emerge in two different sites. The first is a rural site in the region of Urabá in northwestern Colombia, where stories about the dryness of the soil became the foundation for titling practices that put thousands of hectares of "new land" onto the formal land market. The second is an urban site in the upper comuna of the city of Medellín, where stories not just of streams but of the very stability of the soil itself emerged as the primary factor in the historical titling of plots and the ability of residents to retain those homes as the construction of the Green Belt progressed. In both sites, soil stories became crucial elements of both the manufacture and foreclosure of new forms of property and land consolidation.

My analysis is based on ethnographic fieldwork in both Urabá and Medellín around the ways that property became central to the state's efforts to prepare for a post-conflict peace. This fieldwork explicitly straddled both urban and rural sites, in part because it is difficult to even begin to understand the dynamics of conflict in Colombia—and the role of property in it—without having some insight into both rural and urban life and the ways they are intertwined, even as they refuse analytical collapsing into each other. The dynamics of the war, and of efforts to achieve peace, make the kind of integrated analysis of rural and urban that this volume calls for a theoretical, political, and empirical imperative for work in Colombia—one that I take seriously in the analysis in this chapter. The juxtaposition of these two sites in this chapter sheds light on the ways that the soil becomes a crucial player in war and peace, as Serres suggests, through its foundational role in the property rules that come to redefine both rural and urban land markets in the unfolding of the conflict and attempts to bring it to a close.

Disappearing Rivers

The day had been hot, the air still and sticky around the area of packed earth where a commission of state officials from different land agencies had met with the rural community of Las Guayabas in Urabá. The meeting had concluded and just a few community members were left at the end of the day. Many had a long walk or bus ride awaiting them, their homes dispersed far from the dirt country road that led to the meeting place, the center of the village from which many of them had been displaced fifteen years before. The road was flanked by large cattle ranches held by a few local elites, which had replaced most of the small plots community members had farmed before their displacement.

Others had left early out of frustration, wary of the commission's promise to help them return to the land they had lost during the war. Colombia had initiated a national land restitution process, which aimed to return more than 6 million hectares of rural land to people who had been dispossessed or forced to abandon their land due to the country's ongoing armed conflict. While this meeting had been organized to provide further information about the process to the community, there were deep divisions and ongoing power struggles within the community itself around who had the right to which land. This rendered the prospect of restitution appealing to some, while others remained skeptical, worried that restitution might actually cause them to lose the small farms that a few people had been able to establish after their initial displacement.

As the meeting concluded, the visiting officials gathered around a set of papers. Don Fernando, a community member, had shoved them at one of the officials in an act of frustration during the meeting, singling out other community members as in part responsible for what the papers illustrated. He had then left in a huff, clearly unconvinced that the commission would be able to change his situation.

The papers turned out to be a copy of a land title, dated several years back. Like all titles in Colombia, this one indicated at the top the notary's office where the title had been produced, and went on to cite the names and identification numbers of the individuals who came to the notary's office to adjust the title. Any adjustment to a title in Colombia—be it mortgage, purchase, sale, change in boundary, or something else—must be first filed at a notary's office and subsequently recorded at a public land registry in order to be legally recognized. In this sense, the title appeared perfectly standard.

The remainder of the title also seemed, at first glance, nothing out of the ordinary. It described the land, a rural plot of just over forty hectares, located nearby. It then proceeded to describe the adjustment processed at the notary's office: a clarification of area and boundaries. This was a common process, used to correct the boundaries of plots present in a title if they had been recorded incorrectly, or to adjust slightly the boundaries between neighbors, for example. The title then had signatures and fingerprints of the notary and of the plot owner at the end, with the array of stamps that generally accompany documents emitted by notary's offices.

Upon closer examination, however, there was something strange about the title. It described the reason for the clarification of area and boundaries as the drying up of a river. According to the title, this drying had generated more land. This land had not previously been included in the title, as the river had served as the boundary between two plots. Now that it had dried completely, the owner was including the area of the riverbed in the total area of the titled plot, necessitating a clarification of area and boundaries. The new area, according to the title, was nineteen hundred hectares.

This section of the title gave the officials pause. One of them called over a lingering community member, asking her if it were plausible that a river in the region would dry up completely. Yes, she said. She knew rivers that had dried up. He then asked how much dry land would generally be created through such a process. Could a dry riverbed be over eighteen hundred hectares? She seemed skeptical about this. Eighteen hundred hectares was a lot of land, bigger than the total area of Las Guayabas and the farms that had once surrounded it. The official thanked her and turned back to the papers, convinced that something was off.

The claims made in this title were not anomalous, but were rather part of a broader pattern of titling in Urabá based on the same theory: "alluvial accession." This particular title followed the basic alluvial accession argument common to that pattern: a river dries up, is bifurcated, or changes course. These changes create more dry land, which is then integrated into an existing title through the clarification of area and boundaries at the notary's office. While plausible in principle, many of the title adjustments involving alluvial accession in Urabá expanded the total titled area by implausibly large amounts. Title registrations I collected involving alluvial accession recorded expansions of hundreds and even thousands of hectares, just like the one presented by Don Fernando.

Alluvial accession was used in the 2000s to expand possession of land in various parts of the region of Urabá. These expansions, rather than constituting accessions of previously unowned riverbed, were often takeovers of neighboring land titled or informally owned by others. In some cases, this neighboring land was held by private individuals. In others, accession was used specifically to expand possession of land within territories that were collectively titled to black communities.[5] While there are legal restrictions on the private purchase and sale of collectively titled territory, plots within collective territories that were individually titled prior to the establishment of collective title are respected as individually held land, which may be bought and sold. Often, however, these individually titled plots are relatively small, ranging from a few hectares to a few hundred. Alluvial accession allowed these small individually titled plots to be expanded exponentially, resulting in the absorption of thousands of hectares of collectively titled land into individual private titles that could be bought and sold. In the case of one black community with collective title, Curvaradó, the national rural development agency (Incoder) documented five cases of illicit land acquisition through alluvial accession, which expanded private titled areas totaling 185 hectares into areas totaling over 18,000 hectares (Incoder 2012).

This use of alluvial accession to expand individual private property involved a broad set of actors, including state officials, paramilitaries, community associations, businessmen, agroindustrial companies, and lawyers. Incoder's documentation of the Curvaradó cases, for example, alleges that several of the plots were expanded through accession and sold immediately to an association of farmers of African palm and to a private ranching business.

The Incoder report also alleges the complicity of the notary publics and registry officials themselves, who presided over these dubious expansions of titled areas (Incoder 2012). The notary public involved in the most infamous case of accession in Curvaradó—in which the title holder, a small farmer, expanded an 18-hectare plot into a 5,908 hectare plot and sold it to the same African palm association in 2000—was described in a newspaper article as being a person to whom "biblical powers are attributed. They say that he brought someone back from the dead and multiplied land" (Congote Gutiérrez 2011). Not only had the notary public performed the miracle of turning 18 hectares into 5,908 hectares, but he had also presided over a title transfer allegedly conducted in person by a small farmer. The farmer named on the title had in fact been dead for five years, drowned in a river in 1995 under circumstances his family described as "questionable" (Congote Gutiérrez 2011).

Alluvial accession was just one of a range of titling schemes employed in Urabá to facilitate the consolidation of land by a handful of large landholders. From the 1960s, Urabá had been home to the country's banana industry, which brought an influx of migrants from neighboring regions such as Córdoba and the Chocó to work. Other small farmers came looking for *baldíos* (idle state-owned lands), felling tropical forest or making informal purchases from other small farmers to plant small plots of rice, plantain, and other subsistence crops on Urabá's famously fertile soils. While left-wing guerrilla groups such as the Revolutionary Armed Forces of Colombia (FARC) and the Popular Liberation Army (EPL) exerted control over much of Urabá in the 1970s and 1980s, by the late 1980s right-wing paramilitary groups had been formed in the department of Córdoba by landholding elites and narco-traffickers (Duncan 2006, 2014). These groups eventually established their center of operations in Urabá and actively contested guerrillas' territorial control.

The entry of paramilitaries began a new wave of violence in Urabá, marked by massacres of banana workers, the targeting of unionists and small farmers as supposed guerrilla collaborators, and the flight of thousands of people from the countryside. During the particularly bloody period of 1996–97—a time that locals call *la violencia* (the violence)—nearly all of the people living in rural villages like Las Guayabas were forced to flee, often to larger towns in Urabá or cities like Medellín, leaving their farms behind.[6] Some simply abandoned their land without selling it, fleeing for their lives. Other farmers from the region talk about how they were approached at the time by *comisiones* (commissions) who were looking to purchase land. Some of these commissions included individuals people said they recognized as paramilitaries. Locals often sold their land for little or nothing. Subsequently, a few of these plots were expanded through alluvial accession.

In cases of illicit acquisition, the recording of title at the public registry itself was crucial to the ability of new owners to conceal the nature of transfers. In many cases of acquisition of land through alluvial accession, for example, those performing the accession would then break up the resulting larger plot into a series of smaller plots, which they might sell or transfer to other companies or individuals. These new plots would then each be recorded at the public registry under a new number. Teo Ballvé (2013) calls this process "land laundering," illustrating how this series of transfers and changes in registrations can hide illicit land acquisitions.

These methods also reveal the extent to which processes of land acquisition and consolidation, like alluvial accession, involved collaboration between state and private actors and armed groups. Even schemes that involved purchases or falsification by people associated with paramilitaries often also eventually included participation by bureaucrats such as rural development officials, notary publics, or public registry officials. This reflects a broader pattern of collaboration between paramilitaries and state and private actors that has been widely documented (Romero 2011, 2007; López 2007).

Through a combination of these and other methods, over the course of a few years, thousands of hectares of land in Urabá were consolidated into the hands of just a few large landholders. While some of this land had already been part of an active informal land market—subject to purchase and sale between small farmers and neighbors using unregistered bills of sale—these titling schemes brought many hectares of land into the formal market for the first time. This was crucial for elites interested in initiating agroindustrial projects on the land, as formal land title allowed them to receive credit from state agencies and banks. The credit that new landholders would receive in many cases went toward the preparation of the soil for agroindustrial projects. For a number of these projects, this credit financed the establishment of canals to drain wet soil, which was necessary in order to keep the roots of palm and banana crops well-drained.

For farms acquired through alluvial accession, the use of credit to finance the draining of the soil laid bare the extent to which arguments around accession relied on fictions about the ground—fictions that, as Haraway describes, sat at the interstices of the true and the counterfeit. On the one hand, those acquiring land through alluvial accession claimed that the soil had dried up—that an area that was once so wet that a river coursed through it had desiccated, leaving thousands of hectares of "new" dry land, now available to be acquired and titled. On the other hand, once acquired, they claimed that the soil was too wet for farming something like palm, and required significant investment to drain the soil and make it productive.

Even as these claims revolved around fictions, it was their proximity to possible truths that made them plausible on their face—plausible enough that even a visiting state commission focused on land would have to ask a local in Las Guayabas whether, indeed, a dried riverbed could yield over eighteen hundred hectares of newly titleable land, rather than rejecting the possibility immediately. The plausibility of the claims rested on the fact that the wetness or dryness of the soil in Urabá had been a matter of constant change and management since the region's widespread colonization in the 1950s. When the earliest banana plantation owners arrived, the tropical forest soil was so wet that they had to dig canals to drain the fields in order to plant banana, which has roots that will swiftly rot in poorly drained soil. By the 1970s, the canals of the banana industry zig-zagged across the center of Urabá, draining the region's enormous volumes of fresh water to the sea. The felling of the forest for logging and to establish the small farms that began to appear in areas like Las Guayabas had a significant drying effect on Urabá's soils (Leal and Restrepo 2003). This was exacerbated in the wake of the paramilitary violence of the late 1990s, when the consolidation of land in the region and the conversion of small farms into plantations and ranches came along with new investment in canals.

Between the canal cutting by the banana industry, the felling of forests by loggers and small farmers, and the later construction of new canals in the 1990s, Urabá was drained of much of its water in the second half of the twentieth century. While water remains in abundance, it is heavily managed through canals by everyone from medium-scale plantain farmers to agroindustrial palm plantation owners. The historical management of water in Urabá rendered the ground itself—even prior to arguments around alluvial accession—something of an artifact rather than a static fact, a product of human action that was deliberately built and rebuilt over time.

The historically shifting nature of Urabá's soils provided part of the foundation for the legal storytelling that emerged through arguments around alluvial accession. The notion that a river would dry up, revealing "new" dry land, was not necessarily in and of itself an implausible claim. Many long-time residents of Urabá could name a river or stream that had once existed and was now dried up, just as the woman the commission consulted in Las Guayabas confirmed. This made the alluvial accession argument proximate to something that could resemble the truth. At the same time, titling through alluvial accession clearly involved the production of counterfeits. These ranged from clear counterfeits, such as the signatures of already deceased former owners, to those related to the scope of the claims to title, as it was highly unlikely, if not impossible, that a dried riverbed in Urabá would reveal over eighteen hundred hectares of freshly available land.

These claims, which sit between the factual and the artifactual, are an example of what I call here a ground fiction. They are fictions about the material form of the soil—particularly its wetness and dryness—that are rooted in specific histories of the colonization of Urabá and establishment of the banana industry in the 1960s through the 1980s, the paramilitary violence of the 1990s, and the consolidation of land in the 2000s. These histories had particular effects on Urabá's soil, granting the ground a shapeshifting quality that allows the soil to be a subject of fictions.[7] These fictions become crucial elements of novel or repurposed forms of property such as extensive alluvial accession, turning thousands of hectares of informally held land into titled plots or inalienable collectively titled land into expanded individual plots. These property forms, in turn, allow land to be brought into the formal land market either for the first time or in new ways and by new actors.

The ways these fictions are intertwined with both historical and present forms of colonization and violence also make them part of a larger story about the long arc of the country's ongoing war and current efforts to build peace. The importance of these ground fictions to the relationship between land and conflict in Urabá indicates the crucial role that apparently benign, stable things—such as the wetness of soil—can play in this larger story of war and peace. In the next section, I illustrate how this comes to be the case not just with rural land, which has largely been the focus of public conversation in Colombia around peacebuilding, but also in urban space.

Risky Soil

The room was packed with residents of Loma Linda, a neighborhood in the upper comuna of Medellín, with late arrivals spilling into the open space behind the white plastic chairs where other residents were seated. The meeting with the city development corporation (CDC) had been going on for over an hour, with the CDC engineer in his official vest marching through a PowerPoint presentation about the housing benefits that would come along with the Green Belt project. He showed photograph after photograph of apartment towers where residents could be relocated in other parts of the city, and several smaller towers that would be built in Loma Linda as part of the Green Belt construction.

Residents had been asking almost from the beginning for more information about who might be removed from Loma Linda as construction proceeded, with little response from the CDC. Finally, the audience couldn't take it anymore. A woman attending interrupted the presentation, asking "and if we're in a *zona de alto riesgo* [zone of high risk], what happens?" The CDC official was visibly annoyed, responding that they didn't yet have a finalized risk map for the neighborhood. He went on to describe the general problem with high risk zones: "What do we want with this project? To deal in some way with all the situations here, which is the situation in all the upper *comunas* . . . the illegal occupation of the land, the loss of environmental goods and services, people occupying the banks of streams generating risks with their trash . . . we don't want housing in high risk zones." The audience became even more restless, demanding to know which houses were in zones of high risk. The CDC officials refused, confirming that a number of residents of Loma Linda were living in zones of high risk, but that they needed additional studies to determine which residents would need to be removed.

The city's determination of "zones of high risk," such as the banks of streams like the one Elvia's house abutted, relied in part on soil studies conducted by experts in hydrology and geology, some contracted through the CDC. These studies had become a point of contention in the upper comuna, as risk was being used by the CDC to justify the removal of some residents from their homes as Green Belt construction proceeded, but precisely what areas of the upper comuna had been determined to be risky had not been revealed. Some residents in the direct path of Green Belt construction had already received removal notices; unsure what to do, several had signed, agreeing to leave their homes for compensation or eventual relocation in apartment towers.

The material instability of the ground beneath residents' feet was thus the crux of fears and desires in the upper comuna, even as proof of its instability remained opaque. As in Austin Zeiderman's (2016) eloquent analysis of the fluid assessments of the stability of the ground that emerged from encounters between technocrats and residents of zones of high risk in Bogotá, the changing nature of both the ground itself in the upper comuna and technical assessments of it meant that the determination of risky soil was not about clear, static threat. Rather, as Zeiderman (2016, 76) notes, it was part of "an ongoing effort to render the uncertain future an object of official decision-making in the present." The notion of risky soil undergirded residents' fears of displacement by the Green Belt and their distrust of the city, as well as the desire by the CDC to prioritize specific resident removals as Green Belt construction proceeded.

The deep concern on the part of the city and the residents about the instability of the soil, combined with the opacity surrounding the actual determination of "risky soil," rendered the ground of the upper comuna a powerful locus of fictions. As with alluvial accession in Urabá, these fictions sat at the intersection of the factual and the artifactual. They drew on specific histories of colonization and violence in the upper comuna in which the instability of the soil had in fact played a crucial role, even as the historic and present instability of the soil in the area remained a matter of contestation.

The event that had precipitated early conversations in Medellín around risky soil was the landslide of Villatina in 1987. Perched on a mountainside overlooking the Aburrá valley, Villatina—like Loma Linda and other neighborhoods in the upper comuna—was full of small, humble homes made of concrete blocks or wooden planks, inhabited largely by the city's poor. One Sunday in 1987, twenty thousand cubic meters of soil came down the mountain onto the neighborhood, burying homes and residents in earth. Hundreds were killed in the landslide, and more than a thousand residents suffered damage or complete destruction of their homes.

Zones of high risk had been established in 1985 across the city, in line with a trend Zeiderman (2016) observes toward an increased focus on risk management and prevention as governmental imperatives in urban Colombia writ large in this period. This trend, Zeiderman notes, followed the eruption of the Nevado de Ruíz volcano and the M-19 guerrilla siege on the Palacio de Justicia (the Bogotá headquarters of the judicial branch), which occurred nearly simultaneously in 1985. The disaster in Villatina, however, provoked the reassessment of these initial zones. Areas in the upper comuna that had not figured as high risk prior to Villatina now appeared on new maps and regulations as high risk (Universidad Nacional et al. 2009), and the notion of risky soil in Medellín became increasingly attached to poor neighborhoods in the upper comunas.

Even as places like Loma Linda or Villatina became the perceived epicenter of risky soil, residents' visions of risk were cast elsewhere. These neighborhoods had long been centers of guerrilla activity in the 1980s and then right-wing paramilitaries in the 1990s, financed in part by narco-trafficking. While some of these paramilitaries demobilized in the mid-2000s, successor groups (officially called "Bacrim" or criminal bands) continue to exert control in the upper comunas to this day. Given the history of armed groups in these neighborhoods, the notion that risk resided in the instability of the soil—rather than in the daily violence residents experienced due to the armed conflict—was unimaginable to some residents. This reflected the intersecting, yet also divergent, notions of endangerment that Zeiderman (2016) theorizes as central to urban governance in Colombia.

The CDC's invocation of risky soil to justify resident removals during initial construction of the Green Belt was thus an argument that sat somewhere between fact and artifact. It was rooted in historical events like the disaster of Villatina, which had drawn attention to the potentially fatal instabilities of soils on Medellín's mountainsides. With this in mind, the removal of residents from high risk zones and the replacement of their vulnerable shacks with parks and green spaces seemed to be a fact-based approach.

At the same time, to many residents' ears, this was at best poorly timed, and at worst entirely fabricated. If the soils were indeed so unstable, why hadn't the city enforced building restrictions in those zones during the past thirty years or built retaining walls to mitigate these risks? Why were CDC officials arriving only now that homes and neighborhoods had already been built, advising people across the upper comuna to halt home improvements? Residents speculated that risky soil was simply a pretext to remove the poor to make way for the Green Belt, which they identified as a project the city wanted to attract tourism. One resident summarized this point of view in a community meeting, arguing that "they [city officials] put in our heads that we don't fit because they want to put in their tourism projects. For them, there's everything. There's land. But when it comes to us, there's no money, and there's no land!"

These arguments about the fabrication of the instability of the soil in order to remove the poor in part correctly identified the relevance of economic vulnerability to the factors included within the city's assessment of risk. Paradoxically, however, the very establishment of zones of high risk based on these criteria had tended to augment the legal and economic vulnerabilities of the residents of the upper comuna and the ability of residents to remain in their homes with the arrival of the Green Belt. This was the case particularly due to the difficulties that residents faced in securing title to homes in zones of high risk.

As in Urabá, many of the plots people acquired in the upper comuna did not have formal title. This was due in part to the circumstances of their acquisition—some people had felled trees to make plots and simply never acquired title, while others purchased plots from armed groups or previous owners using an informal bill of sale. But the notion of risky soil had also played a significant role in the levels of informal tenure in the upper comuna. While in theory plots within zones of high risk could be titled, no construction on them was permitted. This had led to a widespread belief among residents that they could not title the land on which they had built their homes, and few had gone through the steps to attempt to title their plots, believing they would simply be rejected. City officials I spoke with assured me this was not the case, and that plots in zones of high risk could in fact be titled—just not the homes themselves. That said, residents' uncertainty about the city rule, combined with the fact that building a home was the prime reason for which they had acquired plots, contributed to the low rate of titling of plots and homes in the upper comuna.

For many years, the low rate of titling in the upper comuna had few significant impacts on residents. The city did relatively little to stem the conversion of municipal property into informally held private plots or to prevent construction in zones of high risk. As mass displacement from rural areas exploded in the late 1990s and early 2000s, waves of displaced people arrived in the upper comuna and built humble houses and shacks extending far up the mountainside, in and around zones of high risk. Local paramilitaries often participated in the real estate market in the upper comuna as well, staking out small plots on municipal property that they would sell to new arrivals. People frequently transferred their plots using informal bills of sale, which were often notarized but did not require title, facilitating a lively local land market in which titles were few and far between. City enforcement of restrictions in these zones was limited to nonexistent, commensurate with the lack of city presence in the upper comunas during this period.

There was a marked shift in municipal practice and enforcement, however, with the arrival of the Green Belt project. On the one hand, city officials began to monitor and discourage new construction and even home improvements in high risk zones. It was a waste of money, officials said, since residents would not be compensated for any of this new construction when they were removed. In addition, the city began to distribute removal notices, largely to residents who lacked title to their plots and homes. The lack of title put residents in a more difficult negotiating position regarding both removal itself and the compensation they might expect from the city for removal. This demonstrated the long-term effects of the establishment of zones of high risk; these zones had inhibited residents from securing title to their homes, which later facilitated their removal for the Green Belt.

The fictions that had been built around the instability of the soil thus had long-term implications for the kind of property that was possible in the upper comuna. This, in turn, affected the mix of land markets that emerged in the comuna over time. Notions of risky soil had initially facilitated land markets dominated by informal purchases and sales between displaced people and illicit paramilitary real estate schemes. With the arrival of the Green Belt, however, the city reemphasized the notion of risky soil to shift these markets away from informal or illicit private transfers and toward the reestablishment of municipal property.

This shift in city enforcement based on notions of risky soil, however, did not simply imply a strict closing off of private land markets in the upper comuna. There was, on the one hand, the specter of the establishment of a private land market by the city itself with its construction of new apartment towers. Residents looked at pictures of the towers, speculating about the people that would one day live in them and enjoy the view of the valley, when current residents were long gone. More immediately, city enforcement actually also caused an expansion of the paramilitary land market in anticipation of potential removals. As in Urabá, the fictions around the materiality of the soil facilitated particular forms of property that allowed land to shift between different informal, private, public, and illicit land markets.

The notion that the soil of the upper comuna was unstable, like the stories of wet and dry soil in Urabá, was a fiction about the ground that rested on real, specific histories of colonization and disaster, like that of the landslide in Villatina and the subsequent establishment of zones of high risk by municipal experts. At the same time, the idea of risky soil held within it artifactual elements, demonstrated through city officials' inability to precisely identify which soils were and were not risky, and the seemingly pretextual use of zones of high risk to facilitate the removal of poor residents as the Green Belt project proceeded.

These accounts from Urabá and Medellín demonstrate the power of ground fictions. Stories about the soil's materiality become key factors in the ability to bring new forms of property into being, such as extensive alluvial accession, or to close off the possibility of property, such as in the upper comuna's zones of high risk. These property forms—both those that emerge and are foreclosed—in turn become centerpieces of state and paramilitary strategies for land accumulation and development. In Urabá, alluvial accession is used to accumulate and consolidate land for large-scale cattle ranching and palm cultivation, while in Medellín, land in high risk zones becomes central to the expansion of public infrastructure and potential future private housing markets.

Ground fictions thus become a crucial tool for shifting land between markets, which range and also occupy spaces in between private and public, formal and informal, licit and illicit. Alluvial accession turned thousands of hectares of communally titled or informally held land into formally titled, alienable plots overnight. In unexpected ways, moves by Medellín to reclaim public land simultaneously facilitated a shift toward future private housing markets and an increase in the intensity of the paramilitary land market in the upper comuna. These shifts between different markets were facilitated in great part by the property forms that were built and foreclosed based on stories about the materiality of the soil—its wetness and dryness, instability and stability. Here, the question is not whether land can or should be part of "the market"—and if its very existence as a commodity is fictitious—but rather how fictions facilitate what sort of commodity land becomes. This becoming emerges as actors such as paramilitaries, landowners, city officials, and displaced people craft and contest stories about the soil to turn land from a communal ethnic resource into a private palm plantation, or from a home for displaced people into a public park.

These are the kinds of shifts that are made visible when we consider the fictional with respect to land not as a defining element of land as commodity, as in Polanyi's formulation, but rather as a more complex, dialectical relationship between what is factual and artifactual in the stories we tell about land. Haraway attunes us to this dialectic, asking us to consider the elements of both truth and counterfeit that reside within fictions. Doing this allows for an understanding of the ways that stories about the ground emerge from real histories of colonization and war, at the same time as they involve artifactual forms that are specifically designed to accumulate land in certain hands, or shift it between particular markets. This kind of analysis opens up a fine-grained view of the actors, stakes, and markets around land that a denial of land as commodity might foreclose.

An attention to both soil and property is crucial in this analysis. As Lyons (2020) observes, soil is frequently understood as fixed, the characteristics of certain soils a natural, given quality, rather than elements in flux. It is precisely soil's fluidity, however, that makes it possible for multiple, divergent stories about the soil to undergird the ground fictions that emerge as important in these sites. These fictions work because they are rooted in real histories in which wetness, dryness, and instability are crucial factors in colonization and settlement, forms of violence, and patterns of property. At the same time, the shapeshifting quality of the soil that emerges from these histories lends it to the artifactual, such that people in Urabá can claim that soil that was once wet is now dry, or city officials and comuna residents can contest whether or not the soil underfoot is in fact unstable.

The soil's importance in these histories has made it a central subject of fictions as Colombia attempts to forge a post-conflict peace. As people build narratives around how the country might achieve peace—be it through investment in public infrastructure like the Green Belt, or restitution of rural land acquired through illicit forms of alluvial accession—these narratives necessarily refer back to layered histories of war and colonization in which soil played a vital role. As these narratives emerge, we would do well to turn our attention to the new fictions that emerge about the ground, and how they are deployed in the name of peace, even as they have long been central to the cause of war.

5

NARRATIVES OF WASTE

The Fictions and Frictions of Land Commodification in Liberalizing India

Sai Balakrishnan

In 2006, bureaucrats in the Khed *taluka* in western Maharashtra attempted to acquire agricultural land for a new special economic zone (SEZ). The acquisition provoked protests, with agrarian landowners occupying the highways in and around the proposed SEZ for almost two months. These highway interruptions were publicized by the media, and in the wake of negative publicity, the bureaucrats started negotiations with the protesting landowners. This chapter focuses on a specific demand by the landowners, which has now made its way into the national land acquisition act, the 2013 Right to Fair Compensation and Transparency in Land Acquisition, Rehabilitation and Resettlement Act (LARRA). The Khed region has irrigated multicrop fields that grow vegetables for sale in the surrounding cities, including Pune. The protests against the SEZ were spearheaded by landowners belonging to the dominant Maratha-Kunbi caste. The landowners demanded that their fertile agricultural lands be left untouched and that the bureaucrats only acquire the "barren waste land" within their villages for the new SEZ. This demand is now institutionalized in the 2013 LARRA as the "food security" clause, which mandates that

> no irrigated multi-cropped land shall be acquired under this Act. Such land may be acquired subject to the condition that it is being done under exceptional circumstances, as a demonstrable last resort. Whenever multi-crop irrigated land is acquired ... an equivalent area of culturable wasteland shall be developed for agricultural purposes or an amount equivalent to the value of the land acquired shall be depos-

ited with the appropriate Government for investment in agriculture for enhancing food-security.[1]

In Polanyian terms, the agrarian landowners were agitating for a protective countermovement of their fertile agricultural land. Land, Polanyi argued, is a fictitious commodity (Polanyi 2001 [1944]), meaning that while treated as if it were like any other commodity, land is not in fact produced for sale—the standard commodity definition. Any attempt to commodify land, he argued, would be met with countermovements aimed at protecting affected social groups from the social and environmental effects caused by reducing land to a mere asset, or "element of industry," as Polanyi put it. This back-and-forth tension between the pressures of commodification and countermovements to slow or reverse them together form what Polanyi famously termed the double movement of capitalism. For Polanyi, land can never be fully reduced to a mere commodity because, as the negative consequences of an unrestrained land market become apparent, people resist: "They refuse to act like lemmings marching over a cliff to their own destruction" (ibid., xxv). The pressure from an agrarian capitalist class—the dominant-caste landowners in Khed—to protect their land from market-oriented redevelopment might seem unexpected, given that they are the group most invested in systems of commodity production and surplus creation. One would assume that the liberalizing push in the double movement is driven by capitalist fractions, and that propertied capital, like the agrarian landowners, would stand to benefit most from land commodification. Polanyi, though, in his departure from more narrowly class-based accounts of economic development, noted that the task of "protecting" society could fall to different factions of society, including landed capital, and would not necessarily be led by the working class.[2] Less anticipated by Polanyi, though, was the possibility that nonpropertied and working classes might themselves become drivers or at least proponents of land commodification. The Khed conflict exemplifies precisely this arrangement, as Adivasi owners—a self-appellation for the colonial-era category of "tribes"—of the waste lands supported the commodification of land that had long been a source of subsistence needs. Acquiescing to the demands of the agrarian propertied class, the Khed bureaucrats redrew the boundaries of the SEZ to only include waste lands. The Khed Adivasis, who have historically labored on the lands of the dominant-caste landowners, were not only willing, but eager, to have their lands acquired and commodified for the SEZ.

This chapter uses the case of the Khed SEZ to explore these contradictions and unexpected twists in Maharashtra's land commodification tale. It does so by turning to both the fictions and frictions that underpin the conversion of agrarian lands into urban real estate. To understand the unexpected caste/class alignments variously resisting or supporting land commodification, I first turn to an historical analysis of the fictions of "waste," a long-standing, colonial-era label used to mark certain lands as vacant, idle, devalued, or unused and that has historically erased the multiple subsistence land uses of more marginalized, nonpropertied constituents (Gidwani 1992; White et al. 2013; Baka 2013). This erasure has continued to be central to the creation of a real estate market in rural Maharashtra today, which I examine by asking how the categories of fertile and waste land have been produced and maintained, first under colonial rule, then through the postcolonial Green Revolution, and finally in the post-1991 liberalization era. In historicizing the sociolegal construction of the category of wasteland, I also want to link these Lockean narratives of waste to fictions of surplus land. At various historical-geographical junctures, state authorities seek out "surplus" "waste" land that is legitimized as available for economic growth, or in the parlance of economists, for the highest and best land use. In contemporary episodes of land redevelopment, these surplus waste lands may be public land in the neoliberal United Kingdom and Canada (Christophers and Whiteside, this volume), or they may be waste land in liberalizing India's agricultural land frontier (the focus of this chapter). But the surprising twist in the narrative of surplus waste land that I want to highlight is when propertied elites search for countermovements to protect their land from market exposure, and when laboring constituents become willing participants of waste land commodification.

In liberalizing India, agrarian propertied classes adopted a strategic narrative of food security, borrowed from the right to food movement, to apply the brakes on the accelerating processes of land commodification. Food security, so the story goes, needs fertile land, and land urbanization and SEZ formation risk wasting productive agriculture, thereby undermining the security of the rural population and wider national polity. By capturing the more equity-oriented rhetoric of the right to food movement, agrarian capital, I show, has thus used the narrative of food security to defend its irrigated agricultural lands from state expropriation, not so much to maintain an equitable agrarian society, but to set their own terms for possible land sale. Adivasi users and occupants of land, particularly the youth, however, have not been passive actors in waste stories, but have instead selectively reanimated ideas of waste to depict land conversion as an emancipatory way out of a caste-oppressive agrarian order.

Fictions and Frictions: Narratives of Waste

Recalling the Polanyian double movement, the fictions that attempt to produce an expanding land market encounter frictions of various sorts. In liberalizing

India, the creation of a transnational real estate market is interrupted in myriad ways. Benjamin (2008) argues that the diverse land tenure systems in much of the global south, which is generally slotted under the rather unhelpful category of "informal sector" or "slums," actually constitutes tactics of subversion against "high-end infrastructure and mega projects." These multiple de facto land tenures enable what he calls "occupancy urbanism," a form of legal pluralism that "helps poor groups appropriate real estate surpluses via reconstituted land tenure to fuel small businesses whose commodities jeopardize branded chains" (Benjamin 2008). It is these diverse land tenure systems that also make it difficult to seamlessly link India's nascent real estate market with real estate markets elsewhere in the world. A transnational real estate market requires fictions of commensuration: a plot of land which is embedded within specific legal, regulatory, and cultural contexts needs to be standardized in such a way that it can be compared, using a common metric, to another plot of land in a completely different context. Land titles, that is, private property rights, are one way of transforming discrete landed resources into a commensurable and fungible commodity. Searle (2016) highlights the fact that global capital does not simply enter a new land market; instead, she points to the painstaking work involved in valuing, building, accounting, and marketing that helps to integrate local land markets into a globally legible financial asset. Searle points to the complex land tenure conditions in India to explain a puzzle in Indian real estate: why do even the most high-end, "world-class" buildings have "open stairwells, dingy corridors and 'bad' corner details?" Searle argues that Indian real estate developers, whose expertise lies in the difficult task of assembling fragmented plots of land with unclear titles, consider land assembly to be the main determinant of quality. International design and construction firms, on the other hand, place value on architecture and construction quality. Joint ventures then are a fraught exercise as Indian and international real estate partners fundamentally disagree on the common metric—land or building—for valuing the quality of the real estate product.

Of interest to this chapter on the 2014 LARRA, Chatterjee (2008) analyzes India's ongoing "land question" as primitive accumulation, that is, the dissociation of peasants and other direct producers from their means of production, including land. But unlike the enclosures of industrializing Europe and the settler colonialism of the United States, the conditions of an electoral democracy, for instance, make it unacceptable to leave the dispossessed populations to fend for themselves. Chatterjee sees the explosion of rights-based laws, including the 2014 LARRA, at precisely the moment that the Indian state allowed "hegemonic corporate capital" entry into land and labor markets, as the "political management" of the dispossessed: these populist programs are attempts to reverse the effects of primitive accumulation, in the absence of which these dispossessed groups run the risk of becoming "dangerous classes." Though the characterization of ongoing land commodification processes as primitive accumulation is equivocal, the timing of the explosion of rights-based laws enacted under the Congress-led United Progressive Alliance (UPA) between 2004 and 2014 supports Chatterjee's argument of governmental attempts to provide the dispossessed with some basic safety nets. Besides LARRA, other rights-based laws include the National Rural Employment Guarantee Act (NREGA) and the National Food Security Bill (NFSB). These laws are aimed at guaranteeing every citizen access to entitlements like work and food. The National Rural Employment Guarantee Act (NREGA), for instance, is a social welfare program that guarantees all citizens one hundred days of employment on public work at minimum wage. If the NREGA "protects, to a limited extent, entitlements of households with able-bodied persons," the National Food Security Bill seeks to protect the food entitlements of those who are unable to work, including the elderly, the disabled, pregnant and lactating women, and so on" (Khera 2013, 9). Another of these rights-based laws is the Forest Rights Act, a landmark law that recognizes the use rights of forest dependents and reverses the colonial act of forest enclosures.

These rights-based laws are not clear-cut countermovements but contain within them conflicting clauses. A single law, the LARRA is itself a schizophrenic piece of legislation that incorporates within it clauses that represent both the market movement and countermovement. Take for instance the two main clauses in the title: Right to Fair Compensation, and Right to Rehabilitation and Resettlement. The compensation clause centers around finding the right price for land. Agricultural land, which did not have a price in the decades between Independence and liberalization (1947–91), is now getting transformed into a tradable asset. Landowners, who were earlier compensated at prices set by government diktat, are now demanding what they perceive to be a fair compensation. These price demands sometimes reach absurd levels—a landowner in Punjab recently sued the cash-strapped Indian Railways for a higher compensation, and the court adjudicated with "express justice" by ordering the public railways to compensate the landowner with a train (Kumar 2016). The fair compensation clause has a propertied bias: only landowners with private property rights to their land are beneficiaries of compensation. On the other hand, the Right to Rehabilitation and Resettlement clause recognizes the occupancy claims of nonpropertied groups. Tracing its provenance to the 1980s protests by the social movement the Narmada Bachao Andolan, the Rehabilitation and Resettlement clause is unprecedented in the 120-year history of the land acquisition act in including land occupants and dependents among "project affected persons."[3] If the fair compensation clause appeases the organized electoral constituencies of regional dominant-caste landowners, the rehabilitation and resettlement clause was included at the insistence of activists who had earlier been part of pro-poor and even insurgent movements but who had been roped in by the Congress for the drafting of these laws.

Here, I would like to focus on the "food security" clause of the LARRA. The LARRA mandate that multicrop land only be acquired as a "demonstrable last resort" begs the prior question of how these categories of multicrop and waste land were produced in the first place. In this section, I highlight three narratives of waste during the colonial period (late nineteenth and the first half of the twentieth century), the postcolonial agricultural modernization period of the Green Revolution (1960s to 1980s), and the postliberalization urbanization period (post-1991).

Waste Land as Revenue Waste

Whether private property in land existed before the colonial period is contested (D. Kumar 1998). The colonial era was decisive in constructing a taxonomy of revenue-yielding land that continues to be in use to this day. Agricultural land was one of the main sources of public revenue for the colonial state, accounting for more than half of Britain's total government revenue by the mid-nineteenth century (Banerjee and Iyer 2005), and the colonial state instituted an elaborate system of land taxes for these various categories. Though agricultural land tax was abolished in postcolonial India, these land categories have become the basis for determining the compensation price for land acquisition. Even today in Maharashtra, land compensation is pegged to these colonial-era land categories. For instance, the currently used category of bagayat land, which commands the highest compensation price among all land categories, has its provenance in the Bombay Provinces land revenue system. Bagayat lands are defined as lands where more than 50 percent of the land is irrigated by either canals or wells; these are the most agriculturally productive lands, and therefore the most valuable land in terms of revenue.

More fundamentally, the colonial-era land categories differed from precolonial land systems in their ascriptive and moral registers (Gidwani 1992). The colonial land revenue system introduced a new Lockean notion of waste-value-property (ibid.) that conflated categories of land with categories of personhood (Whitehead 2010). The category of wasteland was a "social category" that applied to land that the colonial state perceived to be idle or unproductive, but it also extended beyond land use to land users, in ascribing to these land users a socially undesirable behavior. The zamindar [landowning class] were "indolent, effeminate, ignorant" (Gidwani 1992, PE42); the tribal forest dependents were a "savage lot" (Whitehead 2010). Lands in the commons, which had plural usufruct claims shared by various groups, were reduced to a bounded commodity. The most brazen of these property transformations was the canal colonies of Punjab, where the colonial state introduced massive irrigation projects and incentivized "hardy cultivating classes" (Whitehead 2010) to practice settled agriculture in these newly irrigated frontiers (Bhattacharya 2019). These large-scale hydraulic experiments in transforming surplus waste land into productive agrarian categories of fertile land dispossessed pastoralists and other nonpropertied groups from their land. In their scale and ambition, they rivaled the "frontier colonization" of the settler-colonies of the American Prairies, Australia, and Canada (Amrith 2018), where indigenous property regimes were violently erased by the "colonists' protestant ethic [which] asserted that neither the leisured nor the lazy had a right to land" (Krueckeberg 1995; Cronon 2011).

Colonial narratives on property were not monolithic. From the late nineteenth century onwards, certain colonial narratives opposed the earlier liberal project of "improvement" and argued instead that "native society," including traditional property regimes with communal forms of ownership, be protected from the paternalistic impulses of colonial rule (Mantena 2010; Chatterjee 2011). This often resulted in what Li calls the "communal fix," where the colonial state marked certain groups—in India, the "tribals"—out for special protection, confined them within boundaries, and subjected them to land laws that sought to protect the "child-like tribal [from] the vicious webs of commerce, credit and marketable property" (Chatterjee 2011, 691).

The legacies of these colonial narratives live on in contemporary land regimes. The 1878 Forest Act and the 1894 Land Acquisition Act remained in use even after Independence and it is only now, as part of the wave of rights-based entitlements, that these antiquated laws are being amended. The recent song "poromboke," by the Carnatic singer T. M. Krishna and the environmental activist Nityanand Jayaraman, is an effort to dislodge the stubborn narrative of waste in popular discourse. In colloquial Tamil, *poromboke* is now a word that means worthless. But poromboke has its provenance in colonial-era land revenue systems, where it stood for "land [that is] exempt from assessment, either because it is set aside for communal purposes or because it is uncultivable" (Murugan 2017). The popular song reclaims the communal use of poromboke land by reminding us that "poromboke is not for you, poromboke is not for me, poromboke is for the city, poromboke is for the earth."

Waste Land and Food Scarcity

The categories of fertile and waste land settled into a distinct geography of agrarian capitalism under the agricultural modernization programs of the Green

Revolution from the 1960s to 1980s. The colonial state not only normalized a Lockean property narrative of waste land as revenue waste; it also set the precedent of using massive hydraulic engineering to produce uneven geographies of fertile and waste land. The big dams and irrigation canals which first emerged as famine-protection works (Guha 1985; Ludden 1999) became the sites of a nascent geography of surplus agricultural production, which further developed during the Green Revolution decades.

In the early 1960s, a confluence of events—including severe droughts in the mid-1960s and the death of Nehru in 1964—resulted in a sharp shift in development politics. Minister of Agriculture C. Subramaniam led the vanguard of an agricultural modernization program that came to be known as the Green Revolution. The Green Revolution was a marked departure from the Nehruvian politics of the previous decade. The Nehruvian state had been at the forefront of a Third World political project (Prashad 2007) that had, as an aspirational ideal if not in realpolitik, the aim of eschewing relations of dependency on the West and developing domestic expertise. In order to spur balanced economic growth, the state-led industrialization program of big dams and steel towns located these megadevelopments in "economically backward regions." In contrast, the Green Revolution program pursued a deliberate policy of uneven development. To solve the problem of food shortage, the program selected regions that already had sufficient water, and the subsidized package of water-seed-fertilizer was concentrated in these irrigated regions. The precondition of the region already having irrigated water so as to maximize the "prospects of achieving rapid increases in [food] production" (Frankel 1971, 3) meant that, ironically, arid lands that had received irrigation water as famine-protection works often became the epicenter of surplus food production, and rain-rich regions bypassed by irrigation canals sank into economic decline.

The Green Revolution departed from the earlier Nehruvian ideal in two ways, by abjuring both the ideal of balanced economic growth for uneven development, and the Third World norm of self-sufficiency for an explicit reliance on US aid and expertise. These shifts required new stories. In a discursive analysis of the Green Revolution, Visvanathan (2003, 3) argues that the "technocrats of the Green Revolution were not only storytellers but had a profound understanding of the need to reset narratives to ready society and institutions for new gestalts." C. Subramaniam and others crafted a narrative that expertly linked food scarcity to the nation-state, to the normative obligation of the state to make food available for its citizens, and not to abdicate on its duties as the colonial state had done. In 1965, for instance, soon after the Green Revolution pilot program had been launched, C. Subramaniam came under scathing attack from the Communist Party of India for signing the PL-480 agreement for the import of food grains from the United States to India. Subramaniam used the narrative of food security to justify US dependence:

> [If, in order to sustain ideological purity, we do not import food], it is not we members who would suffer. Once scarcity conditions begin to persist, it would be the people in the lowest ring of the ladder who would be affected first.... So when the Honorable members want me to take the risk of not importing food, they are really asking me to play with the lives of the poorer sections of the people. (ibid., 7)

For a country haunted by the specter of the colonial-era famines, the grafting of the hungry body onto the body politic (Khorakiwala 2017) had the evocative power to gain legitimacy for a program that steered sharply away from Third World ideals.

The strategic but uneven infusion of the Green Revolution technology package of water-seed-fertilizer in formerly arid regions that had received colonial-era irrigation works helped consolidate agrarian land-based social power. These flows of water mapped onto social power: in western Maharashtra, for instance, the irrigation canals were made to pass through the formerly arid lands of the "hardy cultivating class" of the Maratha-Kunbi caste cluster in western Maharashtra, and this routing of irrigation canals in turn helped consolidate the Maratha-Kunbis into one of the most formidable electoral constituencies in the country. The dense network of subsidized irrigation canals not only transformed arid lands of western Maharashtra into cash-crop exporting regions, they also facilitated the rise of the cultivating castes into regional "dominant castes" (Srinivas 1987) that exercised economic and electoral control over the agrarian countryside via land-based sources of power. The Green Revolution decades helped produce a distinct geography of uneven agrarian development: the regional dominant castes appropriated the most agriculturally productive multicrop land, which, often, was formerly arid, and the waste lands were relegated to subordinate caste groups, mainly Dalits and Adivasis. These socially constructed agrarian land categories have today become the basis for new urban land commodification.

The narrative of food scarcity produced a specific form of commodity fiction in agricultural land. In the early 1980s, when agrarian power was at its peak in Indian democratic politics, price and price-related issues were politically charged issues. Agrarian commodity producers lobbied political parties to adjust the price both of available inputs (such as fertilizers) and of marketable food surpluses (Brass 1995; Varshney 1995). The absence of any agitation around wages reflected the class structure of these agrarian movements as being based in propertied, not laboring, classes. Institutions like the Agricultural Price Commission, set up in 1965 as soon as the Green Revolution was launched, were the focus of intense political negotiations over food prices, on the one hand, trying to ensure that farmers were assured a minimum support price for their commodities, and on the other, trying to ensure that consumers could purchase food grains at affordable prices (cf. Varshney 1995). During this period, in order to protect land for food production, land laws imposed strict regulations on the market exchange of agricultural land, in effect decommodifying it. Some state governments, for instance, prohibited nonagriculturalists from purchasing agricultural land, thus restricting the fungibility of land. Land ceiling laws were imposed, both to protect marginal farmers from land speculators and to prevent the creation of a real estate market in the countryside. The price wars during this period were over the price of crops grown on the land and not over the price of land itself. Agricultural land was implicated in global commodity prices via crop capitalism and the price of food, rather than via the price of agricultural land itself. Liberalizing reforms shifted the debate from the price of food to the price of land, thus transforming the form of commodity fiction in land.

Waste Land as the New Frontier

With liberalization reforms, the narrative of food scarcity has resurfaced as food security. Implicit in the discursive shift from food scarcity to food security is a fundamental change in the relationship of commodified food production to the nation-state. Starting in the 1980s, the architects of the Green Revolution, now in its second phase and under the leadership of the scientist, M. S. Swaminathan, had to experiment with a new vocabulary around "sustainability" to deal with the new opposition from ecological activists. As Shiv Visvanathan notes, "If the earlier Green Revolution talked of scarcity, productivity and national security, Swaminathan felt that the activist connotations of the word security must be transferred from the nation to food" (Visvanathan 2003, 16–17). In this new narrative, the security of the nation-state is achieved not through older Third World notions of economic self-sufficiency, but it demands that the boundaries of the nation-state be made porous to global food regimes so that the lives and livelihoods of individuals are secured. In this context, the narrative of food security entered the postliberalization rights-based laws in two conflicting ways: through the Right to Food campaign, and through the "food security" clause in the amended land acquisition law, the LARRA.

The Right to Food campaign was pushed forward, among others, by the welfare economist, Jean Dreze. In advocating for the right to food, Dreze aligns strongly with his frequent co-author, Amartya Sen. In his Nobel Laureate work on famines, Sen challenges the dominant orthodox view that famines are caused by a decline in food availability. The food availability decline thesis is easily debunked when one looks at various examples of famines, including the 1943 Bengal Famine, when certain groups were denied access to food while others within the same society prospered from food exports. The access to food, Sen argues, depends on "exchange entitlements": in a market economy, a person can exchange the bundle of commodities she owns for other sets of commodities (Sen 1981). But her exchange entitlements are adversely affected by factors such as unemployment, low wages, and even increasing inequality where the rising wealth of certain groups can lead to higher purchasing power for food, and thus higher food prices. Most important for Sen, exchange entitlements "depend not merely on market exchanges but also on those exchanges, if any, that the state provides as a part of its social security programme. Given a social security system, an unemployed person may get relief, an old person a pension, and the poor some specified benefits. These affect the commodity bundles over which a person can have command" (ibid, 6). Welfare economists like Sen and Dreze would argue that in contrast to the colonial state, which lacked any accountability to its subjects, one of the most important normative obligations of a liberal democratic state is to step in and secure the exchange entitlements of their most vulnerable citizens. The Right to Food campaign is one such social security program.

It is curious how the rights-based entitlements to food found their way into the LARRA in the form of the "Food Security" clause. By mandating that multicrop land be acquired only as a demonstrable last resort, the LARRA in effect targets waste land for urban expansion. There are many means to achieve the right to food end. For instance, instead of protecting multicrop lands and targeting waste lands, the state could have improved the access of the waste land occupants to credit and other subsidized resources *and* granted them more secure occupancy rights over their lands. In this way, instead of giving the poor access to food grains, the state could have secured their command over food production by granting them control over the means of production, including land. The current LARRA instead exposes waste land occupants to new market relations, while protecting the dominant-caste owners of multicrop land from the vagaries of an uncertain real estate market in the making. If the right to food and work laws were pushed through by welfare economists and activists, it is telling that the LARRA "food security" clause is driven by a different set of constituents, that is, dominant regional castes. The LARRA is a central government act. As a federal polity, India's state governments have to be consulted for any legislative reform. Some of the most vociferous objectors to any change to the "food security" clause have been regional political parties like the Shiromani Akali Dal of Punjab and the Swabhiman Paksh of Maharashtra (Mukherjee 2015), both of which draw their constituents mainly from the Jat and Maratha agrarian propertied classes in these states. The narrative of food security, then, is mobilized by the regional dominant castes and their allied political parties such that commodification of fertile lands is protected from external actors, and agrarian propertied constituents have the voice to set the terms of these new market relations in agricultural land.

At the core of India's ongoing land conflicts is the politics of commodification/decommodification. As liberalization reforms create new regulatory regimes that enable the flows of private capital into formerly protected agricultural land markets, we see a new frontier in market land. As Mitchell (2007, 247) reminds us, the frontier is not a neutral line that divides market and nonmarket, or capitalist and noncapitalist, relations; it is instead "a broad terrain that . . . is the scene of political battles, in which new moral claims, arguments about justice, and forms of entitlement are forged." Mitchell reminds us that certain geographies and categories of land have not been left outside the market as some remnant of a tradition or backward society, but these property arrangements are the outcome of long histories of struggles to protect land and land users from the incursion of the markets. But in India, the most protected category of land is agricultural land, and the transformation of agricultural land into a fungible asset is met with stiff resistance from the organized agrarian propertied constituents who own these lands. These agrarian propertied classes are not against commodification of agricultural land; they would be (and in many cases, are) willing participants of land commodification if the new market relations in land are on their terms and not based on prices set by government diktat. As the regulatory regimes in land remake the boundaries of landed property, it throws up an unexpected outcome of agrarian propertied constituents agitating for the protective countermovements for their fertile land. To get a ground-level view of the new politics of market movement and countermovement, I turn next to the case of the Khed SEZ in the Pune region.

An Unexpected Market Movement and Countermovement: The Khed SEZ, India

In 2006, Bharat Forge, an Indian company that manufactures automobile components, identified 16,800 acres of land in seventeen villages in Khed taluka in western Maharashtra for setting up a multiproduct SEZ. When the industrial parastatal—the Maharashtra Industrial Development Corporation (MIDC)—tried to acquire land for the first phase of the SEZ, the land acquisition was met with vociferous opposition. Spearheaded by the dominant-caste Maratha-Kunbis, agrarian landowners organized swiftly. They took to the streets, blocked highways, and sat in *dharna* [nonviolent sit-in] outside the Khed Revenue

Department bureaucrats' office. Interruptions of this sort by an electorally organized constituency cannot be ignored without grave consequences at the ballot boxes, and the Khed bureaucrats decided to negotiate with the protesting landowners. The landowners had a number of demands and I want to focus here on one in particular, that the boundaries of the SEZ be redrawn so that only *dongarpad* land—uncultivable waste land on the hillocks—be acquired and the irrigated cabbage-growing land on the plains be left untouched. Figure 5.1 shows a map of the redrawn SEZ boundary. After a year of negotiations, the bureaucrats conceded to landowner demands, including the redrawing of the SEZ boundary. Note the 2008 boundary of the SEZ, which moves away from a Cartesian rigidity to a more zig-zagged territory that only encompasses the uncultivable waste lands on the hillocks. Another negotiated solution was that landowners would receive monetary compensation for 85 percent of their acquired land;

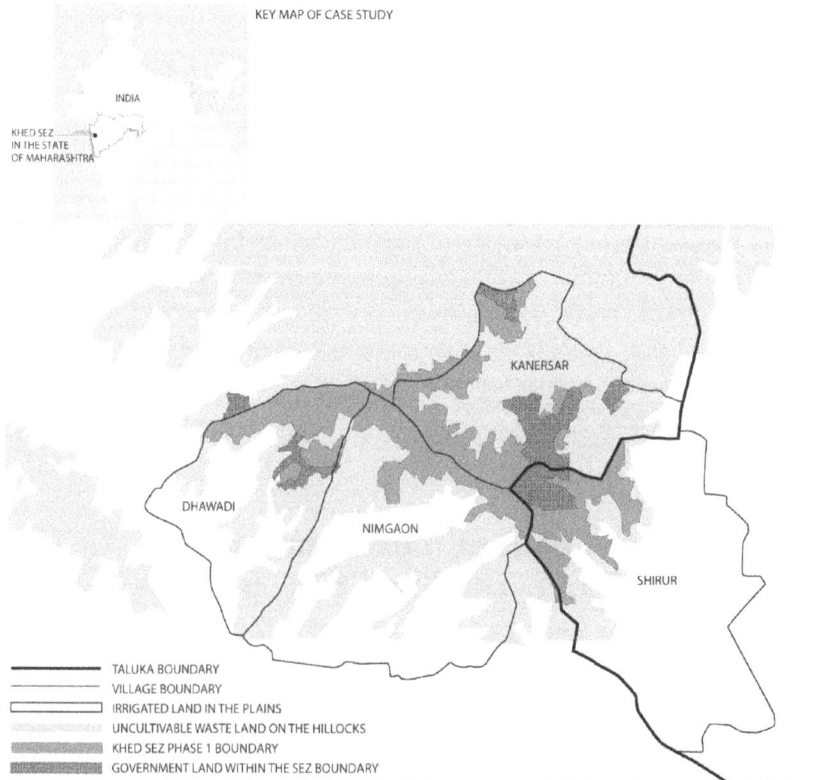

FIGURE 5.1. Jurisdiction of Khed SEZ, encompassing "waste" land in four Gram Panchayats. Map drawn by author based on land acquisition details from the Maharashtra Industrial Development Corporation (MIDC).

for the remaining 15 percent, they would receive pro rata shares in the SEZ company so that they could benefit from the appreciating land price of the SEZ development.

Phase 1 of the Khed SEZ overlaps with the jurisdiction of four Gram Panchayats (rural local governments)—Kanersar, Nimgaon, Dhawadi, and Shirur. The former sarpanch of Kanersar Gram Panchayat, seated in 2006–8, explained the negotiations between the landowners and the bureaucrat, Shyam Patil:

> Kanersar was the first village to agree. The first project report that was prepared of the 17 villages, people felt that this is agricultural area. Patil *saab* told us, "aap logo ko thyaar kijiye; jo kuch chahiye, voh ho jaayega" [you prepare the people; whatever you need, that will be done]. We went around all the farmlands in the village, what to keep and what to remove, we underlined that. Here, most of the land is *dongar—pahaadi illakha* [hilly territory]. All the *dongar* area has gone to the SEZ, and land with water remains with the farmers.[4]

Note that the former sarpanch includes as "farmlands" only the "land with water" and not the pahaadi illakha. Those considered to be "farmers" here are only the landowners, and not the laborers who work on these lands. These categories echo the colonial and postcolonial development narratives of watered and waste land—of waste as revenue waste, and the owners of revenue-rich land as sons-of-the-soil farmers at the exclusion of the laborers who toil on these lands. A look at the land records for the Kanersar Gram Panchayat shows the dominant-caste landowners to own multiple plots of land, often in joint ownership with other members of their joint family, at several geographically dispersed sites. The dominant-caste landowners own both watered multicrop land on the plains and uncultivable waste lands on the hillocks. Of the 876 acres of privately owned waste land in Kanersar, around 50 percent of these lands are owned by Maratha-Kunbis and around 30 percent are owned by an Adivasi group called the Thakkars.

TABLE 5.1. Details of land acquired for the Khed SEZ

VILLAGE	PRIVATELY OWNED 'WASTE' LAND, IN ACRES	GOVERNMENT OWNED LAND, IN ACRES	TOTAL AREA FOR KHED SEZ, IN ACRES
Nimgaon	794	153	947
Kanersar	876	577	1,453
Dhawadi	747	0	747
Shirur	529	390	919
Total	2,946	1,120	4,066

Source: File with the details of landholdings for the SEZ project, compiled by the MIDC. This file contains the names of the landowners, their land survey/title number, and land acreage.

By demanding that their fertile lands remain untouched and that only waste lands be acquired for the SEZ, the dominant-caste landowners were, in effect, seeking a countermovement to protect their agricultural land at a time of frenzied land commodification. Why the demand for a countermovement? In 2011, almost three years after the completion of the negotiations, there were hardly any visible signs of construction on the *dongarpad* lands. A boundary wall had been completed with signs announcing the Khed SEZ, and some construction had started on the resettlement colony for the Thakkars whose lands were within the new SEZ boundary. The slow pace of development was largely due to the 2008 global financial crisis, which negatively affected the promoter's ability to raise capital. When I visited Kanersar in 2011, dominant-caste landowners, including the former and current sarpanch, revealed strong feelings of uncertainty over the project. Those whose lands had been acquired by the SEZ asked me if I had visited MIDC. When I answered in the affirmative, they had many anxious questions on the project:

> Our negotiations were completed in 2008, but we don't see the buildings coming up.
>
> I gave up 15 acres of land four years back. For the three acres for which I am a shareholder [15 percent of the land], I should have received 120,000 rupees in interest. But, for four years, I haven't received anything.
>
> What assurance do we have that the SEZ will be completed?[5]

Besides these delays, agrarian landowners faced the typical market risks of profitability in a real estate development. Changes in interest rates, in material costs, in demand for the industrial services being provided by the SEZ, and a number of other changes can seriously affect expected project returns.

It was in anticipation of these risks that the dominant-caste agrarian landowners protested against the initial Khed proposal in 2006 and demanded that their irrigated lands be protected from SEZ commodification. Though these dominant-caste landowners expressed anxiety over the status of the SEZ project, they continue to grow cabbages and other vegetables for sale in Pune and surrounding cities on their irrigated land in the plains. If the Khed SEZ does not do well and undergoes losses, they have their fertile agricultural lands to fall back on. Commodifying the waste land on the hillocks for the new SEZ offered these landowners the possibility of making profits from revenue waste land. If the SEZ does well, their waste lands, which earlier had little economic value but immense symbolic value that helped maintain agrarian patron-client relations, could become a new source of profit. It has to be underscored that the dominant-caste landowners are not holding on to their cultivable lands for their market value, but because these lands become a crucial safety net during a precarious transition. The preference of these regional agrarian propertied classes has been institutionalized in the new LARRA in its "food security" clause. The clause is justified as a food security measure, but its advantages to the agrarian propertied classes as durable sources of symbolic and economic capital cannot be ignored.

Unlike the dominant-caste landowners who hedge their bets of an uncertain transition through only commodifying their revenue waste land, the Thakkars own single plots of waste land of less than two acres, on which they grow dry crops for subsistence needs. The Thakkars were not a part of the 2006 protests; neither were they consulted during the 2006–8 negotiations. The younger generation Thakkars, however, are favorably inclined to land commodification for two reasons. First, the commodification of their waste land transforms them into the owners of a high-demand market asset. Their control over a desirable commodity increases their negotiating power vis-à-vis dominant-caste landowners and bureaucrats. Though they were not a part of the negotiations, the Thakkars have subsequently negotiated with the "local leaders" of their villages for better access to public services and jobs. Second, the urbanization of the countryside opens up for the Thakkars new economic opportunities, albeit in the informal economy. The new demand for their waste land and the availability of alternative informal work in the construction industry allows the younger generation male Thakkars to break their relations of dependency on the dominant-caste landowners. During the Green Revolution period, when agricultural work was the main source of employment in these villages, the dominant-caste landowners resorted to economic sanctions as a way of quashing caste assertion, but the declining reliance on agricultural work as the only source of income weakens this form of labor control. A Maratha landowner in Kanersar complained about the rising autonomy of the Thakkars: "Earlier, people here had less money; now they have more money and more job opportunities. Earlier, if we asked the laborer to come for work, he would come. Now, we do not find any laborers; 'mazdoor milta nahin' [workers are not found]. Earlier 60 rupees per day for farm work per person was enough; now even for 100 rupees, they do not come."[6]

The younger generation male Thakkars are eager for land commodification; the older generation Thakkars are not. Dairy farming is common in western Maharashtra. Before market-oriented urbanization, the Thakkars in their sixties and seventies used their waste land for grazing their cows and goats. They also grazed their livestock on the waste land owned by the dominant-caste landowners. If their families had been working on the lands of the dominant-caste landowners for generations, norms of reciprocity obliged the dominant-caste landowners to allow their laborers to graze their cattle on their lands for free. The government lands were also used for grazing. Notice in figure 5.1

that government-owned common lands have now been privatized and commodified for the new SEZ. In fact, besides their locational advantage, Kanersar and a few other villages had been identified by the Khed bureaucrats for the SEZ because they had significant acreage of land under government ownership. At a time when organized agrarian propertied constituencies are staging stiff opposition to the acquisition of their lands, these government lands become an easier target for commodification. Both the enclosure of village common lands and the commodification of privately owned waste land deprives the most vulnerable dairy farmers of access to formerly decommodified land. As Thakkars break away from old norms of dependence, the dominant-caste landowners have also started charging a monthly rent for the use of their waste lands outside the SEZ boundary. The denied access to former grazing lands is forcing these vulnerable Thakkars to sell their livestock and lose their only source of livelihood.

If the commodification of formerly waste land is experienced unevenly within the household, it also has differential impacts across wider scales. In the Mulshi taluka, a forested region of the Western Ghats mountain range that is adjacent to the Khed taluka, the Katkari Adivasis have occupancy claims, not ownership rights, over their forest land. Contrary to the emancipatory potential of waste land commodification for some of the Khed Thakkars, the commodification of waste land in Mulshi taluka has resulted in widespread eviction and dispossession of the Katkaris, including the younger generation males (Balakrishnan 2019). Though the commodification of waste land may crack open slivers of possibility for a new politics of recognition for younger generation Adivasis, it is only propertied constituents who can stake their claims on the profits of land redevelopment.

Surplus, Waste, and Voice

In the mid-2000s, India's till-then protected agricultural land became the new frontier for capitalist urban expansion, giving rise to SEZs and other forms of new cities amid croplands (Levien, this volume). Narratives of food security justified the protection of agriculturally productive fertile land, thus making waste lands the target for capitalist urbanization. A persistent theme across colonial and postcolonial property rule is the Lockean narrative of "unused" or "idle" land. If colonial-era Lockean narratives redistributed land from groups with usufruct claims to "hardy cultivating castes," the new "food security" clause exposes the waste lands that were relegated to Adivasis during earlier hydraulic histories of sociospatial segregation to postliberalization capital flows. The lands that were bypassed by irrigation networks during the Green Revolution and that are now occupied by weaker constituents are being framed as new frontiers for capital. When "wasteland" is classified as surplus and available for redevelopment, it echoes Lockean norms of the "property-constituting capacity of labor" (Sartori 2014). The fiction of surplus land is a sociolegal sleight of hand that legitimizes certain forms of labor while delegitimizing others. Indigenous lands during colonial and postcolonial frontier expansions were particularly vulnerable to this narrative, which granted state-authorized priority claims only to those forms of labor that reclaimed property from waste (ibid). The fiction of surplus land, linked via Lockean norms to wasteland, is a forceful reminder that surplus does not mean excess; instead, surplus land is part of a legitimizing narrative that renders certain lands valueless, justifying their redistribution, or in the case of the public land dispositions that Christophers and Whiteside discuss in this volume, from the public to the private sector.

While acknowledging the durability of colonial-era land categories like wasteland, it would be a mistake to trace an unbroken continuity from colonial to postcolonial property regimes. Such a view would elide the role of postcolonial democratic institutions in mediating the fictions of waste and surplus; it would, to borrow a Polanyian concept, fail to explain how postcolonial land markets are embedded in democratic institutions. In liberalizing India, what difference does the condition of an electoral democracy make in arbitrating conflicts over land commodification? Though colonial-era categories of land continue to shape property relations in postcolonial India, the rise of agrarian power and capital as frictions to the fictions of land commodification is itself a triumph of electoral democracy.

As new rushes of private capital enter agricultural land, agrarian capital spearheads the countermovement against marketization. Interestingly, this agrarian countermovement has appropriated the progressive language of "food security," wielding it as an instrument key to reproducing the fiction that multicrop, irrigated land is core to the consumption needs and exchange entitlements of agrarian society as a whole, and thereby reinscribing the colonial fiction that waste land has little use value and is worthy of sacrifice to urban capital. In a liberalizing society, as the "waste-value-property" triad (Gidwani 1992) is rearranged, propertied agrarian constituents and their allied regional political parties are instituting these safeguards of protecting irrigated multicrop land not because of their opposition to land commodification, but rather to retain the power to set the terms for commodification. As Polanyi warned, such countermovements do not have to be necessarily progressive or pro-poor. The new land laws leave open the possibility for agrarian landowners to voluntarily convert their multicrop land to urban real estate developments, as was done by sugarcane growers in the Pune region who became shareholders of a new real estate development called Magarpatta City (Balakrishnan 2019).

But the emergence of agrarian propertied classes as frictions to the fictions of land commodification militates against clean winners versus losers, David versus Goliath narratives. These agrarian propertied classes started off as peasant cultivators under colonial rule. Their thunderous rise to dominance in national electoral politics in the late 1970s, when they for the first time seized power in a hitherto upper caste-dominated Parliament, has been heralded as the "second democratic upsurge" (Yadav 2000, Jaffrelot 2003). If the first democratic surge was the transfer of power from the colonial to the postcolonial state, the second democratic upsurge saw the rise of the backward castes into a formidable electoral constituency, with their own political parties and substantial representation in both state-level and national electoral politics. The rise of regional agrarian power in national politics was enabled both by redistributive land reforms that transferred land from the noncultivating propertied classes (zamindars) to the backward caste cultivators and by the uneven infusion of seeds-fertilizers-water under the Green Revolution. These agrarian propertied classes transformed electoral politics into an arena of legitimate contestation. Referring to these groups as the "dominant castes," as is common in popular and scholarly writing, reveals their disruption of normalized caste hierarchies (see Deshpande 2016).

The agrarian propertied classes, however, are locked in exploitative labor and credit relations with the Dalits and Adivasis who labor on their lands. In a twist that was unanticipated by Polanyi, the Adivasi owners of marginal waste land are capitalizing on the revaluation of their land to subvert agrarian land-based social relations. Certain Adivasis, such as the younger generation Khed Adivasis, are willing to commodify their land both to escape caste-ridden agrarian moral economies of control and out of the desire to enjoy the city life and its imagined freedom from caste hierarchy (cf. Menon and Nigam 2007). But their gains from land commodification are the incidental outcome of the "food security" clause whose primary beneficiaries are propertied constituents. During the Green Revolution, these Adivasis were relegated to classified waste lands, which were themselves sociotechnically produced by the hydraulic state and its biased routing of irrigation canals. Now, even though younger generation Khed Adivasis are amenable to land commodification, weaker household members who do not control land titles risk being deprived of the subsistence land uses they long enjoyed while also being denied the benefits of urbanization and land sale profits.

Electoral politics still retains a property bias; agrarian propertied castes have gained access to the electoral arena, while the owners of devalued land and non-propertied constituents are left out. The core of India's ongoing land conflict is not about either the commodification or decommodification of land, but instead the more fraught question of which lands are to be opened up to market relations, and which ones protected from the market. As Mitchell (2007) reminds us, the frontier is a contestable space over the control and distribution of assets, and as this chapter has shown, fictions about the revenue status and social valuation of different categories of land produce caste/class-segregated hierarchies of land rights and property protections, which in turn maintain uneven geographies of resource access. Agricultural land in liberalizing India is a contested frontier, and unless nonpropertied constituents have the power to exercise their voice in these land commodification decisions, no countermovement can, ex ante, do justice to their needs and desires.

6

RENTAL FICTIONS
Speculating in Rent-Regulated Housing in New York City

Benjamin F. Teresa

During his 2013 campaign for mayor, Bill de Blasio lamented New York City's expanding economic divide as a "tale of two cities": a resurgent financial sector generating spectacular affluence alongside a significant remainder of the city languishing in neglect. This tale of two distinct and disconnected segments of the city resonated electorally, but elided a more complicated and intertwined relationship between the "two cities." In New York City, inequality is most acutely produced and experienced through the housing market. A flood of investment has been pouring into the city's luxury residential market since the 2008 financial crisis (Story and Saul 2015). Yet, belying the two cities narrative, a historically unprecedented wave of investment has also been moving into housing regulated by rent laws that establish tenure protections and rent limits, which has traditionally served as housing for lower-income New Yorkers. Since 2001, investors have been purchasing rent-regulated multifamily buildings, often for historically high prices and with large amounts of debt, anticipating future rent increases. This speculation is transforming the ownership and management structure of the city's rent-regulated housing sector and increasing displacement pressure on tenants. The real "tale of two cities" is not about two separate parts of the city, one ascendant and the other abandoned, but about how the same actors, institutions, and logics produce affluence for some by impoverishing others.

In response to periodic housing crises in New York City over the past century, tenants, landlords, and elected officials have shaped an ever-changing set of laws and practices that regulate the tenant–landlord relationship. This chapter considers the history of the extension and erosion of tenant protections as an example of Karl Polanyi's (2001 [1944]) double movement of capitalism—the historical oscillation between breaking down barriers to the commodification of land, labor, and money on the one hand, and the establishment of social protections in response to the devastations wrought by that same commodification on the other. In the case of New York City rent-regulated housing, Polanyi's theory of the double movement helps frame the erosion of rent regulation during the 1990s as an opening for the financialization of the regulated housing stock that has proceeded since the early 2000s, but also calls our attention to countermovements to that financialization. The particularities of rent-related countermovements in New York City, though, help make evident that the double movement is not a simple, duplicative oscillation between more or less embedded forms of liberal capitalism. Rather, each phase of commodification and associated countermovement can shift the terms on which land fictions are elaborated and contested.

Specifically, while rent regulation offered social protection for tenants from the deleterious effects of unfettered commodification beginning in the 1920s, it maintained housing as a commodity, albeit with new limits, and thereby tended to diffuse the most radical political organizing aimed at securing housing as a collective resource available to all. Rent regulation always contained the potential to be interpreted and used as an individual consumer safeguard rather than as a broad social protection—or as a tool for collective action through such things as rent strikes and tenant-managed buildings. Changes to rent regulation in the 1990s accentuated these individualizing tendencies in rent law, diminishing its collective aspects and creating the conditions for new financialized futures of rent-regulated housing. Protective countermovements to land commodification in the form of rent regulation—despite countering some of the most exclusionary effects of private housing markets—thus partake in the fiction of land as commodity.

I use land fiction in the sense introduced by Ghertner and Lake (this volume), signaling both the social violence necessitated by drives to reduce land's diverse social and material imbrications to an "element of industry" available for exchange like any other commodity via the price mechanism, as well as land's organization as fictitious capital, or a "pure financial asset" that yields rent like any other interest-bearing asset, such as bonds (Harvey 1982). The financialization of land and housing in New York City today rests on the particular financial fiction that circulating forms of capital will garner the rents that lenders assume when they extend credit, even though there is no guarantee that future rents will materialize via real value creation through the productive activities based on the land in question.

I begin the chapter with a review of twentieth-century rent regulation in New York City, which enables me to show how the erosion of rent regulation in the

1990s paved the way for the financialization of housing in the 2000s. Under these new conditions, professional investors took advantage of weakened housing regulations to create new fictions about future rent increases in rent-regulated housing. The changing conditions of ownership and management of rent-regulated housing evident in the shift from local, independent "tenement landlords" to the professional investors connected to financial markets played out unevenly across New York City neighborhoods. In expensive and gentrifying neighborhoods, investors have sought to make large rent increases and deregulate apartments in buildings via a discourse of "undervalued assets." In the outer boroughs of the city, in contrast, where rents and property values are not as high as in core areas of Manhattan and where tenants are poorer and have fewer housing choices, investors narratively construct lower-rent housing as a "mismanaged asset"—buildings that the previous tenement landlords have strategically under-maintained for years. In these buildings, investors systematically exploit avenues for rent increases opened in the rent law changes of the 1990s, increasing displacement pressure on rent-regulated tenants in the form of increasing rent, neglected maintenance, and harassment to vacate. I explore how these narratives of undervalued assets and mismanaged resources operate as fictions driving housing financialization in what follows, but first show how the more enduring land fiction that commodity housing provides the most efficient and optimal allocative mechanism for shelter delivery was built up through twentieth-century rent regulation.

Rent Regulation and Its Erosion as a "Protective Countermovement" in Twentieth-Century New York City

Housing regulations and, in particular, rent control and stabilization are a historical product of political struggle between tenants and landlords for control over the cost of housing. Rent regulation in New York City has been a "protracted saga" (Keating 1998) over the twentieth century, spurred by repeated housing shortage crises that placed pressure on tenants and inspired political activism and policy response. Struggles over housing during and immediately following World War I yielded new regulatory solutions that shaped subsequent efforts to advance tenant protections in the city. The wartime economy redirected labor and materials away from the housing sector, reducing new housing construction and creating shortages of heating fuel. As workers moved to the city for war production and as housing production stagnated, the balance of power in the tenant–landlord relationship, already decisively in the landlord's favor, swung strongly toward apartment building owners, who could command increasing rents in an environment of high-demand and easily replaceable tenants.

Tenants at the time found few legal avenues to address problems of rent increases, lack of heating, and eviction. Up to this point, agricultural common law inherited from England defined the tenant–landlord relationship, which placed no legal obligation on landlords to provide amenities such as heating and plumbing, or to make repairs (Blackmar 1989; Day 1999). Conversely, tenants' obligation was to pay the agreed rent; if the tenant did not pay, then the landlord could evict. During the wartime housing shortage, landlords imposed frequent and large rent increases, and when tenants complained about repairs or heat, withheld rent for repairs, or simply could not pay, landlords swiftly displaced them from the buildings. Local courts that adjudicated dispossession proceedings, both as a matter of practice and law, typically deferred to the landlord's discretion for determining when tenants had violated the lease (Day 1999).

This near-absolute landlord power over tenants caused severe social disruption. Owners increased rent, often multiple times a year. For example, in Brownsville, Brooklyn, in 1919 rents increased from $14 to $23 a month on average (Day 1999). Some tenants grew recalcitrant amid the increasing cost of housing and began to withhold rent to force landlords to address the lack of heat and neglected repairs. But withholding rent was dangerous for individual tenants and households. Rent increases and evictions were not only profit-maximizing practices, but also tactics to discipline tenants; "problem tenants" could be quickly evicted and replaced (Lawson 1986). Landlords could legally evict tenants within three to five days, a time frame that made it practically impossible for tenants to challenge their eviction in court, especially once courts became overwhelmed with eviction cases.

Mass evictions became a part of daily life in New York City from 1918 to 1920. In some parts of the Bronx and Brooklyn, more than half of all tenants were evicted during 1919 (Day 1999). Individually, tenants had almost no power to protect themselves against this dislocation, and they found their only recourse in organizing as a class whose interests were opposed to the landlords'. Tenant leagues based in Brownsville, the Lower East Side of Manhattan, Harlem, and other working-class neighborhoods organized rent strikes and picketed buildings in which landlords had evicted people. These coordinated tenant actions prevented landlords from filling emptied apartments with new tenants and thereby curtailed the profitability of eviction. Open violence erupted in many neighborhoods as landlords sought city marshals to enforce evictions and considered the organized tenant groups a fundamental threat to their property rights (Fogelson 2013).

These material conditions, the social disruption they caused, and the radical socialist politics they inspired ultimately provoked legislative action. Tenants and advocates, elected officials, and even some landlords recognized the housing market was dysfunctional and that "the freedom of contract had been impaired" (Day 1999, 136). The New York state legislature passed reforms in April and September 1920 that substantially shifted the balance of power in the tenant–landlord relationship. These laws provided a new template for tenant activism in subsequent decades.

The Emergency Rent Laws of 1920 contained permanent and temporary features protecting tenants. The law permanently (1) protected lease agreements beyond one month, which had been the previous legal standard and had permitted landlords to raise rents and evict frequently; (2) required landlords to provide services necessary for habitation; and (3) limited landlords' access to evictions by increasing the length of time it took to evict and by placing the burden of proof on the landlord to demonstrate the reason for eviction (Day 1999). The law's temporary measures regulated landlords' ability to set rents and gave tenants a right to renew their lease when it ended. While at first the law limited rent increases to a maximum of 25 percent per year, landlords tended to take this maximum allowance, continuing the displacement pressure on tenants. Eventually, the legislature redefined the standard to be the rent at which landlords could achieve an 8 percent return on their investment (Lawson 1986).

Regulation on setting rents was a temporary protection, its necessity defined by a state of housing emergency. However, the state legislature enacted rent control alongside other tenure protections in the Emergency Rent Laws because tenant displacement did not substantially subside until landlords' ability to increase rents without limit had been curtailed (Lawson 1986). Rent controls and the right for tenants to renew leases effectively prevented landlords from using eviction in a sweeping manner to secure profit and discipline tenants.

Landlords opposed the rent laws as incursions on their property rights. Just as tenant associations grew during this period, so did organizations representing landlords' interests, such as the Real Estate Board of New York (REBNY), and they pressed lawmakers to rescind rent regulations as they came up for renewal. The most acute phase of the housing shortage eased after 1921, as generous tax credits spurred builders to increase housing production, and many tenants, although primarily middle-class renters who moved into newly built and more expensive housing, experienced less pressure from increasing rents and deteriorating conditions (Lawson 1986). The dissipating crisis meant that while legislators did periodically renew the Emergency Rent Laws through most of the 1920s they also yielded some ground to landlords by gradually exempting a larger section of the housing market from rent regulations at each renewal. Finally, the legislature let the temporary limits on rent increases expire in 1929. Nonetheless, the major shift in tenant–landlord relations was intact and the political organizing during this period provided the basis for future activism.

While the tenant movement never gave up advocating for rent regulations after their repeal in 1929, in the 1930s the focus shifted to delivering public housing, as the Depression produced new problems of wide-scale abandonment and deterioration of rental buildings and limited renter incomes. The tenant movement understood that tackling the housing crisis required protections for tenants in private housing through rent regulation alongside a commitment to building new publicly owned housing that could directly compete with private housing for the poorest tenants (Lawson 1986).

The post–World War II era would yield both goals of the tenant movement: rent controls and public housing construction. The Federal Housing Acts of 1949 and 1954 provided funds for the eventual construction of close to 200,000 units of public housing in New York City (Schwartz 2014), but caused significant displacement through slum clearance. During World War II, federal price controls allowed local governments to establish rent control to combat rising prices amid housing shortages, and tenants succeeded in extending rent control to all housing built before 1947. As the tenant movement intersected with and gathered momentum from the Civil Rights movement during the 1960s, New York City also created a system of rent stabilization in 1969 that covered housing built after 1947. This system of rent stabilization, which is the form of rent regulation in place today, typically allows for more flexibility and more generous rent increases than under rent control law.

The private housing stock continued to deteriorate during the postwar era, particularly in poor neighborhoods. Landlords and their advocacy organizations continually seized on these conditions as a rationale for repealing rent controls that they argued prevented profitable operation of their buildings. With abandonment and public concern over urban crisis reaching a peak in the late 1960s and early 1970s, both New York city and state governments' sympathy shifted from the beleaguered tenant to the mythologized "tenement landlord" who was under siege from rising costs and burdensome regulation (Sternlieb 1966, 1975). In 1971, New York governor Nelson Rockefeller signed legislation that decontrolled housing. Vacancy decontrol allowed landlords to remove housing from regulations and increase rents once tenants moved out, and tenants feared that landlords would harass renters to leave to accelerate the process. A report commissioned by State Assembly member Andrew Stein in 1974 validated tenant fears of decontrol and increasing rents, especially for middle-class neighborhoods. Vacancy decontrol did not alleviate the abandonment problem in poorer neighborhoods, as real estate and landlord advocates argued it would (Lawson 1986).

Soon after the decontrol experiment, the legislature passed the 1974 Emergency Tenant Protection Act, which moved hundreds of thousands of apartments built after 1947 back under rent stabilization.

Just as landlords sought regulatory rollback during the 1920s after rent regulations were passed and again in the post–World War II era, so they also sought to shift rent laws to be more amenable to them during the 1990s. While the Urstadt Law, passed with decontrol in 1971, prevented New York State localities from enacting rent regulations more stringent than state law, it did not stand in the way of local efforts in *weakening* rent laws. Landlord and real estate interests found the New York City mayor and city council once again receptive to arguments about the harm rent regulation inflicted on the city's already moribund housing market buffeted by recession in the early 1990s. Landlords won changes to rent control law in 1994 that once again provided routes for the removal of rent stabilization. Once rent hits an established threshold—$2,000 in 1994 and raised periodically, standing at $2,700 as of 2015—and the apartment becomes vacant, the landlord can remove the apartment from rent stabilization. Additionally, in a process termed luxury decontrol, once the rent passes the threshold and the tenant earns more than $250,000, the unit may also be deregulated without vacancy.

State Senate majority leader Joseph Bruno announced his goal of ending rent regulation when it came up for reauthorization in 1997. Instead, the legislature renewed the law, but added a provision that allows landlords to increase rents by as much as 20 percent once an apartment becomes vacant. In renewing the law again in 2003, the legislature distinguished between "preferential" and "legal" rents. Legal rent is the rent for an apartment that a landlord can legally charge a tenant, based on accumulated annual rent increases set by the Rent Guidelines Board. However, if landlords charge a lower, "preferential" rent (because, for example, that is the highest rent the market can bear), landlords could increase the preferential rent to the legal rent even if that increase is higher than the allowed annual increase set by the Rent Guidelines Board. This change allowed landlords to effectively circumvent the maximum annual rent increases allowed by law. As of 2017, nearly a third of all rent-stabilized apartments in New York City have preferential rents and therefore are at risk of not having the protections of controlled rent increases (Podkul 2017).

The erosion of rent regulation during the 1990s and early 2000s precipitated a mass deregulation of rental units. In 1980, nearly two-thirds of all rental housing in the city was rent stabilized; by 2014, regulated units comprised about 45 percent of the approximately 2.1 million rental units in the city (Furman Center 2014). The most common mechanism for the loss of these units was vacancy decontrol—that is, apartments that are deregulated once the rent threshold is reached. The loss of rent-stabilized housing has accelerated since 2002, with more than fourteen thousand stabilized units removed per year on average (Rent Guidelines Board 2014a).

The historical advance and retreat of rent regulations are a clear example of a Polanyian double movement. Under conditions of prolonged and severe housing shortage, the effects of the commodification of land and housing have repeatedly undermined tenant tenure, neighborhood stability, and the functioning of a market in housing. Rent regulations have circumscribed this process of commodification by extending tenant protections. The evolution of regulation, however, has also created the conditions for renewed commodification. Since the 1990s, the movement has once again turned toward commodification, as changes in rent regulation provide landlords with opportunities to increase rent and deregulate apartments. In this phase of the double movement, the erosion of rent regulation coincides with and enables the process of financialization of housing, in which actors with greater appetites for risk and profit enter into the regulated housing market. The search for profits has been sustained by particular rental fictions, enabled by a general trend of deregulated rental housing.

Fictions and the Production of Uneven Development

The erosion of rent regulation provided an opportunity for professional investors tied to financial markets to capitalize on the shifting regulatory landscape in New York City. The change in rent regulation and the entrance of financial actors new to the rent-regulated market play out through two distinctive spaces in the city: "undervalued assets" located in an expanded reinvested urban core and "mismanaged assets" located in the working-class neighborhoods of the city. In the language of investors, "undervalued assets" are the regulated apartment buildings with below-market-rate rents in areas that are near the most expensive housing in the city. Outside these core neighborhoods are where investors find "mismanaged assets," regulated buildings in which the previous generation of landlords either could not or did not maximize all available revenue.

When investors treat land as fictitious capital, they circulate credit through land and housing on the expectation of future rents. They base mortgage credit on expectations about the future value of the property based on future rents. Investors establish expectations about future rent, in part, on the urban context within the geographies of undervalued and mismanaged assets. Within this setting, investors purchase and operate buildings with a set of assumptions about the profitability of the housing and strategies to realize those assumptions, which produce effects that stem from realizing and/or failing to meet those expectations.

"Undervalued Assets" in the Expanding Reinvested Core

Since the late 1970s, Manhattan has experienced the most sustained and intense reinvestment in property markets compared to the other boroughs (Hackworth 2001, 2002; Hackworth and Smith 2001). Hackworth (2002) describes Manhattan south of Ninety-sixth Street as the "reinvested core," an area that by the early 1990s recession had seen increasing rents and property values and substantial investment in new development and renovation. Since the mid-1990s, investment has expanded outward from the reinvested core into northeastern Brooklyn, northwestern Manhattan, and central Bronx (Hackworth 2002). With the most expensive housing in the city within the reinvested core, both capital and people shifted outward during the mid-1990s recovery and economic expansion. Developers and investors could invest in these areas of the expanded, reinvested core more profitably and with less risk than a decade earlier (Schaffer and Smith 1986).

The expansion of investment from the reinvested core below Ninety-sixth Street into northern Manhattan during the 1990s produced a chain effect of displacement of capital and people. By the 2000s, the most expensive housing in the reinvested core was pushing white, middle- and upper-middle-class renters (and homeowners) in search of less expensive housing options into neighborhoods in northern Manhattan. This migration meant the displacement of poor black and Hispanic residents to farther-flung neighborhoods in northern Manhattan, such as Washington Heights, and into southern and central Bronx (Newman and Wyly 2006).

By the early 2000s, a decade of reinvestment in northern Manhattan placed increasing pressure on the rent-regulated housing stock. Rent-regulated stock becomes a site for investment when previous reinvestment exhausts opportunities in the private, unregulated stock. Sustained reinvestment in unregulated housing produces a significant divergence between unregulated and regulated rents. In northern Manhattan, this difference between median unregulated, "market" rents and median regulated rents is larger and increasing at a faster rate than citywide averages. This makes rent-regulated housing an even more attractive investment due to the potential to increase regulated rents that are below market rates. A large share of the housing stock in neighborhoods in northern Manhattan is rent regulated: the neighborhoods of Washington Heights, Harlem, and Morningside Heights each have about twice the share of regulated housing as the city as a whole (Furman Center 2017).

These dynamics of reinvestment and the attendant expectations of rising rents influence how banks and financial markets extend credit in the form of mortgages for investment in the rent-regulated housing stock. All mortgage underwriting involves making assumptions about future income flows. Mortgage underwriting based on anticipated and not current or historical income levels is referred to as pro forma underwriting. Financial documents that provide information to investors about the underlying asset—typically the multifamily building—explicitly state that all mortgage underwriting is inherently speculative, whether the underwritten income is current or anticipated, because creating mortgage credit depends on making judgments about future events that are uncertain. In particular, since "commercial lending is dependent upon net operating income.... repayment of a commercial loan is typically dependent upon the ability of the related mortgaged property to produce cash flow through the collection of rents," which are "often based on assumptions regarding (future) tenant behavior and market conditions" (COMM 2012-CCRE2 2012, S-43). Levitin and Wachter (2013) confirm how pro forma underwriting works: "Pro forma loans calculated the debt coverage ratio based on prospective rents, including leases anticipated, but not in-place and future rent increases, rather than leases in hand. In other words, pro forma loans' debt coverage ratio was solely aspirational" (2013, 24).

In 2006 Rockpoint Group, a private equity firm, and the New York property manager Stellar Properties purchased a large, rent-regulated multifamily complex in northern Manhattan, the Riverton Houses, when nearly all of the eighteen hundred apartments in the complex were rent regulated. Financial institutions that underwrite commercial mortgages and the bundling of those mortgages in commercial mortgage-backed securities (CMBS) write prospectuses for potential investors that detail investment assumptions. Those documents state that for Riverton, property revenues, net operating income, and expenses were "based on certain assumptions, including an annual rate of conversion of units from rent-stabilized units to de-regulated units such that by 2011, 53% of the units will be deregulated and rented at market rents" (CD 2007-CD4 Commercial Mortgage Trust 2007, 73; hereafter "CD 2007-CD4, 2007"). This strategy would increase rents from a weighted average of $894 to $2,261 a month, an increase of more than 150 percent (CD 2007-CD4 2007, 73). The Riverton CMBS documents detail the time schedule for increasing apartment rents, with half of the units deregulated within five years, and assuming an annual net operating income growth of 66 percent to over 100 percent (CD 2007-CD4 2007). The assumptions of growth built into investment prospectuses are larger than the historical rates of growth. Data from the Rent Guidelines Board show that on average from 1983 to 2015 across Manhattan, net operating income for rent-stabilized apartments increased about 2.4 percent a year. The prospectus warns that if these expectations about the rate of deregulation were not met, the building revenue would not cover the debt payments: "Conversion of units from rent-stabilized units to de-regulated units at a rate lower than the assumed rate would have a negative impact on the underwritten NOI [net operating income]" (CD 2007-CD4 2007, 73).

The financial documents also explain the building management strategy: how investors would realize the expectations that underlie the extension of the mortgage credit. The CMBS prospectus describes Stellar Management, the owner and property manager of the Riverton Houses, as having "extensive real estate experience, which enables them to target under-performing/under-marketed assets and profit from value-added opportunities" (CD 2007-CD4 2007, 74). Moreover, Riverton is not the first or only multifamily property that Stellar has purchased with the intent of increasing rents in pursuit of the "value-added opportunity":

> Stellar Management has acquired other properties of a similar scale to the Riverton Apartments Property and has employed their business strategy to purchase assets below replacement costs, reduce operating expenses, manage turnover and rent roll, generate an accretive return on renovation costs and use the firm's centralized accounting and asset management functions. Stellar has generated additional value at Independence Plaza (1,332 units located in the Tribeca area of Manhattan) and the Villas Parkmerced (3,221 units located in San Francisco, California), which are multifamily properties with similar rental regulations to those at the Riverton Apartments Property. (CD 2007-CD4 2007, 75)

The "value-added opportunity" described here relies on seeing latent or suppressed value in rental properties that have perceived below-market rents. The ability to "generate additional value" depends on finding properties like Riverton, Independence Plaza, and Parkmerced with the potential for rent increases. The potential lies in the buildings' location in rental markets with higher and increasing market-rate rents and changes in rent control laws that enable those rent increases through individual apartment improvements (IAI), vacancy bonus when tenants turn over, and major capital improvements (MCI). Increasing rents and eventually deregulating apartments through vacancy decontrol provisions increase property income and hence property value.

Increasing displacement pressure on tenants to meet the expectations of rent growth that the financing of the properties demanded is a fundamental part of the undervalued asset strategy. Changes in rent regulation allow landlords to remove apartments from regulation—if they can get current tenants to leave. In situations where deregulation is not immediately possible, landlords work consistently to increase rents in order to come closer to the rent level legally required for deregulation. Larger rent increases are possible if a tenant vacates, and this provides an incentive for landlords to increase displacement pressure on long-term tenants. From 2007 to 2009, tenants in Riverton and in buildings like it throughout the city reported forms of landlord harassment that included ignored repair requests, unexplained additional fees, and offers of lump-sum cash payments to vacate the apartment, which were frequently accompanied by the threat of eviction if the tenant did not accept. Tenant advocacy and investigations by the New York Attorney General's office led to new regulations and commitments from owners to preserve the properties as affordable housing (Speri 2011; Carmiel 2012; Interview February 20, 2014).[1]

"Mismanaged Assets" in Low-Vacancy, Working-Class Neighborhoods

Landlords employ different strategies to increase building income in neighborhoods with more low-income renters and where rents are generally lower than in the reinvested core and adjacent areas. At least until the late 1990s, the previous generation of tenement landlords in neighborhoods outside of the expanded core made modest returns (compared to core markets) by carrying out only the most basic building maintenance and by leaving individual apartments unimproved for decades (Sternlieb 1966, 1972; Stegman 1972; Salins 1999; Gelman 2007). This systematic and strategic under-maintenance presented an investment opportunity given the changes in these places since the urban crisis in the 1970s when New York City's neighborhoods were emptying and property abandonment was widespread.

Neighborhoods in the Bronx, Brooklyn, and Queens where professional investors have been purchasing rent-regulated buildings since the early 2000s are in general home to racial minorities and immigrants, most of whom are poor and have restricted residential choice for a combination of economic, social, and legal reasons. Additionally, in post-2001 New York City, these neighborhoods are adding residents, no longer losing large portions of the population as was the case in the late 1960s and 1970s. In Brooklyn, for a generation now, immigrants from the Caribbean have been settling in the neighborhoods to the east and south of Prospect Park, including Crown Heights and Flatbush. These places have large shares of regulated housing, high levels of housing in distress, and problems with crowding. Flatbush and Crown Heights are also adjacent to middle- and upper-income neighborhoods like Prospect Heights and Park Slope, now part of the expanded core of reinvestment. Proximity to these expensive neighborhoods contributes to the notion that neighborhoods like Crown Heights and Flatbush represent the next spatial frontier for investment.

Prevailing conditions in the Bronx, Queens, and Brooklyn affect investment strategy because the poorer tenants who live in these places historically limit the possible rents, and so owners must find different routes to profitability where the scope for increasing rent is much more limited than it is in core markets. The strategy hinges on what industry participants call "working the building," which refers to the management practice of pursuing legally allowed rent increases under rent control laws. The strategy also relies on the 2003 change to rent law that allowed new owners to raise preferential rents previously granted to long-term and elderly tenants to the maximum legal rent. Previous under-maintenance of these "mismanaged assets" provided the basis for new owners' assumptions about realizing profits from higher rents allowed by improving conditions in these units.

Tenants had been dealing with systematic under-maintenance of their buildings in the Bronx, Brooklyn, and northern Manhattan for two decades before the latest wave of professional investors began purchasing rent-regulated housing after 2000 (Stantucci 2008; Walsh 2008; Hasty 2012). Buildings had hundreds and thousands of outstanding violations, according to tenant advocacy groups that tracked landlord behavior, and previous owners had consistently appeared in "worst landlord" lists compiled by *The Village Voice* and other news publications (Dwoskin 2010).

Commercial mortgage-backed securities documents describe how underwriting is based on assumptions about the growth in income after improvements are made. The documents state that new owners of regulated buildings in the Bronx "invested approximately $6.4 million to clear building violations, complete capital improvements, and lease-up vacant units. Certain improvements eligible for rent increases and tax abatements per rent stabilization guidelines have been underwritten by lender and are expected to take effect in the next 6–12 months" (COMM 2012-CCRE2 2012, B-99). The prospectus acknowledges that such underwritten revenues "by their nature, are speculative and are based upon certain assumptions and projections. The failure of these assumptions or projections in whole or in part could cause the underwritten or adjusted cash flows to vary substantially from the actual cash flows of a mortgaged property" (COMM 2012-CCRE2 2012, S-43).

Investors justified their expectations of rising rents on the basis of "strong market occupancy," meaning the very low vacancy rates in multifamily housing in New York City and in the tight rental markets of the Bronx, Manhattan, and Brooklyn in particular. They highlighted that the Bronx is ranked as the number one rental submarket in the nation over the past five years based on its 0.9 percent vacancy rate. The document cites "consistent revenue growth" in multifamily buildings with rent-stabilized units, with an average lease renewal increase set by the Rent Guidelines Board of 4.95 percent since 1968.

City housing staff and nonprofit housing developers familiar with the mismanaged asset portfolio recall the strategy as investing in under-maintained and/or poorly managed properties and expecting a large increase in rents and corresponding appreciation in value. These returns would depend on maximizing the allowable rent increases under rent stabilization, pursuing past-due rents, and seeking evictions. What real estate professionals call "professional asset management" includes careful scrutiny of all aspects of the building and tenants with the objective of reducing expenses, increasing rents where possible, and thereby maximizing revenue. This strategy can have disparate effects on tenants, depending on their length of tenure and their ability to pay higher rents. New owners make building-level improvements such as upgrading elevators, doors, and water boilers, and installing a new roof or surveillance cameras, and using such improvements to increase rents through the Major Capital Improvement Program. At the same time, owners withhold repairs and maintenance in apartments that have long-term tenants who pay lower rents than in apartments that have had more turnover (Hasty 2012; Interview A, February 21, 2014; Interview B, February 21, 2014). Increasing preferential rents to maximum legal rents can be a powerful tool to displace tenants who cannot afford the legal rent.

In many rent-regulated buildings purchased with the expectation of increasing value through professional asset management strategies, owners have not met their debt obligations from the income in the buildings and defaulted on their loans. Buildings caught in the foreclosure process often suffered from poor maintenance, and records of building violations document myriad problems including nonfunctioning heating systems and recurring leaks (Hasty 2012). Water damage to ceilings and walls was not fixed but patched over, and apartment floors, walls, and ceilings weakened to the point of collapse. Under these conditions, mold spread throughout the buildings. Trash piled up inside and outside of the buildings without janitorial staff on hand to provide routine property maintenance. Rodent infestations multiplied in the unsanitary conditions (Milbank Tenants Memorandum of Law 2009; Hasty 2012; Interview A February 21, 2014).

In an example of the laissez-faire phase of the double movement, the weakening of rent control laws in the 1990s established conditions for the financialization of rent-regulated housing. Investors created two spatially distinct fictions in the form of undervalued and mismanaged asset strategies, which hinged on increasing building income through rent increases allowed by the alterations in rent regulations. Rent regulations opened new legal avenues for landlords to pursue rent increases on an individual apartment basis, rather than treating the building as an aggregation of rents that increased at a stable annual rate. Investors calculated revenue increases through these new routes and projected them into the future, and lenders extended credit based on these fictions. Specifically, the undervalued asset strategy underpins a fiction based on a future of advancing gentrification and displacement. The mismanaged asset fiction assumes a future of continued and increasing spatial and political-economic constraint on low-income tenants. These fictions also set the terrain on which new countermoves unfold. In this case, the laissez-faire phase of the double movement reconfigured what needed to be protected, and the countermovement proceeded in a decidedly individualistic form, accepting the financialization of rent-regulated housing and focusing protection on tenants as contract holders.

New Countermoves: From Social Protection to Managing Fictions

Viewing rent regulation in a Polanyian frame draws attention to the historical advance and retreat of tenant protection in New York City's rental housing market. New rent regulations and tenancy laws in the 1920s, 1940s, and 1960s marked state responses to the deleterious effects of landlord power in extracting rent, whereas intervening and subsequent periods saw a loosening of rent regulations. Polanyi's theory of the double movement, though, does more than alert us to the oscillations in laissez-faire and its social regulation. It also calls attention to how state power shapes the relative strength of different class factions, while also governing the terms on which market regulation takes place (Block and Summers 1984). Struggles over state regulation, the organization of capital markets, the provision of public goods, and the legal instruments for defining individual and collective damages were some of the arenas of social contestation, then, that variously set the terms for social protections against the commodification of the fictitious commodities. This insight is significant for our understanding of the current period of renewed attention on housing affordability in New York City because previous weakening of regulations has defined the terms of the countermovement and narrowed the social protections it provides.

The changes to rent laws in the 1990s opened rent-regulated housing to new investors and investment strategies, which moved through the housing market during the 2000s. The erosion of rent regulation in the 1990s did not only once again increase pressure on tenants, especially low-income renters, through the displacement pressures of increasing rent, deteriorating conditions, and harassment. It also exacerbated the tension that had always existed within the rent laws between their ability to offer a broad social protection to all tenants as a class and stability across the rental housing market, and the individualizing impulse of the law to confer benefits to a freely contracting renter-as-consumer of a commodity, housing. Much of the policy response to the financialization of housing has framed the problem through this individualized legal framework, which may protect some current tenants but is predicated on the end of rent-regulated housing.

The 1990s changes to rent law in New York fundamentally transformed rent regulations from a market-structuring device into a space for extracting rent through law. As professional investors purchased rent-regulated housing during the 2000s with financial expectations that placed pressure on tenants, community organizations campaigned to bring code enforcement, legal sanction, and other forms of state support to bear on the problem (Fields 2015; Teresa 2016). Increasing public advocacy and political activism around deteriorating housing conditions led to the creation of new housing code enforcement powers and institutions within New York City and state governments to wield them, but could not achieve changes to the state rent laws that would have brought broad tenant protections. The Alternative Enforcement and the Emergency Repair Programs, administered through the city's department of Housing Preservation and Development, focus building inspections and administrative sanctions on the worst-maintained buildings in the city. City officials expected that enhanced policing of housing codes would encourage proper maintenance by increasing the cost of strategically under-maintaining buildings and would provide the foundation for subsequent criminal legal action against landlords who did not adhere to the housing code.

Beyond physical deterioration of buildings, long-term and low-income tenants face other forms of harassment that are designed to force them to leave, such as increased rents and fees, intentional withholding of repairs, and efforts to prevent tenant organizing. Tenant organizing during the housing boom of the middle-2000s brought housing problems to the attention to New York State's chief law enforcement officer, the attorney general. The New York State Office of the Attorney General investigated claims of tenant harassment and illegal landlord activity and found enough evidence to secure several legal settlements with landlords (New York State Attorney General 2010, 2014). These agreements typically do not include admission of guilt, but mandate landlord payments to tenants for improper fees and rent increases and stipulate ownership and management practices, such as scheduled rent increases.

By 2012, amid mounting cases of systematic tenant harassment within the regulated sector, New York governor Andrew Cuomo and Mayor Bill de Blasio announced the formation of the Tenant Protection Unit, formally housed within the state agency responsible for administering rent stabilization, New

York State Homes and Community Renewal (NYSHCR). The unit's mandate includes investigating landlord practices, and it has power to audit building finances and legally sanction owners. By 2016, the Tenant Protection Unit had returned fifty thousand apartments to rent regulation that were found to have been illegally deregulated (New York State Homes and Community Renewal 2016). These various enforcement powers were bureaucratized in 2015 in the Tenant Harassment Prevention Taskforce, an intergovernmental group focused on managing investment in rent-regulated housing as an enforcement problem (New York Governor Press Office 2015). Exposing the link between reinvestment, the extraction of rent, and displacement pressure, Mayor de Blasio's 2015 rezoning proposal included a $36 million allocation for tenant legal services (Office of the Mayor 2015).

When strong rent regulations were passed in the 1920s, 1940s, and 1960s, tenant activism shifted toward assisting renters to navigate the new bureaucracies that these laws created, dissipating the most radical political activism that at times directly threatened the fiction of land as a commodity. More recently, tenant organizations devote substantial resources to helping tenants navigate the expanding enforcement apparatus that includes the Tenant Harrassment Prevention Task Force and Tenant Protection Unit. While these efforts help some tenants, they nonetheless use time and resources that could be spent on other organizing activities that would not just be centered on remedying harm to individual tenants but could work toward strengthened rent regulations and increased public housing. These efforts are underway, of course, but the point is that time and money are diverted from those activities and into helping tenants navigate complex government bureaucracies that only help them after they have already suffered. In response to the financialization of housing in the 2000s, the state has bolstered its enforcement powers to manage the legalized extraction of value from privately owned rent-regulated housing, rather than working to restructure the market through rent control or publicly owned housing that would expand the supply of affordable housing units. Viewing this more recent struggle to address problems of housing investment and displacement in comparison with the twentieth-century history presented earlier in the chapter illustrates how periods of facilitating commodification can also set the terms of the second half of the double movement, social protection. State regulations and their discursive frames can shape the very conception of what is to be socially protected. That is, do all renters as a class have a right to shelter, or do individual contract holders have a right to protection within the law? Both of these relationships can be protected, but they represent fundamentally different conceptualizations of society and so they will carry disparate consequences for tenants and their housing.

The Work of Fiction

Treating land and improvements on land as a commodity undermines the human institutions that are connected to land. Commodification of land also allows it to be comprehended through a financialized logic that values land for the rent it produces and extends credit on assumptions about future rent. There are temporal and spatial dimensions to the commodification and financialization of land. In the case of investment in New York City rent-regulated housing, forms of fictitious capital like mortgage credit circulate through housing on the assumption that the buildings will produce revenues in the future. The circulation of credit through land—in this case via housing—implicates very specific futures of renovated buildings and apartments, higher-income tenancy, and rent growth. These implied futures demand management practices to realize them: using rent law to increase rents, strategically reducing maintenance to encourage tenant attrition, and ultimately eviction.

The financialized logic underlying land as fictitious capital is that creditors extend capital in the present on the basis of fundamentally uncertain events. Either the success or failure to meet expectations that underlie credit has different consequences in different parts of the city. In Manhattan, validating the assumptions about rent growth means increasing displacement pressure on long-term and low-income tenants; if achieved, this changes who lives in these neighborhoods and the expectations about rents and profits. If they are not realized, then physical deterioration is possible. In areas of New York City where the perceived and actual capacities for increasing rents are more modest—in the working-class areas of the Bronx, Brooklyn, and Queens—the expectations of fictitious capital establish specific visions as surely as they do in Manhattan. On an already uneven geography of slum landlording, the expectations about fictitious capital in the rent-regulated buildings that house the poor and working class capitalize on the shortage of housing in New York City and, often, reproduce the long-standing deficiency of decent affordable housing options.

The history of rent regulation and the financialization of regulated housing in New York City tells us, then, something about the double movement, financialization, and the fictions that sustain them. First, the double movement is not symmetrical between periods of more and less embedded forms of liberal capitalism. Responses to the effects of the financialization of rent-regulated housing since the 2000s have taken a much different form than they did in earlier periods of housing crisis. Rather than fiscal and regulatory commitments to treating housing problems as results of the structure of the market and the system of housing production, new legal and enforcement strategies have more narrowly defined the problem as a legal question of harm to tenants. Therefore a central question for the protective countermovement is how it manages commodification: by remedying harm after the fact or by creating alternatives that would avoid the damaging effects in the first place.

Second, this asymmetry in the unfolding of the double movement is relational, with each half of the double movement influencing the other. Changes to rent regulations in the 1990s weakened tenant protections in a specific way that set the discursive and institutional terms of the countermovement. Predicating deregulation on considerations of individual apartment rents and renter income orients rent-stabilized housing as an individualized benefit rather than as public good. It is a regulatory change that renders housing tenure more calculable and turns the rent-stabilized lease contract into a legal tool for progressively extracting more rent. Professional investors estimate rates of rent increases and the number of units deregulated and translate those into revenue projections and ultimately prices for financial instruments backed by those revenues. This suggests that processes of individualization can facilitate financialization; the ability to calculate and project in individual units of account is fundamental to circulating financial capital. Consequently, what may stymie financialization is more cooperative and collective action and institutions that limit this kind of calculability.

Therefore, the underlying logic and material form of the countermovement matters for what is to be socially protected and with what effects for tenants. The current state action in the countermovement frames society as a set of contract holders to be protected under law rather than a broad class of renters who require housing as a basic human need. Government efforts manage the financialization of rent-regulated housing through the housing code, and tenant rights enforcement can, at best, limit the harm to *current* tenants by helping them to stay in decent and affordable housing. These protections not only leave in place broader market dynamics that lead to displacement, but reinforce conditions that make rent-regulated housing attractive investments. State enforcement and legal settlements can secure lower, more affordable rents for some, but simultaneously expand the gap between regulated and market-rate rents in a context of gentrification and thereby increase potential returns from rent-regulated housing. Of course, rather than concluding that protecting tenants is perversely harmful, it calls attention to how the idea and material reality of an "outside" to regulated housing generates value for investors and is the actual source of harm. Therefore, more socially protective countermovements have to focus on eliminating or at least reducing the accessibility of an outside to rent-regulated housing, for example, by removing legal routes to deregulate apartments and to circumvent stabilized rent increases, as tenant organizations have been calling for (Whitford 2015).

The fictions in the double movement implicate an anticipated future. The rental fictions that undervalued and mismanaged asset strategies underpin assume value extracted from housing, made real through building management practices, displacement, and evictions. The prevailing countermovement to these fictions does not substantively challenge this future, but only sets some limits on how uncomfortable the process will be for tenants. Housing code and tenant rights enforcement manage the deregulation of rent-regulated housing stock, which is a form of protection based on a future without regulated housing. While the protections make this decline more palatable in the short term for current tenants, it jeopardizes future tenants and the housing stock as a public good. Rent increases and deregulation not only burden current tenants, but they also constitute a collective, future loss because they reduce affordable, tenure-protected housing available to future renters. Therefore, to not only manage decline and its effects but effectively reverse them, countermovements will need to move beyond a focus on individualized legal harm and to secure housing as a collective resource for all current and future renters. This will require reframing the aims of the countermovement as protecting housing as a public good for future generations, to rescale the legislative efforts from the city to New York State, to engage financial market regulation that governs investment in housing, and center the purpose of housing as shelter. These are the aims, political strategies, and substantive focus of many tenant groups and community organizations in New York City, but the state has not adopted them, which would be necessary to build the kind of sweeping social protection that would meaningfully alter the trajectory of the countermovement.

Finally, fictions in land are tools that facilitate commodification and speculation, and so it would seem as though we can safely discard these tools if we are interested in other kinds of social relations in land. The chapter showed that treating land as fictitious capital, valued for the rent it produces, involves extending credit on the basis of future events that are by their nature uncertain, a process that has devastating consequences for tenants and their communities. But fundamentally, the fiction involves acting in the present in anticipation of an imagined future. An alternative reading of fictions is that the central question is not whether we need them or not, but what kind of futures the fictions imply: are they based in expanding commodification, capital, and rent that serve no purpose other than "accumulation for accumulation's sake," or can we predicate our fictions on an imagined future centered on people's needs.

7

THE FICTION OF FORMALIZATION
Titles, Concessions, and the Politics of Landownership in Cambodia

Michael B. Dwyer

"Sorry uncle!" These are the words of a cadastral officer who appears at the beginning of *Land Is Life*, an educational booklet produced by the Cambodian Ministry of Land Management and handed out to local residents at the beginning of the land titling process (LASSP n.d.).[1] In this fictional narrative, the officer has just told an elderly peasant, Uncle San, that his plans "to clear the bush for planting" are strictly forbidden. Uncle San is landless: sometime in the past, the reader learns, he had mortgaged and lost his single plot of farmland due to a combination of "drought, flood, disease and destitution." After his makeshift apology, the cadastral officer speaks at length in the voice of the state, quoting passages from Cambodia's 2001 Land Law and making Uncle San "extremely scared" by describing the fines and worse that would have befallen him if he and his sons had "encroached ... within the private property of the state." The vignette ends with Uncle San learning about and "expectantly and hopefully" applying for a state-sanctioned "social" land concession to allow him to feed his family while still obeying the law. In the meantime, Uncle San and his family remain "determin[ed] to continue their ordinary living," Uncle San by working as a wage laborer, his wife by "baking cakes for his children to sell."

This episode appears at the beginning of a document that devotes the majority of its attention to people *with* property. What follows the four-page story of Uncle San is a thirty-five-page account of a different family's journey through the multistage process of systematic land titling: community education, parcel registration, the cataloging and resolving of disputes, and ultimately the production and handing out of formal land titles. *Land Is Life* is a morality tale that illustrates the social benefits of legal conformance and formalized transactions, a mode of thought and action that land professionals sometimes call "the culture of land administration." After his opening vignette, Uncle San reappears only once—much later in the story—and his new clothes and homegrown produce convey the message that his social land concession has indeed lifted his family out of poverty. Yet he had not fully disappeared from the story, remaining in the background via his son's marriage into the propertied family whose progression through the titling process is featured in the booklet. Through this liminal presence, Uncle San thus conveys one of *Land Is Life*'s key messages: By working hard, "giving up old ideas" about how legitimate land access should be defined, and forging ties to the propertied, even the landless can benefit from Cambodia's post-2001 land regime. Uncle San's trajectory from encroacher to stakeholder makes it clear that although he is not the story's protagonist, his participation and consent are essential nonetheless to its happy ending.

Even in its abbreviated form, the story of Uncle San gestures to the political work that goes into constructing and maintaining what this chapter calls the fiction of formalization. From government officials to concession holders, from multilateral development institutions to the "properly" propertied families like those of Uncle San's daughter-in-law, a diverse range of actors has invested deeply in the idea that property formalization—the bureaucratic work of measuring, demarcating, authorizing, and inscribing landownership—is merely the technocratic recording of facts that already exist on the ground. Formal property has a certain common-sense inevitability; some version of it seems almost necessary for public order. And following the work of economist Hernando de Soto (2000), formalization is widely seen as a necessary precursor to development, a way to make the value of land legible to the engine of capitalism. And yet, it only takes a few lines about the life of a fictionalized figure like Uncle San to glimpse formalization's darker side—the exclusion produced when the power of the state is mobilized to support one notion of ownership at the expense of others. In Uncle San's case, the same act of land clearing would have had radically different meanings depending when it took place. Before August 30, 2001, it would have begun the five-year process of establishing Uncle San's legal rights of possession; after that date, it would have made Uncle San a criminal. In law, the arbitrary becomes the rule. And in the practice of formalization, the arbitrary rule becomes concrete geography, making once fluid distinctions between legal and illegal hard and fast.

This chapter examines the work of property formalization in Cambodia, read through processes of titling and concession making associated with the global land rush of the late 2000s. As with other authors in this collection, my approach addresses the need noted by Ghertner and Lake in this book's Introduction to denaturalize land commodification practices that can appear necessary, inevitable, and permanent simply because they are done routinely. In the sections that follow, I begin with the discursive work that renders formalization logical, legal, and hegemonic. I then examine the bureaucratic work that gives it a subnational geography. I finish with the political work of enforcing it at the margins where hegemony breaks down and conflicts erupt with those who openly question its fictions. As I elaborate in the conclusion, my goal is not to argue against formalization per se, but to denaturalize it so that its powers can be put to work in better ways.

The Formalization Fix

In the late 2000s, many development institutions identified land titling as a go-to solution to what was variably described as the global land rush or, more politely, "irresponsible agricultural investment." Working within the conceit that requires multilateral institutions to frame governments such as Cambodia's as well intentioned yet lacking in state capacity, the "Principles of Responsible Agricultural Investment" (PRAI) published by the UN Food and Agriculture Organization (FAO), World Bank, and sister organizations in the immediate wake of the global land rush (FAO et al. 2010) described the problem as essentially a shortage of cadastral maps:

> In many countries of interest to investors, the state "owns" large amounts of land, which may make it easier to transfer such land to outsiders in less than fully transparent ways, even if it is still occupied by traditional users. The fact that governments often do not know the extent or location of their holdings, or that by law all land that is not "productively used" can administratively be transferred to other uses, increases such dangers. (FAO et al. 2010, 3)

Framing the problem this way—as a conflict between, on the one hand, the unmapped claims of states that "own" (in scare quotes) land but don't *actually* own it since they don't know where it is (also see Deininger et al. 2012) and, on the other hand, traditional or common property-based claims "to which no formal records exist" (FAO et al. 2010, 3)—anticipates formalization as a preferred solution, helping construct a narrative of a technical resolution to long-intractable political disputes and bureaucratic neglect. Not surprisingly, the authors of the PRAI lay out a vision that sounds a lot like systematic land titling, beginning with "(i) the identification of all rights holders" and "(ii) legal recognition of all rights and uses, together with options for their demarcation and registration or recording" (ibid., 2). While acknowledging that this is an ambitious goal and suggesting that "countries with limited resources may do well to initially focus efforts on areas with high agro-ecological and infrastructure potential and expand from there" (ibid., 2), they position full cadastral coverage—"a countrywide systematic identification and registration of rights" (ibid., 3)—as the ultimate goal. They propose, in short, that titling should focus on fertile and accessible areas—the same areas often targeted by land concessions (Cotula et al. 2009; Borras et al. 2011; Messerli et al. 2014), but that it should do a better job at getting there before the problems of large-scale investment arrive. This is the promise of formalization: that it both facilitates economic investment and minimizes the most unsavory forms of dispossession often associated with private land concessions.

This narrative, constructed in immediate response to the global land rush, proposed a significant reorientation of the way that titling has been pursued across the global south for the better part of the preceding two decades (cf. De Soto 2000; Borras 2007; Bromley 2009). While titling programs regularly acknowledge a number of different benefits that formalization creates—increased tenure security, more efficient land markets, a larger tax base, and increased access to credit—in practice it has been the last two of these that have been consistently prioritized. This prioritization takes the form of actively avoiding areas where tenure is believed to be "complicated" or "contested," and focusing instead on areas where the process will go quickly so as to issue as many titles as possible. Such an approach prioritizes titling's potential to create what Hernando de Soto (2000) called property's "double life" as loan collateral, as well as its potential to generate land tax revenues. Its potential to provide legal weight for communities whose tenure situation is precarious is correspondingly deprioritized, despite the enduring narrative weight that institutions like the World Bank place on formalization's security benefits to the poor and marginalized. This gap between the promise of formalization, or what I call the formalization fix, and the reality of formalization politics' minimal emphasis on enhancing the land rights of the marginalized, is what produces formalization as a fiction: a story that continues to be narrated as both desirable and possible despite evidence that it is not, indeed, doing what it purports.

In practice, the spatial dimensions (and associated trade-offs) of land titling have been slow to emerge, largely due to a shortage of available data about where titling takes place on a subnational level. While land administration projects have tended to target countries with what experts (again politely) call "weak land governance regimes," land titling can undermine the existing tenure rights of smallholders in areas where titling does *not* occur (COHRE 2009; Grimsditch and Henderson 2009). Philip Hirsch calls this land titling's central conundrum:

> While most farmers and other landholders are pleased to obtain formal title over plots of land that they hold individually under more weakly demarcated and state-recognized arrangements, the process of land

> titling in some areas can weaken security in others and can entrench, sharpen and exacerbate existing inequalities in access to land. (Hirsch 2011, 15)

In his research on "titling against [land] grabbing" in Southeast Asia, Hirsch has posited something like a diffusion model for the way that titling moves through the social landscape:

> For the main part, land titling has tended to work outward from core agricultural areas where land and its produce have been commodified for longer than in more peripheral areas. However, [as titling programs in Southeast Asia] have extended titling into the margins, . . . increasingly we see a geographical overlap with areas more commonly associated with land grabbing. (Hirsch 2011, 5)

Hirsch's assertion of core-to-periphery expansion and the growing geographical overlap between titling and concession areas is better thought of as a hypothesis, however, given the data shortages. Most of his examples—untitled swidden land, grazing land, and teak plantations in Laos that are increasingly at risk of concession expansion (Hirsch 2011, 9–11)—tend to fit the pattern of separation rather than convergence, while the case of Cambodia's Boeung Kak Lake that I turn to below is an exception that proves the rule of separation.

Although province-scale maps of titling projects' target areas tend to be relatively common, precise information about their subnational geographies is rarely in the public domain. The World Bank, for example, which tends to be on the more transparent end of the spectrum of development institutions, has yet to fill in the geographical details on its titling projects' public websites. The "map" pages for titling projects in Ghana, Indonesia, Laos, Thailand, and Zimbabwe all recently said—in place of the Google Map data that populate other Bank projects' map pages—that "detailed locations for this project are currently not available."[2] Cambodia, in contrast, is an exception. Its uneven geography of formalization, visible in the data generated out of a high-profile land dispute in the late 2000s, shows how formalization, despite its promises of reducing the negative effects of land grabbing, can deny the very land claims it is thought to protect.

The Uneven Geography of Formalization in Cambodia

In mid-2011, an important map of Cambodia was posted to the website of the World Bank's Inspection Panel. Produced in early 2011 by World Bank cartographers, the map showed the communes where systematic land titling had taken place in Cambodia between 2003 and 2009 under the Bank's Land Management and Administration Project (LMAP). The map was a revision, and it contrasted markedly with an earlier version that had shown the project's target area depicted by province. The new map resolved the project target area two administrative levels downward, to that of the commune, and in doing so added much to the map's information content. But it also changed the map's meaning. In contrast to the original, which showed roughly 60 percent of the country as the project's target area, the new map showed a far more limited geography of titling operations, with the communes shown in the revised map covering only a small fraction of Cambodian territory.[3]

Cambodia is one of the few places in the world where a relatively detailed national map of donor-funded land titling efforts is in the public domain. The reason is that the new map was created and *published* only after there was a problem. In early 2007, Phnom Penh city officials had declared a 133-hectare "development zone" over Boeung Kak Lake, a centrally located area that had been recently selected for land title adjudication. Over the two years that followed, the Boeung Kak concession conflict erupted into a battle between radically conflicting modes of development: large-scale land allocation among Cambodian business elites and well-capitalized global investors, and bottom-up development based on the enhanced tenure security of propertied smallholders. The revised project map emerged relatively late in this process: after eviction notices were issued to the residents of the "development zone"; after legal advocates filed a claim with the World Bank's internal watchdog, the Inspection Panel, arguing a lack of due process for potential title recipients (COHRE 2009); and after the resulting investigation largely vindicated this charge, criticizing project managers in Phnom Penh for failing to appreciate the "political economy context" in which they were working and expressing "extreme concern" for "the large number of people who were forcibly evicted, displaced, or [who remained] under threat of eviction in Project areas" (WBIP 2010, xx, 71–72).

Enter the revised map. Confronted with assertions of mismanagement, LMAP's managers countered that their project was a limited contribution to "a very complex development problem," and that it had never intended "to address all of the land transactions and conflicts in the Project provinces" (World Bank 2009, 26–27). The new map provided a spatial reiteration of this claim. It attempted to distance the project from land conflicts—many of which stemmed from land concessions aimed at realizing the value of so-called state land (Hughes 2007, 2008; NGO Forum on Cambodia 2008, 2009, 2010; LICADHO 2009; O'Keefe 2009; Un and So 2009; WBIP 2010)—that occurred in project provinces but not in project communes. In short, project managers were trying to distance their titling activities from the spate of land concessions that increasingly covered the Cambodian countryside.

This episode gestures to the distance that today's defenders of land titling would have to go—quite literally—to make titling a solution to the problem of "irresponsible agricultural investment" that, in the form of land concessions, plagues the Cambodian countryside. The Boeng Kak conflict was, as figure 7.1 shows, one of the few areas in the entire country where titling and land concessions *overlapped*. It was an exception to the rule, elaborated below, that titling and concessions have developed as parallel and essentially separate forms of property formalization. Making sense of these geographies of formalization gives the lie to the fiction of formalization as a technical fix to illegible but ultimately objective property rights, and requires that formalization be reconceptualized as a space in which public authority is contested, albeit on uneven political terrain.

Land concessions have a heterogeneous pedigree that reflects multiple aspects of Cambodia's modern history and geography: its uneven density of settlement and production, which creates the impression (at least for some) that peripheral

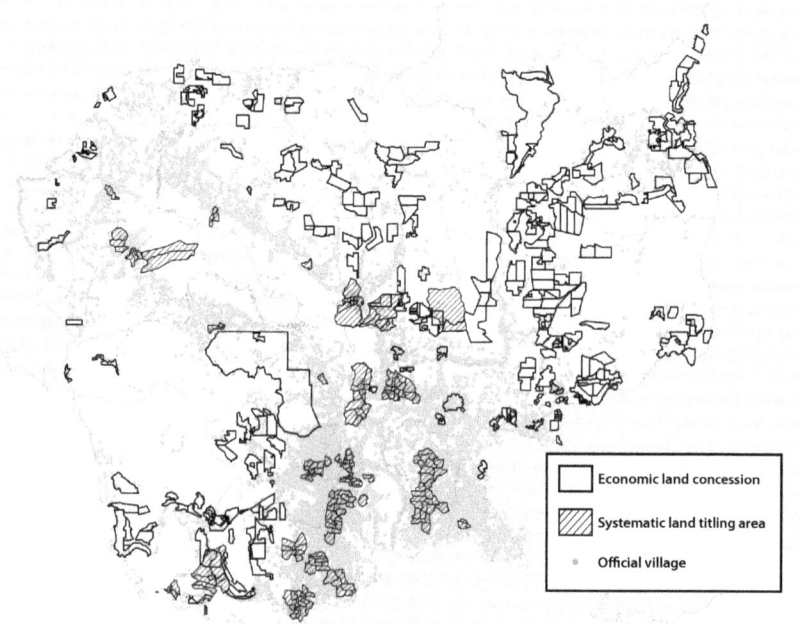

FIGURE 7.1. Titling areas versus economic land concessions in Cambodia. The diagonally hatched polygons are communes where LMAP operated and were extracted from a World Bank map at WBIP (no date) (digitizing by the author).

Source: Figure by the author using data from LICADHO (2012) and the World Bank.

areas have large swaths of "underpopulated" and "available" land; constitutionally mandated state ownership of key natural resources like forests, mountains, rivers, and minerals; the population displacements during and after the Khmer Rouge period, which have been widely interpreted as calling earlier property relations into question in a systemic and fundamental way; and the role of forestry—and particularly forest concessions and the tycoon-centered business networks that developed and exploited them—in the period during the mid- and late-1990s that ultimately brought relative peace to the country (Chandler 1993; Le Billon 2000; Gottesman 2003; Hughes 2007). Each of these attributes, in its own way, has helped legitimize Cambodia's concession boom.

The current round of land concessions began in the late 1990s and early 2000s. These are generally referred to as "economic" land concessions (or ELCs) to distinguish them from the forest concessions that preceded them. Although the two are often distinguished in official policy language—ELCs being framed as rehabilitating and developing the lands that forest concessions exploited and degraded—there is actually a strong continuity between the two in that both foster the impression that much of Cambodia's hinterland is state land. Official estimates of the percentage of Cambodian territory that is state land vary, but 80 percent is a widely cited number (e.g., Council for Land Policy 2002; GTZ 2006; Ministry of Planning and UNDP 2007; USAID 2011; also see Dwyer 2015, 921–23). While challengeable on a number of grounds—the most basic being that Cambodia has not had a full cadastral survey (Suphal, Saravy, and Acharya 2001; Sar 2010) and that such estimates thus put the cart before the horse—the belief that much of the Cambodian countryside belongs to the state gives significant cover to concession-based "development" efforts. Moreover, the widespread belief that great swaths of the countryside are degraded—significant because concessions can legally be granted only on lands that are no longer fit to be what the Land Law defines as "state-public" property—adds to the putative legitimacy of a concession-heavy landscape.[4]

In such a context, scrutiny of the spatial dimensions of Cambodia's land titling project has been almost inevitable. Although the Boeung Kak conflict brought these issues into exceptionally public view, the uneven geography of Cambodia's tenure formalization efforts has been the subject of critique for over half a decade. The debate centers on the project's explicit decision to avoid "areas where disputes are likely" (World Bank 2002, 24) and reflects the mechanisms by which "contested" areas are avoided and the implications of this avoidance.

As a project whose stated goals include the enhancement of land tenure for the poor and vulnerable as a high priority (World Bank 2002), it may come as a surprise that LMAP targeted precisely those areas "in which preexisting tenure systems [were] best embedded, where the least conflict occur[red], and where the interests of the poorer majority [were] least at risk" (Adler and So 2012, 88). Biddulph describes the combination of factors that produce this geography and the central role of provincial authority:

> According to the relevant legislation [a 2002 subdecree], it is provincial governors who must allocate an adjudication area and determine its boundaries, before initiating the work of officials of the Ministry of Land Management Urban Planning and Construction to conduct the registration process. At this stage, therefore, strategic choices may be made about project location on the basis of the sort of vested interests and networks that order the economic development of contemporary Cambodia. (Biddulph 2010, 99)

Biddulph also recalls an interview with the LMAP project director in Phnom Penh who used cock fighting as a way to explain the project's spatial logic:

> [He] said that if a cock is sent to fight and loses, that will be the end of the cock with no second chances. So it is always wise to send the cock out to fight against some weaker opponents first to get some victories and become stronger before fighting a stronger opponent. For this reason, he argued that it is beneficial that the systematic land titling program has been implemented in areas where tenure is already secure. (Biddulph 2010, 98)

Biddulph questions this framing of tenure conservatism as temporary and capacity-building oriented and describes a more permanent and deliberate arrangement in which provincial authority functioned as "a decentralized safety valve which ensures that systematic land titling only travels to places which government feels comfortable with" (Biddulph 2010, 99). Ballard (2010), who interviewed provincial governors in 2007 with colleagues at the Cambodia Development Research Institute, found a similar result: "Most [provincial] administrators were reluctant to title land in areas that were further away from market centers and had poor access, and where there tended to be more disputes. They felt that they could not issue titles as quickly in such areas and that they would receive poor performance ratings, as performance was evaluated on the number of titles issued" (Ballard 2010, 3). In their investigative report that helped ground the request for the World Bank Inspection Panel investigation mentioned above, Grimsditch and Henderson (2009, 4) echoed this emphasis on performance over substantive impact, noting that "LMAP has evaluated the success of the titling program largely based on its outputs, particularly the number of titles issued, rather than its impacts, such as clear improvements in tenure security and a reduction of land-grabbing and disputes." Such a focus articulates the tenure conservatism of land titling projects more generally in Southeast Asia, which according to one expert cited by Biddulph have systematically avoided "complex tenurial situations, as well as complex land types such as forests, so as to be able to concentrate on reaching high production targets in non-contested areas" (Shawn Williams, cited in Biddulph 2010, 99).

The mismatch between concessions and titling shown above in figure 7.1 is only part of the story. Two other interventions are also crucial to the failure of formalization-based efforts to address Cambodia's land problem. These are communal land titles and social land concessions (mentioned in the opening sketch), both of which were rolled out during the 2000s more or less in parallel with LMAP's individual household titles, but which have had far less success in terms of implementation. In the absence of these more equity-oriented projects, economic land concessions have done the bulk of the property formalization in the Cambodian hinterland, often with adverse consequences (*Cambodia Daily* 2012, 2013; Neef et al. 2013; Milne 2014). Despite the narrative enhancement of Uncle San's personhood in the form of improved clothes and homegrown produce via his new social land concession, formalization in much of Cambodia has left landless and land-poor peasants like him high and dry.

The Social Land Concession (SLC) program, despite receiving its operationalizing subdecree before the ELC program, has produced results that verge on negligible, despite the deployment of the (post-LMAP) Land Allocation for Social and Economic Development (LASED) project in 2009. As the LASED project's top foreign adviser complained in his paper for the 2012 World Bank Conference on Land and Poverty,

> Whereas 1.7 million hectares have been officially reported to be distributed as economic land concessions (ELCs) for about 200 rich and powerful investors, only 6 thousand hectares were made available for 1,614 rural poor households as social land concessions by the end of 2011 through . . . donor [support]. In addition, a few thousand retired military staff and their families received land through a so-called "national SLC [social land concession] program" without donor support. As a gross summary it has to be stated that 99% of the distributed [state] land was handed over in long-term leases of up to 99 years to national and international investors to the detriment of the rural poor[,] who got only a 1% share. (Müller 2012, 3–4)

Communal titling has achieved even less thus far. Only three villages had received titles by the time the government issued a moratorium on new ELCs in mid-2012 (Pickardt et al. 2013, 5; also see Ironside 2011). While the number has since climbed to nineteen, this compares unfavorably with the many tens of community title applications still pending (Rabe 2013; Baird 2014; MLMUPC 2017), as well as with the extensive landscape of concessions that were issued prior to the moratorium (see figure 7.1 and LICADHO 2012). As many communal title applications remain bogged down in procedural requirements—including the application for "indigenous" status required by the 2001 Land Law—the systematic ignoring of legal and regulatory process by many concession developers (Müller 2012) has become an increasingly glaring contrast (LICADHO 2009; Cock 2010; BABSEA 2010; HBF 2011; Un and So 2011; Bugalski 2012; Neef et al. 2013). I examine the selective (ab)use of process, which often involves the deployment of formalization, through the high-profile case of the Koh Kong sugar concessions below.

Formality Politics outside the Titling Zone

Western Cambodia has emerged in the last few years as one of the country's most notorious areas for agribusiness-related land grabbing. This is due in part to the rise of sugar as a new "boom crop" (BABSEA 2010; also see Hall et al. 2011), and in particular to the influence in Koh Kong, Kampong Speu, and Oddar Meanchay provinces of Ly Yong Phat, a ruling party senator and "one of Cambodia's most influential businessmen" (BABSEA 2010, 2). According to researchers who have helped bring the story to an international audience, Ly Yong Phat and his business associates have been able to "flout the law at will" in their development of at least 60,000 hectares of sugar plantations in these three provinces, leading to "serious and widespread human rights abuses and environmental damage . . . affecting more than 12,000 people" (ibid., 1, 2). One of those cases—a pair of side-by-side concessions in Koh Kong's Sre Ambel and Botom Sakor districts—forms the backdrop for my analysis of formalization politics here.

The details of the Koh Kong sugar concessions have been extensively documented elsewhere, and are summarized here as a prelude to my discussion of formality and formalization. In mid-2006, a pair of adjacent concessions were demarcated and allocated to Ly Yong Phat and Chamroon Chinthammit, a Thai businessman who, along with a third (unnamed) Taiwanese partner, subsequently developed them into large-scale sugar plantations. Each concession was roughly 9,500 hectares; totaling 19,100 hectares, their separation was "an apparent attempt to circumvent" Cambodia's legal ban on concession holdings larger than 10,000 hectares (BABSEA 2010, 2).[5] Since then, project operations have been disturbingly reminiscent of Marx's classic account of primitive accumulation: documented impacts include loss of farmland and grazing land, destruction of crops (including tree crops), shooting and confiscation of livestock, exclusion of communities from forest areas and water sources, and impoverishment and lack of livelihood alternatives to the point that children have been pulled from school and adults forced to take jobs with the company—a process which entails their renouncing any claims to compensation (BABSEA 2010, 3; also see UNCO-HCHR 2007 and cf. Marx 1990 [1867], 873–913). Adding insult to injury, sugar from these and the other concessions in the region has been receiving duty-free access to the European market under the European Union's "Everything But Arms" trade provisions (BABSEA 2010, 8–9; Danish Church Aid 2011; Clean Sugar Campaign n.d.).

In parallel to its on-the-ground disparities, the on-paper geography of the Koh Kong sugar concessions provides a useful illustration of formalization politics in practice. Not only does the project exemplify the pattern of geographical separation shown in figure 7.1; it helps take the analysis a step further by showing how state land formalization has been pursued selectively and strategically, to the exclusion of other possible formalizations, including counterformalizations that might have protected communities from losing their land.

The boundaries for the two sugar concessions were demarcated in a pair of survey maps that, based on their dates of approval by government authorities, seem to have been made sometime in early 2006.[6] These maps were replete with all the trappings of formality, including official-sounding titles (see source information for figure 7.2 below), embossed stamps and signatures of office. These maps were made to impress, if not with their cartography (see below), then at least with the array of authorities whose approval they symbolically marshal.

Figure 7.2 locates the two survey maps in the wider formalization landscape shown in figure 7.1. As the more zoomed-out maps (top-left and bottom) show, the two sugar concessions are located well away from the systematic titling zone farther to the east. And as evidenced by the intermediate-scale map (bottom), the concessions have been carved out of territory just north of a string of villages that line one of western Cambodia's main roads. Zooming in even closer, based on the upper-right map, the concession areas appear to have been demarcated in such a way as to avoid the large areas of dark space as well. The map legends (not shown here) label these dark areas as "evergreen forest," and specify a few different types of white space not visible on the photocopied versions shown here. The legends that classify the areas inside the two concession polygons are shown in table 7.1.

These numbers track closely to those on the final concession contracts and provide strong evidence that the two concessions were formally allocated based on the official rationality that they avoided the high-quality forest represented by the category "evergreen." Once the evergreen forest is removed from the numbers above, the west concession comes out to be 9,410 hectares, while the right measures 9,731. The two concessions allocated to Ly Yong Phat and Chamroon

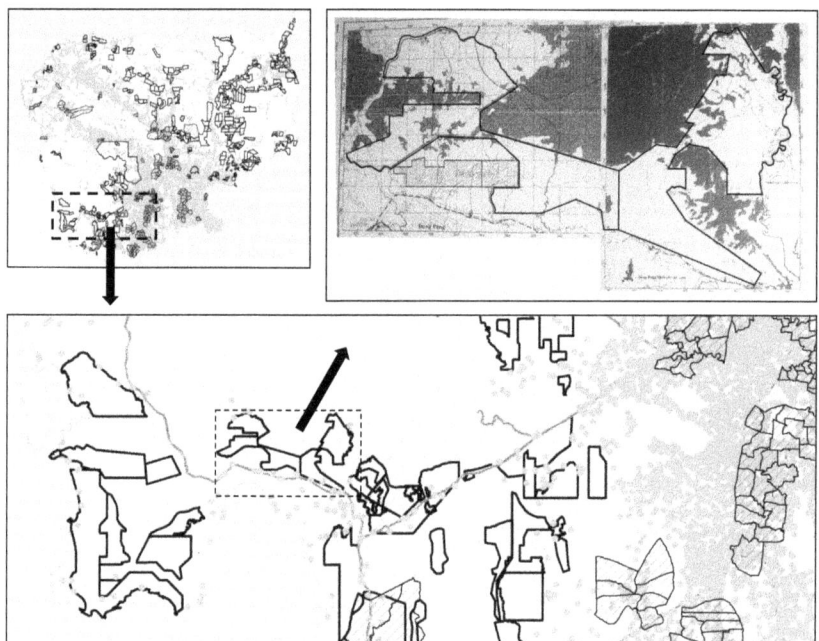

FIGURE 7.2. Location and survey maps of Koh Kong sugar concessions.

Sources: Upper left and bottom: LICADHO (2012) and the World Bank. Upper right, left side: Koh Kong Plantation Co., Ltd., "Land Concession Map for Agro-industrial Crop Investment and Sugar Factory, Koh Kong International Resort Club Cambodia Company, Sre Ambil, Thmar Bang, and Botom Sakor district, Koh Kong Province"; upper right, right side: Koh Kong Sugar Industry Company, Ltd., "Land Concession Map for Agro-industrial Crop Investment and Sugar Factory, Duty-free Shop, Sre Ambil District, Koh Kong Province." Figure by the author.

TABLE 7.1 . Land categorizations in Koh Kong sugar concessions

	WEST (LEFT) CONCESSION	EAST (RIGHT) CONCESSION
Evergreen forest	918 ha	812 ha
Other forest	122 ha	572 ha
Land without forest	9,288 ha	9,159 ha
Total	10,328 ha	10,543 ha

Source: LICADHO (2012) and the World Bank; Koh Kong Plantation Co., Ltd., "Land Concession Map for Agro-industrial Crop Investment and Sugar Factory, Koh Kong International Resort Club Cambodia Company, Sre Ambil, Thmar Bang, and Botom Sakor district, Koh Kong Province; Koh Kong Sugar Industry Company, Ltd., "Land Concession Map for Agro-industrial Crop Investment and Sugar Factory, Duty-free Shop, Sre Ambil District, Koh Kong Province."

Chinthammit, according to the contracts, are 9,400 and 9,700 hectares respectively (Danish Church Aid 2011, 18). What this says is that the formal geography for these two concessions comes primarily from the domain of forestry, and that the official rationale in laying down lines of exclusion was not an effort to avoid smallholder land, but rather to avoid relatively intact forest (also see Dwyer 2013).

In its attention to forest exclusion, the concession demarcation process is notable for doing what LMAP could not: *inventorying large parcels of state land* (Grimsditch and Henderson 2009; Bekhechi and Lund 2009; WBIP 2010). But this "inventory" process is in fact less inventory than *creation* of state land via a selective reading of the landscape. Herein lies a key element of the formalization fiction: property is produced, not merely inventoried or registered, via the formalization process. As evidenced by the categories above, the purpose of the survey was not to address the "state land problem" identified by the FAO et al. (the worry that states "own" large tracts of undemarcated land and thus risk dispossessing smallholders if they act on those rights). Rather, what the survey process shows is an effort to distinguish high-value forest, which Cambodian land law classifies as inalienable "state *public* land," from other areas (classified here as "other forest" and "land without forest") that were classified as "state *private* land," which can legally be alienated to concessions.[7] The formal geography of the Koh Kong concessions thus shows a very different set of priorities being applied to the formalization of hinterland property rights than what is intended by most proponents of formalization. In fact, it shows a different sort of formalization fix entirely. Rather than formalizing property rights *in advance* of large-scale concessions in order to protect smallholders and delimit state claims to land, what we see here is the use of the concession process to *create* state land legibility—just in time for state land to be alienated to private concession holders. Formalization thus becomes a technology for writing smallholders out of the legal picture, creating a "fix" not in the sense of preemptive titling (FAO et al. 2010), but in the sense Harvey (1982) uses to describe capital gaining access to new territory for purposes of surplus disposal. In this case, the territory in question is otherwise occupied and exploited by small-scale land users, and formalization provides a quasi-legal tool to undermine the legitimacy of these uses.

Here, we then see how the just-in-time formalization of state land belies the developmental discourse's presumption that formalization leads to a smooth process of land-rights adjudication. Rather than clarifying already existing land allocations and providing a formal process for transforming or protecting those rights, formalization here erases any premise of local land rights, showing formalization's rights-enhancing premises to be, in this case at least, fictitious. This is evidenced by the fact that just prior to the concession survey, three villages in the eastern ELC were deliberately documented as land under smallholder use through Cambodia's Commune Land Use Planning (CLUP) program. CLUP grew from a donor effort to promote decentralization and deconcentration (D&D) as part of Cambodia's post-conflict reconstruction process; although the process was not widely implemented, one place it *was* deployed was in three of the villages that line the southern edge of the soon-to-be Koh Kong sugar concession.

Figure 7.3 shows one of three village-scale CLUP maps produced in February and March 2006 in an area that ended up just a few months later inside the concessions described above. Using the geo-referencing done by a local NGO,[8] figure 7.3 shows the overlapping claims to the same space, contrasting the simplifying vision of the concession polygon to the variety of smallholder land uses shown in the CLUP map.[9] This attempt at a formalization fix—formalizing local landownership in advance of, and in order to exclude, an outside concession—has proven largely unsuccessful, showing again how the very communities narrated as benefiting from property formalization are often rendered invisible by the cartographic techniques driving the formalization process.

Concessions of this sort thus provide a challenge to the fiction of formalization as a technical remedy to irresponsible investment. Indeed, the case shows the formalization of *state* property rights being deployed for almost opposite ends, as the closely managed relationship between legible and illegible rights is used to paper over the unsavory operations of a plantation company. Managed illegibility paired with the just-in-time formalization of state land is surely not what proponents of formalization have in mind. Formalization thus appears less as an instrument of inclusive growth or as an antidisplacement technology and more as an extension of the neopatrimonial resource politics characteristic of contemporary Cambodia (Hughes 2007; Un and So 2009, 2011; Biddulph 2010;

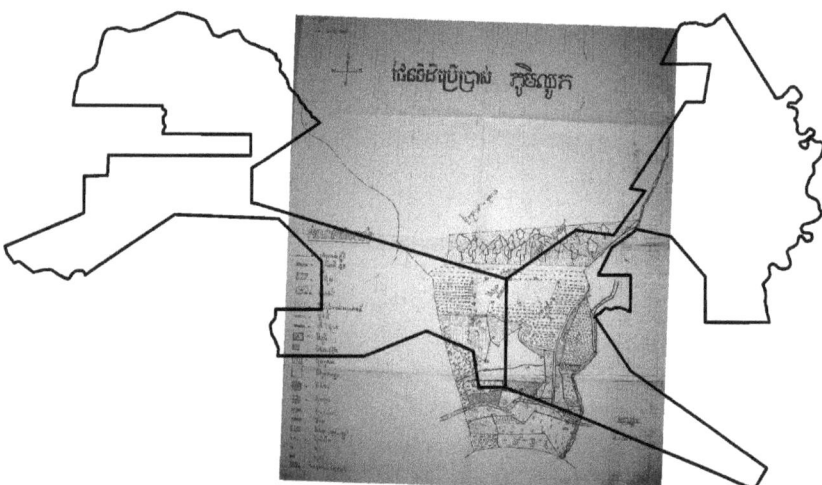

FIGURE 7.3. Commune land-use planning map overlaid with Koh Kong concession.

Sources: CLUP map: Chi Kha Leu Commune, "[Village-Scale] Commune Land Use Planning map" (2006). Concession polygon extracted from LICADHO data set shown in figures 7.1 and 7.2. Figure by the author.

Cock 2010; Springer 2011; Adler and So 2012). Indeed, the legal-cartographic manipulations and exclusions on display above help put the "neo" in neopatrimonialism: they show how elites are able to mobilize the legal-bureaucratic mechanisms of formal state authority in order to support and legitimize dubious business operations.

> [Land] policy requires broad agreement to make it a consensual undertaking which has the support of people in all walks of life, whether they are farmers, fishermen, loggers, builders, soldiers, government officials, lawyers, bankers, tourism operators, industrialists, or workers. It needs the support of minorities and the poor or least visible members of society. With consensus, policy can be implemented in a way that will encourage confidence and security, and foster trust and transparency.
>
> —Council for Land Policy, "Interim Paper on Strategy of Land Policy Framework"

This chapter has presented three lines of evidence through which Cambodia's experience with property rights formalization challenges the fiction of formalization as a technical fix to land conflict. Beginning at the national scale, I examined the geography of systematic land titling and used evidence released in the wake of the Boeung Kak conflict to support critics of the country's land titling project who have argued that it has focused on the wrong areas. This section highlighted the competing priorities—and by extension, political questions—that are rolled into formalization projects; it also reviewed the mechanisms that, in Cambodia's case at least, were used to keep titling and concessions in geographically separate domains.

I then examined these politics of uneven formalization in more detail by focusing on the problem of selective and uneven property rights at the scale of a single agribusiness concession. This case, of sugar concessions in Koh Kong Province, showed how the formal geography of concession surveying can be used to paper over a land grab using the legal discourse of state land. It highlighted the difficulties of using democratic and locally grounded forms of land formalization in a context where the arena of "the formal" is dominated by state-connected business interests, although in doing so, it also pointed to an arena of struggle that remains open to regulatory reform and, perhaps, citizen pressure. Although it is impossible to make across-the-board recommendations, the example of commune-scale land-use planning illustrates the types of land formalization that might be put to use, in combination with better regulatory controls on large-scale investment, to protect common resources and the rights of the socially and politically vulnerable.

The third line, illustrated by the chapter's opening sketch, highlights the ways in which these sorts of cartographic politics hinge on wider political questions of citizenship, enrolling not only the poor and landless but also "people in all walks of life" (epigraph above). The "education" of Uncle San should remind us of the need to pursue the land grab debate beyond legal geography per se, and into the arenas of popular education, social movements, civil society, and donor assistance. Only by taking uneven property formalization into these domains *off the map* can the politics of formalization, and problems of unmapped state land more generally, be adequately confronted.

Finally, a coda: notwithstanding the substantial work that has gone into bringing Cambodia's land problems under greater public scrutiny, it is worth pointing out that the study that most alarmed the World Bank's Inspection Panel in 2010 was never published. This was a study conducted in early 2006, which found that "at least a fifth of households (19.6 percent) in thirteen of the adjudication areas visited [were] being adversely affected by the systematic land titling process, usually through the refusal to register land in household possession or use." The reason for this exclusion was that "the [project] demarcation teams flatly refused to register either their 'claim or possessionary rights' to some of 'their' land due to it being State land" (O'Leary 2006, cited in World Bank Inspection Panel [WBIP] 2010, 49). In light of the analysis presented here, this should not be surprising. Formalization may be part of a sustainable fix to the problem of land grabbing. But without critical scrutiny of past efforts, and without addressing the politics of state land head on, naïvely deployed formalization efforts will surely only produce more of the same problems, or worse.

8

REGULARIZATION AND THE FICTIONS OF PLANNING "UNAUTHORIZED DELHI"

D. Asher Ghertner

This chapter explores mimicry as a planning practice central to the development and occupation of what is rapidly becoming the most popular neighborhood form in Delhi, and indeed much of metropolitan India—the unauthorized colony. Built on land beyond the development area of the master plan, these periurban settlements house more than 30 percent of Delhi's population, or around 6 million people (Sheikh and Banda 2014). They form as developers consolidate rural farmland and cut plots for private sale. Varying drastically in their size and income level, the category "unauthorized colony" encompasses everything from peripheral neighborhoods with services worse than those found in slums to vast, manicured enclaves composed of elite "farmhouses"—off-grid manors where the rich and famous go to escape the city's bustle, building codes, and property tax. Although land owners in unauthorized colonies possess formal documents showing detailed payments for their property—thereby making them more secure than squatter settlements—these transactions cannot be registered with the state because unauthorized colonies are not included in the city's master plan, or because they exist on land not zoned for residential use (Bhan 2013).

From their earliest beginnings, middle-class unauthorized colonies mimic the appearance of planned neighborhoods through use of both the same hierarchy of spatial units (individual streets form pockets or blocks, which fit into sectors or phases of a wider colony), as well as the same materials and design elements that make up what has historically been their principal architectural form: the bungalow (see figure 8.1). Developers mimic in this way to appeal to middle-class aesthetic standards, but also with a partial eye toward the possibility

FIGURE 8.1. A bungalow in a middle-class unauthorized colony in South Delhi, borrowing architectural and design elements (tiered iron gates, Grecian balustrades, single-person balconies) common in planned Delhi colonies. Photograph by author, June 8, 2013.

of future "regularization," a contested process by which town planners—often at the behest of politicians—retroactively approve the layout plans for unauthorized colonies. The idea behind regularization is to attempt to align colonies and individual buildings within them with planning norms and building codes to which they have never formally been subjected: unauthorized colonies are "unauthorized" not necessarily because they violate code (although they often do), but rather because they exist in areas not subject to plan oversight or code enforcement. Mimicking code in anticipation of regularization is thus a prefigurative act of producing the appearance of being "planned" in areas that have never been evaluated for their plannedness. The regularization process allows unauthorized colonies to be registered with the revenue department, thereby making their residents' property titles legal and providing eligibility for state service provision such as water, sanitation, road paving, and street lighting—which must be privately arranged prior to regularization (Zimmer 2012). So-called "regularized unauthorized colonies" remain officially unplanned based on the fact that they remain outside the city's development area, but they benefit from improved neighborhood stability and services, as well as associated property price increases.

The increase in ground rent potential delivered via regularization sustains the wider commodity fiction that land should be organized according to the logics of the market. This marks a deviation from the longer standing valuation of peri-urban land in India for agricultural uses, as a green belt expected to deliver environmental amenities to the built-up area of the city, and for fostering extant forms of India's culturally hallowed village life. Regularization sustains land commodification but is also a product of that commodification, to the extent that rising ground rents and the capital invested in sustaining them generate political pressure to secure legal protections that only regularization can offer. Each new piped water connection or sewer line laid via regularization, in this sense, is an infrastructure that sustains the commodified future of the urban periphery.

Unauthorized colonies represent a preeminent form of improvisational urbanism to which increasing numbers of people—lower-income and middle-class alike—have turned.[1] Settled as they are on rural land and with densities far exceeding the village infrastructures to which they only sometimes have access, everything from the plotting of individual housing lots, to the paving of roads, to the installation of water lines, to the disposal of household sewage must be built up incrementally in unauthorized colonies—a pattern of self-organization characteristic of the "auto-constructed" peripheries prominent across much of the world (Caldeira 2016; Harms 2011; Silver 2014; Zanfi 2013). This range of improvised neighborhood-making practices represents a multifaceted and decentralized planning process oriented toward balancing a range of competing interests. The developers who have historically initiated unauthorized development—often called land colonizers, given their role in aggregating village lands into the residential "colony" model typical of Delhi (Tiwari and Rao 2017)—often hire architects to prepare layout plans that superficially resemble those in planned colonies. However, key requirements of neighborhood design are often left out of these plans so as to maximize the area of private, sellable lots. Space for schools, parks, and other social infrastructure tends to be limited, and developers often squeeze road widths and setbacks, thereby constraining community livability.

Unauthorized colonies are thus designed outside of planning norms, but by selectively borrowing from and copying those norms, they reveal them to be unstable elements of city making, not fixed rules or a rigid code (the formal) from which informal practices necessarily deviate or spill over. The regularization of unauthorized colonies is an historic action of acknowledging that such norms are an impossible achievement for most of Delhi, and indeed most of urban India (Bhide 2015; Cowan 2018; Ranganathan 2014; Sundaresan 2017). But, regularization also maintains the performance of planning by affirming the power of the expert to continue to uphold those impossible norms in as-yet unregularized areas. Regularization thus authorizes a copy or approximation of the not-quite or never-fully-realized norm, showing the imagination and making of the city to be founded on the historically and geographically specific capacity to copy, draw on the power of the other, and even become the other—what Walter Benjamin (1999) calls the mimetic faculty. This mimetic faculty, as I set out to show, is central to planning in contemporary India, informing professional standards as much as community interpretations of "authentic" form, and thereby showing the formal city and the planning instruments presumed to underpin it to operate as what Ananya Roy (2009, 84), writing about the "impossibility" of planning in India, provocatively calls "fictions, moments of fixture in otherwise volatile, ambiguous, and uncertain systems" of city making.

Treating planning as a regulatory fiction, or set of idealized and reified norms (Haraway 1991, 135), means examining planning as "a set of repeated acts within a highly rigid regulatory frame that congeal over time to produce the appearance of substance, of a natural sort of being" (Butler 1990, 33). According to Judith Butler, who theorizes the regulatory fiction of heteronormativity, it is the reiteration of norms that produce that which they name. Her classic example is of the midwife cry, "it's a girl," which is not merely a reflection of a biological given, but also a performative act, binding a gender onto the body (Butler 1993). To the extent that performativity, or the reiteration of those norms, "acquires an act-like status in the present, it conceals or dissimulates the conventions of which it is a repetition" (ibid., 12). This is the case whether the norms in question pertain to the assignation of a fixed gender to a body or the aesthetic and spatial criteria for delineating legitimate residential land uses—things like a house's setback from a road or the adequate amount of green space for a neighborhood. While the regulatory fiction to which Butler refers is "the heterosexual original," we might say that the plan, as a model to which all land uses are expected to conform, acquires a similar natural being, maintaining the constructed distinction between planned and unplanned, formal and informal, on which land price differentials depend in rapidly urbanizing areas. While the discursive forms through which heteronormativity and city planning are built are obviously radically different, as are the bodily stakes and sites of contestation for each, Butler's reading of the "original" as, ultimately, itself a copy offers a generative method for following the performance of planning. As she puts it (Butler 1990, 31), "The replication of heterosexual constructs in non-heterosexual frames brings into relief the utterly constructed status of the so-called heterosexual origin. Thus, gay is to straight *not* as copy is to the original, but, rather, as copy is to copy."

That planning in India's capital city operates as a regulatory fiction is most evident in the official acknowledgment that more than three-quarters of Delhi properties are "unauthorized" (Government of Delhi 2009). This includes properties that violate official land-use categories by being located in squatter settlements and unauthorized colonies, as well as the huge number of buildings in planned colonies that violate building codes through illegal additions, faulty layout plans, sidewalk or setback encroachments, or other structural or service violations now widespread across urban India (Sundaresan 2017). The fact that the outcome of Delhi's extensive planning apparatus has been a largely unauthorized city, and the further fact that the formal planning apparatus has become increasingly attuned to regularizing that unauthorized city, reveals the extent to which planning is implicated in and even productive of the informal (Verma 2002; Bhan 2015; Ghertner 2015a). The fiction of a distinction between the formal and informal is hence maintained by performative acts of naming that reify a difference that has become materially difficult to uphold, but that is responsible for producing a highly uneven land system defined by inflated ground rents and premium services in the "planned" core and strained social infrastructures and planned insecurities elsewhere.

Much of the literature on urban informality and vernacular planning frames the informal through the lenses of resistance and insurgency (Bayat 2007; Benjamin 2008; Cruz 2007; Miraftab 2009) or else presumes that planning "sweeps the poor [and informal] away" (Watson 2009). Examining planning as a regulatory fiction, in contrast, skirts the question of normative intention (Is the state "pro-poor" enough? Is regularization a product of sovereign will or a popular triumph over it?) and allows us to attend to the routine performances—by state agents and everyday citizens alike—that while not necessarily aimed at subverting official rules, sometimes achieve that end. This is the notion of political agency Butler's theory of performativity offers, where resistance is not the willed practice of an individual seeking to challenge a norm, but a performative effect of a norm's iterability, wherein repetitions take on unexpected or infelicitous valences, failing to assume their expected pattern. Butler's examples of such infelicitous performances include parodic repetitions of gender norms such as "cultural practices of drag, cross-dressing, and the sexual stylization of butch/femme identities" (1990, 137), as well as a range of performances that simply fail to reinscribe heteronormativity. In the context of unauthorized colonies explored below, we find that the mimicry of official norms has a similar parodic effect, even when executed by planning experts seemingly operating within felicitous conditions—that is, the field of official planning.

To explore how urban mimicry sustains and mocks the regulatory fiction of land-use planning in Delhi, I build on four months of fieldwork carried out in 2013–15 in the Chhatarpur area of South Delhi, where the most rapidly growing middle-class unauthorized colonies exist today. I specifically examine three different planning spaces, which together show how the making of unauthorized colonies emerges through the improvisational practices by which diverse actors—from developers, to homeowners, to town planners—mimic an original plan that exists only through its many scattered imitations. The first space I examine is the town planning department, where planners compelled by pressures to regularize unauthorized colonies create maps depicting those colonies in conformance with planning norms while knowing these "imaginary maps" will never be implemented. Drawing hypothetical roads, parks, and dispensaries, state planning becomes a practice centered on the reproduction of an open fiction. The second space is the site of the unauthorized building, where multistory apartments on designated agricultural and village lands are demolished not because they violate building code and zoning rules—which all such structures do—but because they are as-yet unoccupied. Mimicking occupancy, developers respond by installing air conditioning units, hanging laundry, and adding religious iconography on vacant or incomplete buildings to avoid site demolition. Surface embellishments and signs of occupation thus become design features central to successful project completion, showing aesthetic appearance to be potentially as significant as calculative protocols of building inspection—such as the measurement of setback or the determination of floor area ratios—for the adjudication of legality. The third space consists of the improvised water systems of unauthorized colonies, which mimic state systems and develop through collaboration with state agents, even though such systems are illegal in unauthorized colonies. The postregularization ability to network this privately built infrastructure into state water lines raises the question of when the copy becomes the original. Taken together, these three spaces show the planning of unauthorized colonies to mock power as much as they centralize or appropriate it. India's most rapidly urbanizing lands today are hence expanding through a regulatory fiction that stigmatizes and threatens "unplanned" areas, but simultaneously provides avenues for them to participate in India's expanding game of speculative urbanism (Goldman 2011), wherein the legitimacy of land development is based on ground rent potential as much as legality or formal planning codes.

Space 1—Town Planning

In the summer of 2012 the beleaguered chief minister of Delhi, Sheila Dikshit, ordered the issuance of a plan for regularizing Delhi's unauthorized colonies. This was not the first time that a chief minister pandered to the unauthorized colony vote through the offer of regularization, but it was a uniquely ambitious one. Whereas the town planning department in the municipal corporation had previously been charged with finalizing regularization lists on the basis of existing regularization guidelines, in this case, the chief minister took the lead, issuing her own list of 895 "regularizable" unauthorized colonies without any consideration of their relationship with regularization guidelines, which historically put in place terms for bringing unauthorized colonies into approximate alignment with master plan norms.[2] The town planning department was subsequently handed this list and given the new task of evaluating the layout plans for colonies already deemed regularizable. While some unauthorized colonies already had layout plans, most did not, and once unauthorized colonies were added to the regularization list, their resident welfare associations—informal governance bodies that typically organize local service delivery and interface with elected officials and bureaucrats (Zimmer 2012)—were given a mere fifteen days to submit layout plans for approval.

I visited the town planning department in the summer of 2013, just months after the chief minister's list was transferred to its chief town planner and his team. Staff at the time were busy looking over the layout plans for unauthorized colonies that had already been declared "regularizable" to the plan. Put another way, planners were seeking ways of depicting unplanned neighborhoods with faulty and hastily assembled layout plans as aligning with town planning requirements. As an engineer in the department told me, "We haven't found a single layout plan done properly. Most of them have basic errors of scale, North/South, colony boundaries, and the size of plots." The whole process, he said, "is entirely against planning principles" (personal communication, June 5, 2013).

Each time new regularization guidelines have been established, a new date has been set by which time colonies have to be built up in order to be eligible for regularization. In 1977, when Delhi's first wave of regularizations took place, this cutoff date was set at 1975. The construction cutoff date was later advanced to 1992, then to 1997, and then to 2002. To be eligible for regularization, colonies must have at least 50 percent of their area built up by the cutoff date, as confirmed by aerial photographs. There are three main problems with the notion of 50 percent built-up area, however, which helps set the stage for understanding unauthorized colony development as a process of simultaneous mimicry and mockery. First, aerial photographs are not always accurate or comprehensive. Second, the definition of "built-up area" has changed over time. In unauthorized colonies, even though most plots are established and sold off at a very early stage, they often remain vacant until land prices rise and resident welfare associations form and can organize basic infrastructure provision. In 2008, as part of the chief minister's effort to win the unauthorized colony vote, the definition of "built-up area" was relaxed, such that if somebody owned a large plot, so long as they had constructed even a small shed on it, that entire plot could be included within the measure of the overall colony's built-up area. As a result of this change, colonies or sectors of colonies with minimal development saw their property prices skyrocket as the promise of state services and property registration came on offer.

The third problem with the cutoff date is that politicians regularly declare that they will eventually advance it, so that even if a colony were to miss the 2008 regularization list, its residents could rest assured that they would make the next list once neighborhood development had progressed. This indeed happened in 2015 when the upstart Aam Aadmi Party won the state assembly election, forcing Dikshit's Congress Party out of office. The new Aam Aadmi Party government advanced the regularization cutoff date from 2002 up to 2008, making scores of unauthorized colonies suddenly "regularizable." This condition, what Amita Bhide (2015) calls "the regularizing state" (also see Zanfi 2013), allows land owners in unauthorized colonies to avoid regulatory oversight, taxation, and building codes early in the development of a colony, only to later be regularized, at which point town planners are forced to somehow reconcile unauthorized construction with a planning and building regime that these colonies, by their very definition, violate.

Can we describe this as a "state of exception," as much of the urban informality literature might urge us to do? Is this process best described as a condition under which the state suspends the rule of law to build up sovereign command and retain discretionary authority? Perhaps, but from the perspective of state officials, regularization appears anything but a coherent strategy to build sovereign authority and synoptic control. Consider the perspective of the chief town planner in 2013, a soft-spoken man who kept a copy of Delhi's land-use plan stretched out beneath glass on the surface of his desk. Expressing deep frustration with the regularization process, the planner half-jokingly told me of his plans to write a book upon retirement called "How to Unplan a City" (personal communication, July 3, 2013).

At the time of my visits to his office in the summer of 2013, the chief town planner noted that most of the layout plans he had received from unauthorized colonies on the regularization list suffered from major problems, including basic errors of cardinal direction and colony boundary identification. But, he was nonetheless expected to give these colonies provisional approval. How did he and his staff of senior planners proceed? How did they reconcile hundreds of plan-violating settlements with a plan they were schooled and hired to uphold and even venerate?

They began by taking the unauthorized colonies' submitted layout plans and overlaying them on government-supplied aerial photographs and land-use data. The problem is that government records at the time were based on a 2007 aerial survey, which often indicated adequate space for the social infrastructure—such as parking and green space—required to meet colony layout norms. However, when the planners (or, more often, the universities to whom they contracted this work) visited the colonies to confirm the ground reality, they almost universally found that the areas they had assumed to be vacant were already built up.[3] Instead of trying to reconcile such discrepancies and being dragged into an extensive ground-truthing process, these planners proceeded by acting as if the reality in the present was the same as was displayed in the 2007 photograph. In other words, they made plans that resembled not reality, but a photograph of the recent past, reproducing a fiction as a means of accepting (or ignoring) the factual obstacles on the ground. This took place through the simple design practice of drawing traces on digitized versions of the layout plans, producing hypothetical maps for these colonies that mimicked master plan norms for such things as road width, green space, and medical dispensaries, knowing full well that existing land development and construction already violated the maps. This was done by marking with dashed lines "proposed roads" wide enough to meet code—the irony being that such roads would have required the demolition of the hundreds of structures already built up to the edges of the existing, narrow roads.

Consider, for example, Shiv Ram Park Extension, an unauthorized colony located in West Delhi, the layout plan for which is shown in figure 8.2. The heavily dashed lines going from the bottom-left to the upper-center of the map, indicated as a "proposed master planned road" on the legend, show that the colony encroaches approximately ten meters onto what is supposed to be a thirty-six-meter-wide main trunk road. The thin, dashed lines on the inner-colony roads

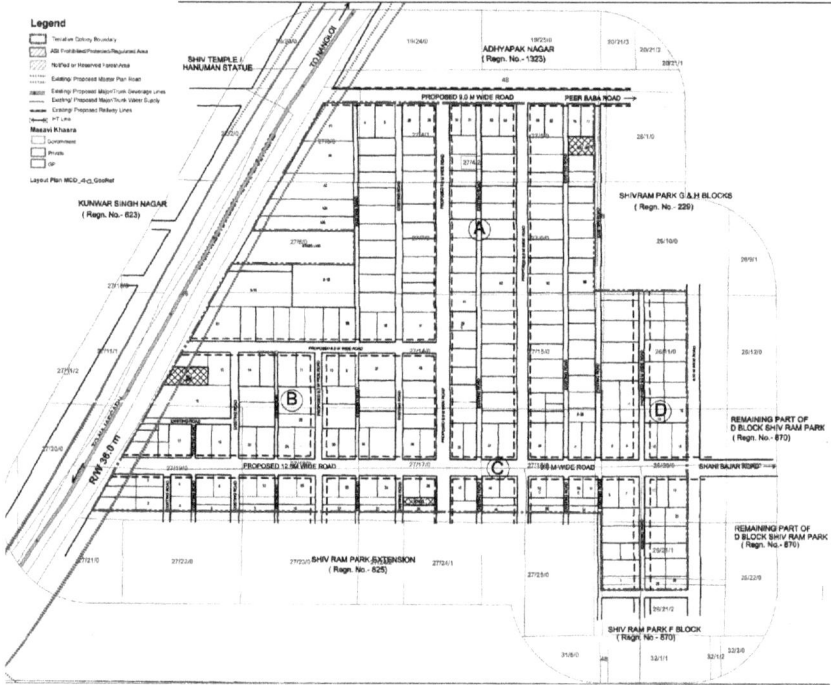

FIGURE 8.2. Section of "Scrutinized Layout Plan for Shiv Ram Park Extension," an unauthorized colony in West Delhi, produced by the town planning department, Municipal Corporation of Delhi. The dashed lines shown inside the colony boundaries indicate where proposed, code-conforming roads would be located. Given that most structures are built up to the edges of the existing roads, nearly every colony structure would have to be at least partially demolished to fulfill the "proposal."

Source: "Unauthorised Colonies Cell," Department of Urban Development, Government of the National Capital Territory of Delhi

show where existing six- and nine-meter-wide roads are "proposed" to be widened into nine- and twelve-meter-wide roads, respectively. Were these proposals to ever be implemented, every structure in the colony would have to be at least partially demolished, since nearly all structures, as shown in the aerial photographs that accompanied the layout plan, were built up to the very edge of the existing, narrower roads.

The planners next added to their layout plans necessary social infrastructure—such as parks and medical dispensaries—to what appeared as vacant or unused lands on the layout plan. However, these vacant lands were in almost all cases privately owned and were often already built up by the time the planners made their amendments. As the chief planner told me about this process,

> On paper we do it, for the sake of planning. [The Delhi Development] Authority [which prepares and maintains the Delhi master plan] will say "ensure all these things [like roads and parks] are there [on the layout plan]." If we ever try to implement the layout plan, the politician [who represents the people] will come and do *dharna* [sit-in]. So we are left making this layout plan knowing it will never become reality. Ours is a paper game.

And so, town planning in Delhi operates through the production of fake maps, which mimic planning norms but bear little resemblance to reality, showing how one key aspect of urban land use—the location of social infrastructures and the functional organization of neighborhood space—operates not as a monumental state performance but rather as a tentative representation of an ideal state that is simultaneously disavowed; it is a paper game.

I am here drawing on postcolonial theorist Homi Bhabha (1994, 122), according to whom "mimicry emerges as the representation of a difference that is itself a process of disavowal." In Delhi, the representation of difference emerges as the exemplary form of the unauthorized colony, whose very condition of being is its definition as "unplanned," and yet whose surface resemblance to planned neighborhoods—which by the early 2000s also featured widespread building and plan violations—and "regularizability" call into question what, indeed, is so different about it. "In order to be effective," Bhabha writes, "mimicry must always produce its slippage, its excess, its difference." This slippage gives the mimicking subject—the one who copies—an incomplete and virtual presence. Bhabha writes about mimicry as a British colonial discourse through which Indian colonial subjects were brought into the sphere of liberal law, but never fully integrated. The virtual presence of the mimicking subject, in other words, is defined by his position both inside and outside the law, by the condition of being *similar*, but never same. In Delhi's urban planning space, this virtual presence is visible in the dashed lines outlining the virtual road that upholds the planning code but that will never meet it. For Bhabha, mimicry is an "ironic compromise" that conflicts with the assumptions that authorize it. We see this in the town planning department, where the planner himself mimics the plan he was trained and hired to uphold. Urban mimicry in unauthorized Delhi seeks resemblance, but in failing to achieve this perfect condition, or in rendering transparent the imitability of the original, also mocks that original. Or, as the anthropologist Taussig (1993, xiii) puts it, "The wonder of mimesis lies in the copy drawing on the character and power of the original, to the point whereby the representation may even assume that character and that power."

As the unauthorized colony "passes," via regularization, the power of the original diminishes, as does the system of rules on which it depends. The planned colony hence becomes itself a fiction, as unplanned development more and more acquires the backing of the planning apparatus and, as we shall see, begins to itself mimic the unauthorized colony. Informality here is not a deviation from the formal, then, but rather its inappropriate performance. While declared "unplanned" from the beginning, the drafting of layout plans, the allocation of social infrastructure, the application of building codes, and the ground-truthing and plan verification steps all function as reiterations of planning that authorize unauthorized colonies as somehow "regular." In gaining this authorization, though, they simultaneously mock the plan for its impossibility on the ground. Delhi's rapidly expanding peri-urban developments necessarily generate these inappropriate performances, not as excesses, but as essential components of growth, constituting the leading edge of an urban revolution that carries with it the promises of mass housing and endless profitability, and that arguably hold the Indian political economy together today (Levien 2018; Ghertner 2015a; Searle 2016).

For Bhabha, mimicry's success depends precisely on the proliferation of what he calls *inappropriate objects*, which ultimately also ensure its failure. Bhabha's point is that efforts at appropriation, be they by those in power or those marginal to it, cannot evade this menace—mimicry always produces a mocking double, or in Butler's parlance, infelicitous acts. In Delhi, the unauthorized yet "regularizable" colony is the plan's double—a figure that has a virtual presence within planning but whose inherent unplannedness destabilizes and mocks planning power. This is evident in the fact that, while unauthorized colonies are unplanned in the sense that they do not conform with code, they are very much an expected outcome of planning. Delhi's planning authority, the Delhi Development Authority, after all, has approved historically far fewer planned housing units than the master plan itself projected to be necessary, leaving a large mass of the population to rely necessarily on unauthorized development (Verma 2002; Ghertner 2005). Unauthorized colonies, in other words, are an internal product of the planning process, what Bhan (2013) calls a "planned illegality." The regularization of unauthorized colonies confirms that planning depends on state performances that merely imitate, but that cannot replicate, the plan, and that the viability of the plan itself rests on ongoing inappropriate performances. For this mimicry to work, it must be open to a number of such performances, including at the scale of the unauthorized building.

Space 2—The Unauthorized Building

In the wake of a rise in property prices in unauthorized colonies that received regularization guarantees in 2008 and 2012, a boom took place in the construction and sale of "builder flats"—apartments constructed by outside developers in eight-, twelve-, or sixteen-unit, multistory high-rises. This building form emerged in these colonies well after the 2002 construction cutoff date in place at the time. Such structures have contributed to a massive increase in density (and associated congestion and infrastructure problems) in the middle-class unauthorized colonies where they have become prominent. It is now common to see what are formally categorized as agricultural or village lands dominated by five-story apartment buildings, with undeveloped agricultural land and older bungalows of the sort shown in figure 8.1 flanking and interspersed with such dense residential growth. Roads have since become jammed with parked cars and are prone to waterlogging due to limited drainage; water systems are more strained; and resident welfare associations now divide up once integrated neighborhoods to define territorial control and to try to protect local service provision. Even within the commodified, privately plotted space of the bungalowed colony—the dominant built form of the middle-class unauthorized colony until the late 2000s—the builder flat represented an intensified expression of rent-driven development, a revaluation of the social function and image of land—a deepening of the commodity fiction—that excised the bucolic vision of the rural farmhouse that drew many early residents to these areas in the first place.

Responding to this escalation of illegal construction, in 2011 the lieutenant governor of Delhi—an official appointed by the central government to a state-level oversight role that is independent of the elected chief minister (who is the head of the state government)—constituted special task forces for each city district charged with "acting against unauthorized/unsafe constructions whether on public or private lands."[4] Over the following two years, the special task force in South Delhi, where I was carrying out fieldwork at the time, ordered the demolition of hundreds of buildings under construction in unauthorized colonies (see figure 8.3) (also see Yardley 2013). In response to serious complaints by occupants of builder flats whose homes were threatened by demolition and who claimed to have unknowingly bought what were illegal flats from small-scale and often difficult-to-track developers, the task force assumed the position that once a structure was built, sold off, and occupied, it could not on humanitarian grounds be demolished. The Delhi high court similarly granted relief to individuals who had purchased finished flats from builders, arguing that liability for plan violation lay with the builder, not the purchaser.

FIGURE 8.3. A mix of vacant lots (foreground), finished single-family homes (middle ground, right), and partially demolished "builder flats" (background) in the outskirts of a middle-class unauthorized colony in the Chhatarpur area of South Delhi during the 2013 summer of demolitions. Photograph by author, June 19, 2013.

Developers, recognizing this occupancy loophole, hence began mimicking occupation. They did so by transforming their construction approach where possible so that after the basic shells of their buildings were completed, they would quickly finish the ground floors so that they could be sold, sometimes at a concessionary rate to try to add a building occupant while the upper floors were being finalized over subsequent months. Finished ground floors, replete with marble cladding or faux brick—common middle-class design elements used to cover up or personalize poured concrete—or Hindu markings indicative that a home-warming ceremony had taken place, thus became visible in buildings even before elevators were installed or upper-floor windows and balconies were added. In multiple buildings I visited in a rapidly developing, middle-class unauthorized colony in the Chhatarpur area, where I spent most of my fieldwork time, security guards took advantage of developers' offers of free housing and moved their families into ground- or first-floor flats or parking spaces, usually before running water or electricity was supplied or a bathroom had been built. Occupancy, from the builder's perspective, was secured.

When such efforts to secure occupancy were not enough to deter the task-force-initiated demolition crews from attacking the upper floors with sledgehammers, developers began a practice of affixing satellite television dishes and air conditioners on unfinished or unsold upper-floor units. In some cases, they hung laundry over balcony rails to produce the appearance of occupancy (see figure 8.4).

Developers hence found a way to complete building projects through a simple semiotic shift: embellishing the facades of their structures with the resemblance of occupation. Installing family names on doors and including religious iconography in entranceways were other design techniques that signaled that the basic threshold of occupancy had been met. Hanging strings of green chilies and lemons or displaying masks of the goddess Kali—common Hindu techniques of warding off the evil eye (*buri nazar*)—proved to be materially effective, warding off building inspectors and task force charges of unauthorized construction. Urban design of the most elementary and household sort hence emerged as a most effective tool of illegal building and speculative real estate. Similar improvisations in neighborhood design and construction operate through infrastructure provision in unauthorized colonies as well, the third planning space I discuss.

Space 3—Incremental Infrastructure

One of the greatest benefits of regularization for unauthorized colony households is the promise of future state services, especially drinking water, stormwater drainage, and sewerage. In the years before regularization, though, households must organize and plan for the delivery of these basic services on their own. For lower-income unauthorized colonies, this poses challenges similar to those found in slums: household budgets are stretched to pay for private water delivery, and communicable diseases are higher than they should be due to such neighborhoods' reliance on open drains. Armed with resources far greater than their poorer counterparts, better-off unauthorized colonies, such as those featuring larger bungalows and builder flats of the sorts shown in figures 8.1 and 8.4, improvise their own infrastructures.

Delhi has a rapidly declining water table, and to discourage the formation of new unauthorized colonies, in 2010 the state government passed an order effectively banning the drilling of bore wells there. Yet, in wealthier unauthorized colonies, new wells were being dug regularly during my fieldwork. In the

FIGURE 8.4. A vacant building's "occupied flats," as semiotically evidenced by the presence of air conditioning units and laundry on balcony railings. Photograph by author, December 28, 2014.

colony in Chhatarpur where I spent most of my time, I counted fifteen bore wells, reported to me to be six-hundred-feet deep, pumping water twenty-four hours a day. Many of these illegal wells were overseen by water board officials, who trained local security guards to operate a series of "gate walls" that switched the flow of water from one lane to another according to need. How did water board officials come to operate bore wells in neighborhoods barred from bore well construction?

The officials had what they consider a well-reasoned answer to this question, one in which they—the face of the state—were simultaneously inside and outside of the state (see Ghertner 2017 for an analysis of the new state spaces such improvisational urbanism inaugurates). The local member of the legislative assembly, a politician elected into Delhi's state government, who represented the area, paid the officials using his discretionary fund, a non–water board source. As water board employees, they operated the bore wells legitimately, in the sense that as specialized state officials, they had the competence and know-how to run bore wells without significant technical or political interruption. The water board could claim noninvolvement, however, by noting that none of its funds were allocated to unauthorized colony wells. As state officials who first exited the formal employ of the state, but then reconstituted a cloak of state authority around their practices, these officials improvised a vast, informal infrastructure that provided reliable ground water to thousands of households. Resembling Anand's (2017, 188) observation from Mumbai that leaking pipes can enable state formation, here a state was engineered for the purposes of leaking technical capacity (and groundwater) out of official spaces of oversight and into the unauthorized city.

Regularization brings with it the promise that these colonies will become eligible for municipal water supply, but old, privately built water lines do not always become redundant when this occurs. When extensive excavation is required to lay new pipes or when buildings are at risk of structural compromise from digging, state water mains can instead be linked into existing, self-built neighborhood pipes, which have almost always been designed to code, often with the oversight of water board engineers. Most middle-class households in Delhi's planned neighborhoods use bore wells as informal/illegal backups to the irregular and intermittent municipal water that is their formal/legal source of water. Unauthorized water systems have an inverse relationship with the formal/informal: an illegal system first mimics state systems and then becomes redefined/repurposed as planned urban development, serving as the very vehicle for state water delivery, a perfect example of the mimetic capacity of the copy not just to draw on the power of the other, but also become the other (Benjamin 1999).

Contemporary Delhi, like so many postcolonial metropolises today, is a city where the political energies of the unauthorized peripheries are absorbing increasing state bureaucratic attention. Accelerating regularization—which retroactively authorizes unplanned growth—marks a similar shift in the focus of the planning apparatus from the core to the periphery. It further reveals that urban planning in the postcolony might be best understood as part of a mimetic drama in which dominant rules of neighborhood form and layout are inappropriately performed. This takes place not as a deliberate strategy to challenge those rules, but as a form of "symbolic piracy" (see Romberg 2005)—a borrowing of signs and rituals of legitimacy—that encompasses them. In other words, through the vernacular forms of borrowing evident in unauthorized colonies, rules of neighborhood form and organization intended to exclude the informal and the "unplanned" are rechanneled to advance the development of an unintended settlement type. The picture of informality that emerges from these colonies, then, is not of a monumental state performance or a strategic suspension of the law to enhance state discretionary authority to do as it wishes, but rather of an improvisational mechanism for pulling a diverse range of practices into the field of urban planning. Be it the production of virtual regularization maps, the installation of an air conditioner on an unauthorized building, or the private employment of state workers, Delhi's unauthorized colonies mimic the formal city, but in so doing extend a land-use pattern that threatens the core principles of planning.

But what is the alternative? Where else would the 6 million inhabitants of unauthorized colonies go for shelter? What political rifts might open up in such a highly unequal city, where there is an estimated 400,000 unit shorting of affordable housing, were the prospect of unauthorized property ownership foreclosed for everyone from those just escaping life in slums to those with architectural dreams of secluded, gated oases? Urban mimicry of the sorts evident in Delhi's unauthorized colonies hence represent an "ironic compromise," in Bhaba's terms, that conflicts with the assumptions that authorize it. This is the regulatory fiction of planning in contemporary India. Rather than denying or overturning the original, such performances reveal the extent to which the original depends on the copy in the end. Planned Delhi cannot exist without unplanned Delhi; the city cannot grow without regularization. And yet, as Bhabha reminds us, mimicry always risks slipping into mockery, a worry recently articulated by the supreme court of India.

In a high-profile case focused on the question of incorporating regularized unauthorized colonies into the master plan via a plan amendment, the supreme court appointed an *amicus curiae*, or friend of the court, to assist it in evaluating the technicalities of regularization. In an April 2018 hearing, the amicus curiae, a senior lawyer, noted how the failure to enforce building codes in unauthorized colonies was beginning to lead residents of planned neighborhoods to flout rules similarly, adding illegal structures to their rooftops, encroaching on required road setbacks, or converting gardens into living spaces. In other words, he openly worried that "planned" development was mimicking unauthorized colonies, a practice that threatened to lay bare the regulatory fiction of planned development. Even imperfect copies, as Taussig (1993, 17) reminds us, can be effective in acquiring the power of the original. In Delhi, a copy considered grotesque by most trained planners has become the model for increasing floor area ratios and ground rent everywhere. "At least, even if they want to regularise these unauthorized colonies, there should be some sanctity [of planning]," the amicus curiae told the bench. "The situation today is that there is lawlessness in these colonies," he continued, warning that "lawlessness" would become the norm that might spread into the core of all planning (quoted in *The Hindu* 2018). As Space 1—Town Planning above shows, the expert domain of planning has already become marked by a considerable degree of lawlessness, but for the regulatory fiction to go on, the performance of law must endure. And so, the supreme court bench ordered the relevant authorities to enforce building codes in regularized unauthorized colonies, as if the country's oldest planning authority needed its apex court to remind it of its basic duties! Lest fiction becomes fabulation—departing from the conventions of realism and openly trucking in artifice or allegory—it must retain at least some narrative or normative felicity to an original: the true, the authentic, the divine, the real—or in this case, the plan. Or, perhaps Delhi's planning will enter a true phase of magical realism, accepting fabulations of the sort already proffered by developers promising to transform Delhi into a world-class, smart city through architectural grandeur or technological upgrades, if only pesky regulations could be completely ignored.

9

THE SANCTUARY OF THE COLLECTIVE
Contesting the Fictions of State-Led Land Commodification in Peri-Urban Guangzhou

Mi Shih

In the summer of 2017, I took my usual three-hour trip—first by subway train, then by bus—to Yonghe village from my hostel near the city center in Guangzhou, as I had done many times in previous summers. Walking across the bridge leading away from the city's economic development zone (EDZ), Yonghe's industrial landscape straddled the river in front of me. The scene was familiar: smoke stacks and coal power plants imposing on villagers' four- to five-story, shoulder-to-shoulder, brick-structured houses. Thick smog lingered in the air, bringing the factories, giant pipes, and elevated, open-faced coal transport belts all around into tactile proximity. Yonghe was once a farming and fishing village sitting on the bank of the expanding marsh of the Zhujiang River. It lost all of its farmland to the EDZ in the mid-1980s. Three decades later, Yonghe villagers still call themselves "families on the water" (*shuishang renjia*), but their relationship to the water became estranged after the marsh was filled in by concrete embankments and the river became heavily polluted. Since the establishment of the EDZ, pollution has been the greatest grievance in Yonghe. This year something had changed in the skyline: two high-rising, huge, glass-curtain-wall buildings were emerging right behind Yonghe. The new construction was part of a private-oriented real estate development project carried out by a state-owned enterprise.

The entrance of the new real estate development and the back of Yonghe were only a few meters apart. Mr. Fang took me in and we strolled around the massive ground in front of the new buildings. Both of us were awed by the verticality of the new development. The land on which the glass towers now stood was Yonghe's farmland before the city government expropriated the village's collective land for a steel power plant. After the shutdown of the plant about ten years ago, this area had been mostly an abandoned site until recently. Mr. Fang was a longtime local villager and also a communist party member. He had been the village official of Yonghe since 2005 after he left, without a pension, the manufacturing job he worked for eighteen years in the EDZ. In Yonghe and villages elsewhere in China, the interrelated processes of transformation, including state expropriation of collectively owned farmland, industrialization of villages and towns, the breakdown of collective organization and agrarian economies, the absorption of the now-made-surplus village population into the manufacturing sector, the capitalization built on migrant workers' labor and bodies, and the recent commodification of land and development of the real estate market clearly show that urbanization is a state-led process in China (Buck 2007; Hsing 2010).

Since the mid-2000s, a series of village redevelopment policies have intensified state expropriation and commodification of land development in peri-urban Guangzhou. These policies target villages in favorable city locations sought by real estate interests or those in peri-urban areas slated by the state for new town development. The goal of the redevelopment policy is to convert all village land to state ownership so that it can be leased to real estate developers, while rehousing villagers in high-rise apartments financed by land-leasing rent. In China, the state is the only agent vested with the power to expropriate villagers' collectively owned land, and land expropriation is the only legal channel through which collective land can become commodified. The official rationalization for village redevelopment is that villagers' ongoing reliance on collective land represents both backward rurality and an obstacle to the deepening of marketization in China. Since these villages are already in highly urbanized areas or will soon undergo urbanization projects, there is no reason why they should not relinquish collective land. Administrative reshuffling of the rural population to the urban sphere dominated by the state has greatly underpinned the state's discourse on and practice of statization and commodification of collective land (Andreas and Zhan 2016; Chuang 2014; Shih 2019). Two administrative practices have particularly helped actualize state-led urbanization. The first is granting urban *hukou* (household registration) to villagers so that they are officially registered as city residents (*chengshi jumin*); the other is reclassifying villages (*cun*) as urban communities (*shequ*) so that the residential committee (*jumin weiyuanhui*) replaces the village collective to become the grassroots governing body under the street office (*jiedao banshichu*) of the city government, the lowest urban governance level in China. In the official discourse, these two practices are called "urbanization of people" (*ren de chengzhenhua*) and are said to be most central in achieving China's national development goal of urbanizing people in tandem with urbanizing land (State Council 2014). Recent scholarship has shown that the commodification of village land, through a combined employment of state expropriation, hukou reform, and new town development, has given rise to the dispossession of livelihoods, environmental pollution and degradation, political othering, and the breakdown of village-based mutual support networks in China (Andreas and Zhan 2016; Chuang 2014; Shih 2017; Smith 2014; Tilt 2010).

This chapter is about the social meaning and function of collective land to Yonghe villagers—or the "sanctuary of the collective" (*jiti de bihu*), a term expressed to me by an interviewee during fieldwork research in Guangzhou. Of the meanings and functions of the phrase, the most crucial is the noncommodified use of land as an anchor point for rural forms of exchange and sociality—that is, a sanctuary—in a city undergoing rapid and forceful state-led urbanization. Detailed later through ethnographic accounts, the social value of noncommodified land use came through most clearly in villagers' years-long, difficult struggles in choosing between relocating to commodity housing and staying where Yonghe was. The former allowed villagers to escape environmental pollution but also required them to relinquish the collective land located in the latter. Villagers' struggle to decide between the two injustices also demystifies the regulatory fiction that organizes state-led urbanization and urban land management in China.

"Regulatory fiction" describes the imagined and assumed alignment between collective land and rurality on the one hand, and between state-owned land and the urban on the other. This regulatory fiction rests on the often-quoted article 6 of the Land Administration Law, which says that "land in the urban area in the city is state owned, land in the rural area is collectively owned." As urbanization has accelerated in China, the urban-rural boundary has become more fluid, and this regulatory shorthand rarely holds up in practice. To the extent that it is assumed to be true or in the process of becoming true, though, it functions as an active fiction, performing a legal and ideological role in shaping perceptions of land's proper use.

I once asked a planning scholar in Guangzhou how he squared with the untruth in "land in the urban area in the city is state owned" in Land Administrative Law, as the common term *chengzongcun* (villages in the city) shows precisely that much of the urban land is still collectively owned in Guangzhou. He answered "[the law] just gives a discourse [*shuofa*]. The state still has many things to do to make [the discourse] a reality" (interview, May 2014). This regulatory fiction in the Chinese context works, then, as Ghertner and Lake argue, to "morph variable and contextual social history into ontological inevitability" (this volume). The reality referred to by the local scholar is the statization of collective land through expropriation. At the same time, an ideological construct that relegates villagers' continuous holding of and reliance on collective land to the historical baggage of backward rurality has helped legitimize state expropriation. As villagers become more urban via participation in nonagricultural employment, the possession of urban hukou, and administrative classification as an urban community, this fiction also produces an expectation that their rural citizenship and rural ways of life based on collective land use will also necessarily come to an end, even if this is against their own interests. Noncommodified uses of collective land are hence inscribed in state and popular discourse as both an obstacle to and a divergence from the commodification of the city. Seeing collective landownership as anything but urban and fully commodifiable hence becomes not just anachronistic, but politically unviable. In this sense, the regulatory fiction of urban land becomes the narrative and ideological vehicle for performing the fiction that land can operate as a purely marketable commodity in peri-urban Guangzhou.

To show the challenges that villagers face in confronting the regulatory fiction of urban land, as well as the political stakes of their practices that expose it as a fiction, I use "the sanctuary of the collective" (jiti de bihu) to describe what collective land and relationships do for villagers in the face of the profound changes that rapid urbanization has brought to them. Building on ethnographic fieldwork in Yonghe village conducted in 2012–17, I show that villagers find a sanctuary first in the economic protection that collective land provides. This includes the managerial control of the village-owned childcare center and market as well as land-based income from the village's collective assets. More important, villagers also find a sanctuary in what anthropologist Li Zhang (2006) calls *renqi*, or human vitality, that is so crucial for communities. Yonghe has over the years become a gathering ground and a small marketplace where villagers from elsewhere come to sell fruits, vegetables, garments, and hardware to migrant workers, Yonghe villagers, and local residents living nearby. These villager-vendors usually travel a long way, pedaling rickshaws and riding motorbikes with their goods from as far as the agricultural areas in northern Guangzhou and across the river in Guangdong Province. Viewed from the center of Guangzhou, Yonghe is a backward village enclave in a large development zone, now symbolically dominated by commodity housing and industry. In the vast peri-urban region outside the city, however, Yonghe is a sanctuary for the marginal and marginalized villagers, serving as an anchor point for rural forms of exchange and sociality in a city now booming with speculative real estate.

While no developer was interested in Yonghe village as a real estate redevelopment project, Yonghe villagers' years-long struggle with pollution had moved the role of collective land to the center of an intense debate over their relationship with urbanization. Between 2008 and 2015, Yonghe villagers were engaged in an internal debate over whether to relocate the whole village elsewhere in order to escape the long-term, cross-generational problem of pollution from the nearby factories. After years of protests against pollution in the development zone, the district government took a "self-determination" (*zizhu*) approach to the pollution problem, asking villagers to make a voluntary choice between continued exposure to environmental hazards in their original site or acceptance of voluntary state relocation to a new site. The final decision came down to a village vote. At the center of the debate was each family's own calculations of how and whether it was possible to rebuild life in a new site without jiti de bihu. I argue that it is those moments of debate, negotiation, and struggle that most clearly reveal the absurdity of the idea that urbanization and marketization are capable substitutes for collective landownership and relationships. Those moments also make clear the regulatory fiction of urban land as an ahistorical and power-reinscribing construct of the state.

Regulatory Fiction and Land Expropriation in China

In this section I discuss two meanings of regulatory fiction. One is the legal construct that grants the state a consolidated power over all land in the city. The other is the ideological construct that allows the state to relegate collective land to backward rurality and market constraint, both of which are depicted as problems of historical baggage correctable through landownership conversion. In these two senses, regulatory fiction has legitimized land expropriation as a practice that either realizes what is left to be done—that is, to statize collective land still in the hands of villages—or tackles what is perceived to be an entrenched social defect—in other words, the stubborn persistence of rurality in relation to marketization.

A Legal Construct–State Power over All Land in the City?

The following laws have produced an imagined alignment between urbanization and state ownership and between rurality and collective land. The 1982 revised Constitution for the first time legally stipulated that "land in the city is state owned." The 1986 Land Administrative Law further demarcated state-owned land from collectively owned land. Article 6 reads, "Land in the urban area [*shiqu*] of the city belongs to the state. Land in rural villages [*nongcun*] and the outskirts [*jiaoqu*] of the city ... belongs to collective ownership."[1] In other words, the Land Administrative Law equates the geographical urban-rural boundary with the administrative state-collective boundary. Here, it is important to be precise about the legal definitions of "city" and "urban area" used in Article 6, because this forms the basis of local states' expropriation of collective land in urbanizing areas as nothing more than those states' realization of de jure land rights. "City" refers to "municipalities directly under the central government" (such as Shanghai), as well as cities and towns set up administratively by the state (such as Guangzhou), whereas "urban area" means "the built-up area in the city" (Ho 2001, 410). Yonghe village is located in an administratively designated city district where several development zones are located, making it easy to classify as a built-up area even though villages still dominate much of the land use and landscape. The 1989 Land Use Rights Reform specified that only state-owned land could be leased to private developers for profit-oriented purposes. This made off-budget revenue from land leasing a stable political-economic structure of land-based finance (*tudi caizheng*) for local states, driving an aggressive wave of urbanization projects and land expropriation (Yeh and Wu 1996). The 1999 Enforcement Rules for the Land Administration Law clarified further what types of land fall under state land ownership, detailing six unique types.[2] Among these types are land in the urban areas of the city (type 1), land expropriated or confiscated by the state (types 2 and 3), and "land of rural villages whose collective-economy members have been transferred to become urban residents" (type 5).[3] Type 5 specifically pertains to villages that have been engulfed by industrial and urban development, whose collective economies based on farming have been eliminated, and whose rural hukou registrations have been transferred to urban ones. Peri-urban villages, such as Yonghe, or already highly urbanized villages in urban districts, such as *chengzhongcun*, are in this category. Rapid urbanization has left most villages in the city in the type 5 category, facilitating the expropriation of peri-urban village land.

These legislative acts form the basis of China's legal land regime and collectively maintain, in theory, a clear-cut spatiality of state ownership and its uniform expansion through urbanization. Such an alignment is a fiction in Guangzhou, however. A 1995 city monograph (*shizhi*) archived in the Guangzhou City Local Studies Room shows that in 1993 the Guangzhou city government owned 20 percent of the total land in Guangzhou, while the remaining 80 percent of the city territory was in the hands of village collectives (Guangzhou Municipal Government 2011). To my knowledge, this single archival text offers the only publicly available information on the distribution of state-versus-collective landownership in Guangzhou, even though the urban-rural spatiality of the city has undergone an inside-out transformation since the country's 1979 economic reforms. Among the eight city districts in Guangzhou, only the three innermost districts—Liwan, Dongshan, and Yuexiu—had high percentages of state-owned land (99.67 percent, 88.56 percent and 81.55 percent, respectively). These three districts together accounted for a mere 0.52 percent of the total city land, however, and the remaining five city districts and four counties comprised lands that fell largely under collective ownership (see table 9.1). In Guangzhou,

TABLE 9.1 State-owned land and collectively owned land in Guangzhou as of December 1993

	GUANGZHOU	LIWAN DISTRICT	DONGSHAN DISTRICT	YUEXIU DISTRICT	HAIZHU DISTRICT	TIANHE DISTRICT	FANGCUN DISTRICT	HUANGPU DISTRICT	BAIYUN DISTRICT	PANYU COUNTY	ZENGCHENG COUNTY	CONGHUA COUNTY	HUADU COUNTY
Land area	7,284.59	12.21	17.12	8.48	91.77	147.93	46.28	118.03	907.71	1,246.62	1,744.19	1,984.58	959.69
State-owned land	1,474.49	12.17	15.16	6.91	47.88	65.27	18.99	41.29	193.92	399.55	319.3	259.96	94.09
	20.24%	99.67%	88.56%	81.55%	52.17%	44.12%	41.03%	34.98%	21.36%	32.05%	18.31%	13.10%	9.80%
Collective-owned land	5,800.45	0.04	1.96	1.56	43.9	82.06	27.27	76.42	705.08	847.06	1,424.88	1,724.62	865.59
	79.63%	0.33%	11.44%	18.45%	47.83%	55.47%	58.93%	64.75%	77.68%	67.95%	81.69%	86.90%	99.20%
Not determined	9.65	–	–	–	–	0.6	0.02	0.32	8.71	–	–	–	–
	0.13%	–	–	–	–	0.41%	0.04%	0.27%	0.96%	–	–	–	–

Unit: km^2

Source: Guangzhou Municipal Government (2011, 123)

villages were scattered throughout, even in highly urbanized, built-up districts such as Tianhe and Haizhu. Archival data clearly show that state land ownership was not the norm well into the reform years.

There are two major reasons why state land ownership is not as consolidated as the law projects. First, a quick historical review of the early rural industrialization process in the larger Pearl River Delta (PRD) region shows that a complete dismantlement of rural villages was not in the interest of the development of Town and Village Enterprises (TVEs). In the 1980s, the development strategy of "leaving the field without leaving the land" (*litubulixiang*)—which expropriated village farmland while leaving housing allotments (*zhaijidi*) intact—allowed local states to squeeze "surplus" agricultural populations into the new industrial sectors, utilize existing village housing and infrastructure, and reduce conditions for social instability due to rapid structural changes. In the 1990s, the land practice of "return land for economic development [*jingjifanhaidi*]" (hereinafter "return land") was implemented, under which 8 to 10 percent of the total expropriated land was "returned" to the villagers to serve as a new land basis for collective economic development, since farming had been made impossible. Some scholars have called this process "accumulation without dispossession" (Hart 2002) and "*in situ* urbanization" (Zhu 2000). Second, villages, especially those with large landholdings and strong kinship networks, have engaged in what Hsing (2010) calls civic territoriality to contest state land expropriation. Building on their return land and drawing from networks with overseas Chinese capital, peri-urban villages have practiced a wide range of land-based activities, including warehouses, factories, workers and migrant housing, hotels, office buildings, and rental properties that bring urban uses to collective land. Revenue generated from this returned land is redistributed back to villagers as land dividends (*fenhong*) and used to subsidize village facilities, schools, social programs, and cultural activities that make urbanization a process of village entrenchment, not elimination.

The result of rural industrialization and urbanization in the past three decades is a spatially fragmented state-collective landownership pattern in the PRD, reflecting the historically contested power relations between the two in the region (Hsing 2010, Siu 2007). Zhujiang New Town—the new city center through which Guangzhou hopes to become a global city of the twenty-first century—represents such a contested urban process. It is entirely built on expropriated village land. This might be taken as a sign of state dominance over the collective. However, three villages (Liede, Xiancun, and Tancun) have remained permanently settled within Zhujiang New Town, despite early city government efforts to relocate these villages. The persistence of collective land in the core of urban areas thus shows the expectation that urban areas are state controlled to be a regulatory fiction whose realization relies on not just legal instruments, but also the popular denigration and symbolic downgrading of rurality, what I will show to be an unstable ideological project.

An Ideological Construct—Collective Land as the All-in-One Problem in Urbanization?

Since the mid-2000s, peri-urban villages and their collective land in the city have become the policy focus at the central and local levels. Initially, collective land in the city was described as a challenge to urban governance based on its lack of uniformity, mixed land uses, and incompatibility with the city's master planning. A policy report by the Ministry of Construction in 2007 stated that "peri-urban villages are a product of urbanization[,] and what [the villages] reflect is the backwardness in societal governance in places where the city and the countryside meet" (10). The report used this framing to ask local governments to create more effective planning regulations to build controls over land-use activities in villages. In this early stage of their problematization, peri-urban villages were seen as an effect of poor local-state governance, and the techniques of urban planning were framed as the instruments necessary to secure their elimination—or at least rationalization. Since the 2010s, the very existence of collective landownership has been increasingly seen as an obstacle to urbanization and marketization but is no longer seen as a result of failed state governance. In 2011, the Ministry of Land and Resources released a report on the landownership problem in peri-urban village redevelopment, with Guangzhou highlighted as a key case study. To redevelop peri-urban villages, the report prescribed an approach characterized by "four kinds of legal transfers." These four transfers include: converting collective landownership into state ownership, transforming villagers' rural household registrations (hukou) into urban ones, assigning village collectives' social responsibilities to respective municipal bureaus, and redeveloping villages according to city planning guidelines. Significantly, the report gives new impetus to the institutional change (*gaizhi*) of peri-urban villages' landownership, stating the need to

> thoroughly break away from the conditions that restrain urban development in Guangzhou and also to effectively accelerate the bottlenecks in urbanization in Guangzhou . . . [because] ownership conversion is conducive to dismantling the closed-off situation in the village as well as to changing villagers' petty-peasantry mentality [*xiaonong yishi*] so as to genuinely integrate the masses of villagers into the economic society and life of modern cities. (ibid.)

These restraining conditions consist of the legal prohibition that collective land be used for profit-oriented functions. This report marks a shift in the problematization of urban villages away from an early technical focus on governance challenges to a framing of collective land as an obstacle to marketization. Whereas collective land had long been legally defined as a non-market-oriented means to protect segments of society from the pressures of land commodification, by 2011 the administrative barrier to full commodification was reframed as a holdover of an earlier era, one that locked the beneficiaries of collective land in a "petty-peasantry mentality" in need of modernization and correction via market exposure. Underpinning this particular problematization of collective landownership is China's popular disdain for rurality, a "quality" (*suzhi*) coding of people presumed to be behind in development (Siu 2007; Yeh 2013). In other words, urbanization is not only a progression toward a development object, but also promises to improve the suzhi of villagers. Thus, the report signals a policy attempt to perform the commodity fiction of subordinating social relations around collective land to market logics; it does so not just as a means of increasing commodity real estate in Guangzhou, but also as a social correction to rural backwardness.

In 2012, the Guangzhou municipal government completed a study on land problems in villages.[4] The most important policy recommendation listed in the study was to implement capitalization (*zibenhua*) on collective land owned by the village. Specifically, the report recommended that collectively owned land in villages in Guangzhou's urban center and peri-urban areas be converted to state-owned land so that land could be monetized and exchanged. The goal was to "enter an urban-rural-integrated land market which has the same land [*tongdi*], same right [*tongquan*], and same price [*tongjia*]" (Guangzhou Social Science Planning Leadership Office 2011, 6). Here "same land" means state-owned land; "same right" refers to the tradable, state-owned land-use rights; and "same price" refers to the market price. Here, past systems of facilitating collective economies and modes of village life emerge as regulatory holdovers from a previous era, denying equal access to market forces and the social benefits they are presumed to deliver.

The Sanctuary of the Collective in Yonghe Village

A villager once described to me the territorial size and soil quality of Yonghe prior to land expropriation: "All of what is today's development zone was our farmland, from where we stand here all the way to the river. The soil was neither waterlogged nor droughty [*bulao buhan*]." The EDZ built on Yonghe's farmland is approximately 10 square kilometers. The post-expropriation Yonghe is a fraction of this size, occupying only 0.19 square kilometers of land. Among the 700 households, or 1,800 villagers, in Yonghe today, there is no "surname in the majority [*daxin*]," which reflects the history of Yonghe as a settlement of migrant fishermen on the water. As a village of "multiple surnames," there are no prominent lineages, no ancestral halls, and no kinship-based activities or customs in the village. One local scholar jokily called Yonghe "a village of no culture [*meiyou wenhua de cun*]." What she actually meant was that, compared to other powerful villages in favorable city locations, Yonghe is in a particularly difficult position, as there are no cultural, economic, geographical, or overseas resources villagers could summon for protecting themselves from the force of urbanization. Almost three decades after land expropriation in the mid-1980s, Yonghe village has been identified by the government as one of the poorest villages in the district.

It is against this deeply penetrating process of urbanization that the collective provides a sanctuary, critical to sustaining Yonghe livelihoods and enhancing, from the villagers' perspective, human vitality (renqi). Even though a new Yonghe was the only foreseeable way out of generational struggles of environmental pollution, the tremendous difficulties and hesitation villagers experienced in accepting a relocation plan to a newly developed area is evidence of the value they place in the socioeconomic relationships that have formed around collectively owned land.

Livelihoods Protection

When land expropriation took place in Yonghe village in the mid-1980s in preparation for the expansion of the EDZ, the material and discursive understanding of "urbanity" was not based on the marketability of land. At the time, the Land Use Rights Reform Act of 1989, which opened up a frantic market for private-oriented land sales and development, had not yet been adopted. Yonghe villagers—farmers and fishing boatmen on the Zhujiang River—understood the term *urban* to apply to city residents and factory workers, those holding urban hukou and receiving benefits from state pensions, job security, health care benefits, housing subsidies, and access to urban schools and hospitals. Seeing the benefits privileged by urban status with urban hukou, the villagers yearned to become "urban." As a result, Yonghe villagers embraced the expropriation of their land and the shift to an administratively "urban" life, and they voiced little opposition when their farmland was taken, leaving only the individual villagers' allotted housing sites (zhaijidi) and three economic return land lots designated for the purpose of village economic development. The combined area of the three return land lots is 0.037 square kilometers, 19 percent of the 0.19 square kilometers of land that Yonghe now owns.

In the early 1990s, following the official completion of land expropriation, Yonghe villagers' hukou was converted from rural to urban, listing them as "residents" (*jumin*) rather than "villagers" (*cunmin*) on their identification cards. However, urbanization of hukou status, despite popular perceptions, is not automatically accompanied by the statization of social benefits.[5] On the contrary, the early 1990s also saw the beginning of large-scale privatization in China, leading to a fundamental restructuring of how income could be secured. While urban infrastructure such as tap water, street lights, paved roads, and transportation were installed in Yonghe, most villagers struggled to secure reliable employment, pension plans, or social insurance. At the very moment that collective and subsistence forms of livelihood were ceded for urban hukou, Yonghe villagers found themselves in a highly disciplined labor market, competing with an influx of migrant workers for contract-based, relatively insecure jobs (Shih 2017). Mr. Li worked at different jobs in both Taiwanese and Hong Kong factories before taking a position as the director (*shezhang*) of an economic cooperative in the village several years before our 2016 meeting. He argued that village residents in their fifties and sixties were most affected by land expropriation because "they were downright peasants when [land expropriation] happened. They just did not learn the skills to work in the factory.... I was one of them, and I believe I was one of those who adapted better, and I am still here. Imagine how others have fared" (Interview, June 2016). A village official whom I interviewed told me that only about seventy villagers received secure positions for factory jobs in the development zone, mostly because of their status as party members or collective officials.

These market insecurities have made annual dividends (*fenhong*) from the three return land lots extremely important for villagers. These lots are leased to nearby factories for metal waste recycling, pipe molding, and garment production. In recent years, villagers have received between 400 and 2,000 renminbi (about US $300) as an annual land dividend, figures considered very small when compared to other land-rich villages. The calculation of the amount of land dividend a villager can receive is based on how many years that person worked as a farmer on Yonghe's collectively owned farmland before land expropriation. Therefore, the older a villager, the higher the land dividend received. Villagers born after 1988, the year that land expropriation was completed, are not eligible to receive land dividends, as they did not contribute to the village collective. While almost all villages have similar age-based structures for distributing land dividends, for Yonghe villagers in their fifties and sixties—those Mr. Li described as least prepared to enter the industrial labor market—this modest income is especially crucial.

Collective land has also helped stabilize market insecurities through context-sensitive building practices. In the mid-1990s, a housing shortage was becoming a serious problem in the village. As villagers rented out available rooms to migrant workers for rental income, married children were left without independent living spaces. Villagers developed the creative solution of demolishing a few village houses and building "collectively funded apartments" (*jizifang*) in their place. These were six-floor apartment buildings with minimal design features and no elevators, public spaces, or balconies—a design decision made to maximize the usable interior spaces of apartments. Villagers pooled together money needed for building the apartments and contributed directly to their construction. Yonghe village built forty-eight apartments in total, half of which were sold at a subsidized price to Yonghe villagers, the other half sold at regular rates to migrant workers and other non-Yonghe villagers. The existing law, however, banned selling village housing to nonvillager buyers—an early legal design aimed to prevent the loss of control of collective land to marketization. While Yonghe villagers needed to raise funds for the village by selling village housing, they were also cautious about opening the village to outside buyers. When I asked Mr. Fang about the nonvillager buyers, he said they were "people who have worked here and people we sort of knew." To ensure the transactions were understood as a contact between the individual non-Yonghe buyers and Yonghe village as a whole, all apartment sales included paperwork carrying a stamp of the Yonghe village collective office, now a defunct entity, but the signature of which produced the effect of an intracollective transfer.

Yonghe's "collectively funded apartments" project is similar to the township-initiated projects Hsing (2010) has observed in Beijing, which were constructed without proper approvals from the central government, but nonetheless gained unofficial sanction. Whereas the large scale of the township projects in Beijing led Hsing to describe them as part of a territorial strategy of township government gaining influence beyond rural spaces, Yonghe's innovation was more narrowly focused on helping the village economy and fostering conditions for collective survival. Villagers used village spaces and built their social relationships according to their own rules of governance and knowledge about the local population. In other words, Yonghe villagers found a way to make sure the market economy served the social needs of villagers, not the other way around.

Renqi—A Gathering Ground and a Marketplace

In her work on spatial modernity in Kumning, Zhang (2006) argued that renqi, the breath and energy of human beings, is crucial to local community and business prosperity and is inseparable from the spatial form of a place. Comprehensive city planning, she noted, often ends up making dynamic living spaces cold and bleak, sanitizing them and removing their organic renqi. In Yonghe, renqi is most evident in its public spaces. The village-run market sits next to the childcare center, fish ponds, and the basketball court, and these facilities are grouped around the village's most important public gathering space: the village park, featuring siting benches, tables, and playground facilities. Surrounding these public spaces are village houses. Private homes, public spaces, and any activities in between the private and the public are tightly packed in the small village space. Every time I visited Yonghe, I felt and observed a sense of chaotic order: men (not women) playing mahjong with money in the park, with bystanders watching; new migrants exploring the area and having some fun as they took turns playing ping-pong (their suitcases together with bamboo mats, buckets, and handheld fans revealed their status as newcomers); wet blankets and clothes spread on the benches in the park, showing that villagers used and reappropriated the space fully; and migrant workers crowded into the park after work in the afternoon, talking to each other in Mandarin (*putonghua*), as distinct from the Cantonese (*yueyu*) villagers spoke out of both habit and to maintain social difference.

Renqi is also evident in Yonghe's market activities. As the end of morning shifts in the EDZ approaches, vendors come to set up stands, carts, and stalls to sell fruits, vegetables, meat, garments, hardware, small appliances, and all kinds of goods to shift workers. While there was an official wholesale market in the EDZ, Yonghe villagers rarely shopped there. Along the sidewalks on the bridge that connected the EDZ to Yonghe were several vegetable stands attended by women from other villages in the hilly areas in the district. At the village gate, a girl selling bananas out of a bike was from Dongguan, a prefecture-level city across the river in Guangdong Province. Dongguan has turned into a major manufacturing hub, despite being a rural town in recent decades. Each afternoon she started pedaling from her village in Dongguan until she reached Yonghe, telling me she preferred coming here because Dongguan city was further from her home and more competitive. A man spreading some kind of kiwilike fruits on the ground at the edge of the park rode his motorbike down from the areas still in agricultural production in northern Guangzhou. He came to Yonghe because motorbikes were banned from entering in the city, and there was no way for him to get a booth in the wholesale market in the EDZ. Close to the park, the ground floor of a village house had been converted into a workshop where three women and one man hand-assembled frames for lanterns and carefully hand-pasted white papers around each frame. They were in their fifties, migrant workers from different inland provinces speaking Mandarin to each other. They told me the workshop was a downsized version of a factory previously located in the development zone. Export demand for these handmade, Japanese-style, white lanterns had dropped quite significantly in recent years. The boss lived in Shenzhen, about a hundred kilometers from Guangzhou, and only came to check their work once a week.

All of them rented housing in Yonghe, and when the factory closed, they started working in Yonghe, too. When I asked why they did not search for new jobs in the development zone, one of the women—with her hand swiftly spinning the frame while applying glue—told me, "We are too old to work [in the development zone], but we cannot go back to our old homes either. We have worked here [Guangzhou] for decades already." In one of the small eating places in Yonghe, the cook-proprietor told me that her old home near the river had been demolished for a city greenery project several years ago. With her husband and their four kids, they rented a place in a community somewhere sixty minutes away from Yonghe by bike. They did not want to live in Yonghe because the pollution was too bad, so they used the compensation money from her demolished home to rent a place in Yonghe, where she opened and continued to run a restaurant. Her husband worked as a cook in a factory in the EDZ and helped her in the restaurant in the afternoons. She raised chickens in cages in the back of the restaurant, purchased perishable ingredients daily from vendors in Yonghe, and bought less-perishable foods from the market in the development zone.

The kinds of socioeconomic relationships that have formed around Yonghe are certainly market oriented, but are experienced as less subordinate to harsh market logics and more accommodating to villagers struggling with rapid urbanization. Seen from the angle of villagers, Yonghe is a small center in a vast peri-urban area.

Choosing between Two Evils

One profoundly detrimental impact that industrialization has had on the Yonghe villagers that even the socioeconomic sanctuary Yonghe provides cannot abate is severe environmental pollution. Smog from the several stacks surrounding the village; two rows of high-voltage power lines flanking the village; airborne particulates from the open-faced, elevated coal transport belt running along the western boundary of the village; and noise, dust, and speeding problems caused by heavy trailers in the area are just some of the environmental challenges villagers face. Organized protests in the past have led to only temporary improvements, such as speed restrictions and fines for traffic violations. Limited monetary compensation paid by polluting factories in response to villagers' individual petitions and official complaints are now subject to regular renegotiation (Shih 2017).

At a meeting with the district government in 2008, Yonghe villagers raised the possibility of moving the whole village to a new location to escape these unresolved environmental problems. Tired of villagers' petitions and protests over many years, the district government eventually agreed to initiate a plan to relocate the whole village to commodity housing. In a survey conducted in 2009, more than 90 percent of Yonghe villagers voted in favor of proceeding with the plan. The survey questions did not include details of the relocation plan, but simply asked villagers whether the village should be moved elsewhere. By the time the survey was conducted, the villagers had arrived at a point where they believed moving away was the only way to escape from multigenerational environmental hazards, even though redevelopment of peri-urban villages in Guangzhou for the most part takes place on-site, and proposals for relocation usually receive outright rejection from villagers.

Details of the redevelopment plan of a new Yonghe gradually took shape between 2013 and 2014. In a nutshell, villagers would live in high-rise apartments in a newly developed residential area. The residential area was to be one of the new, large-scale real estate developments in peri-urban Guangzhou, thirty minutes away from Yonghe by car, and located off a major highway. Villagers would receive monetary compensation for their houses in old Yonghe, which could be used to pay for the new apartments. The new Yonghe community would sit on state-owned land, which meant that after paying the government an unspecified-at-the-time land-use fee, villagers would be able to register their apartments as commodity housing (*shanpinfang*) and would be legally allowed to sell their property on the private housing market. According to the law on community governance, a private property management company needed to be hired to handle building maintenance affairs related to high-rise, commodity buildings. Therefore, villagers would need to pay monthly fees to the company. Because the new Yonghe would no longer own collective land, what were previously collective facilities—such as the childcare center, vegetable and meat market, and elementary school—would be treated as individual, market services. Villagers hence would need to pay much higher fees, tuitions, and prices for these facilities and services. These fees and more individualized service delivery options were part and parcel of what becoming new urban residents and consumers meant.

Quarrels over the new Yonghe erupted as soon as the redevelopment plan details were made public. The district government twice in 2014 bussed Yonghe villagers out to visit the redevelopment site, but this only increased villagers' worries. Three aspects of the redevelopment plan were seen as particularly detrimental to Yonghe's future. First, the physical design (both within the new site and in the surrounding area) was not considered friendly to villagers and their needs. A major highway used heavily by trucks transporting goods outside the city separated the new site from the residential complex where most necessary daily facilities, such as the childcare center, were to be located. Without a pedestrian cross-over bridge connecting the two locations, Yonghe villagers worried for their children's safety. Second, living costs after redevelopment were expected to rise. As one villager put it, if they accepted the redevelopment plan, their lifestyle would be dictated by a reality where "every morning once you open your eyes, you are off to make money to pay off fees." These fees, including the parking fees, property management fees, and expected high costs of childcare and shopping, were either nonexistent or very low in Yonghe village.

Finally, the redevelopment plan represented the beginning of a fundamental livelihood change. Right across from the entrance to the site were clusters of high-end, luxury residential commodity housing, with wide roads separating each gated community and connecting them to an upscale, impressive new housing development. The Yonghe villagers immediately recognized the anticipated increase in real estate value of this new residential area, particularly since all the developers were well-known in Guangzhou for their specialization in high-end housing markets. Taking a quick drive in the area, one could get the clear sense that the area represented the Guangzhou city government's spatial development goal of "advancing to the east" (*dongjin*) by encouraging movement of capital, population, and projects to this previously underpopulated hilly area. However, the villagers did not see themselves as part of the new real estate-based development. The adjectives villagers used to describe the new area included *da* (vast), *buwang* (not flourishing), and lacking in renqi (human vitality). What was missing from the new redevelopment site, for them, was something extremely essential: what Zhang (2006, 470–72) describes as the "breath and energy of human beings" so vital for close-knit communities and bustling small businesses in urban China. A high-end real estate market, lacking a flourishing set of street-level, close-at-hand interactions, and without street markets and small and informal businesses, would never be sought out by migrant workers, the clientele and cultural economy to which Yonghe livelihood habits were most attuned. Yonghe villagers anticipated that this diminished renqi would lead to a loss of rental income as well as incomes earned by operating fruit and vegetable stands, food stands, cart bikes, or working odd jobs within local networks. Compounded by the anticipated increase in living costs, villagers worried about the acute pressure they would face to somehow become competitive job seekers.

Facing an impossible choice between ongoing environmental injustice and anticipated livelihood deterioration, a deep sense of powerlessness arose among Yonghe villagers. Village officials, who usually align their position with that of the government, were ambivalent and torn. One village official, Ms. Ma, described her disoriented feeling:

> Of course, we had meetings to discuss [the redevelopment plan] with everyone, but we did not try to direct [the meetings]; we don't know

anything and therefore cannot say anything out loud. Because you don't know whether it is a good decision to move there, what the benefits are, nobody dared to say with certainty.... The government only says these are the apartments we will live in and gave us the information on the apartments. How to talk villagers into accepting [the redevelopment plan]? It is impossible to tell yes from no. (Interview, June 2015)

Mr. Mai, who was in his forties and had a position in a local government branch office, was inclined to move to the new site for his children. He liked the fact that he would be legally allowed to sell the redevelopment apartment in the private housing market once he paid off the yet-to-be-specified land-use fee. A marketable apartment in a residential area without the presence of heavy industries would be an asset he could pass down to his children. His worry was that monetary compensation for his house allotment in Yonghe village would not be enough to cover the additional living costs in the new site. Therefore, at the several meetings with the developer and officials from the district government, Mr. Mai had a list of very concrete questions and requests. These included: exactly how many years would it take before the redevelopment apartments could become marketable; an estimated figure for the land-use fee villagers would need to pay; a request to replace the doors, windows, and wood frames of the redevelopment apartments that were already damaged by termites; and a request for a pedestrian cross-over bridge so villagers would not be excluded from the residential complex. Among these requests, the developer only agreed to replace the termite-damaged parts of the new buildings. The officials from the district government told Mr. Mai that only a higher authority could respond to his other requests. When Mr. Mai raised his voice out of frustration at the meeting, the villagers were warned by the government officials not to display "barbarian" (*yeman*) behavior.

Mr. Luo, who was in his sixties and worked as a security guard in the village, strongly opposed the redevelopment plan. A long-term communist party member, he explained that he had participated in protests against the EDZ out of rage because "pollution is a real problem, but all environmental impact assessment reports say otherwise" and "even a communist party member of many years cannot stand it" (Interview, June 2014). Mr. Luo did not believe his family could survive in the new site. In recent years, he had seen more than half of his rental rooms sit vacant, as the relocation of many labor-intensive assembly lines to the north of the city had taken a great number of migrant workers with it. His salary as a security guard was small, and his son did odd jobs in the area to contribute to the household budget. Both generations relied on rental income and local networks to get by, and the redevelopment plan ignored both.

In 2013 and 2014, Yonghe villagers voted twice on the redevelopment plan. Both times, the rate in favor of the plan was slightly above 70 percent, a rate considered too low from the "hard indicator" (*yingzhibiao*) of 90 percent set by the city government. Passing the 90-percent threshold, according to the official reasoning, was a necessary demonstration of villagers' collective determination and indicated a choice of their own accord—the so-called self-determination (*zizhu*) approach—even though a decision between two equally unjust options is itself a form of oppression. Based on the results of the two votes, the district government called a halt to the redevelopment plan. After five years of waiting, suspending all construction projects in the village in preparation for redevelopment, and weighing the costs and benefits of a new urban life, Yonghe village was back to square one.

In this chapter I have shown that China's urban development and land commodification is predicated on numerous shrinking villages such as Yonghe, where collective land in the village is expropriated by the state. What Guangzhou city government did in dismantling Yonghe's collective landownership as an obstacle to urbanization is strikingly similar to how Levien describes the use of eminent domain by the Rajasthan state government for a private Special Economic Zone in Rajpura village (this volume) in that both the Chinese and Indian governments ultimately aim to transform rural land into a commodity. Polanyi argues that to include land "in the market mechanism means to subordinate the substance of society itself to the laws of the market" (2001 [1944], 75) and draws an analogy between separating land from man to a man "being born without hands and feet" (ibid, 187).

To get a sense of the fictitiousness of land commodification, one only needs to step inside and outside of Yonghe to wonder at the complete lack of explanation for why only real estate development outside Yonghe is considered legal and desirable. The wonder of urban land commodification helps make evident the extent to which China's rapid land commodification rests on a legal and ideological regulatory fiction. As a legal construct, this regulatory fiction establishes a legal landownership structure that grants the state consolidated power over land in the city. As an ideological construct, it relegates collective land to backward rurality and treats it as a necessary market constraint associated with the historical baggage of prereform socialism. In its first sense, this regulatory fiction legitimizes land expropriation as a practice through which the state completes the process of urbanization by statizing collective land still in the hands of villages and ushering in a modern era of development. In its second, more ideological function, this regulatory fiction legitimizes land expropriation as an improvement on the all-in-one problem of collective land: a collective governance failure, the associated petty-peasantry mentality, and cumbersome restrictions on marketization deemed essential to regional and national economic growth. In Guangzhou, where state-collective relations have been highly contested and fragmented historically—with 80 percent of land in the city still collectively owned as recently as the mid-1990s—this regulatory fiction depicts state ownership as an inevitability, even though its means of execution is far from certain and its effects largely contested. By casting any collective land within an urban area of China as backward and out of place, despite its ubiquity, the burden of fitting in, or eking out an existence in a city increasingly geared toward profit making rather than labor absorption or collective welfare, is transferred from the state to members of the collective. Rather than dealing with the real challenges of building viable alternatives to collective land in urban villages, the regulatory fiction of urban land presents urban villages as impediments themselves: their dispossession is necessary for their own betterment. This serves ideologically to minimize the concerns of China's large population unprepared to compete in the commodity market of land and labor.

In Yonghe, the sanctuary of the collective—the durable positive attributes of village life—has helped villagers respond to the regulatory fiction of urban land and the deeper commodity fiction on which it relies, despite the environmental hardships and symbolic isolation they must endure by being surrounded by dense industrial development and through their location outside the high-rise commodity housing increasingly common in the city. Villagers have found a sanctuary in livelihood security afforded by a more localized economy in which market transactions are mediated by migrant socialities and shared cultures of exchange. More important, Yonghe has over the years developed into a gathering ground and economic space where people come for its renqi, a human vitality critical for local communities accustomed to more spontaneous, interpersonal, and informal exchange. Viewed from the center of Guangzhou, Yonghe appears to be a left-behind village enclave in a large development zone, a holdover from a bygone era. From the perspective of the vast peri-urban region outside the city, however, Yonghe is a sanctuary for marginal and marginalized villagers and other urban outcasts.

10

RIGHTS GONE WRONG ON THE CITY'S EDGE

The Fictions and Fetishes of Land Documents in Ho Chi Minh City

Erik Harms

> **It is nothing but the definite social relation between men themselves which assumes here, for them, the fantastic form of a relation between things. . . . I call this the fetishism which attaches itself to the products of labour as soon as they are produced as commodities.**
>
> —Karl Marx, *Capital: A Critique of Political Economy,* Vol. 1

> **To accuse something of being a fetish is the ultimate gratuitous, disrespectful, insane, and barbarous gesture.**
>
> —Bruno Latour, "Why Has Critique Run out of Steam?"

One day in early 2011, I was talking to a resident in a newly developing part of Ho Chi Minh City about the fact that he was about to be evicted from his home. He lived in the middle of a neighborhood where 737 hectares of land were being "cleared" in order to build an urban development project called the Thủ Thiêm New Urban Zone. To express the sense of injustice he was feeling, he showed me a document he had saved on his computer. The document had been written by a woman who had already sent several petitions addressed to government offices. This time, however, instead of addressing the government authorities who were clearly ignoring her complaints, she addressed her petition to the public. The resulting document was something of a hybrid: the header and first several paragraphs adopted the conventions of a formal bureaucratic text, but the rest read partly like a formal petition and partly like an open appeal. The appeal portion read like this:

> I sent this call for help to the functionary offices of the City, but not a single place has bothered to listen to my cries!

[One morning in] 2010, District 2 mobilized hundreds of people to come and forcefully occupy my home! Pushed me out onto the street! Only compensated me 1,000,000 đồng per square meter [approximately US$50 per square meter]. After that they took my piece of land and sold it to businesses at a price of several hundred million đồng! The proceeds from this difference are not going to the state! They flow directly into the pockets of those corrupt rascal bureaucrats (bọn quan liêu tham nhũng)! Precisely because of this they are so deeply engrossed in the work of stealing land from the poor people, regardless of the law, no longer possessing human sentiments. These gangsters have money and position, [and] they have protection (có ô có dù; Lit. "have umbrellas"), so they can inconsiderately steal in the middle of the day!

Attached please find several photos, taken by stealth![1]

The photos attached to the appeal depicted a crowd of people gathered around a plot of land watching a bulldozer smash apart a home. There were policemen standing around in gruff poses. There were also several photos of a woman, sitting up defiantly in one photo and then lying on the ground in another, clearly distressed. This woman, it turns out, was the author of the appeal. The man who had shared the appeal with me had received the appeal and photos by email from a friend who was also angry about the low level of compensation offered to evictees. While the appeal highlighted a number of unsavory practices, especially the use of force by authorities, the central injustice it denounced was the discrepancy between the amount of compensation given for the land and the amount for which it was later sold. According to the appeal, the land was essentially being "stolen" (cướp đất).

I received scores of similar documents while conducting fieldwork in Thủ Thiêm between 2010 and 2012, and many of the people I met in the area had sent appeals to district authorities, to the city, and even as far as the Prime Minister's Office in Hanoi. As early as 2009, well before the final push to complete the eviction process began, a report from the Vietnamese Ministry of Justice on land petitions had identified Thủ Thiêm as one of the most sensitive places of concern in the whole country (Vietnamese Ministry of Justice [Bộ Tư Pháp] 2009, 7). The appeals and petitions I collected raised a range of different complaints—such as how the project dimensions were expanding beyond officially approved limits, how land was being classified, and how the people were being treated by land officials. However, all of them focused explicitly on the problem of low compensation. For example, a petition I collected on a different occasion directly addresses the land compensation authorities. It uses very polite language to appeal to their sense of fairness.² Like the previous case, it also focuses on compensation:

> I make this petition at this time in the hopes that the respected organ of the authorized branch review this and make a decision on behalf of my family that correctly calculates the size of the home and courtyard at 150 m² and compensate according to the 100% coefficient rate so that my family does not suffer injury and has the proper conditions in order to soon move according to the decision and find stability in a different place. Please accept my heartfelt gratitude.

The polite language used here recalls the idioms of "righteous resistance" O'Brien has described in China (O'Brien 1996; O'Brien and Li 2006). It also invokes a similarly righteous focus on "justice" and rights claims that Vietnam scholars have more recently described in land cases across the country (Gillespie 2012; Kerkvliet 2014; Labbé 2015; Schwenkel 2015). At the same time, it is worth noting here how this author focused on the so-called "coefficient rate" (hệ số) used to calculate land compensation. This term alludes to how the total compensation rates assigned for some types of property are calculated in government-sponsored land appropriation cases. Across Vietnam, the land law stipulates that general land values for all areas must first be assigned by government agencies at the city or provincial level. From this base value, the value of individual plots is subsequently determined by multiplying it by a set percentage—called the "coefficient rate"—which is determined according to various locally determined criteria, such as when the land was occupied, whether it had been squatted on, how far it is from a major road, if it is bisected by a riverbed, and so on.

This process for calculating land compensation angered many residents. They criticized the seemingly arbitrary ways in which officials made their calculations or chose to apply the coefficient rate. There was good reason for this, because simple decisions about calculation could profoundly affect how much compensation a displaced household would receive. According to the compensation regulations, in 2002 the base rate of compensation for residential land in Thủ Thiêm was set at around 2 million đồng (approximately US $100). However, these totals could be reduced according to various criteria. For example, lands squatted on (i.e., occupied without obtaining formal registration papers at a local People's Committee) before Vietnam's new land laws went into effect in 1993 would be compensated at 80 percent of the base rate; lands squatted on between 1993 and 1998 would be compensated at 50 percent of the base rate; and those squatted on after 1998, when the plans for the Thủ Thiêm project were officially announced, would get 0 percent, or no compensation at all. Other reductions could be made based on various criteria related to various features of the plot and the position of the land in question. If the land was not facing a road, for example, its compensation value could be reduced by 60 to 80 percent. Land bisected by a canal or eroded by the banks of the river would not even be considered "residential land" and would be compensated at much lower agricultural rates; and in some cases, such land would not be eligible for any compensation at all. All of these factors could dramatically alter the amount of compensation a household would be granted for their land.[3] In this context, with so much money riding on the way one's land or occupancy status was classified, even a "coefficient" could be seen as a villain worth fighting against.

I was initially surprised by the bold language that appeared in these petitions and appeals. In contemporary Vietnam, political discourse remains largely absent in the official media, especially in newspapers, television, and online media channels, which remain controlled by the single-party state. While active online dissident communities do exist in Vietnam, the large majority of citizens avoid protesting government supported actions because open political dissent or critique of government policy is actively criminalized. To publicly print and circulate a petition like the ones described above is no small matter. Doing so makes one vulnerable to state-surveillance, harassment by the police, and possible imprisonment. Indeed, in recent years, numerous activists have been jailed for writing blogs the state deems subversive. Even media spaces not overtly controlled by the state sometimes reproduce certain dominant ideologies, and "activism" often shies away from politics and devolves into playful engagements with pop culture (Phuong 2017, 826–28). Unlike India, the "world's largest democracy," where land protests form part of the formal political landscape, and even become tools in party politics, it is difficult to identify a broader political or intellectual movement behind the voices of resistance being expressed in these petitions, which are largely the product of risk-taking individuals or small cells of activists.[4]

While some scholars studying land protest elsewhere in Vietnam read such bold claims as evidence of an emerging social movement agitating for justice (Kerkvliet 2014), much of the protest one sees in the country actually depends on the bravery of identifiable individuals who are willing to risk putting their name on open petitions. Regardless of whether these petitions are seen as part of a nascent social movement or as atomized individual responses, it is not clear that they actually help residents stay on their land. As time went on, and as the Thủ Thiêm development project continued moving forward, the more it became clear that the rubble-strewn landscapes from within which these documents were coming were growing bigger and bigger. As the number of documents proliferated, so too did the extent of the dispossession. The disconnect between the bold resistance evoked by the documents and the ever-increasing extent of dispossession prompted an obvious question: were these documents actually doing what they claimed to be doing?

Looking around at the landscape in Thủ Thiêm revealed that the cries denouncing injustice were not stemming the tide of dispossession (figure 10.1). At the same time that residents were expressing their resistance in these petitions and appeals, the landscape of Thủ Thiêm was being changed forever and the writing on the wall was clear (figure 10.2). The forces of urban development were too big to fail and it was clear that there was no way these petitions would ever stem the forces of dispossession steamrolling their way through Thủ Thiêm. Furthermore, while their focus on the right to receive fair compensation gave these petitions a voice, this very language depended on an idiom of market-based property value that actually reinforced the terms of their dispossession in the first place. Texts, in the form of petitions or legal documents, came to play an important role in channeling people's resistance, and people seemed to believe that these documents carried a certain agency and force. But there was one problem—these texts weren't actually doing the things people wanted them to do. The documents acted like fetish objects in the classic sense described by Marx in his discussion of commodity fetishism; they represent a case in which "the products of the human brain appear as autonomous figures endowed with a life of their own"

FIGURE 10.1. The demolition of Thủ Thiêm District, Ho Chi Minh City, Vietnam. 2012. Author's photo.

FIGURE 10.2. "The Writing on the wall was clear": Here, the writing reads "đập nhà" (knock this house down). Thủ Thiêm District, Ho Chi Minh City, Vietnam. 2010. Author's photo.

(Marx 1990 [1867], 165). People themselves had made these documents, and they treated the documents as if they had the capacity to act on the world. But as the Thủ Thiêm case shows, the documents did not in fact act on the world in the ways people hoped they would.

In this chapter, I show how land-related documents—including petitions, titles, government-issued reclamation orders, and a labyrinthine array of legal papers—simultaneously do and do not have the power to act on the world. While the documents described in this chapter often spur people into action, they just as often lead them to distraction. The active mobilization for rights they inspire is thus both real and illusory. In this way, in addition to offering a novel way of looking at land fictions in Vietnam, the chapter argues for a reconciliation of what have heretofore been seen as antagonistic Latourian and Marxist perspectives on fetishism. On the one hand, a Latourian perspective would rightly highlight how the land documents in this case engender novel forms of action. But such an approach would only capture part of the story, because the evidence also shows that documents like these also contribute to forms of mystification. This suggests that while Latour's perspectives on the agency of nonhuman things is useful, his critique of the concept of the fetish needs to be reconsidered.

The Case of Thủ Thiêm

Thủ Thiêm lies across the Saigon River from Ho Chi Minh City's District 1, the city's thriving downtown (figure 10.3).[5] Long the heart of this former "Paris of the East," District 1 is the famous downtown Saigon of Graham Greene novels and the Vietnam War era, and now the site of cosmopolitan culture, international hotels, boutiques, art spaces, music venues, great restaurants, and because of all these things, intense real estate speculation. Until they were demolished, the neighborhoods across the river in Thủ Thiêm were decidedly less glamorous. The homes there were simple affairs, mostly one-story boxes, largely built by their owners. Thủ Thiêm was not a slum by any stretch of the imagination, but some of the homes were rudimentary wooden structures, and some even had leaf roofs. Still, most of the houses were made of brick and cement, and there were some beautiful old French colonial bungalows. Many of the homes were two stories tall, and there was a Catholic church, other religious structures, and markets

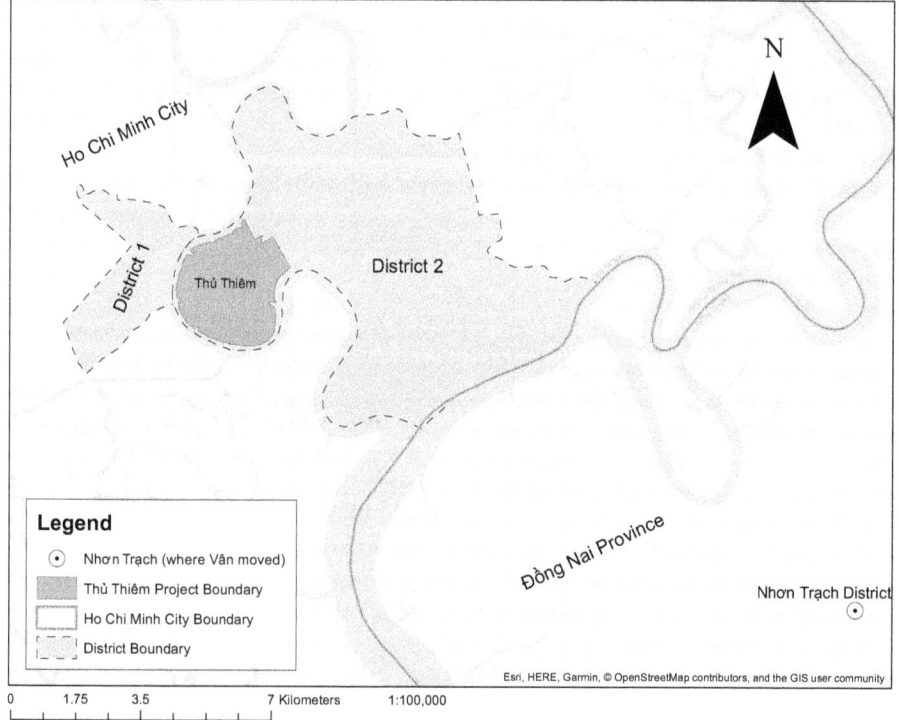

FIGURE 10.3. Map of Thủ Thiêm in relation to Ho Chi Minh City's District 1 and Nhơn Trạch District in Đồng Nai Province. Prepared by the author.

within the district. The main roads were paved, but smaller pathways were mostly muddy and potholed, and there were large swaths of swampy, inundated land crisscrossed by canals and dotted with ponds. If you cupped your hands around your eyes to block the urban horizon and only looked in some specific directions, it was possible to imagine that you were in the middle of the Vietnamese countryside. But when you uncupped your hands, the city once again unfolded before you. For working-class residents of the city, it was possible to live simply yet comfortably on a working-class budget but still enjoy the pleasures of a cosmopolitan city. There were also cool river breezes in the neighborhoods and the view across the river to the city was (and still is) spectacular. The tall skyscrapers of downtown were just a five-minute ferry ride from the center of the city, the ferry cost almost nothing, and it ran all day and all night (figure 10.4).

Between 2002 and 2012, 14,600 households were forced to move from their homes in Thủ Thiêm so that the city could clear the land in order to begin building a massive utopian urban showcase. In response to this situation, many Thủ Thiêm residents fought for their rights and demanded justice. In many cases, their resistance and stubbornness was profound—they successfully slowed the project down, and it took more than a decade and several large increases in the level of compensation to get people to move. By the time most of the Thủ Thiêm residents had been evicted, around late 2012, many of the residents had achieved many of their stated goals—compensation had been raised from 2 million đồng per square meter to as much as 20 million (approximately US $1,000), and residents managed to mobilize aspects of the law on their behalf. By the end of the land clearance period, the total compensation paid out was estimated at 16.4 billion Vietnamese đồng, or approximately US $820 million, which averages to just over US $56,000 per household.

In the final instance, however, the fact remained that all of the residents eventually ended up displaced from their homes, and the great majority found themselves living in circumstances much worse than those they had been forced to leave. It is true that their compensation levels rose dramatically thanks to their expressions of dissent and their noncompliance with early eviction notices. Nevertheless, it is also true that land values in the area rose at even faster rates, so much so that their increased compensation ended up being worth less, in terms of the land it allowed them to buy, than it was at the beginning of the process. This meant that the longer people stayed to fight for gains in compensation, the less they were able to purchase suitable places to live within the city limits. Officially, the resettlement rules stipulated in Vietnam's land laws and the policies to regulate the specifics of the Thủ Thiêm case accord clear rights to compensation for those who occupy lands reclaimed for projects deemed to be in the

FIGURE 10.4. The view from Thủ Thiêm toward Ho Chi Minh City. Note the Thủ Thiêm ferry crossing the Saigon River. Thủ Thiêm District, Ho Chi Minh City, Vietnam. 2010. Author's photo.

public interest. In this way, the Vietnamese regulations are similar to the eminent domain clauses present in most land laws around the world. However, interpreting what counts as fair compensation becomes a central conflict in all such cases, because land values are determined by government-appointed land valuation authorities that regularly value land well below the prices a parcel would receive if it were to be sold through existing real estate markets. While economists have criticized this "two price system" and called for the government to base all land valuation on market mechanisms (Thien Thu and Perera 2011), the rapid transformation in land prices makes even that method untenable because it is the market itself that drives the rapid price increases. Every rise in compensation is always accompanied by even greater rises in market values.

In the Thủ Thiêm case, the situation was further complicated by the fact that full authority for developing a compensation plan rested in the hands of a parastatal agency called the "committee for compensating losses due to project land clearance" (Hội đồng đền bù thiệt hại giải phóng mặt bằng của dự án). This committee was created as a subsidiary of the Thủ Thiêm Investment and Construction Authority (ICA), an organization tasked with clearing the land for the development and also with recruiting investors. The fact that the ICA was charged with both compensation and investor recruitment led to a situation in which the whole economic logic of the project depended on keeping the value of land low during the compensation phase while maximizing the value of land during the period of recruiting investors. In the end, residents recognized this situation and engaged in stubborn resistance that led, incrementally yet steadily, to higher levels of compensation. Nevertheless, those negotiations took time, and the gains achieved in fighting for their "right" to fair compensation were always several steps behind the speed at which land prices were rising. By the time residents gained a victory in demanding fair compensation at what they understood to be fair market values, the land values had once again rocketed to prices well above the gains they achieved. Thus, when all was said and done, even though residents successfully demanded that base compensation rates be raised to 20 million đồng per square meter, once that victory was achieved in 2012 land values in nearby areas had surpassed 60 million đồng per square meter. On paper, they had fought for their rights, mobilized the rule of law, and achieved justice; but in practice they were all evicted against their will and still ended up with compensation that was far too little for rebuilding their lives.

How is it possible that fighting for and in many ways successfully defending one's rights still ends up leaving someone evicted from house and home? To answer this question it is useful to focus on the mediating role played by documents and by abstract conceptions of "rights" and "the law." My ethnographic work shows how the documents in this case channeled the fight for rights in such a way that the very concept of rights became conflated with the act of gaining fair monetary compensation. These documents clearly encouraged people to act in certain ways that they would not have acted without the documents. As such, they can be profitably understood using some of the tools developed by Bruno Latour and others associated with the intellectual movement known as Actor-Network Theory (Latour 2005). In Latour's terms, "every time you want to know what a nonhuman does, simply imagine what other humans or other nonhumans would have to do were this character not present" (Latour 2008, 155). Clearly, in the case of Thủ Thiêm, a host of activities was instigated by the prompts and demands of documents, which made it possible for people to communicate their rights and their demands on paper, and to send those papers to offices, circulate them on the internet and thereby generate a discursive world in which aggrieved residents were able to assert certain claims they might not have been able to make without them. In this way, the documents looked and indeed "acted" very much like those the anthropologist Matthew Hull (2012) has described in urban Pakistan, where the interaction of residents and urban planning bureaucracy produced a "regime of paper documents" that not only express human relations but actually instantiate and produce new relations, new kinds of agency, and new forms of governance. This is clearly the case in Thủ Thiêm, where documents are entangled in all aspects of people's lives and in many ways guide their responses to eviction.

There is, however, a twist: in the case of Thủ Thiêm, the evidence suggests that the agency induced by these documents developed into a form of distracted agency. Like the kinds of action inspired by a classic fetish object, the documents incited people to organize their efforts around terms set by the demands of the documents themselves. These documents are able to do this because people have ascribed to them power not only to represent but in fact to demand something called rights. The documents that express and claim an ability to deliver these rights, however, both produce and are the product of the commodification of land, which is itself dependent on preserving the rights supposedly inscribed in the documents for some, while stripping those rights from others. The commodification of land is itself the end result of a complex process which extracts land from social relations of care, labor, cultivation, improvement, and habitation and transforms it into a commodified, quantifiable unit of financial investment value that can be claimed by some and stripped from others.[6]

In this way, documents both produce new forms of agency and also conceal a host of existing social relations. What is important to recognize, and ultimately quite troubling to watch in this case, is how the documents calling for rights and deploying the language of the law start to proliferate precisely as the land becomes stripped from people. Of course, it is common that rights become objects of intense debate precisely when they are under threat. However, in this case, it is precisely the absence of rights in lived action that leads people to intensify their focus on the existence of rights on paper. While the discourse that emerges may certainly be construed as a form of resistance, this discourse actually draws people deeper into the very commodification process that started their dispossession in the first place. Hull states the problem well in his study of Pakistan: "Whatever the utility of the dominance-resistance framework elsewhere, it is not productive here" (Hull 2012, 163). This is not because people passively accept the loss of their land. By contrast, they are quite vocal and they place great emphasis on the production of petitions and other forms of righteous resistance. However, in the process of generating all this paperwork, people end up replacing what has been lost with piles of paper declaring their rights, placing extraordinary faith in the importance of fighting for the right to compensation, while their actual right to live on their land vanishes under their feet. The piles of documents grow ever larger at the same time that their homes are reduced to rubble.

Meanwhile, the reliance on legal documents and formal language for expressing grievances reframes the way land is conceptualized. Land is increasingly seen as little more than a valuable commodity that can be classified and enumerated in terms that correspond to market values. In the case of Thủ Thiêm, as the quest to achieve rights became increasingly synonymous with the struggle over land values, the notion of rights themselves became flattened into a quantifiable idiom that conflated "rights" with property value. Instead of a right to the city, in which residents might be seen as equal partners in the larger planning of the world in which they lived, or a right to livelihood, or to an ability to reproduce themselves as social persons, a bureaucratic paperwork version of rights was reduced to a calculation of money and meters. In the end, paperwork versions of law and justice delivered residents a Pyrrhic ideological victory, granting evictees "rights" and a large but still insufficient pile of money while stripping them of house and home.

Paperwork in the Cemetery

The argument I am building here hints at the limits of Western liberal conceptions of rights and forces us to think critically about the hidden costs associated with the rule of law. While such a critical perspective on rights is not new in itself, applying it to urban land disputes adds a critical perspective to what are often ideologically driven debates about the supposed correlation between property rights and democratization.[7] The case of Thủ Thiêm, furthermore, highlights what the literature on rights widely recognizes: namely, that concepts like "rights" or "rule of law" must not only be studied at the level of discourse and logical argumentation, but must be understood in terms of lived experiences. Rights are not things that people "have" but must continually be demanded and acknowledged—and in this case, the more that people made claims on their rights, the more it was clear that they did not have them. Over the course of interviewing one hundred and forty-eight evicted residents in Thủ Thiêm, watching the way they handled legal documents related to their land, and listening to how they spoke about their rights, I started to realize that the more they fixated on petitions and legal documents as a way of articulating their rights, the more they were drawn into debates over compensation values and quantifiable numbers of square meters of land. Additionally, the more they became fixated on property values and their legal rights, the more they became drawn into a form of negotiation in which dispossession seemed to be the only foreseeable outcome. When land became converted to something valued primarily in terms of money and meters, fighting for rights became little more than a game of "Let's make a deal." And the terms in this deal were almost always skewed in favor of interests that were more powerful than the evicted residents. Even in those rare cases where residents did negotiate a good deal, such deals were always contingent on them relinquishing their land.

This realization first came to me during the middle of fieldwork when I found myself in a cemetery on the edge of the city. It was late October 2010 and my research partner and I had been led across town to the corner of a desolate and dusty graveyard by a woman and her ten-year-old son. They had been evicted from their home in Thủ Thiêm, and we were visiting the small house she had purchased on land encroaching this cemetery, just beyond the administrative borders of Ho Chi Minh City, over the ferry crossing at Cát Lái, across the Nhà Bè River, in Nhơn Trạch district, part of Đồng Nai Province. The woman's husband had died in 2001 and, on the meager single income she scraped together through odd jobs, this small, distant plot of land, which land speculators had illegally usurped from the dead, was the only place she could afford. She had brought us there to tell us the story of her fight for her rights. She ended up showing us a pile of documents.

The mother, who I will call Vân, was forty-six years old. The wrinkles on her face showed that she had once known how to smile, but those marks of happier times had grown rigid and stiff. On that day at the edge of the cemetery, she mainly had sadness to share. She lamented the dust and the heat and complained about how far this desolate spot was from her old home, and how she was now cut off from the personal networks she had cultivated over half a lifetime living in Thủ Thiêm before being forced to leave. There was no work out there in Nhơn

Trạch, the schools were terrible, her son had no friends, and she didn't feel like she could trust any of her new neighbors, who didn't seem to trust her either. As we talked, her son went off by himself to play in the cemetery, where he climbed across tombstones as if they were playground equipment, and we sat down in her living room to discuss how she had ended up where she was. As commonly happens when people discuss their eviction, she pulled out her paperwork, and she walked us through the documents in reverse chronological order.

Vân lingered on the most recent document, which she described as a kind of victory (figure 10.5). It was handwritten on lined notebook paper, with the words "Socialist Republic of Vietnam: Independence—Freedom—Happiness" carefully printed in two lines across the top. The document also had a title, carefully centered on the page, which she had printed in block letters, all capitalized, as if trying to mimic the words of a typewriter: "ĐƠN XIN XÁC NHẬN" (REQUEST FOR CONFIRMATION). It was signed by the local police department in her new district, who had also stamped their red seal over their signatures. Its sole purpose was to affirm that Vân lived in the district. This paper was a victory, she said, because she had been fighting for months with the Thủ Thiêm authorities over her right to receive special additional compensation legally entitled to those

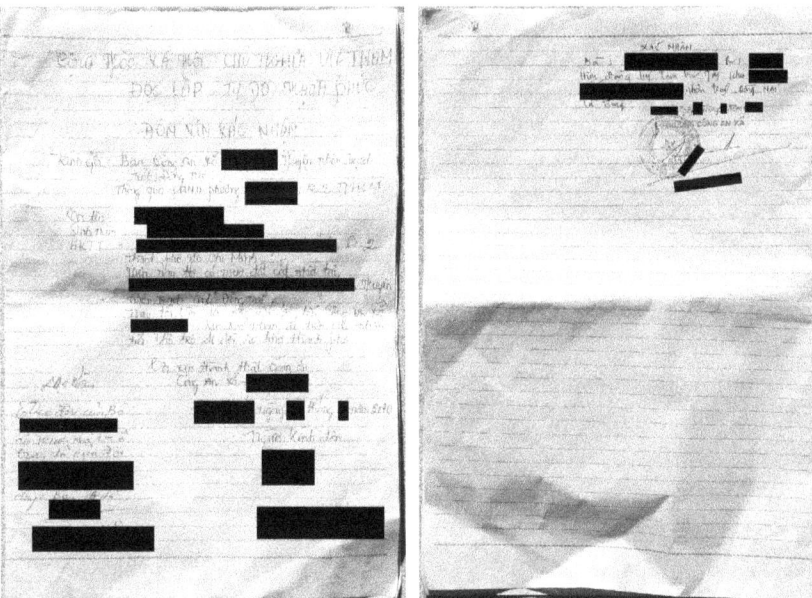

FIGURE 10.5. Handwritten documents from an evicted Thủ Thiêm resident trying to establish residency in her newly relocated area. Ho Chi Minh City, Vietnam. 2010. Author's photo.

who had been forced by circumstances to relocate to districts beyond the boundaries of the city. The problem she had been facing until this point was simple yet frustrating: the house she bought on the cemetery land had been built on an informal plot of land, not formally registered in the cadastral land registry. But in order to claim her extra compensation, she needed formal residence papers to prove where she had moved. Although the policy of offering extra compensation for those forced to move great distances had been designed to help the most disadvantaged among the evictees, the irony here was plain to see: the reason she lacked the papers to prove that she was needy was because she was so needy. It was precisely because her compensation had been so low that she had been forced to purchase a piece of land lacking full and complete land-use right certificates. After countless trips back and forth to the Thủ Thiêm land compensation office in District 2, each time being rejected for not providing adequate proof of her residence beyond the borders of the city, she had finally managed to get the local police to sign the paper. It was handwritten, but it still had the official government seal. This was her huge victory.

But what kind of victory was this? The paper she clutched so triumphantly confirmed the fact that she now lived in a district she never wanted to live in in the first place. As she spoke, she began to pull out further documents, all detailing the nature of her displacement, telling the story of how she ended up where she was. The documents she had received from the government were all expert legal contrivances, laying out in legal terminology the careful reasoning and legal basis for the low level of compensation she had been offered. The most important document was the one she had received in January 2007, which described and itemized the level of compensation she would receive, which added up to a total of 137 million đồng (approximately US $7,000) divided into two sums: 121 million đồng (ca. US $6,000) for her house and property, and an additional 16 million đồng (about US $800) for her move. The document, like all official Vietnamese documents, including her own handwritten ones, had the words "Socialist Republic of Vietnam: Independence—Freedom—Happiness" written across the header. Beneath that was an official alphanumeric document identifier indicating the case number and the particular ward where she had lived before the eviction. Beneath that was the title of the document: "Calculation Worksheet for Additional Compensation for Resettlement Expenses and Other Losses due to the Construction of the Thủ Thiêm New Urban Zone."[8]

The document did two things at once: First, it laid out extremely low levels of compensation. Second, it managed to envelope this low compensation in a discursive shield of legal terminology, obscuring the nastiness of eviction and the insufficient compensation in the formal and distancing language of legal detachment. The first lines of the document set the stage for the rest of the document's legal performance by opening up with a list of legal declarations. They read like this: "Pursuant to Decision No. 1997/QD-UB on May 10th, 2002 of the Municipal People's Committee on land recovery and reallocation for the Thủ Thiêm New Urban Center Project," pursuant to Decision X, pursuant to Decision Y, and so on. And then the document laid out a long series of calculations, carefully itemizing the legal basis on which the decision to grant the 121 million had been arrived at: 81 million (about US $4,000) for the land, 6 million (US $300) for the actual house and other "architectural objects," 5 million for agreeing to move without dispute and for abiding by the law, and so on. Total compensation and support was listed point by point in a clear and seemingly transparent calculation: Item one plus item two plus item three plus item four . . . plus five plus six plus seven. Together all these items added up to the total: 121 million plus 16 million.

These clear and rational calculations, however, obscured the financial burden this whole process was placing on Vân. The new house in the cemetery had cost her 125 million đồng—4 million more than she had so far received. This meant that without the 16 million in extra assistance she was really scraping by, and her struggle was compounded by the expenses she had incurred undertaking the move itself, and by the fact that she had no work or support network in the new area. She desperately needed that 16 million, but the District 2 authorities had demanded papers to verify her residence. This is what had sent her on these several months of negotiating with the District 2 authorities, struggling to claim that extra 16 million. Riding her motorbike from office to office, from the local police in her new district to the authorities in the old district, she eventually managed to get that signed piece of paper. It was indeed a victory—she had secured her right to compensation. But the victory itself was subsumed under the larger loss, the fact that she had been forced to move from a house along the Saigon River with a view looking at the Ho Chi Minh City skyline, a short few minutes away from work opportunities downtown, evicted along with all her friends and neighbors and shunted off to the dusty margins of the city. On paper, Vân's was a case in which her rights had been delivered, but the dejection on her face as she told me the story, and the material deprivation and displacement she experienced as a result of the process, indicated that she still felt like her right to the city had been violated.

Nevertheless, Vân clutched those documents with care. She asked me to use my camera to photograph them so that she would have a digital back-up of her records. And then she wrapped them carefully in a plastic bag to protect them from the dust, and placed that bag inside one of those plastic file folders with the firm snap clasp that nearly every Vietnamese household has for the purpose of storing these documents. As she snapped her "My Clear Bag" closed, she had both earned her right to stay in the cemetery and sealed her fate by closing the case on her eviction.[9]

The Pull of the Document

This encounter with Vân in her house in the cemetery was not unique. I had similar exchanges in the course of meeting and talking to Thủ Thiêm residents undergoing eviction. On many occasions, when my research partners and I would meet persons being evicted from their home, whether it was in the rubble fields of Thủ Thiêm or in the distant and desolate neighborhoods into which they had been displaced, they would pull out their documents, unsnap their "My Clear Bag," and lay their papers out before us, describing similar stories of dispossession documented in the very legal documents they clutched with such care. The documents all referred to long lists of laws, laid out calculations in carefully itemized fashion, and were replete with official signatures, signed and countersigned, and stamped with red stamps. Then, after laying the documents out before us, these evicted residents would tell of the many fruitless trips they had made between offices at all levels of the city, the petitions they had sent, the requests for reconsiderations, the one-on-one meetings they attended with district officials, and the disputes about how many square meters they were told their property measured, or how some parts of their land were worth so many đồng while different parts were worth different amounts, and how many đồng certain types of built construction were worth, based on when it was built, all pursuant to Decision X, Decision Y, Decision Z and often long lists of other decisions. They would then delve into heated debates about the meaning of those decisions, which they had tried to look up and read, but which, they often admitted, they rarely understood. Still, in spite of it all, they ceaselessly combed through the documents and even tracked down and read the laws that the documents counter-referenced, proceeding line by line with fine-toothed combs but no legal training, searching for loopholes or missed clauses—searching, of course, for something that would help soften the blow of their eviction.

Many of the residents undergoing eviction became fixated on the documents they had received. In the process they became pulled into a legal labyrinth like Joseph K in Kafka's *Trial*. Their plight recalls the scene when "the priest" recounts a parable to the protagonist K: "In front of the law there is a doorkeeper. A man from the countryside comes up to the door and asks for entry. But the doorkeeper says he can't let him in to the law right now" (Kafka 2012, 154). Likewise, the Thủ Thiêm residents have their papers and stand before the doorway. But their papers do not let them into the law. Nevertheless, the language and the form of the documents themselves altered people's mode of articulating their sense of injustice. Two things started to happen. First, people began to adopt a quasi-legalistic language, which enabled them to speak of "justice," "rights," and "the law." Mobilizing this language, they found a voice that emboldened them to insist that they had a right to defend themselves and to be treated fairly before the law. Second, as they did this, they also started talking a great deal about money and square meters. As a result, while they spoke quite loudly about rights, it was also clear that "rights," "justice," and money began to blend in with each other. On the one hand, they began to experience what Annelise Riles (2011, 8) has called the "pull of documents." On the other hand, those documents were not letting them into the law.

Shortchanged by a Long List

Documents related to land management in Vietnam, as elsewhere, are characterized by legalistic language, lists, and enumeration. Given this, it is not difficult to understand how residents are drawn into a form of discourse that conceptualizes land primarily in terms of property values, and where rights are largely flattened into a debate over how land value is calculated according to legal terms. Because the very format in which the legal documents are written demands itemization and quantification, any conscientious engagement with the documents shapes the way in which "rights," "justice," "fairness," and other such concepts become articulated. In the process, essentially humanistic concepts become math problems, exercises in quantification.

Consider, for example, one of the most important kinds of documents in the eviction process that took place in Thủ Thiêm, a document called the "VALUE WORKSHEET FOR COMPENSATION, ASSISTANCE FOR DAMAGES AND RELOCATION" (figure 10.6).[10] The same document was issued to all households facing eviction by an agency called the Land Clearance and Compensation Committee, which was created as a parastatal authority, acting under the supervision of the District 2 People's Committee and the Thủ Thiêm Investment and Construction Authority. In all of the eviction cases, this "Value worksheet" (*Bảng chiết tính giá trị*) was used to detail and itemize the results of drawings and tabulations carried out by the survey and cadastral records office. Like all the other documents issued by formal government authorities, the worksheet opens with a long list of legal decisions and orders before setting out an itemized inventory of the property in question. The inventories could be quite extensive

218 CHAPTER 10

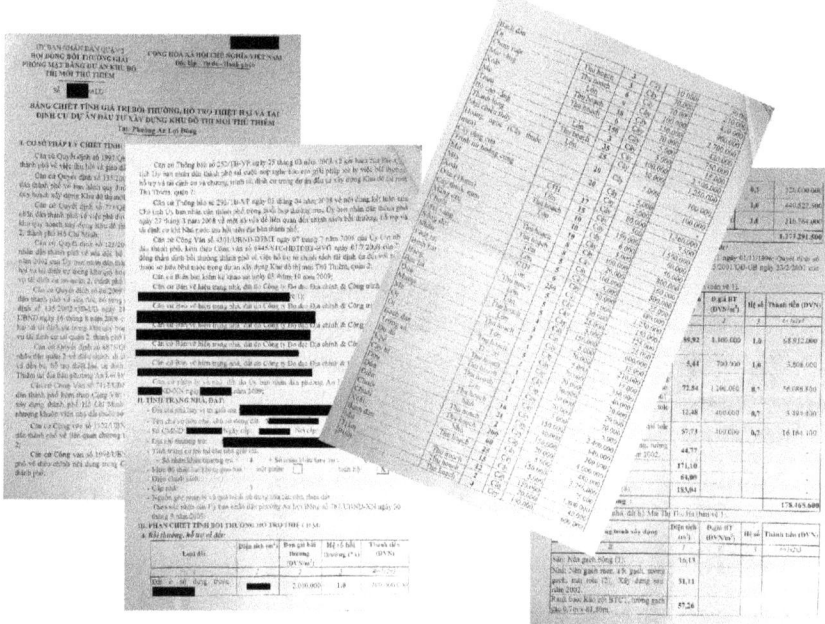

FIGURE 10.6. "Value worksheet" (Bảng chiết tính giá trị) used to calculate compensation for houses being demolished. Ho Chi Minh City, Vietnam. 2010. Author's photo.

and sometimes continued for several pages, where lists on lists systematically itemized every small detail of a household's property.

These documents drew their recipients directly into a process of enumeration and legal discourse that worked to channel the dispute in a particular manner. An example can be seen in the case of an extended multigenerational family living together in a cluster of five patrilocal compounds on a large, nearly five-thousand-square-meter plot of land. This family had carefully preserved land papers proving that they had occupied the land since long before the end of the Vietnam War in 1975, when Saigon was the capital of the Republic of Vietnam. Members of the family had moved there in 1959 as tenant farmers. The family preserved these papers with extraordinary care because they clearly demonstrated the family's long-term occupation of the land. They also showed that they had long been engaged in a complex mix of agricultural and urban activities. With such a large plot of land, some members of the family actively cultivated a wide assortment of fruit trees and perennials, grew vegetables and a little rice, and raised pigs, free-range chickens, fish, and even alligators. At the same time, because they lived so close to the city, more than half the family was also engaged in nonagricultural activity with a mix of occupations. Family members included taxi-drivers, office workers, and schoolteachers. All of the children in the family had at one time attended primary schools in District 2 and some of the older ones attended high school and college across the river in District 1.

When all of this diverse land use was enumerated on the calculation worksheet, all of this extended family's occupational diversity was simultaneously recorded in great detail and also flattened and obscured. On the one hand, the detail was extraordinary: the worksheet carefully noted and assigned a value to every single tree and plant on the plot of land, and the enumeration went on for four single-spaced pages. The end result of this process of listing everything in painstaking detail, on the other hand, was that most of the land ended up being classified as "agricultural land," which drastically reduced its value. As a result, the entire extended multihousehold family was eventually offered a grand total of 1.6 billion đồng (approximately US $75,000) for this especially large plot of land. While this sum might seem like a large amount, it was meant to compensate for nearly 5,000 square meters (half a hectare, just shy of one and a quarter acre), and would have to be split among five separate households, all descendants of the original patriarch who had worked the land in Thủ Thiêm several generations earlier. Divided by five, this amounted to US$15,000 per household in a city where land in even the most distant areas commonly costs well over a thousand dollars per square meter, and much more in areas equivalent to the one from which they were being asked to vacate.

This case, which was quite typical of cases in Thủ Thiêm, helps explain how the same enumerated list that spurs people to *act* may in fact act to *distract*. As I stared at the list with members of the family, it seemed as if the scrupulous detail was so carefully itemized primarily as a way for the authorities to show that they were being fair and careful in their methods of handing out extremely low compensation. The list masqueraded as a fair accounting of compensation due, but in real terms it acted as a screen concealing a bad deal.

A document like this demands a response. And it got one. The members of the household carefully went through the itemizations and calculations, disputed them one by one, and then prepared a response letter detailing and itemizing their disagreement. Responding to a document like the one they had received, it's no surprise that they became fixated on numbers and calculations, and that their cries of injustice took the form of disputes about square meters and money, because this is exactly what the document demands. As a result, when these kinds of documents draw the Thủ Thiêm residents into fights for their rights, these fights for rights become math problems, exercises in classification, and disputes over lists. The only way they can fight for their rights is to bicker over meters and money.

And that is precisely what they did. Thủ Thiêm residents responded to the documents, addressed the discrepancies, made public appeals, and petitioned the authorities with their own documents. They constructed paperwork responses to these lists, and clutched those papers with great care, tending to them as if the papers themselves would deliver something called rights, which would in turn stem the tide of their dispossession. Their actions clearly parallel research from other contexts that shows the important role that documents play in framing and instigating new forms of social action. Writing about the conflict between planners and residents in Islamabad, and building from the work of Bruno Latour, for example, the anthropologist Matthew Hull has powerfully argued that documents, especially those used in land conflicts, actually mobilize people to act. Documents do not simply mediate the relationship between state and society, but actually instantiate and constitute those relationships. Like Hull, I also insist that ethnographic attention to the way petitions and legal texts "perdure, circulate, change, and cease to exist takes us beyond notions of information 'storage' to an understanding of how material artifacts shape the discourses they mediate" (Hull 2012, 23). Documents do not simply represent the world but become part of the association between persons, places, and things that actually makes up the world.

In the ethnographic examples described in this chapter, the documents people receive and produce draw them into a particular way of engaging with the acts of dispossession that are transforming their lives. Their responses to those transformations are in many ways shaped by the form and material qualities of the documents themselves. The ethnographic data from Vietnam thus support a central aspect of the "actor-network-theory" suggested by Latour, which clearly describes and theorizes the socially productive associations that develop through the interrelation between people and things. Clearly, the documents prompt people to do things they would not do without the documents.

However, this Latourian framework has limits. By focusing primarily on cases in which the agency of things productively engages with the agency of humans, Latour's approach actively ignores cases in which humans and things work at cross-purposes. For example, in describing the agentive capacity of nonhuman actants, Latour instructively uses the example of a door hinge (which enables a wall to be turned into a hole; that is, for a door to be opened) or the example of a hammer (which "hits" the nail) (Latour 2008, 155). In other words, he turns to examples that "work," that essentially do what the humans who invented them wanted them to do, and in ways they expect them to do. In such examples, it is clear that humans delegate their agency to these nonhuman actors, and that if you "want to know what a nonhuman does" in such a case, all one has to do is "simply imagine what other humans or nonhumans would have to do were this character not present" (Latour 2008, 155). However, it is important to remember that there are nonhuman things that are much trickier than door hinges and hammers, things that engage in, and enable humans to engage in, illusions and deceptions too. There are things like bad checks, fake products, or disingenuous legal pronouncements that make it seem as if one is doing one thing when in fact they promote the doing of other things. These are the kinds of things that enable humans to engage in deceptive relationships with each other, and to conceal those relationships behind the things themselves.

As this chapter has shown, in addition to attending to what nonhuman things like documents do, it is also important to imagine what kinds of acts the presence of certain nonhumans sometimes work to obscure. We might reframe Latour's comment by asking ourselves to imagine what kinds of actions humans might engage in among each other if certain nonhumans were not present. What, for example, might you do if a group of men came and took you and your neighbors' land and you and your neighbors responded to them directly, and not with a collection of documents that are in fact not really backed up by the law? Latour's sometimes uncritical focus on the productive generation of agency among both humans and nonhuman things risks deflecting or negating critical attention to the nefarious things people do to each other when they hide behind nonhumans. It is equally important to recognize how people regularly deploy things as screens or blockades that conceal the unsavory ways they treat each other. In the case of Thủ Thiêm, one might think of land documents as the functional equivalent of a bad check—and in this case, they are like bad checks that people keep trying to cash even after they have proven not to be backed up by any substance. Even though these documents continually fail to deliver the rights that they promise, people continue to place faith in them. Those who have received these bad checks keep returning to the bank, day after day, making deposits that are never realized—maintaining the belief that the document, by virtue of its material existence alone has the capacity to act. In cases like this, when the agency of documents and the agency of people become theorized as equal partners in the production of social action, it becomes increasingly difficult to call out the ways in which documents distract people from the very causes they are fighting for. It is true that documents can spur people to act, but there are many ways in which documents distract.

In my interaction with evicted residents in the Thủ Thiêm case, I regularly witnessed people treating their documents as if the pieces of paper themselves actually contained a host of sentiments variously called "rights," "justice," "fairness," and so on. My interlocutors would pull them out, hold them up, and declare that they had rights by virtue of possessing the documents. In the Vietnamese legal system, however, as in most places, rights, justice, and fairness are not things that people "have." They always emerge out of social relations, politics, networks of patronage, and battles fought over access to land, the right to the city, and so forth. In this context, while the documents may prompt people to act in particular ways, they also prompt people to act in ways they cannot deliver on. They draw residents into a paperwork maze in which the human actors being evicted direct the bulk of their attention to, and interact ceaselessly with, the documents. Meanwhile, the humans doing the evicting evade direct confrontation with those they are displacing. The evictees come into social relations with the documents, which are themselves divorced from the social relations, deal making, and brokering going on behind the scenes that are actually driving the development of the Thủ Thiêm project. While the residents wield their documents and raise their voices about their rights, the project developers rapidly accumulate land and engage in corrupt yet largely concealed social relations with real estate investors and other powerful government agents. It is in this way that I suggest that the documents not only prompt novel forms of action in the world, but do indeed operate as fetish objects. They perpetuate the illusion that they are able to act on the world in magical ways, all while concealing a world of social action that hides behind the very aura generated by the documents themselves.

While Actor Network Theory clearly supports the conclusion that documents are part of a network of agency involving both human and nonhuman actors, Latour himself would likely reject my conception of documents as fetish objects. In his formulation, objects can never distract or form the basis of illusions because there is no such thing as "the fact." He denounces scholars who look to unmask relations of mystification as naïve promulgators of "factishes" or "antifetishists." "To accuse something of being a fetish," he writes, "is the ultimate gratuitous, disrespectful, insane, and barbarous gesture" (Latour 2004, 243). Given this pronouncement, Latour rejects the notion that documents and rights claims—or anything, for that matter—might possibly operate like fetish objects. But making such a declaration in this case requires ignoring the evidence for how the Thủ Thiêm case played out. All one needs to do is look at the landscape. There once was a neighborhood, and now, despite all the power ascribed to the documents, and despite all the agitated action the documents inspired, the neighborhood is gone. By the end of the case, despite the great power ascribed to them, and despite the great care taken to preserve them, the appeals and documents that were supposedly mobilized to fight the process of dispossession were unable to effect real change that would stop the bulldozers of development and eviction. By 2014, nearly everyone was removed from Thủ Thiêm. In the process, many of the residents most active in fighting for higher compensation had boldly fought for their "rights" but still ended up in distant margins of the city on plots of land they despised. In very real ways, the very act of engaging the authorities in legal discourse only further solidified the legal basis of their dispossession. Fighting for their rights had cost them their homes.

11

WHERE MATERIALITY MEETS SUBJECTIVITY

Locating the Political in the Contested Fiction of Urban Land in Camden, New Jersey

Robert W. Lake

On May 6, 1795, as Polanyi relates, the justices of Berkshire, England, meeting "in Speenhamland, near Newbury," enacted the Speenhamland scale, providing a subsidy to wages to be paid from the local rates (i.e., taxes), "so that a minimum income should be assured to the poor *irrespective of their earnings*" (Polanyi 2001 [1944], 82, emphasis in original). Speenhamland, on Polanyi's account, established a "right to live" for the increasing numbers of dispossessed laborers who, evicted from feudal estates through the widespread enclosure of land, sought employment for wages in the rapidly forming labor markets of the industrial revolution. If the forced displacement of feudal peasants accelerated the commodification of labor in an expanding industrial labor market, Speenhamland represented a countermovement protecting the laboring poor from the debilitating effects of market expansion under conditions in which a burgeoning labor supply forced wages below subsistence.

Speenhamland's subsidy for wages, keyed to the price of bread, comprised one in a series of enactments seeking in various ways and at various times to control the constitution, subjectivity, and mobility of laboring people in the course of England's tumultuous transformation from agrarian feudalism to industrial capitalism through the commodification of land and labor geared to the institution of a market society (Rogan 2017; Thompson 1966; Toulmin 2001). Antivagrancy laws, the Poor Laws, the establishment of pauperism as a legal category distinct from poverty, and other measures constituted what Polanyi memorably characterized as the double movement involving the expansion of the market system and its retardation aimed at ameliorating its most harmful effects. As Polanyi explained,

> Under Speenhamland, society was rent by two opposing influences: the one emanating from paternalism and protecting labor from the dangers of the market system; the other organizing the elements of production, including land, under a market system, and thus divesting the common people of their former status, compelling them to gain a living by offering their labor for sale, while at the same time depriving their labor of its market value. (Polanyi 2001 [1944], 84)

Neither the expansion of market society nor the protective countermeasures emerged spontaneously in the absence of political conflict, contestation, and debate. Strangely missing from Polanyi's historical account is an explication of the contentious politics through which the aims and logics of the double movement were debated, competing aims were even provisionally resolved, and specific measures were enacted to accelerate and/or retard the commodification of land and labor and the embedding of society in the market. He relegates to "the sociological background" the political conflict between market liberalism and its antithesis that, he says, nevertheless "made up the political history of Continental Europe in the nineteenth century" (2001 [1944], 194). Implicit in this sociological background was a series of foundational assumptions that constituted human beings—the actual people whose lived experiences and life chances were poorly captured by such impersonal abstractions as urbanization, commodification, and industrialization—as particular kinds of human subjects required by and conducive to the political-economic transformations underway in the establishment and expansion of a market society (Hoffman 2014; Rodgers et al. 2014). Market liberals, as Rogan (2017, 4) recounts, "reconstructed human persons 'solely as beings who desire to possess wealth,' an outcome achieved (in the words of the young J. S. Mill) by the 'entire abstraction of every other human passion or motive.'" Polanyi explicitly rejected, on both moral and historical grounds, the utilitarian, consequentialist ethic that reduced individuals to the status of a utility-maximizing means to benefit the numerical majority (Block 2018; Polanyi 2002 [1947]; Rogan 2017),[1] and he railed against the assumed inevitability of economic laws that produced in the worker an "abject readiness to be shoved and pushed about indiscriminately (subject to) complete dependence on the whims of the market." The commodification of labor, Polanyi held, produced a dehumanization in which "it is not for the commodity to decide where it should be offered for sale, to what purpose it should be used, at what price it should be allowed to change hands, and in what manner it should be consumed or destroyed" (Polanyi 2001 [1944], 185).

Against the simplified, even caricatured, representation of human subjectivity underlying and implicit in the expansion of market rationality, the reality of lived experience offers a more complicated picture. As Block asserts, "People resist: they refuse to act like lemmings marching over a cliff to their own destruction" (Block 2001, xxv). The result, contrary to claims of the ascendancy of the postpolitical (Rancière 1995; Swyngedouw 2011), is a complex politics of contestation in the enactment of the double movement mediating the commodity fictions enabling the expansion and contraction of the market system. Now the questions become: what sort of politics, located in what political arena, with what consequences for the enactment of a market economy and for the lives of those caught up in its embrace? Posing these questions in this way emphasizes the nonteleological aspect of political contestation and directs attention to its performance in particular situated contexts where outcomes are open-ended and possibilities remain for stories to unfold in different ways (Muellerleile 2013; Peck 2013b; Smith 2013).

In this chapter, accordingly, I trace the unfolding of the double movement through three interrelated moments of political contestation over its form and content. First, a *politics of commodification*, as widely described throughout this volume, negotiates the contentious process of calibrating, coordinating, and constructing the fictions through which life and nature are transformed into the marketable commodities of labor and land. Political conflict arises from the contradictory character of these fictitious commodities, in which the tradable properties of land and labor conflict with the noncommodifiable (i.e., natural, human) foundations on which they are based. The deleterious effects of this inherent contradiction—"the demolition of society," in Polanyi's words (2001 [1944], 76)—produce, second, a *politics of the countermovement* through which society works out the form, substance, speed, and intensity of the institutionalization of the market mechanism and the protective countermeasures designed to ameliorate its destructive manifestations. Yet, as noted above, the politically contentious and often contested processes of commodification and marketization do not proceed in the abstract but must be performed by situated subjects aligned with the ideological presuppositions, embedded logics, and practical demands of the politically designated practices. The formation of appropriately situated subjects is itself contested rather than singularly legislated from above (or outside), generating, third, a *politics of subjectification* through which subject positions are imposed and resisted. Describing the confounding effects of the Speenhamland scale, for example, Polanyi recounted the unexpected rejection of the subsidy by those who might have benefited from higher wages but refused to accept the identity of the pauper: "On the face of it the 'right to live' should have stopped wage labor altogether.... But this was an essentially pre-capitalistic age, when the common people were still traditionally minded, and far from being directed in their behavior by monetary motives alone. The majority of the countryfolk ... preferred any kind of existence to the status of a pauper" (Polanyi 2001 [1944], 85). The possibility that nonmonetary values might undergird behaviors informed both Polanyi's conception of freedom and the moral roots of his condemnation of the unregulated market (Block 2018; Rogan 2017).[2]

Locating the Politics of the Double Movement

Tracing the politics of the double movement through the three interrelated moments of commodification, protectionism, and subjectification belies simple deterministic imputations of interests or intentions on the part of actors engaged in the process. Central to Polanyi's historical account is his recognition that the countermovement slowing market expansion included but was certainly not limited to acts of resistance mounted by those most harmed by the deleterious effects of commodification and market making. As Fred Block (2001, xxviii, emphasis added) observes in his introduction to Polanyi's *The Great Transformation*, "Although the working-class movement has been a key part of the protective countermovement, Polanyi explicitly states that *all groups in society* have participated in this project." The Speenhamland justices used their public authority to allocate local tax revenues to fund the wage subsidy. Describing the massive and often brutal expulsion of laborers from the land during the period of enclosures in England, Polanyi (2001 [1944], 40) explained that "England withstood without grave damage the calamity of the enclosures only because the Tudors and early Stuarts used the power of the Crown to slow down the process of economic improvement until it became socially bearable—employing the power of the central government to relieve the victims of the transformation ... so as to make its course less devastating." A century later, on Polanyi's account, "Wretched Irish tenants and London slum-dwellers were rescued from the grip of the laws of the market by legislative acts designed to protect their habitation against the juggernaut, improvement" (2001 [1944], 191). Such persistent countermovements did not necessarily proceed against but were often in alignment with the needs and wishes of market proponents. Returning to Block's explanation, "Even capitalists periodically resist the uncertainty and fluctuations that market self-regulation produces and participate in efforts to increase stability and predictability through forms of protection" (Block 2001, xxviii). As Polanyi affirmed: "Most of those who carried out these (counter)measures were convinced supporters of laissez-faire, and certainly did not wish their consent ... to imply a protest against the principles of economic liberalism" (2001 [1944], 153). A reductively dichotomized view of the double movement as simply the struggle between opposing factions supporting and resisting marketization thus elides the contentious politics through which the process is negotiated in each particular instance.

Further complicating matters, while the politics of commodification, countermovement, and subjectification address somewhat different substantive spheres, they are not only interrelated but co-constitutive and cannot be separated in practice. Commodification produces the harmful effects necessitating a protective response that in turn alters the process of commodification; the need for protection arises when affected subjects espouse values that evade or exceed the boundaries and logic of "economic man." Additionally, political contestation over the commodification of land and labor is not corralled into separate spheres but expresses two sides of the same coin. Referring to societies organized along principles of organic interdependence, reciprocity, and redistribution, Polanyi observed that "traditionally, land and labor are not separated; labor forms part of life, land remains part of nature, life and nature form an articulate whole" (2001 [1944], 187). The commodification of land and life required for the expansion of a market society, however, requires the fictional disaggregation of land and labor as distinct commodities traded in separate markets: "To detach man from the soil meant the dissolution of the body economic into its elements so that each element could fit into that part of the system where it was most useful" (ibid., 188). The construction of separate markets for land and labor is required by and reflects the unique material attributes of land and labor in their commodity form, in particular the fixity of land and the mobility of labor. A problem arises, however, when the distinct operations of land and labor markets meet their inevitable juxtaposition in time and space. The process of rule and market making corresponding to the materiality and spatial fixity of urban land requires intense coordination with the parallel and equivalent process of rule and market making establishing the embodied subjectivity of urban labor. The necessary coordination occurs by aligning the subjectivity of labor—occupying land as a site of habitation—with the requirements of urban land as a marketable commodity. The performance of an urban land market, in short, proceeds through the construction of subjects willing and capable of occupying the roles and performing the rules required of them. This highly contentious process locates the urban political in the contested domain in which the materiality of land meets the subjectivity of labor in the fictitious construction of urban space.

Making the Land Market in Camden, New Jersey

In what follows, accordingly, I trace the politics of the double movement through a case study of land development politics in Camden, New Jersey, a deindustrialized city struggling to align the subjectivities of city residents with the demands of a resurgent land market following decades of decommodification and disinvestment. If, on Polanyi's account, the wretched Irish tenants and London slum dwellers were rescued from the grip of the market by legislative interventions designed to protect them, the tenants and inhabitants of Camden have not been as fortunate. Located on the Delaware River with a waterfront view of the Philadelphia skyline, Camden was until World War II a thriving industrial city comprised of neat rows of working-class houses in working-class neighborhoods supported by a diversified industrial economy producing ships, electronics, furniture, condensed soup, steel, cigars, fountain pens, and myriad other industrial commodities. In the two decades after World War II, the city experienced a massive wave of deindustrialization, disinvestment, and capital flight as employers closed their manufacturing facilities or relocated in search of cheaper, nonunionized labor. Between 1950 and 1970, the city lost 157,000 manufacturing jobs and a third of its population; experienced near-total white flight; lost virtually its entire retail and commercial sector; saw its land and property values—and attendant tax revenues—plummet in the absence of demand; and became entirely dependent on state transfer payments to provide municipal services and balance its municipal budget. In the complete absence of private capital investment, Camden had become a city without a functioning land market, unable to raise local property tax revenues and dependent on public subsidies as the last bulwark against municipal bankruptcy (Cowie 1999; Gillette 2005; Kromer 2001; Lake et al. 2007).[3] At the beginning of the twenty-first century, the state and city governments led a series of attempts to (re)create a market economy in Camden through a variety of successive strategies: first, through (re)construction of an urban land market; second, through an intermediate strategy of human capital development at the neighborhood level; and third, through massive tax incentives for private capital investment. Each of these strategies of market making required a recalibration of the subjectivities required of Camden's residents, making the process politically fraught when residents asserted contrary positions and resisted the characterizations imposed on them. The Camden story continues in a still-evolving context with as-yet unknown consequences for those affected by the attempted reintroduction of the market mechanism in Camden.

Constructing an Urban Land Market

The massive scale of capital flight and a prolonged series of failed urban renewal projects in the 1960s and 1970s produced an urban landscape of abandoned houses, deserted industrial structures, vacant land, derelict landfills, and acres of unused parking lots throughout the city.[4] By the beginning of the twenty-first century, the potential ground rent (Smith 1979) stored in the abundance of unused and underutilized land had become Camden's most valuable remaining asset and provided the material basis for state action aimed at re-creating a market economy. The MRERA legislation enacted by the New Jersey state legislature in 2002 justified the state's takeover of Camden's municipal government on the grounds of a "fiscal emergency" stemming from the insufficiency of local property tax revenues, and lawmakers posited the (re)creation of an urban land market through private investment in land development as the solution to the fiscal crisis.[5] Within two years of MRERA's adoption, the entire nine-square-mile land area of the city of Camden was contained within approved or proposed redevelopment plans prepared by the Camden Redevelopment Agency (CRA).[6] Under New Jersey land-use law, designation of an area as "in need of redevelopment" empowers a public body such as the CRA to acquire privately owned land within the area through negotiated purchase or through the threatened or actual use of eminent domain.[7] Designating the entire city of Camden as a redevelopment area rendered every land parcel—whether occupied or vacant—vulnerable to acquisition and each redevelopment plan prepared by CRA contained extensive lists of specific land parcels, identified by tax lot and block number, "To Be Acquired" or that "May Be Acquired" for purposes of redevelopment. Land thus acquired by the city would be turned over to private developers and building companies for the construction of new for-profit market-rate housing and other projects according to the terms of the approved redevelopment plan.

Impeding implementation of the proposed redevelopment schemes was the fact that the land encompassed in the plans was not simply standing idle awaiting the return of private capital: some eighty thousand remaining Camden residents inhabited the land slated for redevelopment. Because a substantial proportion of land parcels to be acquired were occupied, designation of the entire city as an area "in need of redevelopment" presaged the displacement of a significant number of Camden's households, and the threat of displacement quickly became a contentious political issue (Lake 2018). A legal brief challenging the redevelopment designation in Camden's Cramer Hill neighborhood (more on this below) summarized the issue succinctly:

The principal issues are as follows:

1) The designation of the entire (area) as a redevelopment area, allowing widespread use of eminent domain, is ... excessive and unnecessary;
2) Implementation of the Plan, which calls for acquisition and demolition of at least 700 homes, would result in the ... forced displacement of many ... residents, causing them severe hardship;

3) The Plan proposes drastic changes to the social and economic fabric of the neighborhood . . . ;
4) The designation of the entire . . . neighborhood as an area in need of redevelopment and adoption of the proposed redevelopment Plan is contrary to the general welfare and to the interests of . . . residents. (Pomar et al. 2004)

City officials and popular media justified the strategy of large-scale displacement as an unfortunate but unavoidable measure required to address the concentration of poverty, economic stagnation, social disfunction, and personal irresponsibility characterizing the city of Camden and its residents. Between 2005 and 2016, local news media repeatedly headlined the city's position at or near the top of national lists of crime and homicide and its status as the "most dangerous city in the United States" (e.g., Gargan 1981; Kelly 2015; May 2014; *Philadelphia Inquirer* 2015). Under the headline, "The Untold Tragedy of Camden, NJ," the *Huffington Post* averred that "Camden, New Jersey maintains a reputation as a violent morass that swallows economic opportunity" (Law 2016). A lurid article in *Rolling Stone* called Camden "America's most desperate town. . . . an un-Fantasy Island of extreme poverty and violence. . . . a major metropolitan area run by armed teenagers. . . . almost completely ungoverned. . . . (a) crumbling dead-poor dopescape of barred row homes and deserted factories. . . . (where) hundreds of industries have been replaced by about 175 open-air drug markets. . . . making it the most dangerous place in America" (Taibbi 2013).

The repeated and prolonged caricaturing of an entire population in terms of crime, drugs, and deviance offered an easy rationalization for displacement, in which the city's residents were identified as the leading impediment that must be removed to allow a land and housing market to reemerge in Camden. In frequent public statements and written reports, city leaders ascribed the threat of displacement to the "hard choices" they were required to make to achieve the city's renewed economic vitality (Primas 2006). Many residents recognized, not without irony, that their displacement was a precondition for market expansion. This view was explicitly expressed by a resident at a community information meeting who challenged a CRA staffer to acknowledge the disparate effects of redevelopment in her neighborhood: "You talk about this game that you're playing but what good will it do if we're not here to take advantage of it? You cannot mess around with people's lives" (Lanning Square resident, August 21, 2007).[8] Over the course of numerous informational meetings convened by Camden officials throughout 2006 and 2007, residents repeatedly charged that the wholesale designation of entire neighborhoods—indeed, the entire city—as "in need of redevelopment" ignored the diversity of land uses and housing conditions within neighborhoods, threatened the demolition of sound, occupied housing, and would reduce rather than expand the supply of affordable housing in the city (see also Pomar et al. 2004).

The strategy of areawide designation, however, supported the rapid assemblage of large land parcels on behalf of the large-scale development that city leaders and CRA viewed as necessary to re-create a land market in Camden.[9] In his first progress report following the city's takeover under MRERA, the chief operating officer (COO) complained that "CRA has not been able to move as quickly as desired in advancing the critical area of activity of the acquisition of real estate for redevelopment purposes. . . . Litigation resulting from public apprehension about the use of eminent domain in redevelopment areas has delayed the adoption of critical redevelopment plans (and) without such a tool large scale acquisition is virtually impossible." In his list of recommendations for further action, the COO asked the state to "support the use of foreclosure and, when needed, eminent domain to assemble sites for development" (Primas 2006, 15–16, 50).

The proposed redevelopment of Camden's Cramer Hill neighborhood illustrates the citywide experience during this period. Located on the Delaware River in north Camden, Cramer Hill is a residential community of about ten thousand residents, with a homeownership rate well above, and a vacancy rate well below, the city averages. CRA issued a request for proposals (RFQ/P) for the redevelopment of Cramer Hill in August 2003, received seven responses, and in December announced the selection of Cherokee Investment Partners LLC, of Raleigh, NC, as Master Developer for a $1.2 billion, ten-year development proposal for the neighborhood. Included in the plan were 5,000 units of market-rate and luxury housing, 500,000 square feet of new retail and commercial space, a marina, and an eighteen-hole golf course to be located on a remediated landfill. Specializing in remediating environmentally damaged sites, Cherokee described itself as a "horizontal developer" responsible for acquiring and preparing land, installing needed infrastructure, and selling land to "vertical developers" to construct the housing and other uses proposed for the site. Cherokee contracted Robert A. M. Stern Architects to prepare the redevelopment Master Plan, which would "transform an . . . environmentally degraded neighborhood of rundown housing into a viable, dynamic community (and) give Camden a much-needed jolt of activity and prosperity."[10] Camden's COO hailed the proposal as "a signature project for Camden (that) could set the tone for what happens in other sections of town" (*Courier-Post* 2005b).

Implicit in the plan, however, was the prospect that the scale of land acquisition, clearance, and demolition required for its implementation would displace nearly a thousand households, or 40 percent of the area's residents. Rejecting their characterization as poverty-stricken, disorganized, and dysfunctional,

Cramer Hill residents organized an effective political opposition protesting their exclusion from the planning process, the scale of displacement, the lack of relocation assistance, and the destruction of their community. Residents voiced their concerns at a series of informational meetings held by CRA in Cramer Hill in late 2006 and early 2007 aimed to assuage community opposition to the proposed redevelopment:

> We shouldn't have to suffer because of redevelopment. We're sitting on some good real estate. We got it. It's ours. We have what you want: the location. (Cramer Hill resident, November 29, 2006)

> If the people can be heard, we know the area and we know what's wrong with the area. If the city will listen to us, we can help produce better plans. (Cramer Hill resident, November 29, 2006)

> It's our land. You have to work with the people. We are not about to leave Cramer Hill. We have to bring things for the people who live here. (Cramer Hill resident, February 28, 2007)

> Here are things the community cannot support: the lack of information, the process of eminent domain, losing our greatest community asset—our residents. (Cramer Hill resident, November 29, 2006)

Residents directed their most scathing comments at the proposed golf course to be located in the neighborhood:

> If that green golf course is not a statement for gentrification, then I don't know what is. I know I don't want this for Cramer Hill. I don't think we need a golf course. (Cramer Hill resident, November 29, 2006)

> The golf course benefits need to be itemized. What are the benefits for us? We need to figure out how this will be beneficial to residents. Golf is traditionally an upper-class sport. There's a fear that the community has that this is not for us. What's in it for us? How will this help us? (Cramer Hill resident, November 29, 2006)

The residents' concerns were not assuaged by the city official at the meeting who explained that:

> There will be jobs, opportunities for neighborhood youth to work as caddies, as groundskeepers, opportunities for local schools to learn about landscape architecture. (City Planner, November 29, 2006)

The concerns raised by Cramer Hill residents reflected a legacy of distrust built up over several years of experience with the city's attempts to acquire land for redevelopment at the expense of large-scale resident displacement. In the weeks leading up to a Planning Board hearing on Cherokee's redevelopment plan for Cramer Hill scheduled for May 18, 2004, and *prior to the plan's approval,* neighborhood residents had received letters notifying them that their property would be acquired by the city and that they had fourteen days to accept the city's offer or "we will assume that settlement by agreement cannot be reached and condemnation proceedings will, as a matter of necessity, be instituted" (*Philadelphia Inquirer* 2004). In July 2004, attorneys from South Jersey Legal Services, representing two hundred Cramer Hill families and four businesses, filed suit to block implementation of the proposed redevelopment plan. The suit challenged the scale of the project, the amount of displacement required, and the lack of relocation assistance, among other matters.[11] Nearly two years later, in January 2006, a Superior Court judge ruled that the city's approval of the plan was invalid because witnesses from CRA and Cherokee who had presented the proposal before the Planning Board had not been sworn in, a legal technicality that effectively stalled implementation of the $1.2 billion project (*Philadelphia Business Journal* 2006).[12] The ruling also blocked redevelopment proposals in two other Camden neighborhoods on the same grounds, and the subsequent onset of the 2008 global economic recession effectively ended the city's ambitions for large-scale land and property development as a solution to the city's fiscal problems.

Building Human Capital for the Land Market

The widespread political opposition to large-scale redevelopment and urban renewal–style displacement prompted the appointment of a new COO and a new head of the CRA in 2007. In an effort to assuage community protest, the new leadership declared that neighborhood redevelopment plans would now include human capital planning alongside physical redevelopment. Under the new strategy, Camden's residents had suddenly been transformed from poverty to be displaced to capital to be developed. The CRA director told a neighborhood meeting in July 2007 that "human capital planning and bricks-and-mortar redevelopment are two sides of the same coin" and a CRA staffer added that "tonight is the beginning of connecting people to the bricks-and-mortar part of the plan." According to a planning consultant hired to implement human capital planning in Camden, "Our job is to make certain there is a deep connection between what people in these communities want for redevelopment," and she promised that "we start working with you all on that tonight" (Field notes, Lanning Square information meeting, July 26, 2007).

The concept of human capital dates to the classical political economy of Adam Smith who, in his *Inquiry into the Nature and Causes of the Wealth of Nations*, written in 1776, counted the stock of skills and abilities among inhabitants as a type of capital "fixed and realized" in the body of the person. The French economist Leon Walras, one of the founders of general equilibrium theory, "included all human beings in the concept of capital (and considered that) the value, or price, of these human beings ... is determined like that of any other capital good" (Kiker 1966, 487). It is only a small step, then, from viewing the human being as a form of embodied capital to understanding the aggregate stock of embodied capital as an attribute of a place or neighborhood, and devising strategies to increase the stock of human capital in place through a process of human capital planning (e.g., Becker 1964). By the early 2000s, both the Ford Foundation and the Annie E. Casey Foundation had enthusiastically adopted human capital planning in their overall approach to urban and neighborhood revitalization and the two foundations funded a consultant to integrate the concept into redevelopment planning in Camden (Lake et al. 2007). In late 2008, the Camden city council approved a municipal ordinance requiring human capital planning as a component of any neighborhood redevelopment plan.

As implemented in Camden, the practice of human capital planning had both a substantive and a procedural component. Substantively, in the tradition from Adam Smith to Gary Becker, human capital referred to the stock of productive capacity embodied in Camden's residents. A flyer distributed at a community meeting organized by the planning consultant defined human capital in this way:

> Q. What is Human Capital?
>
> A. People and their ability to be economically and socially productive. Education, training and health care can help increase human capital. As with physical capital, such as buildings and machinery, human capital is the result of investment. But unlike physical capital, human capital is always owned by the people who have it. It is the constant source of creativity, innovation and the ability to change.

Based on this substantive definition, human capital planning in Camden involved a process of community meetings, data gathering, and survey research to document existing neighborhood conditions constituting a resource to be mobilized in support of brick-and-mortar redevelopment and to identify neighborhood problems—defined as human capital deficits—to be solved through brick-and-mortar redevelopment. The information flyer distributed at the community meeting explained that data to be obtained through a community survey "tells us the current needs families are facing, the community's strengths that can be built on and the community's vision for the future. The survey will help us determine programming and service priorities, physical needs that residents desire (ex. A new community center) and what has already worked or not worked for residents." Yet when the planning consultant referred to "connecting people to the bricks-and-mortar part of the plan," the direction of causality was reversed. Rather than community needs and desires informing the physical redevelopment plan, human capital planning meant preparing residents to align with the requirements of the land development slated for the neighborhood. The planning consultant's draft human capital plan prepared for Camden's Lanning Square neighborhood in 2008, for example, described the physical and material ("bricks-and-mortar") plan, and then asserted that "this redevelopment will take place in and around the . . . neighborhood, making it essential that current residents . . . develop the human capital necessary to allow them to integrate seamlessly into the newly revitalized neighborhood" (Urban Strategies, Inc. 2008, 3). Now the imperatives of land development defined the requisite kinds of human subjects bearing the necessary kinds of human capital that would allow them to "integrate seamlessly" into the new materiality of land being produced in Camden. Rather than a resource informing the practice of land development, people were still an impediment and human capital planning would prepare them to better align with the land development priorities being implanted in the neighborhood. In a marked departure from the earlier strategy of land development, this alignment could be accomplished not by displacement and relocation, with their political and financial costs, but through the better coordination of neighborhood residents with the needs of the land market.

In addition to these substantive elements, human capital planning also incorporated a procedural component necessitated by the unfolding politics of the land development process. As explained in the consultant's draft plan, "the decision to incorporate Human Capital Planning into the redevelopment process came as a result of the need for greater resident inclusion in the redevelopment process" (Urban Strategies, Inc. 2008, 3). What this meant in practice was that the introduction of a participatory and inclusive process to discuss human capital planning served to deflect attention away from the far more contentious issues of property acquisition and displacement. A series of community meetings organized by CRA and the planning consultant throughout the summer of 2008 combined discussion of physical land development and human capital planning on the same agenda, thus blurring the distinction between them. The meetings followed a push-pull format, pushing information *to* residents about the contours of the land redevelopment plan and pulling information *from* residents to flesh out the human capital plan. The meetings took on a predictable rhythm, with CRA staff presenting PowerPoint depictions of proposed land uses and property acquisition maps and the consultant's staff inviting discussion of residents' priorities for the human capital plan. The process allowed the appearance of resident engagement and participation while forcefully channeling that participation away from the controversial topics that residents had come to the meeting to discuss. The sharp directional bifurcation in the flow of information was highly functional for the city and its consultant. The offer of a forum to discuss property acquisition and displacement—the most contentious aspects of redevelopment—was what brought residents to the meeting, but control of the meeting agenda allowed the city's staff to deflect attention away from those topics and onto human capital, while still claiming to encourage resident participation and engagement. Residents objected to the deflection of their concerns, prompting the comment quoted earlier:

> It's really important that we understand what people want and people need and connect it to redevelopment planning, so that's what (we're) here to talk about. (CRA staffer, August 21, 2007)

> We are very appreciative that you've come to these meetings. Your contribution to this process is wonderful. And we hope you will see the results of this in the redevelopment plan. That's been the focus of these meetings—to connect the human capital planning to the redevelopment plan. So that you feel at the end of the day that your needs have been heard. (Planning consultant, August 21, 2007)

> You talk about this game that you're playing but what good will it do if we're not here to take advantage of it? You cannot mess around with people's lives. (You're) here to take the focus away from what's real. (Lanning Square resident, August 21, 2007)

> The human capital plan will be incorporated into the redevelopment plan. (Planning consultant, August 21, 2007)

> We bought our homes here because we thought this was where we would be. We bought these homes because this is where we want to be. How can you come in and tell these older people: "We want your home?" (Lanning Square resident, August 21, 2007)

The Camden Planning Board and the City Council approved a redevelopment plan for the city's Lanning Square neighborhood in 2008, with a Human Capital Plan included as an appendix. The redevelopment plan called for construction of four hundred market-rate single-family homes and declared the entire neighborhood an area in need of redevelopment, making every property vulnerable to public taking through eminent domain throughout the project's twenty-five-year lifetime. The appended Human Capital Plan identified four priority projects for the neighborhood, including rebuilding an elementary school, increasing employment and educational opportunities, "stabilizing" the community, and improving safety and security. The plan estimated a five-year cost of nearly $48 million to implement these priority projects but was silent on possible sources for these funds. The plan instead recommended formation of an Executive Policy Group "charged ... with the task of creating and funding the strategies outlined in this Human Capital Plan." Members of the Executive Policy Group "would consist of executives from key stakeholders to include public sector leaders, philanthropic organizations, corporations and major institutions that have the ability to move the planning forward, drive implementation and bring resource potential to the implementation strategy." Neighborhood residents were notably absent from this list of "key stakeholders" but they were recognized in the plan as members of a Resident Leadership Team charged with "inform(ing) residents of the HCP and its components" (Urban Strategies, Inc. 2008, 50–51).

The introduction of human capital planning in Camden represented a rhetorical strategy of subjectification that constituted the city's residents as a resource to be developed rather than a barrier to be removed. As implemented in practice, however, CRA's redevelopment plans continued to itemize long lists of properties to be acquired but now the displacement of neighborhood residents no longer involved the removal of a problem population but, rather, the alignment of human capital with the requirements of the plan. As in the earlier case, this subjectivity was also rejected by the city's residents who continued to mount a political campaign to protect themselves from the destructive effects of land commodification on behalf of redevelopment.

Land Development through the Labor Market

For a period of several years at the height of the economic crisis after 2008, land redevelopment in Camden—as with most economic activity in the region—stagnated under the combined effects of political insecurity, financial illiquidity, and a general aversion to risk in the local and national economies. Then, in 2013, a reenergized state legislature passed a statute again seeking to reestablish a market society in Camden. This time, the New Jersey Economic Opportunity Act (EOA) authorized the state Economic Development Authority (EDA) to provide ten-year tax credits to private firms in return for job creation or retention in specially designated districts within the state.[13] The 2013 statute, and subsequent amendments adopted the following year, expanded an earlier program, called Grow New Jersey, by altering the eligibility criteria to direct a larger share of tax credits and subsidies to firms moving jobs specifically to Camden. The jobs strategy was still linked to creation of a land market but now the recipients of the tax credits were firms moving jobs to vacant and undeveloped land (much of it held in temporary parking lots) on former industrial sites on the Delaware River waterfront, thus side-stepping the political minefield of resident displacement from occupied neighborhoods that had paralyzed earlier land development efforts.

Within two years following enactment of the new subsidy program, the EDA approved $630 million in tax credits to companies relocating to Camden (NJ.com 2014; Philly.com 2015). Approval of the first several tax credit applications was celebrated by Camden's mayor as "a catalyst for change" and a county freeholder hailed the program as "a game changer for the city and region," asserting that "it's now clear that the city and county are on the rise and bringing Camden back to its former glory one day at a time" (*Courier-Post* 2015a). Recipients of tax credits included, among others, the Philadelphia 76ers professional basketball team ($82 million) for building a practice facility in Camden; Holtec International ($260 million), a nuclear energy technology company, for opening a manufacturing facility on the Camden waterfront; Subaru of America ($118 million) for moving its US headquarters to Camden from the nearby suburbs; the aerospace company Lockheed Martin ($107 million) for consolidating laboratory facilities in Camden; and Cooper University Hospital ($40 million) for expanding its downtown Camden campus.

Despite the celebratory rhetoric that greeted the announcement of these projects, signs of concern also began to emerge almost immediately. Because most of the projects receiving tax benefits relocated existing jobs to Camden from the nearby suburbs, very few new jobs were being created for Camden residents. As an assessment of the new basketball training facility for the Philadelphia 76ers disparagingly noted:

> In a city that was ranked the poorest in the country last year and where the unemployment rate is 16.6 percent . . . New Jersey's Economic Development Authority is going to spend $82 million in tax subsidies to build a state-of-the-art venue in a deal that will deliver approximately 250 jobs. With 200 of those positions already filled . . . the state is paying a whopping $1.6 million per new job created. (Lind 2014)

The substantial scale of the tax credits provided meant that the state and the city would receive little fiscal benefit over the life of the subsidy. An analysis of the Holtec project concluded, for example, that "the state expects Holtec to produce a net benefit of $155,520 over 35 years" (Philly.com 2014; *New York Times* 2019). Community leaders in Camden objected to EDA's failure to include a community-benefits requirement in any of the projects. On the day of the announcement of the 76ers project, the executive director of Camden Churches Organized for People (CCOP), a citywide community advocacy organization, published a "Contract for Camden" that, among other provisions, held that "efforts to assemble and remediate land should be reserved for small-to-large employers committed to bringing low-skilled and no-skilled jobs to Camden" (*Courier-Post* 2015b, 2019).

Extending beyond these substantive concerns, however, a longer and louder objection was raised over the politics of the program's design and implementation. The sponsor of the EOA statute in the state legislature in 2013 was State Senator Donald Norcross;[14] his brother, Philip Norcross, an attorney, drafted the subsequent amendments that significantly increased the size and share of tax credits going to firms relocating to the Camden waterfront; and older brother George Norcross, while holding no elected office, is widely acknowledged as a power broker and one of the most politically powerful individuals in the state (Solomon and Pillets 2019; Sullivan 2014). By early 2019, several investigations by news media and a task force appointed by the governor revealed that $1.1 billion of the $1.6 billion in tax credits awarded by EDA to firms moving to the Camden waterfront went to firms with which the Norcross family had a close connection (New Jersey, Office of the Governor 2019; Solomon and Pillets 2019; see also Whiten 2014). The governor's task force appointed in 2018 to investigate EDA's administration of the EOA program reported numerous allegations of fraud and abuse in tax credit applications (New Jersey, Office of the Governor 2019). Philip Norcross's law firm represented the 76ers basketball team in its application for $82 million in tax credits. His lobbying firm was paid $854,000 since 2012 by American Water Works, a public utility that received $164 million in tax credits in 2018 for relocating to Camden. According to a *New York Times* analysis, one of the 2014 EOA amendments recommended by Philip Norcross's law firm provided a tax credit for "'a qualified business facility . . . housing the U.S. headquarters . . . of an automobile manufacturer,' . . . language (that) appeared intended to benefit just one company, Subaru of America, which ended up reaping a $118 million tax credit from the state" (*New York Times* 2019). George Norcross is chairman of the board of Cooper University Hospital, which received $40 million in tax credits from EDA, and also serves on the board of Holtec International ($260 million in tax credits), while the CEO of Holtec, K. P. Singh, serves as a trustee of Cooper University Hospital. In early 2019, George Norcross's insurance company and two partner firms received tax credits worth $245 million toward construction of a new fifteen-story headquarters building on the Camden waterfront.

The substantial scale of new public and private investment concentrated on the Camden waterfront through EOA produced a broader effect beyond the direct monetary benefits allegedly reaped by the Norcross family. Their successful manipulation of the state-market nexus for personal gain produced a sharp increase in land values on the Camden waterfront as a consequence of the sudden spate of investment in the area. A 2016 assessment of the program reported that

> one of the more pernicious effects of the EOA has been to cause a dramatic rise in land prices in Camden. Since the State gave exorbitant sums of money to corporations to develop the city, a vacant lot in Camden that might have been worth $20,000 five years ago is now worth millions. Because of this rise in land value, property taxes are also rising. But the property taxes aren't going up for the corporations. (*Huffington Post* 2016)

In the underlying logic of the EOA program, Camden's residents were once again mobilized on behalf of the market mechanism. Here the mantra of job creation and retention in the context of high unemployment and a weak labor market provided a legitimating mechanism that enabled both personal enrichment for the few and a substantial stimulus for the land market on the Camden waterfront.

Camden's story situates urban politics in the Polanyian double movement comprising the contentious process of constructing a market society and protecting against its pernicious effects. The commodification of land for neighborhood redevelopment produced a countermovement protecting residents from the threat of displacement. The proposed accumulation of human capital in support of land development generated a countermovement by residents prioritizing their right of habitation over the demands of redevelopment. Massive public subsidy of private investment propelled a countermovement asserting the priority of neighborhood needs over private profit.

The double movement doesn't proceed in the abstract but unfolds through specific enactments enlisting specific subjects in the performance of the market and its protective countermovements. That contentious politics unfolded in Camden through an evolving series of market initiatives and policy interventions over several decades that aimed to align the subjectivities of Camden's residents with the requirements of the land market. The identities and subjectivities of the city's residents were repeatedly redefined and realigned in the process, from poverty to be displaced, to human capital to be accumulated, and finally, to units of labor to be enrolled in support of building a land market on the Camden waterfront. Land and labor markets were repeatedly disaggregated and reaggregated in the process, accomplishing, as Polanyi noted (and as quoted at the outset of this chapter), "the dissolution of the body economic into its elements so that each element could fit into that part of the system where it was most useful" (2001 [1944], 188).

From a longer-term perspective, the process described in this chapter was not confined to the two decades since the state's takeover of Camden's municipal government in 2002. In the industrial city of the early twentieth century, Camden's residents constituted a class of labor empowered to negotiate the sale of their labor power with employers whose ability to realize a profit from investment depended on reproduction of the capital-labor relation. This politics was, of course, also highly contentious. Workers at RCA formed a nine-hundred-member unit of the Industrial Workers of the World (IWW) in 1932. They were instrumental in the early industrial union movement and formed one of the charter locals of the United Electrical Workers Union in 1936 (Cowie 1999). These and similar actions both created and reflected an empowered subjectivity situated in the structural conditions prevailing at the time. The massive disinvestment and capital flight that subsequently transformed Camden from an industrial powerhouse to a city "in need of redevelopment" (or "the most dangerous city in America") similarly transformed the subjectivities of Camden's residents in line with the structural transformations underway.

But Camden's residents were not merely passive subjects buffeted by the imperatives of structural transformation and their resistance created a politics of the double movement. The conclusion may be that political contestation is not simply over the expansion of the market per se but rather over the subjectivities required by the evolving fictions of land attempted by the state and capital in expanding the market society, and the rejection of those subjectivities by the human subjects refusing to be so easily commodified.

12

THE STATE OF LAND GRABS
Regulatory Fictions in Ghana's "Small-Scale" Gold Mining Sector

Heidi Hausermann and David Ferring

Gold-backed reserves became a "safe haven" for capital investment during the 2008 financial crisis, causing the price of gold to hit a historic high of US $1,900/ounce in September 2011. Globally, "small-scale" gold mining activities proliferated as prices climbed. Along Ghana's Offin River, unremediated mining pits stretch for kilometers where cocoa, subsistence crops, and other land uses recently existed. Crops were cleared without farmers' permission and, often, without compensation. Rural communities, homes, and churches have been flooded and surrounded by mining pits (figure 12.1). The irreversible socioenvironmental impacts of recent gold mining practices cannot be overemphasized.

In direct conflict with Ghanaian minerals law, many of these mining sites are foreign-operated. In 2010, people from the United States, Canada, Spain, Turkey, India, and China openly prospected and mined along the Offin River in response to high gold prices. By 2012, only Chinese miners remained, and an estimated fifty thousand Chinese citizens were mining gold in Ghana (Hilson et al. 2014).[1] In 2013, one government official with intimate knowledge of the mining sector estimated Chinese nationals held 70 percent of small-scale concessions. This contradicted other official representations and speech acts that claimed small-scale gold mining was a right reserved for Ghanaian citizens.

Many state officials we interviewed between 2012 and 2017 claimed Chinese miners operate illegally, without official licenses and paperwork. Concession licensing protocols were often portrayed as transparent and democratic, backed by public notifications and waiting periods wherein land users could dispute proposed concessions. The "official" doings and sayings of many government

FIGURE 12.1. Boys fishing in abandoned mining pits behind their community on the Offin River. Photograph by Heidi Hausermann.

officials often reified Ghanaian minerals law, performing an exercise of state regulatory power. Mineral and environmental policies, however, are examples of what this volume refers to as regulatory fictions. In practice, rapid land dispossession for small-scale mining is ubiquitous, and Chinese miners often possess legal concessions and paperwork. Many of the same state actors—who claim Chinese mining is illegal and publicly reproduce mining's regulatory fictions—enable foreign gold mining by weaving together legal and illegal domains.

Ghana, the first African nation to implement structural adjustment policies in 1983, has long been internationally acclaimed as an African "success story" (Obeng-Odoom 2015). Western politicians, development agencies, and others praise Ghana for its political stability, democratic institutions, commitment to neoliberal reform, and other "rational" and "modern" Western ideals. Yet, some Ghanaian government officials are complicit in producing foreign-run mining activities and related socioenvironmental ramifications, ranging from increased malaria incidence (Ferring and Hausermann 2019) to food insecurity and environmental degradation (Hausermann et al. 2018). And while some government elites are intimately involved in mining, other actors and community members express fear in the face of powerful mining interests. These practices and experiences contrast starkly with representations of Ghana as a transparent, rational, and democratic state.[2]

Drawing from long-term observation in Ghana since 2010 and 127 semi-structured interviews conducted between 2012 and 2017,[3] this chapter explores the shifting practices and subjectivities of *big men, frontmen,* and *secretaries* who, in relation with others, mediate foreign mining.[4] While farmers and traditional authorities can also shape land deals, these actors are often uncritically enrolled in regulatory fictions as characters of blame (Hausermann et al. 2018). In government offices and the popular press, rural land users and traditional authorities are often accused of "giving away land" to miners to "get rich quick." However, blaming rural people diverts attention from other actors, spaces, and practices facilitating foreign land grabbing.

This research contributes to understandings of the state vis-à-vis land grabs by directing attention to the actual conditions under which foreigners control concessions.[5] Not all Chinese operations are unlicensed (Hilson et al. 2014), nor is land simply acquired by foreign entities "scrambling" for Africa's subterranean resources (Carmody 2011). Narratives of top-down foreign land deals and extractive practices gloss over the complicity of state actors, national elites, and others. In Ghana, big men, frontmen, and secretaries are key agents who help Chinese miners procure official paperwork and concessions. For instance, high-ranking government officials and wealthy businessmen known as big men provide financial backing for foreign operations, while Ghanaian frontmen apply for licenses. Secretaries, meanwhile, manage Chinese miners' interactions with state officials in various spaces, deftly negotiating regulatory fictions to maintain the appearance of legality where necessary, even when on-the-ground practices are anything but legal.

Empirically detailing the shifting performances and practices of these and other actors illuminates the fiction of mining and environmental regulations. For instance, in government offices and workshops, Minerals Commission officials portray concession licensing procedures as "straightforward" via linear and bureaucratic hoop-jumping, including a promise to the Environmental Protection Agency (EPA) to reclaim pits.[6] Under this fictitious regulatory system, no foreigners should control small-scale mining sites. However, some officials who perform "straightforward" procedures also, in other moments and spaces, collaborate with frontmen and Chinese investors to enable foreign mining. Examining concession allocation highlights the actual sites and practices mediating destructive land grabs.[7] Specifically, we argue maintenance of mining's regulatory fictions serves to reinforce the neutrality of domestic and foreign agents of capital and power, while reproducing the historic and problematic narrative that farmers and traditional authorities "give away land" and are ignorant of existing laws.

The State of Land Deals

The term *land grab* refers to cross-border deals initiated by foreign individuals, governments, or corporations to produce natural resource commodities (food, biofuel, minerals) (Zoomers 2010; Peluso and Lund 2013). These transactions include long-term lease, concession, or outright purchase of land. In 2011, Oxfam estimated that more than 227 million hectares of land exchanged hands since 2001 (Oxfam 2011). Due to the "closed door" nature of most land deals, estimates vary and may be exaggerated.[8] Although data are problematic, and not all announced deals move forward, recent years reflect an inarguable increase in foreign land acquisition (Li 2014). Scholars have focused primarily on large-scale deals involving thousands of hectares of land, thereby missing other important transactions. From the profits generated to the spatial extent of activities and socioenvironmental impact, nothing about Ghana's recent gold rush is small in scale. These transactions also occur quickly with less time for public participation, organized resistance, or opposition from "below" (Hall et al. 2015).

Globally, foreigners acquire land that is represented as vacant, marginal, inefficiently cultivated, and so on. These categorizations enable land grabs (Hall 2011; Baka 2014) and contribute to discursive framings of political-economic possibility (Hausermann 2018). The Ethiopian state, for instance, displaced more than 500,000 citizens so foreign investors could "use land more efficiently" (Thomson 2014). Traditional authorities in Ghana, despite existing landholdings, approved the lease of thousands of "marginal, unused" hectares for biofuel production as a "potential engine of development for deprived rural communities" (Boamah 2014). Yet, classifications of land as "marginal" and "unused" are processes of obfuscation and exclusion. Sales, leases, and concessions are often granted on land already claimed and used by local people (e.g., Cotula et al. 2009; Sulle and Nelson 2009). Scholars have thus largely characterized land deals as occurring through theft and dispossession (Cochrane 2011; Kenney-Lazar 2011; Benjaminsen and Bryceson 2012).

Along the Offin River, rural land users recalled arriving at farms to find foreigners clearing crops in a first step toward gold extraction. When farmers complained, they were shown official paperwork from Accra indicating the Minerals Commission approved the concession. The miners, moreover, often offered little or no compensation, resulting in ad hoc negotiations following crop removal (Hausermann et al. 2018). Chiefs and local leaders similarly reported that they are thrust into reactionary positions vis-à-vis miners carrying documents approved by authorities in Accra.

Ghana's gold rush has resulted in profound health and livelihood impacts, from increased local malaria incidence (Ferring and Hausermann 2019) and local land conflicts (Van de Camp 2016) to women's increased marginalization in agriculture (Hausermann et al. 2018). The same mining operations that cause these injustices yield enormous wealth generation for foreigners, state officials, and other actors. One Canadian miner with two consecutive twenty-five-acre concessions estimated he would make US $6 million in a year, exporting twenty-four-carat bars (Wilson 2016). A Chinese miner working along the Offin River claimed, on a good day, he and colleagues extracted gold worth more than US $100,000.

Rather than abstractly framing dispossessory land deals as global neocolonial encounters, scholars have begun to empirically unpack land grabbing processes (Fairbairn 2013; Sud 2014).[9] As Wolford et al. (2013, 192) argued, "States are not simply passive victims in these deals: they are not coerced into accessing foreign capital by selling off pieces of their national territory to more powerful economic or political players. State actors are active, calculating partners in land deals." Middlemen, for instance, play dynamic roles in brokering land deals in India (Sud 2014) where the state itself straddles formality and informality (Sud 2014). Tanzanian state and local actors facilitate *and* resist highly contingent land grabs in "polycentric governance" arrangements (Pedersen 2016). In Ghana, state actors are entangled in complicated relationships and practices shaping foreign control of small-scale concessions. Untangling these dynamics reveals the state not as a monolithic entity; rather, it is a constellation of diverse agencies and individuals rife with shifting, contradictory interests and performances (see also Hausermann 2015; Ogden 2011).

Our understanding of the state thus diverges from scholars' ongoing characterizations of African governments as "weak" states due to "neopatrimonialism," bureaucratic "inefficiency" and "poor" delivery of services (Bayart 1993; Reno 2001). Gross categorizations and a priori assumptions are problematic for various reasons, including reification of Western ideals such as "efficiency" as the "right" way to govern. Sweeping characterizations of governments fail to capture the incredible spatiotemporal complexity of state–society dynamics. We argue there is nothing coherent or a priori about the state; rather, governments are made up of diverse, often contradictory, subjects and practices (Hausermann 2015; Ogden 2011; Secor 2007). An understanding of "prosaic stateness" reveals complex, subtle, and uneven geographies of state power (Painter 2006, 775). Abandoning metacategorizations and studying practice is key to such analyses.

Official Policies and Procedures

Mineral deposits were vested in the state with Ghana's 1962 Minerals Act. The federal government, via the Minerals Commission and in concert with other agencies, thus controls mineral access and concession allocation. Neoliberal formalization of small-scale mining in 1989 aimed to capitalize on the country's mineral deposits and empower entrepreneurial mining subjects.[10] Ghanaian citizens were thus framed by policymakers as "rational," neoliberal subjects capable of making choices to further individual interest in formalized mining markets. However, lengthy licensing procedures and associated fees hinder most Ghanaians' ability to obtain small-scale licences, and state institutions provide no technical or financing assistance (Hilson and Pardie 2006; Hilson et al. 2014).

Foreigners can only legally participate in the small-scale sector as registered "mine support service companies" that provide equipment, technical knowledge, or contracted services (e.g., blasting, waste removal). Neoliberal reforms promoted by the World Bank and International Monetary Fund removed tariffs and quotas on mining equipment importation to promote foreign investment. Yet, today, foreigners' roles extend far beyond technological support, as they obtain complete control of the operation of concessions, capturing gold and profits flowing from the land.[11]

To acquire small-scale concessions of up to twenty-five acres, prospective miners must apply for a license from the Minerals Commission and undergo permitting procedures in other agencies, including the Environmental Protection Agency (EPA). After prospecting, miners develop site plans for approval by district-level Minerals Commission officials.[12] If the proposed site plan does not overlap with an existing concession (small or large), district officials forward the application to the national government. In Accra, the site plan is again referenced against master geologic and concession maps of Ghana. Then, as an informant who helps Chinese acquire concessions told us: "They [MC officials] say, 'That's okay; the area is not occupied, so therefore you can release it to the person who is requesting the land.' And that's an official letter [license]." According to this and other informants, the Mineral Commission's primary concern is whether the proposed mining site overlaps with an existing concession. If no overlap exists, licenses are approved and mining can begin. Existing land uses—cash crops, subsistence farms, family compounds, etc.—are irrelevant in licensing processes. There is thus the unspoken assumption that extraction of valuable minerals—represented and legitimized through site plans, geologic maps, and other official documents—is a more effective, profitable way of using land than smallholder agriculture, despite the many people it sustains.

The Minerals Commission often depicts concession licensing procedures as straightforward (figure 12.2), an important part of the regulatory fiction. One Minerals Commission officer, echoing the common government line, stated, "It is a straightforward market; the stray people outside . . . see it as a complex institution." Yet, little about the actual licensing process is as simple as it appears; the regulatory fiction obfuscates complex, often backroom negotiations and creates obstacles for those ignorant of de facto licensing practices. When an individual applies for a mining license, for instance, law requires a twenty-one-day waiting period while notice of the proposed concession is posted publicly. If no objections are raised, the registration process continues. When asked about concession licensing procedures, a Minerals Commission official in Accra explained: "We should make sure all relevant stakeholders are informed. In Ghana, in fact, we are partnered with the District Chief Executives. ... You need to publicize this [proposed concession] at a post office, maybe community noticeboard, the chief's palace, the paramount seat, and all that, to make sure that everybody is informed of such activity coming on board."

This official describes minerals law as a process deeply interwoven into local governance and public administration. State actors imagine and represent district assemblymen, local leaders, farmers and others as involved in public dialogue over proposed concessions.[13] In interviews and government-sponsored mining workshops, Minerals Commission officials consistently upheld these legal framings, claiming the twenty-one-day posting enabled public participation and concession contestation. Such speech acts work to bring an understanding of law and public participation into being, resonating with media coverage and governmental discourse to form a public transcript of mineral transparency foundational to mining's regulatory fiction. The "routinization" of performances of an authoritative, functional state thus gives the "appearance of necessity and permanence" (Ghertner and Lake, this volume; see also Butler 1990, 1993).

In practice, however, the twenty-one-day public posting rarely, if ever, happens. Not one respondent in rural communities with whom we engaged reported seeing such an announcement. Rather than public notices, community members recalled arriving at farms to see miners bulldozing subsistence and tree crops unannounced. When farmers protested, they were told the land was permitted for mining, in some cases two years beforehand. Researchers similarly identified the state's lack of information-sharing with local land users as a common practice in foreign land grabbing (e.g., Cotula 2012; White et al. 2013). Even one national-level Minerals Commission official confessed that the twenty-one-day policy does not play out as law requires: "The [district] assembly should make ... people aware of some of these [mining] activities. It should be done, so that people should be conscious of [a proposed site], we were aware, at times, the provocation notice goes to the assembly, it then sits on the desk of the officer. He doesn't put it anywhere—twenty-one days, he signs, and then they bring it back to us."

This official acknowledges the procedure's failure, placing blame on a district-level assemblyman. Blaming other agencies and actors was a common theme in our interviews, whether at the Minerals Commission, EPA, or district assemblies, or with community leaders. Lack of transparency is often attributed to local governance failures, laziness, or bureaucratic inefficiency, reinforcing the regulatory fiction of mining as a coherent system of resource extraction. Within this conflictual institutional landscape, big men, secretaries, frontmen, and other influential brokers build relationships to facilitate foreign control of small-scale concessions, operating, as we show in the next section, under the cover of a regulatory fiction that presumes logical connections between minerals law, capital investment, and local land use.

Big Men

Small-scale concessions are often backed by big men: wealthy and powerful Ghanaian businessmen or government officials. Foreign investors, including wealthy Chinese, can also operate as big men. Big men provide start-up capital for prospecting and concession procurement. Operating behind the scenes, these powerful individuals arrange political cover for foreign miners through personal associations. Several informants reported that big men use power and connections to shepherd Chinese miners from Accra to rural mining sites they (or political affiliates) own, moving foreigners by busloads at night, accompanied by state police and/or military vehicles. As a Ministry of Agriculture official described, "Most of them [foreign miners], they have big men behind them. So, even when the local police arrest them, nothing happens. Because you'll be there and your regional [police] commander or somebody in Accra will say, 'Oh, it's for this people. Release them.'"

The "big men" category, moreover, is gendered and classed in predictable ways, and must be situated historically and culturally. The term is deployed across postcolonial sub-Saharan Africa to refer to charismatic leaders perpetuating "weak" or "hollowed-out" states through the (re)constructions of networks of political power (Hydén 2006; Utas 2012). In Ghana specifically, big man connotes elements of Akan masculinity, including accumulation *and* dissemination of personal wealth. Historically and at the community level, one became a big man, a position of personal and societal achievement, through the performance of generosity. Miescher (2005) demonstrates shifts with the centralized state's emergence, wherein individuals were granted the title ɔbirɛpɔn ("big man") through displays of wealth commitment to the Asante kingdom. By the early twentieth century the senior masculinity of big men no longer depended on age and locally acquired status, but was rather linked to wage labor, migration, and the new cash economy. Urban workers evoked older images of big men, retaining performative elements of the old kin-based and patronage networks, while redefining the status of the figure through an emphasis not on traditional power but on modern aesthetics such as Western-style clothing and vehicles used to reflect big men's increased political and economic power (Miescher 2005).

Big man subjectivities and practices have been reformulated in Ghana's gold rush, bypassing traditional authorities that long structured access to local land, and rearticulating the social relations through which these positions form. One informant, a government official self-identifying as a big man, described wealth generated through "business transactions" with Chinese miners. He recounted using political connections with senior mining officials to obtain concessions and recent luxury purchases and foreign travel funded with gold mining profits. Opposed to the performative redistributions of wealth that once defined the big man, for this individual, status is gained by wielding power in, and profiting from, foreign mining and state institutions. The ability to work the system, to extract profit while maintaining the regulatory fiction of mining as a rational procedure governed by transparency and law, helped define the big man.

Due to big men's political power, enforcing environmental and land tenure regulations has become increasingly difficult in rural Ghana. One regional Cocobod representative, a parastatal agency managing Ghana's cocoa production and exportation, stated:

> So if a minister [high-ranking official] acquires land and has given it to a Chinese . . . he will help the Chinese get all the necessary documents. The government officials are very much involved. They are very much involved. I know one high official of Cocobod who is backing *galamsey*.[14] He sends his boys to get the concession and they turn it over to Chinese. His job is to protect cocoa, and he is spoiling it in his spare time for big money.

Publicly, this big man performs his bureaucratic role as a Cocobod employee, managing a tree crop that sustains 3.2 million Ghanaian smallholders. However, in a world where subjectivities and practices are often contradictory and shift in space and time, he also enables Chinese mining activities that destroy the land use he publicly protects.

Other state officials expressed frustration and fear associated with land-use conversions such as those mediated by the Cocobod big man. A regional Ministry of Agriculture employee, from an area greatly transformed by gold mining, lamented, "On Farmers' Day, if I am to give an address, I will like to mention the degradation and long-term effects of *galamsey*. But what if the politicians or the mining stakeholders were there? I have to be very careful; either I may lose my job or [be] transferred." A forestry official also expressed frustration with his inability to enforce laws prohibiting mining within forest reserves. If he arrested foreigners mining in protected areas, a big man from Accra would call and demand their release.

Thus, while historic big man subject positions have been reformulated to promote personal wealth accumulation and ecological destruction, other officials lament these transformations. Big men have become so powerful and brazen, foresters, agricultural extension agents, and others fear punishment and being sacked should they speak out against mining-mediated degradation of agricultural lands and ecosystems. Officials' restricted ability to speak freely about, and respond to, changing land-use conditions and mining politics reflect uneven power dynamics within the government, and conflicts between state actors and agencies. The regulatory fictions of mineral and environmental laws—as "straightforward," transparent and a vehicle for entrepreneurial empowerment—are in tension with the actual practices mediating foreign mining and the embodied experiences of various actors, including fear and anxiety expressed by people within forestry, agricultural, and other agencies.

Frontmen

Foreign operators and big men employ frontmen to go through formal hoops and obtain concessions. One professor, with extensive mining-sector knowledge, knew a frontman with thirty-two concessions in his name. After frontmen obtain official paperwork, foreigners take over concessions for a "goodwill" fee ranging between US $10,000–$15,000. In other instances, foreign miners invest capital in the equipment necessary for digging and washing large amounts of sediment (excavators, washing plants, etc.). This includes foreigners' importation of mining equipment, rendered tariff-free to promote "foreign investment" in the 1990s.[15] Foreigners thus have an advantage over big men and frontmen in the procurement of mining technologies, and work in collaboration with these other actors.

When mining begins, the frontman takes between 12 to 20 percent of raw gold or cash from its sale. These profits are then redistributed to big men backers. Individual mining operations do not represent capital intensive investments often associated with subsurface resource extraction (e.g., Ferguson 2006; Emel et al. 2011); rather, these sites are operationalized through relatively small capital inputs, including goodwill fees and bribes.

Frontmen are typically male and from the region where mining takes place. We identified only one woman in this role. Compared to big men backers or foreign businessmen, frontmen possess limited financial resources, but truck in their valuable ability to navigate official and/or traditional political structures. As one gold buyer put it: "When they [Chinese] come, they hide.... But they will put Ghana man in front ... register with his name and then cooperate with the guy and work. And at the same time Ghanaian man can explain anything, what is going on around the environment and what is going on around the town or what is going on around the country ... so that they will get access to do their mining." Through frontmen, foreigners gain access to much more than gold ore itself: they gain a Ghanaian identity for paperwork and an intimate knowledge of the things and people that make extraction possible.

As the names and identities of frontmen are tied to concessions, these individuals bear the long-term responsibility for mining operations. For instance, after a concession application arrives at the Minerals Commission in Accra, the frontman must then register with the EPA and obtain an environmental permit for mining. Linked to the EPA permit is a written promise that no mining will take place within three hundred meters of a natural water body and land will be reclaimed and rehabilitated, by filling pits with soil, when mining ends. These environmental regulations represent another regulatory fiction, since land reclamation rarely happens and abandoned, waterlogged pits snake for kilometers along the Offin and other rivers. No informant had heard of a frontman held responsible for failure to follow environmental or other regulations. Rather, law breaking and failure to fulfill licensing promises become status quo despite official laws and policies. With powerful big men backing operations, there is little enforcement incentive. Through processes and practices of pinning paperwork and long-term responsibility on one individual, the larger political-economic connections of mining land grabs, such as the role of foreign capital and big men, are obscured.

Secretaries

Secretaries are responsible for arranging paperwork and local negotiations. Originally from a rural community, secretary informants moved to the gold rush town of Dunkwa-on-Offin specifically to help foreigners navigate concession access. One secretary described his interactions with Minerals Commission officials in Accra when applying for mining licenses:

> HH: So if you want to mine ... you go straight to Minerals Commission?
> Secretary: Yeah.... They will ask you to go and demarcate the area.... You draw the site plan and send it to them. They will wait for twenty-one days, then nobody comes to tell them the area belongs to them,

> they will ask you to pay money before they will give you the license before you can start mining [sic].
>
> HH: How much do you pay for the license?
>
> Secretary: Sometimes some people collect 10,000 GHC [about US $5,347 at time of interview in 2013].
>
> HH: That's a high amount! Is that average?
>
> Secretary: It's variable, depending on who you see.
>
> HH: So there's no set amount?
>
> Secretary: Not at all. . . . You have to be familiar with someone in the office. If maybe this is the first time you're going there. As for that one, you have to give an envelope. Because if you don't open your palm, you'll find it difficult to get your documents. You must work hard to get in.

This secretary understood relationships built in government spaces as vital to license procurement success. This shows how the actual practices mediating concession allocation for small-scale mining contradict the narrative of straightforward licensing procedures maintained by officials. Moreover, in government offices, chiefs' palaces, and at mining sites to state actors, cash-filled envelopes are widely understood and commonly used objects for acquiring concessions. Officials accept envelopes in the same urban offices where they perform and reify regulatory fictions of transparency and good governance, citing minerals law and environmental regulations as rational state practices that structure their behavior and all those below them.

Once extraction begins, secretaries also mediate interactions between Chinese investors and state officials. One secretary, working at a Chinese-run mining site, described how he deals with visiting EPA officials: "I call my boss these people has come to the site. So my boss will say to pay them something. It's a money matter. . . . The EPA says, 'You have big problem here. You should come to office.' No one wants to go to the office. Then it becomes a big money matter. So we dash them something when they come to the site—5 million, 4 million.[16] We pay them, they leave [sic]." Scholars have demonstrated the ways bribes and other illicit practices are de facto institutions in the governance of natural resources (Robbins et al. 2009; Yaro 2013; Boamah and Williams 2017). In Cameroon, "extralegal" payments to national park guards enabled forest resource access, thereby shaping "insider" subjectivities (A. Kelly 2015). In Ghana, passing envelopes and managing "money matters" (in spaces ranging from mining sites to government offices) enable foreign gold extraction. These de facto practices contrast with the regulatory fiction of transparent chains of command and bureaucratic proceduralism.

One secretary described his "fellowship" with Chinese miners as sustaining his career in small-scale mining. He is the only Ghanaian allowed at the Chinese mining site when the day's production is tabulated, indicating trust between actors. He argued that his ability to communicate effectively in "Chinese-English," a hybrid language, is illustrative of the intimate relationship he shared with Chinese partners. He laughed, "'Come, come, come. You, go here. Dig this catch here . . . go, go, go . . . me you go see.' The way I talk . . . is it right? Sometimes I don't come home for three days. When I come home, I can't remember anything but Chinese-English." While the secretary joked about this new way of speaking, his remarks reflect the complex social relations and language formulations that emerge from regulatory fictions.

Regulatory fictions, upheld by problematic legal/illegal binaries, create conflicts for some subjects involved in mining. Secretaries in particular often expressed contradictory views vis-à-vis their positionalities within mining relations. One secretary claimed the gold rush was a "good thing" because it created jobs, but also expressed shame regarding his role in the destruction of land and water resources. He also complained bitterly about the low prices his boss, a Chinese site owner, paid farmers for destroyed farmland. He proudly recounted how he secretly visited farmers to coach them on what to do and say to receive the most money for farmland. Similarly, while the secretary highlighted above sometimes expressed friendship with, and respect for, Chinese colleagues, at other times he made harsh and derogatory comments about foreign miners. While official laws and policies—from "straightforward" licensing procedures to environmental permits promising land reclamation—represent regulatory fictions, it is the shifting and complicated positionalities of male subjects that bring land grabbing and foreign mining into being.

Recent mining activities have wrought significant socioecological changes along the Offin River. As small-scale concessions and the monetary benefits they yield are a legal right reserved for Ghanaian citizens, these foreign mining sites are illegal in their presence *and* failure to follow reclamation, compensation and environmental regulations. However, such land grabbing processes do not happen in a vacuum. Big men, frontmen, secretaries, Chinese miners, EPA officials, police and others work cooperatively, despite linguistic, class, and cultural divides, to enable foreign mining. Making and entangled with these subjects and social relationships, moreover, are various objects and practices, including envelopes, uniforms, concession transfers, goodwill fees, survey instruments, and hybrid language. These entities combine as the real, de facto instruments and institutions mediating mining.

State actors shift between performances of legal and bureaucratic state procedure and the actual practices producing foreign mining. Officials discursively reify regulatory fictions like linear licensing procedures and land reclamation while, in other spaces and moments, they actively facilitate foreign mining that violates those procedures. The regulatory division between what is legal and what is not clearly fails to capture the shifting practices and performances of Ghanaian state actors. Sweeping accounts of the "everyday corruption" of "weak" African states (e.g., Crawford and Botchwey 2016) fail to acknowledge the actual sites, performances, and interactions precipitating injustices and, crucially, how agents of supposed "illegalities" act in accordance with principles of national development and natural resource use. Detailing coproductions between "legal" and "illegal" domains in concession licensing procedures complicates understandings of the state, breaking down the discursive and ontological binaries— e.g., legal/illegal, rational/irrational, official/unofficial—used to uphold an image of state legitimacy and cohesion.

Furthermore, officials from agricultural, cocoa and forestry agencies lament land-use conversions and ensuing ecological impacts. Some state actors fear speaking publicly about their anxieties and frustrations due to powerful individuals, including those from their own agencies, involved in mining. These tensions further illustrate the highly uneven and contradictory relationships between land grabbing processes and the state. Feelings of fear and impotence expressed by community members, traditional authorities, and state actors contrast powerfully with Ghana's heralded democratic ideals of transparency and citizen participation.

Ghana's recent gold rush and associated landscape transformations have wrought complex and serious implications for rural people and ecologies. Yet, many scholars and development experts continue to abstractly label these processes as "global" neocolonial encounters, the result of sub-Saharan Africa's "resource curse" or "weak," inefficient governance. Such simplistic explanations fail to capture complex empirical realities and "open moments" in which laws and access are reworked (Lund 1998, 2). The regulatory fiction of mining governance in Ghana both upholds formal narratives of law while particularly positioned actors violate them in practice. This tension unfolds through the cultivation of complex and shifting social relations and subjectivities that are glossed over through abstract framings of land grabbing, economic development, official mining regulations, reckless *galamseyers* scheming to get rich quick, and so on. The articulation of regulatory fictions and actual practices and sites coproducing foreign mining highlights the spaces and conditions under which envelopes are passed and decisions made, leading to a clearer understanding of where resistance and action might help seek justice and reform.

Afterword

LAND FICTIONS IN THE *LONGUE DURÉE*

Michael John Watts

> **Fiction**: early 15c., ficcioun, "that which is invented or imagined in the mind," from Old French ficcion "dissimulation, ruse; invention, fabrication" (13c.) and directly from Latin fictionem (nominative fictio) "a fashioning or feigning," noun of action from past participle stem of fingere "to shape, form, devise, feign," originally "to knead, form out of clay," from root "to form, build." A belief or statement that is false, but that is often held to be true because it is expedient to do so. **Fictitious**: 1610s, "artificial, counterfeit;" 1620s, "existing only in imagination," from Medieval Latin fictitius, a misspelling of Latin ficticius "artificial, counterfeit," from fictus "feigned, fictitious, false," past participle of fingere "to shape, form, devise, feign." It was first used in English as an antonym for "natural."
>
> —Cambridge English Dictionary

> The history of landed property, which would demonstrate the gradual transformation of the feudal landlord into the landowner, of the hereditary, semi-tributary and often unfree tenant for life into the modern farmer, and of the resident serfs, bondsmen and villeins who belonged to the property into agricultural day-labourers, would indeed be the history of the formation of modern capital.
>
> —Karl Marx, *Grundrisse*

One of the first references to "fake" is in a dictionary of criminal slang compiled by James Hardy Vaux, published in 1819 as *A New and Comprehensive Vocabulary of the Flash Language*. "Flash" was there understood as veiled criminal jargon deployed by the underworld to keep its activities secret from the authorities, victims, and bystanders, and fake was deployed as a sort of insider's language to refer to all manner of fabrications, counterfeits, and sleaze: "To fake any person or place, may signify to rob them; to fake a person, may also imply to shoot, wound, or cut; to fake a man out and out, is to kill him; . . . it also describes the doing of any act, or the fabricating anything, as, to fake your slangs, is to cut your irons in order to escape from custody."[1] While *fake* began life two centuries ago as a part of the flash lexicon of the criminal underworld, in our political moment it has come above ground into the bright light of national politics.

The fake or fakeness is central to the stories told in *Land Fictions*, although the word rarely appears in the text. It speaks in an admittedly moral tone to the notion of counterfeit and subterfuge; something appearing as if it were something other than what it actually is. The book's starting point, as the editors make clear, is Karl Polanyi's notion of fictitious commodities—the notion that land, labor, and money were not the product of the commodity economy but are transmuted into a commodity form as prerequisites for the creation and operation of the self-regulating market. This fiction both organizes actual markets, said Polanyi, and constitutes a plank of market hegemony (a market calculus "affecting the whole of society"). The editors see such fictive qualities as exemplars of reified norms and conventions of governance, as categories of being and conduct that render them—the notion that land is indeed a commodity and nothing else—as a sort of ontological necessity. It makes the "weirdness" Polanyi described seem normal and common sense. Fiction in these senses has family resemblances to ideology, normalization, habitus, and regimes of truth. It is, I suppose, quite Nietzschean.

The fictions described in these chapters trace the ways in which land is invented (differently over time and space); rendered objective, standardized, and discrete; converted (into capitalist property); and stripped of its "natural" (of nature) qualities and repurposed for the social imaginary of improvement and, in the present at least, turbo-charged capitalism. Land in these accounts is made through multiple fictions: it has to be rendered legible and visible (for market purposes); it requires legal standing; it must be abstracted, simplified, standardized, mapped, and logged. It as a veritable "provisional assemblage of heterogeneous elements," as Tania Li (2014b, 589) has it (which frankly makes it seem like a bit of a mess). Semiosis, rhetoric, narrative, representation, iteration, discourse, and market making become the vehicles for creating and exposing the land fictions at work. As Walter Benjamin said, commodities arrive at the market with their price tag. How land comes with its price tag—its valuations and its various qualities (productivity, improvement, world-class cities, a terroir, an ocean view!)—is what this book seeks to address.

It bears repeating that Polanyi's framing of "fictitious commodities" comes with baggage. The first is that commodity fictions, for Polanyi, are inseparable from countermovements. But these reactive sorts of defensive protections have, in Polanyi's account, something of a tautological character: much of what is normalized as struggles in and around capitalism could be seen as expressions of the double movement. Polanyi also had a rather monochrome view of the forms of state or regulated capitalism, and tends "towards voluntarism in his account of the rise of the market and towards functionalism in his explanation of the counter-movement" (Dale 2010, 79). Polanyi's focus on fictitious commodities, in other words, reduces countermovements to a "natural" response to the "artificiality" of the "ravages of the satanic mill" and the "demolition of society" instead of identifying the complex political mediations (which Polanyi largely neglected) and the variety of reactive forms (authoritarian populisms, xenophobic nationalism) at play, some of which do not resemble ways in which "society protects itself against the perils of the self-regulating market system" (Polanyi 2001 [1944], 76). In the same way, Polanyi construed the fictive character of land through what he called an "empirical definition" of the commodity and, in a footnote, explicitly rejects the Marxist notion of the fetishistic qualities of the commodity under capitalism (Polanyi 2001 [1944], 72n3). Put differently, he saw the commodity as a thing and not a social relation, contributing to a reified understanding of social reality.

While Polanyi talks of "crude fictions," *Land Fictions* opens these up, identifying all manner of subtleties—fantastical, enigmatic, mystical, and metaphysical properties that Marx (1990 [1867]) describes in chapter 1 of volume 1 of *Capital*. In other words, it endows the power of the fake and of fabulation to the givenness—the "real"—of Polanyi's commodity fiction. This is as it should be given that Polanyi's treatment of land as a fictive thing rested on his reading of land as nature and addresses questions of safety, habitation, landscape, and stability (2001 [1944], 187). Unlike labor and money, about which he had much to say, Polanyi largely ignored the moral, cultural, political, and institutional integuments associated with noncapitalist land relations (Marx's "precapitalist swamp") and the consequences of the rise of capitalist landed property and markets in land. This is not simply a primitive accumulation story but precisely an account of all the rhetorics, discourses, and conjurings that appear in this book.

In this sense, this book is dependent on Polanyi and commodity fictions but also pushes well beyond empirical definitions of commodities, entering the sanctum of the fetish broadly construed. Marx too had little to say about the inventions of land and the complex non- or paramarket relations in which land is embedded. While not Polanyian in cast, much of the diet of "the anthropology of peasants" I was fed in the 1970s precisely addressed these nonfictive qualities: books like Reichel-Dolmatoff's (1971) *Amazonian Cosmos* or Roy Rappaport's *Pigs for the Ancestors* examine the semiosis of land (often wrapped up with large and more capacious spiritual and cosmological world views). It is a trend one can see running through Native American land struggles. Others examining commodification in peasant societies—I was one—were struck by how land transactions were shrouded in secrecy, dishonor, and shame: it was the cultural and familial attachments to land that rendered land sale a sticky and uneven process. Here, land fictions operated as a way of talking about land transactions to obscure or hide the operations of the market. Such ideas remain important in, to take one example, contemporary discussions of land in Africa. There has certainly been an avalanche of work on large-scale land grabs of various sorts—many exhibiting the shady deals, elastic legality, and dodgy cartography that populate the chapters in this book. But even more central has been the ways in which land titling or efforts at land nationalization have foundered because of how land is encased in changing forms of customary and "modern" authority. These nested, overlapping, and intersecting forms of social, juridical and political control—Lund's (2008) work on shadow or twilight institutions and the complexity of land negotiations is a powerful case in point (see also Berry 1989, 2009)—provide a rich soil in which the sorts of narratives and semiotic fictions described in this book flourish.

It is also worth noting—and I shall return to this later—that *Land Fictions* lays out a rather broad palette of fictions. Sometimes it is not clear whether and how they share family resemblances. The book begins with an example of fraud (how did 3.26 acres become 326 through the actions of the Pune collector?); other examples explore the process of boundaries or cartographic representations; others describe the ways in which the powerful "work the system" or conjure up particular futures (rents, yields) operating under the sign of a particular social imaginary (development, the world-class city). The fictive in these accounts is a capacious category. At the same time, for the most part land here is horizontal and surficial: things are located on, built on, or grown from the land. Other ways of thinking of land as vertical or what has been called "volumetric" receive less attention. By the same token, there is inevitably slippage between land and resources (that which is the product or located within the surface) or on the environmental consequences of capitalist landed property as a source of profit (this has historically been the domain of political ecology). And finally it is worth flagging that Polanyi's point of distinction of fictitious commodities—in this case land as nature—has been approached in different registers. The most obvious would be a hermeneutic approach of a phenomenological sort that starts from the "givenness" of land (the ground which precedes us). Mei's (2017, 115) *Land and the Given Economy*, using Heidegger's view of land as ontological, argues that "land allows us to recognize how we dwell," not simply what humans do on land but "the awareness of our dependency on it." Mei interestingly invokes Polanyi but argues that insofar as land is "in the position of the subject" the "excess" of land should be, as proposed by Henry George, subject to a radical taxation of ground rent. My point is simply that there are other ways—in this instance philosophical—of seeing the differences which make a difference in regard to land as a commodity.

Land is, of course, central to what is usually referred to as the classical agrarian question (see Levien, Hairong, and Watts 2019), which is both about the rise of capitalist property and primitive accumulation but also, to use the language of Karl Kautsky's classic *The Agrarian Question*, "whether and how capital is seizing hold of agriculture, revolutionizing it, making old forms of production and property untenable and creating the necessity for new ones" (1989 [1899], 2). Kautsky was a Czech-Austrian Marxist and a controversial figure in any account of Marxism. Most closely associated with the evolutionary and deterministic views of the Second International, by the latter part of his life Kautsky was a pariah (a "renegade" as Lenin put it) having assumed the role of outspoken critic of the Bolshevik Revolution, the Soviet State, and the likes of Lenin and Trotsky while being shunned by the Social Democratic Party of Germany with which he was associated. Nevertheless, upon its publication, Kautsky's *Die Agrarfrage* was described by Lenin as "the most important event . . . since the third volume of *Capital*" (cited in Ramey 2017, 302). In many respects it defined the debate over the political economy of agriculture in the twentieth century. In Kautsky's book, land and the figure (and future) of the smallholder commanded center stage, especially the question of whether the ubiquity of peasants was a sign of peasant capacity to resist competition and in doing so challenge classical conceptions of agrarian capitalism and large-scale wage-based production (Djurfeldt 1982). Peasant survival, even expansion, necessarily had implications for landed property and rent under capitalism.

Kautsky's intervention had a robust Polanyian cast in one profound sense. He saw, as Polanyi did, land "as nature" as much as property or a crucible for accumulation (the latter being the conventional points of reference for both classical political economy and Marx for thinking about agrarian capitalism). Biology, climate, and the qualities of land led Kautsky to question an orthodoxy that industry was, as Marx argued, "daily doing away with [peasants]" and, as an 1869 meeting of the First International had it, that the smallholder was facing "extinction without appeal and without mercy" (cited in Mitrany 1951, 36). Engels could write in 1894 that among socialists the peasant question and the land question had been placed "upon the order of the day." But land figured in Kautsky because Marxian theory assumed both land market and land concentration over time. The picture in the late nineteenth century during the growth, integration, and completion of a world market in agricultural commodities turned out to be something of a conundrum. Kautsky witnessed the growth of integrated peasant cooperatives, which seemed to point to what Djurfeldt (1982, 146) calls "capitalism without capitalists." The agrarian crisis (opening up of trade) created advantages for middle peasants and for new forms of production (intensive cattle and dairy farming) also compatible with small forms of production. It also drew capital out of agriculture and into agroindustry. Industry, said Kautsky, was the "motor force" of agriculture, but much land-based production remained in the hands of more or less capitalized and fully commodified family farms and smallholders (rather than factories in the fields).

But all this pointed to the otherness of land—its "as if" qualities. Kautsky presented rich statistical and survey evidence at odds with the Marxist orthodoxy on the superior productivity of large-scale estates and on the complete dissolution of "the old peasantry": the 1895 census indicated that the small farm had not lost ground since the 1850s and in some areas was flourishing (1989 [1899], 11). Why then did the peasantry persist; why and how did "the limited nature of the soil" (land as nonreproducible) retard the processes of concentration of land and capital; and why was household production in agriculture structurally differentiated from manufacturing? His answer was in many respects heretical and turned, in part, on the fictive character of land. Kautsky did not, of course, use this Polanyian language but rather focused on the question of biology and nature and how these constitutive properties of land shaped the dynamics of agriculture.[2] As he put it, agriculture "does not develop according to the pattern of industry: *it follows its own laws*" (ibid., emphasis added). Seasonality, climatic and other risks, and the limits to mechanization for some crops made factories in the field difficult for capital. Peasants could moreover overexploit their labor, accepting "underconsumption" and "excessive labor" and underbidding permanent wage workers, therefore providing a source of "continuous primitive accumulation" (Alavi and Shanin 1988, xvi). And not least, Kautsky saw "two souls" in the breast of the peasant—worker and property owner—which implied that the smallholder would only under some circumstances align with revolutionary movements and proletarian parties. It was, if you will, another expression of the commodity fiction at work. Peasant or smallholder identity in this sense might be seen too as "fake" (as opposed to, say, Lenin who saw them as contradictory "propertied laborers"). It was the commodity fiction that, through the operations of biology among other things, in effect constituted another sort of countermovement: less the reembedding of land in nonmarket institutions than the resistance to the evisceration of small-scale property.

Naturally, the disembedding of land and what it took to convert land into a commodity and into capitalist property are central to both classical political economy and to Marxist analysis of the transition from feudalism to capitalism. This book explores, among other things, the narrative, rhetoric, slights of hand and counterfeiture, semiosis, and the grand architecture fictions of regulation and the law: all of the hard work entailed in the historical present to retain land as property and to maintain the fakeness. Marx—and even Adam Smith— showed what a long slog it has been: it historically demanded all the "regulatory, legal and narrative fictions" to strip away customs, commons, and precapitalist institutions. Marx himself had described in his notebooks—the *Grundrisse*—the variety of conditions under agrarian capitalism that could emerge from the "swamp" of precapitalist relations. As Edward Thompson showed, this was a Titanic struggle, uneven and jagged, in which the enclosures and the struggle between different forms of law and property—the moral economy question, in short—revealed once again the ways in which the "givenness" of land threw up all sorts of hurdles and obstacles to the "stripping away" (as the editors describe the process) of nonmarket use values.

But the key question in *Capital* was Marx's discussion of ground rent and the rise of what he called the capitalist form of landed property (Marx 1990 [1867]). Whereas capital, Marx argued, subsumes the labor process in whatever form it finds it—for example, sharecropping, bonded labor, systems of labor rent—agrarian capitalism requires *capitalist* landed property. In early modern Europe, landed property was enmeshed in feudal relations of production, and Marx traces the evolution of these precapitalist forms from labor rent—where the peasant producer is obliged to work for the lord for certain periods—into modern ground rent based on capitalist tenant farming. Labor rent rests on the application of extra-economic coercion and on personal subjugation to the lord, whereas rent-in-kind, where the peasant contributes produce rather than labor-time, is a mutated form of rent that offers peasants the possibility of accumulation (and triggers forms of social differentiation). Marx refers to these evolving forms of labor process associated with agrarian commercialization as the "formal subsumption of labor to capital" insofar as the labor process (the actual mode of working) carries on much as it did prior to the entry of capital and yet increasingly work is mediated through the wage relation. As he put it, "Wage labour in its totality is initially created by the action of capital on landed property, and then, as soon as the latter has been produced as a form, by the proprietor of the land himself. This latter then 'clears' . . . the land of its excess mouths" (Marx 1973, 276). Modern landed property appears as a "form" when capitalist farmers appear, at which point the "proprietor," the landlord, completes the task (removing excess mouths). All along the way the emergence of agrarian capitalism was constrained by the traditional force of customary rights—what Brenner (1986) called the solidity of precapitalist relations of property—to which peasants and workers alike clung. Feudal social relations of production could fetter the forces of production because lords controlled extra-economic powers to compel peasants to work longer or harder or succumb to increased rents. The logic worked against the need to systematically improve efficiency, productivity, and competitiveness. How then was this "solidity" of feudalism's social property relations broken?[3]

The long arc of these complex historical processes is what Marx refers to, in shorthand, as "primitive accumulation," which he explores through the enclosure movements by which "the great masses of men are suddenly and forcibly torn from their means of subsistence" (1990 [1867], 716), becoming in due course "unprotected and rightless proletarians." Marx emphasized the role of violence and of the state in this dispossessing and freeing of labor and the disembedding of land and was surely deeply attentive to the commodity registers, semiotic slights of hand, legal fictions, and social imaginaries covered in this book. And none of this—whether the enclosures, technical innovation, or enhanced farmer productivity—was smooth or without struggle and contention.

Land was also central to classical political economy of the seventeenth century onward, though naturally endowed with a rather different conceptual toolkit and normative expectations. The economy was envisaged as a circular flow of wealth triggered by agrarian surpluses derived from farmers, landlords, and laborers. Adam Smith's (1990 [1776]) *The Wealth of Nations* is a textbook case of such physiocratic thought, privileging the foundational role of agriculture for any commercial society. On the one hand, Smith denounced the monopolizing tendencies of merchants and manufacturers who distorted natural market laws; and on the other promoted "perfect liberty" to ensure there was no discrimination against laborers, farmers, and landlords who constituted the most productive economic sector. Smith preferred the habits and practices of those social classes associated with agriculture and saw his laissez-faire capitalism as representing a sustained attack on industrial capitalists; indeed it was "an argument for agrarian-based capitalist development ruled by prosperous and public-spirited country gentlemen" (McNally 1990, 263). Another foundational land fiction.

The contrariness of land, the contradictions of its commodity status, and what the editors refer to in their Introduction as the commodity register of land (both material and the semiotic), has never really disappeared from the agrarian world. The fictions are alive and well and visible just about every day in the press. We might turn to the appropriation of EU farm subsidies to lubricate "mafialike" land deals enriching political elites and cronies within the orbit of right-wing authoritarians such as Hungarian President Orban, all in the name of defending small farmers (Gebrekidan, Apuzzo, and Novak 2019). Alternatively, we might observe that 89 percent of farms in the United States are small, where land is assuredly property but also has familial nature bound up with ethical, moral, and cultural attachments to "family land," highlighting the resistances and frictions around the process by which the commodity fiction organizes actual markets. And then there is China, where a new trend of the "fading family farms" points to the gradual demise of "traditional" farming communities, as an older generation of post-Mao peasants leases land to larger-scale capitalist growers (Schuman

2018). Here land that was reembedded in communal relations via the prohibition of land commercialization was subsequently pulled away from giant communes and redistributed to individual households, while further changes in government policy in the mid-1990s made those land rights secure enough for farmers and others to have the confidence to rent land on a wide scale. Land has not been fully privatized, but the story of disembedding, reembedding, and disembedding points to the shifting commodity registers of land, as the editors properly put it. All of these dynamics show not only how land as commodity is continually invented and reinvented but also how the nonmarket aspects of land seem sticky, resistant, and contrarian and how the impulse to measure, abstract, and standardize was bloody hard work at best, and not infrequently cloaked in failure. These sorts of land fictions are seen clearly in this book, especially in the chapters by Dwyer, Morris, Levien, and Balakrishnan.

My remarks have focused here on the *longue durée* of the creation of land as a commodity and its various fictional expressions. *Land Fictions* rightly and properly explores across space (Global North and South) and across sectors and regions (the city, the country). The book is intent to show how these fictions are put to work to disembed land from its nonmarket functions, to reembed in the market, to embed market thinking as a common-sense hegemony ("the whole of society"), and not least to *keep* land embedded in the market. I want to conclude by focusing briefly on two themes—the frontier and the vertical—which in various ways run across the chapters but which are worthy of some consideration. The concept of frontier appears throughout this book and is deeply imbricated in the genesis and character of the fictions that surround land's emergence as a commodity. Frontiers are particular sorts of social space produced by particular sets of spatial practices, forms of representation, and lived experiences.[4] Historically frontiers are often seen to stand in relation to nation building and the modern state (see Turner 1893): the reference point is imperial, and commerce advances typically into geographical border zones in which populations are presumed to be (or constructed as) scant or "primitive," property rights unformed, and resources unexploited: in short, a zone of contact between "barbarism" and "civilization." Frontiers are assumed to stand at the peripheries of expanding states or empires, exemplars of what Carl Schmitt (2006) called *Landnahme*, the land appropriating state (see Korf, Hagmann and Doevenspeck 2013). Such appropriations are naturally synonymous with new horizons for accumulation and, often, settler colonialism. As Lund (2008, 511) puts it, the frontier denotes "an influx and presence of non-native private actors in pursuit of the newly discovered resources [and] offers a reconfiguration of the conditions of possibility."

Not surprisingly, much of the work on frontiers is centrally concerned with land. Li's (2014b) *Land's End* is such a land frontier story (the "indigenous frontier") in which capitalist relations (and enclosure and dispossession) take on what she sees as a surprisingly stark and unmediated form. What according to Li is surprising is the speed at which this happens and the degree to which it runs against a conventional narrative of the resilience of common property and peasant endurance. In her account (which she sees as unusual), indigenous people actively engage in the land market out of a desire for the benefits of modernity, not state compulsion, even if what they got was inequality and loss of land. This story is not terribly surprising at all, though. Peasants and indeed indigenous peoples often want what modernity can bring (education, roads, consumer goods), and the history of, say, the dispossession of Native Americans in the United States or the historical emergence of the groundnut and cocoa trade in West Africa reveals the agency with which some peasants threw themselves headlong into the market. Banner's (2005) powerful analysis of how American Indians lost their land on the frontier properly emphasizes the intersection of law and power as a form of rule shaped by uneven and incomplete centralized authority. Whites acquired land within a legal framework of their own construction, but some Native Americans also actively engaged in land transactions. Campbell's (2015) brilliant account of land and land fictions in Amazonia shows a similar story, where, despite differing "theories of property" among peasants and ranchers, both groups have a shared belief in enclosure and consolidation of property. Property, he says, is conjured—made through "material and discursive innovations in a speculative register" (ibid., 193), an argument deeply resonant with this book: "In Amazonia the allure of property lies not only in controlling and potentially profiting from land but also in land's status as an historical threshold that promises participation in a broader political economy" (ibid.,198).

The land frontier is surrounded by social imaginaries often promoted by the state apparatuses. Eilenberg's (2014) fine account of the palm oil colonization along the Indonesia-Malaysian borderlands shows how much of the discursive framing of what he calls the "frontier constellation" is redolent with the imagery of Frederick Jackson Turner (1893)—uncivilized, wild, insecure, and so on. Of course the land frontier in these settings is typically shrouded in myth: "The frontier was a state of mind, a cultural zone, a sociological term of comparison, a type of society, an adjective, a noun, a national myth, a disciplining mechanism, an abstraction, and an aspiration" (Grandin 2019). In Turner's account, circumstances peculiar to the American frontier—such as free land, opportunity, and common danger from Indians—shaped American character and institutions in specific ways: the frontier quickened assimilation of immigrants, had a "nationalizing" effect on young America, and promoted democracy. According to Turner, the push of an expanding people and the conquest of land gave to the American intellect its characteristic inventiveness, practicality, restlessness, optimism, and individualism. Land and property in the Lockean sense emerged at the frontier in this particular fiction. But Turner's frontier, says Grandin (2019), was more James Stewart than John Wayne. The reality was that "the state *preceded* the frontier.... Before the settlers arrived, the government had bought the land and surveyed it and built roads across it. Above all, the United States Army removed Native Americans and Mexicans from the settlers' way, in brutal and deadly fashion" (ibid., 147). The Turnerian origin story of America was at the same time a massive land fiction, narrated so as to shroud land, liberty, and property in mythos.

The frontier constellation is an example of what Weizman (2007, 7), describing a very different situation in Israel and the West Bank, calls a unique territorial ecosystem in which "various other zones ... of political piracy.... barbaric violence ... weak citizenship.... exist adjacent to, within or over each other." The frontier can resemble an archipelago of splintered and fragmented spaces. What *Land Fictions* shows is that frontierness may arise in all manner of situations that are neither peripheral nor remote nor a result of the inability or weakness of the state to project its powers. Frontiers can and do arise in circumstances in which the capabilities of states, for a raft of quite different reasons (economic shocks, external intervention such as structural adjustment, fiscal crises, struggles and conflicts in the political settlement), may contract, wither, or simply be withdrawn. "Frontierness," then, turns on dynamic and shifting state goals and capacities, what Barker and Van Klinken (2009) describe as "institutional patchiness." As such, frontiers need not be historicized by confining them to early state-building but rather are defined in relation to the constantly shifting configurations of all modern and postcolonial states. Land fictions might be thought in this sense as frontier fictions of sorts.

My final point about land and land fictions invokes the vertical as opposed to the horizontal. Extraction raises these sorts of vertical fictions quite dramatically. The geological and the subsurface stratigraphy of land has been central to nation building and other forms of land fiction, namely nationalism (land as territory, in other words). Nature and nationalism, and resources and nationhood are common themes in state-building discourses. But the rise of the term Anthropocene has also triggered an interest in thinking about land and earth history, what has been dubbed political geology (Youssof 2018; Bobette and Donovan 2019). The oil frontier provides a compelling case. A geological province, a large area often of several thousand square kilometers with a common geological history, becomes a petroleum province when a "working petroleum system" has been discovered. A commercial petroleum system (or "play") consists of a number of core features: a source rock with rich carbon content and a geological depth capable of converting organic carbon to petroleum; a sedimentary reservoir rock with sufficient pore space to hold significant volumes of petroleum and sufficient permeability to allow petroleum to flow to a well bore; a nonporous sedimentary rock as effective barrier to petroleum migration and a structural trapping mechanism to capture and retain petroleum; and fortuitous geological timing such that trap formation preceded the migration of petroleum. At this point, the oil frontier takes on a new life within the play, attended by a new raft of fictions and discourses. The discovery of a petroleum field begins a process of appraisal and development, namely drilling many new wells to confirm the extent and properties of the reservoirs and fluids and also whether configuration warrants the larger investment needed to develop the field. The development of the initial fields in a new province is replete with technical uncertainties—and associated speculative imaginings—that collectively shape the ultimate volume of oil that can be recovered. Uncertainties around each of these field variables translate into uncertainty in ultimate recovery volumes; peak production from the field; the life of the field; well flow rates; the density of wells required; required capacities of production, storage, and export systems; and when secondary and perhaps tertiary recovery might ultimately be appropriate. With the development of one or more commercial fields, a frontier becomes "proven" and uncertainty about adjacent fields goes down, often inducing an influx of new entrant companies and investors that were deterred when entry barriers were high. The vertical produces its own fictions around not just unimaginable future wealth, but discourses and narratives around "first oil" and the changing registers of the reservoir and the field as uncertainties are reduced, and the vertical takes on a market value, bringing the subsurface further into play. As reserves are "booked" so the stratigraphy becomes a sort of asset class.

Vertical land fictions appear in especially vivid forms in the work of several geographers. Denizen (2019) describes what he calls Baroque soils in Mexico and how not only are some soils the product of human activity (using post-earthquake materials) but the constantly shifting subsurface geology as a consequence of draining the aquifer in the Valley of Mexico produces complex patterns of subsidence and cracking (of walls and housing structures). All of this becomes, as he shows, legal, financial, and political. It is a strange account of stratigraphy as a complex intersection of what he calls English case law, Mexican mortgage insurance policies, and "baroque hydrological miracles" (Denizen 2019, 73). Marston's (2019) work on artisan and cooperative tin miners in Bolivia reveals how in the wake of the crisis of state and corporate large-scale tin mining, farmers and familial surface configurations around land and farming crystallized into "new social striations" in the form of "subsoil family farms." The vertical cartography of tin mining resembles a complex case of subsurface transference, and along with this come all manner of land (and labor) fictions from above ground. Rodenbiker (2019) offers an intriguing case of a more volumetric approach to land, tracing how speculative land acquisitions in Chinese villages and peri-urban frontiers for horizontal commodifications (sales, leases, and village shareholding) vary according to the land compensation calculations for anticipated vertical growth in the form of "sky fees," subsurface fees, and the associated fears and promises of high-rise buildings.

And not least this extractive and vertical sensibility inevitable draws land and land fictions into the marine and oceanic worlds. Subsea mining and the new frontiers opened up by the melting of the Arctic produce new sorts of land and marine fictions. Arroyo (2019) shows how new systems of global oceanic and atmospheric circulation, a vast constellation of satellites, drones, buoys, cables, supercomputers, servers, and sensors will give form to the New Arctic, a "digital ocean" whose geoeconomic and geostrategic value inheres in its rendering as a calculative, computational domain. A liquid Arctic is both a knowledge and infrastructural frontier—forms of "environmental intelligence" and a logistical order of extraction, circulation, and securitization yet to come into being—but also a new frontier of accumulation. Guggenheim Investment Partners LLC, a New York firm, offered the first Arctic-specific investment portfolio while China published its first comprehensive Arctic strategy for a "Polar Silk Road." This emergent "geography of speculation" rests, then, on what lies beneath the surface. If you think of Wall Street as capitalism's symbolic headquarters, says Henely (2010), the sea is capitalism's trading floor writ large. These speculative geographies are the very stuff of *Land Fictions* and point to the need for further delving into the subtleties, metaphysics, and intricacies of the commodity invoked by Marx 150 years ago.

Notes

INTRODUCTION

1. The meeting with Prime Minister Abe prompted its own ethics concerns, as Abe had a private meeting with Ivanka Trump, who had not yet relinquished her role in the Trump Organization (Lima 2016).

2. The Camden Redevelopment Agency webpage detailed all of the city's redevelopment plans, http://camdenredevelopment.org/Plans/Plans/Redevelopment-Plan.aspx, accessed June 25, 2019.

3. "Land grabbing" emerged in the late-2000s as a broad term for describing the lease, concession, or outright purchase of domestic land by foreign bodies. These cross-border transactions were primarily agricultural in nature and gained scholarly and policy attention after a "land rush" triggered by a boom in food and biofuel prices at the time (United Nations 2007; Borras Jr. and Franco 2011). Mineral extraction later became incorporated into this conversation as part of a rising international concern about China's influence in Africa (Cotula 2013a). Once commodity prices cooled off, scholarship sought to unpack the land grab "black box" by challenging presumptions that it constituted a single process. The "foreignization of space" (Zoomers 2010), which presumes that land deals are driven by foreign capital rather than domestic elites, is no longer integral to descriptions of land grabbing. Earlier definitions focused on large-scale transactions have also been dispensed with (Hall 2011), as has a narrow conception of the state as either a singularly passive agent, or corrupt supplicant, of foreign capital (Wolford et al. 2013). Land grabbing now operates as a stand-in category for a range of land transactions emerging via land-market liberalization; the conversion of collective or customary land rights into private property rights; and land privatization and financialization, all under conditions of questionable consent among—or forced displacement of—traditional land users. To the extent that urban and periurban land transactions focused on infrastructure development, property speculation, and real estate growth are now being brought into the "land grab" fold (see Perry 2013; Zoomers et al. 2017; Steel et al. 2017), land grabbing and conversations around accumulation by dispossession and "global gentrification" are becoming increasingly interconnected (see Levien 2018; Lees et al. 2015). We retain more generalist usage of "land grabbing" for two reasons. First, the productive ambiguity it offers in not differentiating between the type of land grabbed helps pull together analysis of the techniques and narratives of land commodification across rural and urban geographies. We note that market actors often learn from their counterparts in different geographical and regional settings—such as the World Bank's (2007b) efforts to coordinate its urban and rural interventions, particularly regarding integrated land administration, periurban land conversion, and compensation for land acquisition—and thereby demand scholarly attention to the same dynamics. Second, land grabbing is evocative of a struggle, a grabbing and grabbing back. It thus brings to immediate attention the core struggle in land transactions between those doing the grabbing and those struggling to retain possession, much like the double movement metaphor Polanyi (2001 [1944]) uses to describe the push-and-pull dynamics of capitalist development.

4. In Wallerstein's (2012, 6) words, "The land was there before the existence of a capitalist world-economy."

5. "The commodity fiction," Polanyi asserted, "handed over the fate of man and nature to the play of an automaton running in its own grooves and governed by its own laws. Nothing similar had ever been witnessed before" (2002 [1947], 109).

6. The Bombay Tenancy and Agricultural Lands Act of 1948 and its subsequent revision in 1956 facilitated a "land to the tiller" policy that drove the ownership transfer of land to over 150,000 landless households and barred nonagriculturalists from purchasing agricultural land (Balasaheb 2013, 10–11).

7. The effects of urbanizing land rents do not end there. Indian agricultural companies, facing rising land prices, were early leaders in the so-called "global land rush." India's largest sugar manufacturer, Shree Renuka Sugar Ltd., based in Maharashtra, for example, invested in more than 120,000 hectares of sugar-cane-growing land in southwest Brazil. Urbanizing land rents via Trump Tower–like projects first displace domestic agriculture, which in turn displaces traditional land users elsewhere. Each investment step is sustained by narratives of efficiency, land-use maximization, and wider social good. Whereas land urbanization is narrated as a process to close internationally benchmarked rent gaps and make Indian real estate "bankable" (Government of India 2017), transnational land deals promise to close yield gaps; infuse capital-poor markets with development money; and bring technology, food security, and productivity gains to the developing world (see Deininger and Byerlee 2011).

8. For more on agrarian developmentalism and its relation to land as framed in peasant studies, see McMichael 1997. For more on spatial Keynesianism, see Brenner 2004. Value theory is core to the study of political economy, centering on the value form, or the social construction of the commodity. Contemporary work on value theory has done much to expand our understanding of the generation of value in production under conditions of advanced capitalism, specifically related to financialization and the accelerating significance of immaterial labor (see Bigger and Robertson 2017; Christophers 2015; Elson 2015; Purcell et al. 2019). Our focus in this book, as elucidated further below, is not on the study of value creation as such, but rather on processes of social valuation, or how international, national, regional, and local development stories proffer implicit theories of the social function of land, which in turn creates the conditions for value to be realized on the real estate market. See Harvey 2014 for more on the contradictory unity that he, following Marx, poses between value creation and realization.

CHAPTER 1. FICTITIOUS BUT NOT UTOPIAN

1. For other discussions of knowledge as a fictitious commodity, see Jessop 2007; Irzik 2007; Brown-Keyser 2007; and Burawoy 2015.

2. I do think it is difficult to escape the conclusion that the earth's ontological status as the very basis of human existence means that it will always exceed its commodity form, but my argument here does not depend on this.

3. Despite Polanyi's criticisms of Marx, there are many parallels between his account of land commodification and Marx's discussion of "primitive accumulation." Indeed, it seems improbable that Polanyi did not have section 8 of *Capital* fresh in his mind when writing these sections of *The Great Transformation*. I point out some of these parallels in the footnotes below.

4. Marx similarly observed that the government of Henry VII "shrunk back in the face of this immense change," but attributes this to a not-yet-capitalist state that "did not yet stand at that high level of civilization where the 'wealth of the nation' (i.e. the formation of capital and the reckless exploitation and impoverishment of the mass of the people) figures as the *ultima Thule* (uttermost limit) of all statecraft" (Marx 1990 [1867], 879). The Glorious Revolution of 1688, however, brought into power "the landed and capitalist

profit-grubbers" who "inaugurated the new era by practicing on a colossal scale the theft of state lands which had hitherto been managed more modestly" (ibid., 885). For the best empirical account of the enclosures, see Neeson 1993.

5. Compare again to Marx (1990 [1867], 931): "In Western Europe, the homeland of political economy, the process of primitive accumulation has more or less been accomplished. . . . It is otherwise in the colonies. There the capitalist regime constantly comes up against the obstacle presented by the producer, who, as owner of his own conditions of labor, employs that labor to enrich himself instead of the capitalist. The contradiction between these two diametrically opposed economic systems has its practical manifestation here in the struggle between them. Where the capitalist has behind him the power of the mother country, he tries to use force to clear out of the way the modes of production and appropriation which rest on the personal labor of the independent producer."

6. Marx (1990 [1867], 885) similarly observes that "the advance made by the 18th century shows itself in this, that the law itself now becomes the instrument by which the people's land is stolen, although the big farmers made use of their little independent methods as well."

7. This is very similar to Marx's (1990 [1867], 876) observation that "the history of this expropriation assumes different aspects in different countries, and runs through its various phases in different orders of succession, and at different historical epochs."

8. One can also see a close analogy with Durkheim's (1984) progression from mechanical to organic solidarity, contingent on overcoming a period of anomie. But while Durkheim emphasized the importance of corporatism in achieving organic solidarity (in the "organs" of society), Polanyi places greater emphasis on the role of the state in reembedding the market.

9. Dale (2016, 23–29) usefully emphasizes Polanyi's debt to Tönnies but underappreciates how Polanyi's own conception of fictitious commodities greatly expands on Tönnies's. For Tönnies, what is fictitious about the labor contract is that it gives the impression that "the manufacturer . . . is the real author and producer and hires workers only as helpers" (Tönnies 2002 [1887], 98)—it mystifies, in other words, the real source of value. This is a far more restricted conception than Polanyi's, as should be clear from the above—and Tönnies did not explicitly use the language of fictitiousness in reference to land and money.

10. And similarly: "Leaving the fate of the soil and people to the market would be tantamount to annihilating them. Accordingly, the counter-move consisted in checking the action of the market in respect to the factors of production, labor and land" (Polanyi 2001 [1944], 137).

11. This, I believe, is the basis of the notable divergence in Polanyian scholarship between those who read Polanyi as a theorist of commodification (Burawoy 2003, 2015) and those who read him as a theorist of "embeddedness" (Granovetter 1985; Block 2001; Krippner et al. 2004; Krippner and Alvarez 2007; Block and Sommers 2014).

12. Block (2001, xxvi) similarly points to government management of agricultural prices and adds environmental land-use management. But neither amount to decommodification.

13. It is thus not the case that "efforts to disembed the economy from society inevitibly encounter resistance" (Block 2001, xxviii).

14. *Jagirdari* tenure covered approximately 60 percent of Rajasthan's total area (Government of Rajasthan 1959, 7) and contained about 70 percent of Jaipur State's peasantry (Stern 1988, 242). Much of the remainder was *khalsa*, or crown land, which was directly controlled by the princes. In Jaipur district, most of the *khalsa* land was mapped and settled under *ryotwari* (cultivator as opposed to landlord) tenure before Independence (ibid., 244).

15. Singh (1964) documents twenty-nine different kinds.

16. The most important act was the Rajasthan Land Reforms and Resumption of Jagir Act of 1952, which had already been amended twelve times by 1959 (Government of Rajasthan 1959).

17. However, many did retain de facto political influence in their villages for decades.

CHAPTER 2. FICTIONS OF SURPLUS

1. A variety of Acts and Agreements between the Government of Canada and indigenous peoples determine the land management schemes and associated codes, freedoms, and responsibilities germane to First Nations, Inuit, and Métis land rights. With its settler-colonial origins, Canadian land regimes—whether public or private—are a clear indicator of Polanyi's (2001 [1944], 187) "separation of land from man" foregrounded in the Introduction to this book. And yet, to continue the quote, Polanyi includes the caveat that land as a fictitious commodity is a means of "satisfy[ing] the requirements of a real-estate market" (ibid.) which was clearly not the case in proto-capitalist British North America of the eighteenth and nineteenth centuries when legal constructs of Canadian public land came into being. Ambitions at that time were more directly connected to the territorial conquests of an imperial state than to the profit imperatives of a free market. Thus a fair application of Polanyi to the Canadian land story can only be partial at best.

2. Unused and abused "surplus" CNR land was retained by the state in 1995 for the express purpose of reducing the company's liabilities, thus maximizing share sales revenue during privatization.

3. Elsewhere, one of us (Christophers 2016) has offered a sympathetic critique of the concept of the fictitious commodity.

4. http://www.telerealtrillium.com/business-areas/development/strategic-land/public-sector-land, Accessed June 1, 2016.

CHAPTER 3. FICTIONS OF SAFETY

1. I draw here on the classic definition of "real property" under Anglo-American common law (sometimes called "immovable property" to distinguish it from personal property), which encompasses both land and the structures affixed to it. This definition is useful in that it encompasses "land" in the broad sense relevant to investors here, interested as they often are in the value characteristics of buildings and material infrastructures as well as urban and rural land itself.

2. Helping engender Friedrich Engels's famous denunciation of residential property and subsistence garden-style landholding as both exploitive in an absolute sense—allowing capitalists to pay wages below the costs of social reproduction—and politically conservative (Engels 1997 [1872]; and see Herring and Rosenman 2016).

3. Often attuned to other forces now destabilizing US population security and property relations, such as Green New Deal proposals for addressing the threat of global climate change.

4. Although Vanguard has been, typical of its industry reputation, far more cautious about alternatives (e.g., Vanguard 2014), it has also expanded its activities, launching a new alternatives fund in 2015.

5. Although, again, the "real" in real estate and real property has deeper etymological and legal roots in the Anglo-American common law tradition.

6. This is another strategic reason for Chinese government investment in US assets (Brenner 2009).

7. Of course, that gap is itself a fiction in the sense that much of the "wealth" of private-label safe assets was illusory. Familiar imputations of fiscal discipline also crop up in this rhetoric, suggesting safe assets talk as a new vehicle for legitimizing creditor interests.

8. And congruent ones such as concern over aging populations, although these "demographic" pressures are themselves partly a construct, the veiled result of particular choices made in (re)organizing retirement funds (Clark 2000).

CHAPTER 4. GROUND FICTIONS

1. Names and details that might identify individuals and some locations have been changed throughout the chapter to protect anonymity. Although many of them remain unnamed here, I am grateful to the people and organizations in both Urabá and Medellín who welcomed me into their homes and lives over the course of my fieldwork. This research would not have been possible without them. My thanks to Asher Ghertner and Robert Lake for welcoming me to the stimulating conversations that led to this book. I am also grateful to the two anonymous reviewers, along with Asher and Bob, for their thoughtful comments on this chapter. Generous funding for research and writing for this project came from the Social Science Research Council; the Wenner-Gren Foundation; the Inter-American Foundation; the Land Deal Politics Initiative; the University of Chicago Center for Latin American Studies, Department of Anthropology, and Pozen Family Center for Human Rights; the American Bar Foundation; and the National Science Foundation under Grant No. SES-1655497.

2. For a detailed analysis of the emergence and governance of zones of high risk in urban Colombia, see Zeiderman 2013, 2016.

3. For further discussion on the notion of the shadow of the post-conflict, see Morris 2019.

4. Elsewhere (see Morris 2018), I draw on theories of state fictions and violence (Aretxaga 1999; Taussig 1997; Siegel 1998) to discuss how soil becomes part of narratives of paramilitary terror, state violence, and spectral remains, making soil a central locus for stories about a violent past and fantasies of a future peace.

5. Law 70 of 1993 identified black communities in Colombia—descended from the country's former slave population—as an ethnic group and established the possibility for these communities to solicit inalienable collective land title. For a detailed discussion of this matter, see, for example, Arocha 2004; Escobar 2008; Paschel 2016; Restrepo 2013.

6. This reference is in distinction from the mid-twentieth century period of bipartisan political violence known nationally and internationally as La Violencia.

7. This shapeshifting quality resonates with that described by Kristina Lyons (2016) in her analysis of farmers' narratives of the soil in the Putumayo as "seemingly left for dead"—a state that simultaneously evokes death and the potential for regeneration.

CHAPTER 5. NARRATIVES OF WASTE

1. Right to Fair Compensation and Transparency in Land Acquisition, Rehabilitation and Resettlement Act, no. 30 of 2013, The Gazette of India (Ministry of Law and Justice, Legislative Department, Sept 27, 2013), chapter III.

2. See for instance, Block's (2001, 147) introduction to Polanyi's *The Great Transformation*: "Although the working-class movement has been a key part of the protective countermovement, Polanyi explicitly states that all groups in society have participated in this project. When periodic economic downturns destroyed the banking system, for example, business groups insisted that central banking be strengthened to insulate the domestic supply of credit from the pressures of the global market. In a word even capitalists periodically resist the uncertainty and fluctuations that market self-regulation produces and participate in efforts to increase stability and predictability through forms of protection" (xxviii). This then leads to the influential Polanyian argument that it was statecraft that shaped the market, that is, "laissez-faire was planned."

3. Right to Fair Compensation and Transparency in Land Acquisition, Rehabilitation and Resettlement Act, no. 30 of 2013, The Gazette of India (Ministry of Law and Justice, Legislative Department, Sept 27, 2013). Also see Ramesh and Khan 2015.

4. Interview with the author, March 10, 2011.

5. Interview with the author, June 19, 2012.

6. Interview with the author, April 23, 2011.

CHAPTER 6. RENTAL FICTIONS

1. I conducted eighteen semistructured, in-depth interviews from January 2013 through August 2014. I interviewed four senior staff members of tenant organizations, five senior staff of affordable housing development organizations, two attorneys that work on behalf of tenants, and two senior staff from the NYC local government. I conducted interviews with five experts in the real estate finance industry: a principal of a private equity firm, a commercial real estate attorney, a real estate attorney who worked for a special servicer, a real estate broker, and a real estate investor and consultant. In the interviews with nonprofit and government experts, I asked questions about specific buildings, including living conditions, building ownership history, and the efforts to stabilize properties. After conducting this set of interviews and constructing narratives of building ownership, I returned to five key informants from this set of eighteen interviews and, through email messages or brief phone conversations, I asked additional questions that my analyses prompted about specific buildings and practices. My interviews with real estate finance experts involved asking them to explain or clarify industry practices that I learned about from attending the industry conferences, and also asking them about how these business practices apply to the rent-regulated housing sector. I also asked the real estate and financial experts to critique my financial analyses of the investments.

7. THE FICTION OF FORMALIZATION

1. This chapter is derived, in part, from an article published in the *Journal of Peasant Studies* on April 30, 2015, available online at http://wwww.tandfonline.com/10.1080/03066150.2014.994510. To the original acknowledgments, I would like to add a special thanks to Asher Ghertner and Bob Lake for their invitation to the Land Fictions workshop at Rutgers and editorial advice in revising the chapter for the present volume.

2. See, for example, World Bank 2014.

3. Both maps (pictured as figure 1 in Dwyer 2015) are available from the World Bank Inspection Panel (WBIP no date). The revised map is the Management Report and Recommendations Map 1; the original is the Eligibility Report Map 1. On the World Bank Inspection Panel more generally, see Clark et al. 2003.

4. Although my focus is not on the legal dimensions, it is worth comparing the doctrine of state land laid out in the 1993 Constitution with that explicated in the 2001 Land Law. The former mentions neither concessions nor "state-private" land, the legal category on which they are based in the latter. What the constitution calls state property (art. 58) becomes "state *public*" property in the 2001 Land Law.

5. See Open Development Cambodia 2013. This information was formerly available at a website maintained by the Cambodian Ministry of Agriculture, Forestry and Fisheries (MAFF no date) but has since been taken down.

6. The approval dates are in late April 2006; copies of these maps are in the author's possession.

7. Land Law (2001), art. 16–17 and 48–62.

8. Interview, Phnom Penh, September 1, 2011.

9. A more detailed excerpt of figure 7.3, focusing on this variety of local land uses, is provided in Dwyer 2015 as figure 6.

8. REGULARIZATION AND THE FICTIONS OF PLANNING "UNAUTHORIZED DELHI"

1. Unauthorized colonies are one of the main "solutions" to the shortfall of planned housing in Delhi, which the 2021 Delhi Master Plan estimates at 400,000 units (Delhi Development Authority 2007). Bhan (2013, 60) explains a deeper problem of historically insufficient availability of land zoned for planned development. Specifically, he notes how no new land was notified for urban development between 1962 and 1990. Four thousand hectares were added to the city's development area in 1990, but this was a mere 4.5 percent expansion, despite the city's population growing by 3.5 million over the preceding period. An additional 20,000 hectares were added in 2007, when the population grew by another 4 million. In 1990, when the updated Delhi Master Plan 2001 was issued, and in 2007, when the current Delhi Master Plan 2021 was issued, "areas far beyond the notified area in the master plan were already built up. Both [plans] chose not to include already built-up areas as development areas within the plan" (ibid.). These officially unrecognized but built-up areas are the principal spaces where unauthorized colonies exist today. They mostly appear as unshaded spaces on the master plan's land-use map; they are the blank spots on the map.

2. There are 567 previously regularized unauthorized colonies in Delhi (Sheikh and Banda 2014), which house just shy of 13 percent of the city's population (GNCTD 2009). Dikshit's initial list included 1,208 unauthorized colonies, but those that obviously encroached on green spaces, institutional lands, or other protected areas were excluded.

3. Official requirements for regularization, besides the preparation of a layout plan, include the assembly of land records for the properties in question, a statement by the resident welfare association that they shall abide by the layout plans, and that they shall transfer any available land to the relevant municipal body free of cost so that the government might provide social infrastructure (Sheikh and Banda 2014, 4).

4. For the order constituting the special task forces, see Government of the National Capital Territory of Delhi, order No. F-27/SDM/KJ/2010/96, March 30, 2011, http://delhi.gov.in/wps/wcm/connect/e9b5290047d5252b93d8df0fed934187/stf+order.pdf?MOD=AJPERES&lmod=-1825763891.

9. THE SANCTUARY OF THE COLLECTIVE

1. In both academic and general works, the Chinese terms *nongcun* (*nong* means agrarian and *cun* is village) and *jiaoqu* (*jiao* and *qu* roughly mean fringe and area respectively) are often translated as "rural area" and "suburban area." I believe these translations are imprecise and misleading: "rural area" does not reflect the village as a human settlement (as in *cun*), which may be situated in rural areas, periurban areas, or urbanized areas; "suburban area" is a term based on the US context of large-scale suburbanization under Fordism and poorly characterizes the historical context of land regulatory regimes in China. I therefore have chosen "rural village" and "outskirts" for the translations for "nongcun" and "jiaoqu" in this chapter.

2. Promulgation number 256, the State Council in 1998.

3. Type 4 includes "forests, grasslands, wastelands, marshlands and other kinds of lands that are not legally owned by the collectives"; type 6 includes "land previously under collective ownership by villagers and collectives but no longer in use after state-organized relocations or natural disasters."

4. I reviewed and took detailed notes of this study at the Guangzhou Local Studies Room in the Guangzhou Municipal Library in 2016.

5. For the significance of China's *hukou* system in creating income inequality, social stratification, differentiated citizenship, and a process of cultural and political othering, see Chan 1994; and Siu 2007.

10. RIGHTS GONE WRONG ON THE CITY'S EDGE

1. A copy of this appeal, dated September 2010, is part of my personal collection of similar documents. I have withheld the names of authors on the appeal, even though they were widely circulated via email and online forums. In this and other appeals cited in this essay, some of the exact dates of events described have been obscured or slightly altered to protect the identity of the subjects.

2. It is in fact written like a "petition" to government authorities. I call it an "appeal" here, because I acquired it from a resident who had received it himself as an email attachment. The document was clearly being circulated for public consumption, implying that the author is appealing to a wider audience for sympathy, and also trying to shame the government for failing to listen to the petition.

3. The full set of criteria for calculating compensation is laid out in detail in an elaborate pamphlet issued by the District 2 People's Committee (Ban Bồi Thường Giải Phóng Mặt Bằng Quận 2 [Committee for the Compensation and Liberation of Land Surface in District 2] ca. 2006).

4. The writing of someone like Amita Baviskar (2006, 2010), an intellectual deeply committed to resisting evictions and publicly critical of state policy in India, does not have a counterpart in Vietnam. One might say that critical Marxist critiques of accumulation by dispossession have less influence within "actually existing" socialist states, where idioms of resistance are much more muted and forced into more circuitous modes of "talking back" through the media (Kim 2011; Labbé 2015).

5. The following descriptions of Thủ Thiêm are based on my own long-term fieldwork. For more detailed discussion of Thủ Thiêm history, see Harms 2016, 117–82, and Tôn Nữ Quỳnh Trân 2010.

6. On the processes through which individual pieces of land become transformed into commensurable units of exchange value that can be bought and sold on global financial markets, see Searle 2014.

7. Compare, for example, the claims made by De Soto (2000) with the counterclaims made by Davis (2006) and Neuwirth (2006).

8. The title of the document in Vietnamese reads: BẢNG CHIẾT TÍNH BỔ SUNG GIÁ TRỊ BỒI THƯỜNG, HỖ TRỢ THIỆT HẠI VÀ TÁI ĐỊNH CƯ DỰ ÁN ĐẦU TƯ XÂY DỰNG KHU ĐÔ THỊ MỚI THỦ THIÊM.

9. For a similar example of residents carefully protecting their documents, only this time in a Delhi slum community, see Ghertner's (2015a, 134) description of how residents often believed that documents about their proof of residence "was a right not just known and felt, but also possessed in the form of the plastic folder-encased collections of ration cards, voter-ID cards, tokens, school lists, and other civic insignia stored in steel cases tucked beneath beds."

10. The name of this type of document in Vietnamese is: "Bảng chiết tính giá trị bồi thường, hỗ trợ thiệt hại và tái định cư."

11. WHERE MATERIALITY MEETS SUBJECTIVITY

1. As Rogan (2017, 7) writes, "Utilitarianism... could not condemn exploitative labor practices; if the misery of the few enriched the many, it was defensible."

2. Polanyi (2001 [1944], 265) rejected the conflation of freedom and free enterprise, in an explicit rejection of Hayek's (1944) market liberalism: "The passing of market-economy can become the beginning of an era of unprecedented freedom.... yet we find the path blocked by a moral obstacle.... With the liberal idea of freedom... degenerates into a mere advocacy of free enterprise.... This means the fullness of freedom for those whose income, leisure, and security need no enhancing, and a mere pittance of liberty for

the people, who may in vain attempt to make use of their democratic rights to gain shelter from the power of the owners of property."

3. Land and housing values in Camden approached zero by the 1980s in the face of skyrocketing vacancies and massive property abandonment, with the result that nonprofit community-based organizations routinely acquired city-owned property for a nominal $1 payment prior to the state's takeover of city government in 2002 (Gillette 2005; Lake et al. 2007).

4. Federally funded urban renewal projects in the 1960s demolished seventeen hundred occupied homes but nothing was built on the cleared land, while two thousand additional homes were destroyed for construction of Interstate 676 (Catlin 1999; Gillette 2005; Kirp, Dwyer, and Rosenthal 1995).

5. The Municipal Rehabilitation and Economic Recovery Act (MRERA) P.L.2002, c.43 (C.52:27BBB-1 et seq.).

6. http://camdenredevelopment.org/Plans/Plans/Redevelopment-Plan.aspx, last accessed June 25, 2019.

7. The New Jersey Local Redevelopment and Housing Law (N.J.S.A. 40A:12A-1 et. seq.).

8. Field notes, Lanning Square Community Information meeting, August 21, 2007. All remaining excerpts from community meetings are from field notes compiled at fourteen informational meetings convened for residents by CRA and the Camden Department of City Planning in Camden's Cramer Hill and Lanning Square neighborhoods between July 2006 and August 2007.

9. CRA viewed large-scale, for-profit property development as preferable to the practice of community-based nonprofit organizations that, prior to enactment of MRERA, successfully provided small numbers of affordable housing units annually, consistent with their organizational and funding capacity. Leaders of Camden's highly active nonprofits repeatedly reported in field interviews that their access to land for housing had been sharply curtailed by the city's prioritization of large-scale development, which itself was a response to the highly unrealistic five-year time schedule for Camden's economic and fiscal revival stipulated in MRERA.

10. http://www.ramsa.com/project.aspx?id=40, last accessed November 17, 2006. The Cramer Hill project description is no longer included on the firm's website.

11. The logic of the lawsuit presaged Laura Pulido's observation regarding developments in Flint, Michigan, a decade later: "My argument is that the people of Flint are so devalued that their lives are subordinated to the goals of municipal fiscal solvency. This constitutes racial capitalism because this devaluation is based on both their blackness and their surplus status, with the two being mutually constituted" (Pulido 2016, 1; see also Bhandar 2018).

12. The eight community information meetings held in Cramer Hill in late 2006 and early 2007 were part of the city's attempt to restart redevelopment planning in the neighborhood following the unexpected invalidation of Cherokee's plan by the court in January 2006.

13. The New Jersey Economic Opportunity Act of 2013, P.L.2013, c.161 (C.52:27D-489p).

14. Since 2014, a representative of New Jersey's 1st Congressional District in the U.S. House of Representatives.

12. THE STATE OF LAND GRABS

1. Some informants speculated that Chinese citizens were allowed to continue mining due to informal loan conditions. By 2017, while Chinese miners still dominated the sector,

nationalities involved in mining had again diversified. Community members reported nearby sites operated by Russians and Koreans.

2. This tension is not unique to the Ghanaian, or any other, state. Disconnects between discursive state strategies reifying "legality" and "rationality" and practices of state agencies and actors abound in the United States (e.g., Dunbar-Ortiz 2014; Boyce et al. 2015) and beyond (e.g., Ghertner 2015).

3. Interviews were conducted between October 2012 and February 2017 with rural people living and working in areas transformed by mining, and state officials from various agencies, including the Minerals Commission, Cocoa Board (Cocobod), Environmental Protection Agency (EPA), Ministry of Agriculture, and Ministry of Forestry. We also interviewed people with intimate knowledge of, or experience in, the mining sector, including academics, NGO representatives, mining company representatives, gold buyers, small-scale site bosses and miners, including four Chinese miners.

4. Subjectivity refers to the ways people are brought into relations of power, or subjected, which is part of the process through which identities emerge (Nightingale 2011). Subjects are articulated in relationships with other people, objects, practices, and ways of knowing (Foucault 1990; Haraway 1997). Big men, frontmen, and secretaries are terms Ghanaians use. These subject positions are not always mutually exclusive or fixed in time and space.

5. Land deals for foreign gold mining occur through diverse processes, including official concessionization, intimidation, outright dispossession, transfer, and lease. The practices, objects, and performances described in this chapter are not fixed, exclusive, or necessary for a small-scale land grab to occur. While we forefront here the processes through which foreigners come to control "official" small-scale concessions, we do not discount the importance of other, intimately interconnected land grabbing processes of small-scale gold mining in rural Ghana (see Hausermann et al. 2018).

6. For example, Minerals Commission officials, including the CEO, presented this "straightforward" licensing procedure at a workshop held at the University of Mines and Technology, Tarkwa, Ghana, on October 4, 2012. Part of a nationwide series of "Stakeholder Sensitization Workshops," this presentation depicted a step-by-step process of identification, inspection, publication, evaluation, approval, and permitting of a small-scale mining license, including the seamless integration of administrative authorities, courts, and local, regional, and national offices of several ministries and agencies (Minerals Commission 2012).

7. This methodological approach resonates with other narratives of dispossession, such as processes of alluvial accession, enabling acquisition and consolidation of land in Urabá, Colombia, that emerge from encounters and collaborations of variously positioned state and nonstate actors (Morris, this volume).

8. While millions of Tanzanian hectares were rumored to have been acquired by foreign entities (Cotula 2013a), empirical fieldwork only confirmed an exchange of 200,000 hectares (Pederson 2016).

9. Cotula (2013b, 1611), for example, cautions against brushing with too broad a stroke in connecting diverse forms of contemporary land grabbing with the Polanyian processes of land commodification in that, accounting for historical dynamics of local land relations and other factors, the global land rush in certain cases "merely accelerates a pre-existing process of commodification and social differentiation." Yet, while Cotula focuses on the role of international investment law mediating processes of negotiation and acquisition of land, deals resulting from encounters between differently positioned actors that we detail here can also be productive of and dependent on emergent forms of social differentiation and socioecological transformation (Hausermann et al. 2018).

10. While "small-scale" mining dates to precolonial Ghana, these activities were legalized in 1989.

11. Informants largely agreed that foreign miners export gold for sale on international markets; Chinese informants confirmed this.

12. Districts are the most basic unit of government administration in Ghana.

13. While "participatory," the twenty-one day process places undue burden on landowners or farmers to respond to proposed sites.

14. *Galamsey*, or "gather them and sell," is a local term for artisanal and small-scale mining.

15. Spanish miners we met in 2011 swiftly imported two excavators from Colorado before obtaining a concession through a Ghanaian frontman.

16. Many prices in Ghana are given in the "old" New Cedi. Thus 4 million = 400 GH₵, or close to US $200, based on 2013 exchange rates.

AFTERWORD: LAND FICTIONS IN THE *LONGUE DURÉE*

1. See http://mentalfloss.com/article/92556/fake-etymology-story-behind-one-dictionarys-most-intriguing-words.

2. Kautsky's concerns with the biological and ecological preconditions of agriculture was taken up in the 1980s and 1990s and developed into a body of work looking at the constraints, obstacles, and resistances to capital's entry into production presented by natural conditions and rhythms. See, for example, Mann 1990; and Goodman, Sorj, and Wilkinson 1982.

3. The transition from feudalism to capitalism has of course been the object of considerable debate (see, for example, Aston and Philpin 1985; Hilton 1975).

4. The work on frontiers is vast. For a sampling of more recent work, see Redclift 2006; Korf and Raemaekers 2013; Grandin 2019; and Rasmussen, Borg, and Lund 2018.

References

Abasa, Myriam, Baudouin Dupret, and Eric Denis, eds. 2012. *Popular Housing and Urban Land Tenure in the Middle East: Case Studies from Egypt, Syria, Jordan, Lebanon and Turkey.* Cairo: American University in Cairo Press.

Abdallah, Jumanne, Linda Engström, Kjell Havnevik, and Lennart Salomonsson. 2014. "Large-Scale Land Acquisitions in Tanzania: A Critical Analysis of Practices and Dynamics." In *The Global Land Grab: Beyond the Hype,* edited by Mayke Kaag and Annelies Zoomers, 36–53. London: Zed Books.

Abi-Habib, Maria, and Eric Lipton. 2018. "President of Luxury Towers: Either Way, Trump Is the Rage in India." *New York Times,* February 17.

Adler, Daniel, and Sokbunthoeun So. 2012. "Reflections on Legal Pluralism in Cambodia." In *Legal Pluralism and Development Policy: Dialogues for Success,* edited by Brian Tamanaha, Caroline Sage, and Michael Woolcock, 83–94. Cambridge: Cambridge University Press.

Agha, Asif. 2011. "Commodity Registers." *Journal of Linguistic Anthropology* 21 (1): 22–53.

Alavi, Hamza, and Teodor Shanin. 1988. Introduction to *The Agrarian Question,* by Karl Kautsky, xi–xxxix. London: Zwan.

Amrith, Sunil. 2018. *Unruly Waters: How Rains, Rivers, Coasts, and Seas Have Shaped Asia's History.* New York: Basic Books.

Anand, Nikhil. 2017. *Hydraulic City: Water and the Infrastructures of Citizenship in Mumbai.* Durham, NC: Duke University Press.

Andreas, Joel, and Shaohua Zhan. 2016. "Hukou and Land: Market Reform and Rural Displacement in China." *Journal of Peasant Studies* 43 (4): 798–827.

The Annie E. Casey Foundation. 2001. *A Path Forward for Camden.* Baltimore: Annie E. Casey Foundation. Accessed June 25, 2019. https://www.aecf.org/resources/a-path-forward-for-camden.

Anwar, Nausheen. 2018. "Receding Rurality, Booming Periphery." *Economic and Political Weekly* 53 (12): 46–55.

Appadurai, Arjun. 2013. *The Future as Cultural Fact: Essays on Global Connection.* New York: Verso.

Aretxaga, Begoña. 1999. "A Fictional Reality: Paramilitary Death Squads and the Construction of State Terror in Spain." In *Death Squad: The Anthropology of State Terror,* edited by Jeffrey A. Sluka, 46–69. Philadelphia: University of Pennsylvania Press.

Arocha, Jaime. 2004. "Ley 70 de 1993: utopía para afrodescendientes excluidos." In *Utopía para los excluidos: El multiculturalismo en Africa y América Latina,* edited by Jaime Arocha, 159–78. Bogotá: Universidad Nacional de Colombia. Facultad de Ciencias Humanas.

Arrighi, Giovanni. 2010. *The Long Twentieth Century: Money, Power, and the Origins of Our Times.* New and updated edition. New York: Verso.

Arroyo, Alexander. 2019. *Designing a Digital Ocean: Speculative Oceanographies in the New Arctic.* PhD diss., University of California, Berkeley.

Ashton, Philip, Marc Doussard, and Rachel Weber. 2012. "The Financial Engineering of Infrastructure Privatization." *Journal of the American Planning Association* 78 (3): 300–312.

Aston, Trevor, and C.H.E. Philpin, eds. 1987. *The Brenner Debate: Agrarian Class Structure and Economic Development in Pre-Industrial Europe*. London: Cambridge University Press.

Babar, Kailash. 2016. "Donald Trump Meets Indian Partners, Hails PM Modi's Work." *Economic Times*, Mumbai, November 17.

Bailey, F. G. 1957. *Caste and the Economic Frontier*. Manchester: Manchester University Press.

Baird, Ian G. 2014. "Reduced Emissions from Deforestation and Forest Degradation (REDD) and Access and Exclusion: Obstacles and Opportunities in Cambodia and Laos." *Southeast Asian Studies* 3 (3): 643–68.

Baka, Jennifer. 2013. "The Political Construction of Wasteland: Governmentality, Land Acquisition, and Social Inequality in South India." *Development and Change* 44 (2): 409–28.

Baka, Jennifer. 2014. "What Wastelands? A Critique of Biofuel Policy Discourse in South India." *Geoforum* 54: 315–23.

Balakrishnan, Sai. 2018. "Seeing Mumbai through Its Hinterland." *Economic and Political Weekly* 53 (12): 55–60.

Balakrishnan, Sai. 2019. *Shareholder Cities: Agrarian-Urban Land Commodification in India's Corridor Regions*. Philadelphia: University of Pennsylvania Press.

Balasaheb, Tai Deokate. 2013. "Quantification of Yield Gaps in Different Planting Types of Sugarcane in Maharashtra." WP-2013-011. Indira Gandhi Institute of Development Research, Mumbai, http://www.igidr.ac.in/pdf/publication/WP-2013-011.pdf.

Ballard, B. 2010. "Land Titling in Cambodia: Procedural and Administrative Exclusions." Paper presented at the RCSD International Conference on "Revisiting Agrarian Transformations in Southeast Asia: Empirical, Theoretical and Applied Perspectives," May 13–15. Chiang Mai, Thailand. Available online at http://rcsd.soc.cmu.ac.th/InterConf/paper/paperpdf1_497.pdf.

Ballvé, Teo. 2013. "Grassroots Masquerades: Development, Paramilitaries, and Land Laundering in Colombia." *Geoforum* 50: 62–75.

Ban Bồi Thường Giải Phóng Mặt Bằng Quận 2 [Committee for the Compensation and Liberation of Land Surface in District 2] (ca. 2006). Hỏi đáp về Quy định bồi thường, hỗ trợ và tái định cư trong dự án khu đô thị mới Thủ Thiêm: Tài liệu phục vụ công tác tuyên truyền [Questions and Answers about the Regulations for Compensation, Assistance, and Resettlement in the Thu Thiem New Urban Zone Project: Documents in the Service Propaganda Work]. Thành phố Hồ Chí Minh, Ban Bồi Thường Giải Phóng Mặt Bằng Quận 2.

Banaji, Jairus. 1995. "The Farmers Movement: A Critique of Conservative Rural Coalitions." In *New Farmers' Movements in India*, edited by Tom Brass, 228–45. London: Frank Cass.

Banerjee, Abhijit, and Lakshmi Iyer. 2005. "History, Institutions, and Economic Performance: The Legacy of Colonial Land Tenure Systems in India." *American Economic Review* 95 (4): 1190–213.

Banner, Stuart. 2005. *How the Indians Lost their Land*. Cambridge, MA: Harvard University Press.

Barker, Joshua, and Gerry van Klinken. 2009. "Reflections on the State in Indonesia." In *State of Authority: The State in Society in Indonesia*, edited by Gerry and

Joshua van Klinken, 17–46. Ithaca, NY: Southeast Asia Program, Cornell University.
Baviskar, Amita. 2006. "Demolishing Delhi: World Class City in the Making." *Mute* 2 (3): 88–95.
Baviskar, Amita. 2010. "Urban Exclusions: Public Space and the Poor in Delhi." In *Finding Delhi: Loss and Renewal in the Megacity*, edited by Bharati Chaturvedi, 3–16. Delhi, Penguin Books India.
Baviskar, B. S. 1980. *The Politics of Development: Sugar Co-operatives in Rural Maharashtra*. New Delhi: Oxford University Press.
Bayart, Jean-François. 1993. *The State in Africa: The Politics of the Belly*. London: Longman.
Bayat, Asef. 2007. "Radical Religion and the Habitus of the Dispossessed: Does Islamic Militancy Have an Urban Ecology?" *International Journal of Urban and Regional Research* 31 (3): 579–90.
Becker, Gary. 1964. *Human Capital: A Theoretical and Empirical Analysis*. Chicago: University of Chicago Press.
Bekhechi, M. A., and L. Lund. 2009. "Cambodia Land Management and Administration Project: Enhanced Review Report," July 13. Washington, DC: The World Bank.
Benjamin, Solomon. 2008. "Occupancy Urbanism: Radicalizing Politics and Economy Beyond Policy and Programs." *International Journal of Urban and Regional Research* 32 (3): 719–29.
Benjamin, Solomon, and Bhuvaneswari Raman. 2011. "Illegible Claims, Legal Titles, and the Worlding of Bangalore." *Revue Tiers Monde* 206: 37–54.
Benjamin, Walter. 1999. "On the Mimetic Faculty." In *Selected Writings, 1926–1934*, edited by Michael W. Jennings, Howard Eiland, and Gary Smith, 720–22. Cambridge, MA: Belknap Press.
Benjaminsen, Tor A., and Ian Bryceson. 2012. "Conservation, Green/Blue Grabbing and Accumulation by Dispossession in Tanzania." *Journal of Peasant Studies*, 39 (2): 335–55.
Bernanke, Ben S., Carol C. Bertaut, Laurie Demarco, and Steven B. Kamin. 2011. "International Capital Flows and the Returns to Safe Assets in the United States, 2003–2007." International Finance Discussion Papers 1014. Board of Governors of the Federal Reserve System.
Berry, Sara. 1989. "Social Institutions and Access to Resources." *Africa* 59 (1): 41–55.
Berry, Sara. 2006. "Privatization and the Politics of Belonging in West Africa." In *Land and the Politics of Belonging in West Africa*, edited by Richard Kuba and Carola Lentz, 241–61. Leiden: Brill.
Berry, Sara. 2009. "Property, Authority, and Citizenship: Land Claims, Politics, and the Dynamics of Social Division in West Africa." *Development and Change* 40 (1): 23–45.
Bhabha, Homi. 1994. *The Location of Culture*. London: Routledge.
Bhan, Gautam. 2013. "Planned Illegalities: Housing and the 'Failure' of Planning in Delhi: 1947–2010." *Economic and Political Weekly* 48 (24): 58–70.
Bhan, Gautam. 2015. *In The Public's Interest: Evictions, Citizenship, and Inequality in Contemporary Delhi*. Athens, GA: University of Georgia Press.
Bhandar, Brenna. 2018. *Colonial Lives of Property: Law, Land, and Racial Regimes of Ownership*. Durham, NC: Duke University Press.
Bhattacharya, Neeladri. 2019. *The Great Agrarian Conquest: The Colonial Reshaping of a Rural World*. Albany: State University of New York Press.

Bhide, Amita. 2015. "The Regularising State." *Economic and Political Weekly* XLIX (22): 92–100.

Biddulph, R. 2010. *Geographies of Evasion: The Development Industry and Property Rights Interventions in Early 21st Century Cambodia*. Doctoral diss., University of Gothenburg.

Bigger, Patrick, and Morgan Robertson. 2017. "Value is Simple. Valuation is Complex." *Capitalism Nature Socialism* 28 (1): 68–77.

BIS. 2016. "Basel III: International Regulatory Framework for Banks." Accessed May 25, 2016. http://www.bis.org/bcbs/basel3.htm.

Blackmar, Elizabeth. 1991. *Manhattan for Rent, 1785–1850*. Ithaca, NY: Cornell University Press.

BlackRock. 2014. *The Ascent of Real Assets*. New York: BlackRock.

BlackRock. 2015. *Infrastructure Rising: An Asset Class Takes Shape*. New York: BlackRock.

BlackRock. 2016. "About BlackRock." Accessed May 25, 2016. http://www.blackrock.com/corporate/en-us/about-us.

Block, Fred. 1977. *The Origins of International Economic Disorder*. Berkeley: University of California Press.

Block, Fred. 2001. "Introduction." In *The Great Transformation: The Political and Economic Origins of our Time*, by Karl Polanyi, xviii–xxxviii. Boston: Beacon Press.

Block, Fred. 2016. "Karl Polanyi and Twenty-first Century Socialism." *Open Democracy/ISA RC-47: Open Movements*. https://www.opendemocracy.net/fred-block/karl-polanyi-and-twenty-first-century-socialism.

Block, Fred. 2018. "Karl Polanyi and Human Freedom." In *Karl Polanyi's Vision of a Socialist Transformation* edited by Michael Brie and Claus Thomasberger, 168–84. Montreal: Black Rose Books.

Block, Fred, and Margaret Somers 1984. "Beyond the Economistic Fallacy: The Holistics Social Science of Karl Polanyi." In *Vision and Method in Historical Sociology*, edited by Theda Skocpol, ed., 47–84. Cambridge: Cambridge University Press.

Block, Fred, and Margaret R. Somers. 2014. *The Power of Market Fundamentalism: Karl Polanyi's Critique*. Cambridge, MA: Harvard University Press.

Blomley, Nicholas. 2007. "Making Private Property: Enclosure, Common Right and the Work of Hedges." *Rural History* 18: 1–21.

Boamah, F. 2014. "Imageries of the Contested Concepts 'Land Grabbing' and 'Land Transactions': Implications for Biofuels Investments in Ghana." *Geoforum* 54: 324–34.

Boamah, Festus, and Aled Williams. 2017. "Strengthening Institutions against Corruption? Biofuel Deals in Ghana." In *Corruption, Natural Resources, and Development: From Resource Curse to Political Ecology,* edited by Aled Williams and Philippe Le Billion, 117–30. Cheltenham, UK: Edward Elgar.

Bobette, Adam, and Amy Donovan, eds. 2019. *Political Geology: Active Stratigraphies and the Making of Life*. London: Springer.

Borras Jr., Saturnino M. 2007. *Pro-Poor Land Reform: A Critique*. Ottawa: University of Ottawa Press.

Borras Jr., Saturnino M., David Fig, and Sofia M. Suárez. 2011. "The Politics of Agrofuels and Mega-land and Water Deals: Insights from the ProCana Case, Mozambique." *Review of African Political Economy* 38: 215–34.

Borras Jr., Saturnino M., and Jennifer C. Franco. 2012. "Global Land Grabbing and Trajectories of Agrarian Change: A Preliminary Analysis." *Journal of Agrarian Change* 12 (1): 34–59.

Boyce, Geoffrey A., Jeffrey M. Banister, and Jeremy Slack. 2015. "You and What Army? Violence, the State, and Mexico's War on Drugs." *Territory, Politics, Governance* 3 (4): 446–68.

Brara, Rita. 2006. *Shifting Landscapes: The Making and Remaking of Village Commons in India*. New Delhi: Oxford University Press.

Brass, Tom. 1995. *New Farmers' Movements in India*. New York: Routledge.

Brenner, Neil. 2004. *New State Spaces*. New York: Oxford University Press.

Brenner, Robert. 1986. "The Social Basis of Economic Development." In *Analytical Marxism*, edited by John Roemer, 23–53. Cambridge: Cambridge University Press.

Brenner, Robert. 2009. "What's Good for Goldman Sachs Is Good for America." In *The Economics of Global Turbulence*, Spanish Edition, 34–73. Madrid: Akal Ediciones.

Bridges Across Borders Southeast Asia (BABSEA). 2010. "Bittersweet: A Briefing Paper on Industrial Sugar Production, Trade and Human Rights in Cambodia." BABSEA, Phnom Penh.

Bromley, Daniel W. 2009. "Formalising Property Relations in the Developing World: The Wrong Prescription for the Wrong Malady." *Land Use Policy* 26: 20–27.

Brosius, Christiane. 2009. "The Gated Romance of India Shining: Visualising Urban Lifestyle in Images of Residential Housing Development." In *Popular Culture in a Globalised India*, edited by Moti Gokulsing and Wimal Dissanayake, 174–91. London: Routledge.

Brown-Keyser, Virginia. 2007. "Intellectual Property: Commodification and its Discontents." In *Reading Karl Polanyi for the Twenty-First Century: Market Economy as a Political Project,* edited by A. Bugra, and K. Agartan, 155–70. New York: Palgrave Macmillan.

Bryan, Dick, and Michael Rafferty. 2006. *Capitalism With Derivatives: A Political Economy of Financial Derivatives, Capital and Class*. London: Palgrave MacMillan.

Buck, Daniel. 2007. "The Subsumption of Space and the Spatiality of Subsumption: Primitive Accumulation and the Transition to Capitalism in Shanghai, China." *Antipode* 39 (4): 757–74.

Bugalski, N. 2012. "A Human Rights Approach to Development of Cambodia's Land Sector." Bridges Across Borders Cambodia/Equitable Cambodia and Heinrich Böll Stiflung. Phnom Penh, Cambodia.

Burawoy, Michael. 2003. "For a Sociological Marxism: The Complementary Convergence of Antonio Gramsci and Karl Polanyi." *Politics and Society* 31 (2): 193–261.

Burawoy, Michael. 2015. "Facing an Unequal World." *Current Sociology* 63 (1): 5–34.

Butler, Judith. 1990. *Gender Trouble: Feminism and the Subversion of Identity*. New York: Routledge.

Butler, Judith. 1993. *Bodies that Matter: On the Discursive Limits of Sex*. New York: Routledge.

Caballero, Ricardo J., and Emmanuel Farhi. 2014. "The Safety Trap." NBER Working Paper 19927. Cambridge, MA: National Bureau of Economic Research.

Cahill, Kevin. 2001. *Who Owns Britain?* Edinburgh: Canongate.

Cahill, Kevin. 2010. "Who Really Owns Britain?" *Country Life*, November 16. http://www.countrylife.co.uk/articles/who-really-owns-britain-20219.

Caldeira, Teresa. 2016. "Peripheral Urbanization: Autoconstruction, Transversal Logics, and Politics in Cities of the Global South." *Environment and Planning D* 35 (1): 3–20.

Çalışkan, Koray, and Michel Callon. 2009. "Economization, Part 1: Shifting Attention from the Economy Towards Processes of Economization." *Economy and Society* 38 (3): 369–98.

Çalışkan, Koray, and Michel Callon. 2010. "Economization, Part 2: A Research Program for the Study of Markets." *Economy and Society* 39 (1): 1–32.

Callon, Michel. 1998. *The Laws of the Markets*. Oxford: Blackwell.

Cambodia Daily. 2012. "Ethnic Minorities Risk More Than Just Land," December 6.

Cambodia Daily. 2013. "National Program Dropped Communal Titles," February 6.

Campanile, Phillip. 2016. "Land." *Journal of Peasant Studies* 43 (4): 963–67.

Campbell, Jeremy. 2015. *Conjuring Property: Speculation and Environmental Futures in the Brazilian Amazon*. Seattle: University of Washington Press.

Carmiel, O. 2012. "NYC's Savoy Park is Sold to Citigroup-Led Housing Fund." *Bloomberg Business*, June 20. Retrieved from http://www.bloomberg.com/news/articles/2012-06-20/nyc-s-savoy-park-is-sold-to-citigroup-led-housing-fund.

Carmody, Pádraig. 2011. *The New Scramble for Africa*. Cambridge: Polity.

Cassidy, John. 2014. "An Important Step in Taming the Big Banks." *The New Yorker*, April 9.

Castree, Noel. 2003. "Commodifying What Nature?" *Progress in Human Geography* 27 (3): 273–97.

Catlin, Robert. 1999. "Camden, New Jersey: Urban Decay and the Absence of Public-Private Partnerships." In *Rebuilding Urban Neighborhoods: Achievements, Opportunities, and Limits* edited by W. Dennis Keating and Norman Krumholz, 51–66. Thousand Oaks, CA: Sage.

CD 2007-CD4 Commercial Mortgage Trust. 2007. "Prospectus Supplement." Retrieved from http://www.secinfo.com/dsvrn.u1u8.htm#1stPage.

Center on Housing Rights and Evictions (COHRE). 2009. "Request for Inspection by World Bank Inspection Panel" (letter), September 4. Available online at http://go.worldbank.org/IUTVJ7CXG0.

Chakravorty, Sanjoy. 2013. *The Price of Land: Acquisition, Conflict, Consequence*. New Delhi: Oxford University Press.

Chan, Kam Wing. 1994. *Cities with Invisible Walls: Reinterpreting Urbanization in Post-1949 China*. Oxford: Oxford University Press.

Chandler, David P. 1993. *The Tragedy of Cambodian History: Politics, War, and Revolution since 1945*. New Haven: Yale University Press.

Chari, Sharad. 2004. *Fraternal Capital: Peasant-Workers, Self-Made Men, and Globalization in Provincial India*. Stanford: Stanford University Press.

Chatterjee, Partha. 2008. "Democracy and Economic Transformation in India." *Economic and Political Weekly* 43 (16): 53–62.

Chatterjee, Partha. 2011. "The Curious Case of Liberalism in India." *Modern Intellectual History* 8 (3): 687–96.

Christophers, Brett. 2011. "On Voodoo Economics: Theorising Relations of Property, Value and Contemporary Capitalism." *Transactions of the Institute of British Geographers* 35: 94–108.

Christophers, Brett. 2014. "Wild Dragons in the City: Urban Political Economy, Affordable Housing Development and the Performative World-Making of Economic Models." *International Journal of Urban and Regional Research* 38 (1): 79–97.

Christophers, Brett. 2015. "Value Models: Finance, Risk, and Political Economy." *Finance and Society* 1 (2): 1–22.

Christophers, Brett. 2016. "For Real: Land as Capital and Commodity." *Transactions of the Institute of British Geographers* 41: 134–48.

Christophers, Brett. 2017. "The State and Financialization of Public Land in the United Kingdom." *Antipode* 49 (1): 62–85.
Christophers, Brett. 2018. *The New Enclosure: The Appropriation of Public Land in Neoliberal Britain*. London: Verso.
Chuang, Julia. 2014. "China's Rural Land Politics: Bureaucratic Absorption and the Muting of Rightful Resistance." *China Quarterly* 219: 649–69.
Clark, C., J. Fox, and K. Treakle. 2003. *Demanding Accountability: Civil Society Claims and the World Bank Inspection Panel*. Lanham, MD: Rowman and Littlefield.
Clark, Gordon L. 2000. *Pension Fund Capitalism*. New York: Oxford University Press.
Clark, Gordon L., Adam D. Dixon, and Ashby H.B. Monk. 2013. *Sovereign Wealth Funds: Legitimacy, Governance, and Global Power*. Princeton, NJ: Princeton University Press.
Clean Sugar Campaign. n.d. Accessed September 2012. http://www.boycottblood sugar.net.
Cleveland, Cutler J. 1987. "Biophysical Economics." *Ecological Modelling* 38: 47–73.
Cochrane, Logan. 2011. "Food Security or Food Sovereignty: The Case of Land Grabs." *Journal of Humanitarian Assistance* 5. Accessed March 6, 2018. https://sites.tufts.edu/jha/archives/1241.
Cock, A. 2010. "External Actors and the Relative Autonomy of the Ruling Elite in Post-UNTAC Cambodia." *Journal of Southeast Asian Studies* 41: 241–65.
COMM 2012-CCRE2. 2012. Prospectus Supplement. Retrieved from http://www.secinfo.com/d1evd6.pdj.htm#1stPage.
Congote Gutiérrez, Nicolás. 2011. "El notario ante el que convirtieron 18 hectáreas en 5.000. Es investigado porque aceptó supuesto poder otorgado por un campesino para pasar finca a un 'para.'" *El Tiempo*. Bogotá. http://www.eltiempo.com/archivo/documento/CMS-9787360.
Consejo de Estado. 2007. "Concepto del 26 de agosto de 2007." Número de radicación 1825. Sala de Consulta y Servicio Civil.
Corpataux, José, Olivier Crevoisier, and Thierry Theurillat. 2009. "The Expansion of the Finance Industry and Its Impact on the Economy: A Territorial Approach Based on Swiss Pension Funds." *Economic Geography* 85 (3): 313–34.
Cotula, Lorenzo. 2012. "The International Political Economy of the Global Land Rush: A Critical Appraisal of Trends, Scale, Geography and Drivers." *Journal of Peasant Studies* 39 (3–4): 649–80.
Cotula, Lorenzo. 2013a. *The Great African Land Grab? Agricultural Investments and the Global Food System*. London: Zed Books.
Cotula, Lorenzo. 2013b. "The New Enclosures? Polanyi, International Investment Law and the Global Land Rush." *Third World Quarterly* 34 (9): 1605–29.
Cotula, Lorenzo, Sonja Vermeulen, Rebeca Leonard, James Keeley. 2009. *Land Grab or Development Opportunity? Agricultural Investment and International Land Deals in Africa*. IIED. Accessed March 6, 2018. https://pubs.iied.org/12561IIED.
Council for Land Policy. 2002. "Interim Paper on Strategy of Land Policy Framework." Supreme Council of State Reform, Royal Government of Cambodia, Phnom Penh.
Courier-Post. 2005a. "Bryant Is Region's King of Double Dippin," February 13.
Courier-Post. 2005b. "Camden 2015: The Vision, a Two-Page Rendering," November 11.
Courier-Post. 2005c. "Bryant's Firm Gets $200,000 City Contract," January 8.
Courier-Post. 2005d. "Council OK's Contract with Bryant Firm," February 4.
Courier-Post. 2006a. "Bryant's Troubles Started 10 Years Ago," September 26.
Courier-Post. 2006b. "Extra $1 Million for Camden Sparks Probe," September 26.

Courier-Post. 2015a. "EDA Approves $260M for Camden Proposal," May 6.
Courier-Post. 2015b. "Commentary: Invest in Jobs for Camden Residents," May 6.
Courier-Post. 2019. "Months after Promise, No Firm Plan in Place to Match Camden Residents to Job," May 13.
Cowan, Tom. 2018. "Urban Villages, Agrarian Transformation and Rentier Capitalism in Gurgaon, India." *Antipode* 50 (5): 1244–66.
Cowie, Jefferson. 1999. *Capital Moves: RCA's Seventy-Year Quest for Cheap Labor*. New York: New Press.
Crawford, Gordon, and Gabriel Botchwey. 2016. "Conflict, Collusion and Corruption in Small-Scale Gold Mining in Ghana: Chinese Miners and the State." Colloquium Paper No. 48 presented at the International Institute of Social Studies (ISS) International Colloquium: Global Governance/Politics, Climate Justice & Agrarian/Social Justice: Linkages and Challenges, The Hague, The Netherlands, February 4–5.
Cronon, William. 2011. *Changes in the Land: Indians, Colonists and the Ecology of New England*. New York: Hill and Wang.
Crump, Jeff, Kathe Newman, Eric S. Belsky, Phil Ashton, David H. Kaplan, Daniel J. Hammel, and Elvin Wyly. 2008. "Cities Destroyed (Again) For Cash: Forum on the U.S. Foreclosure Crisis." *Urban Geography* 29 (8): 745–84.
Cruz, Teddy. 2007. "Levittown Retrofitted: An Urbanism Beyond the Property Line." In *Writing Urbanism: A Design Reader*, edited by D. Kelbaugh and K. McCullough, 75–79. New York: Routledge.
Culler, Jonathon. 2001. *The Pursuit of Signs: Semiotics, Literature, Deconstruction*. London: Routledge.
Dale, Gareth. 2010. *Karl Polanyi: The Limits of the Market*. London: Polity.
Dale, Gareth. 2016. *Reconstructing Polanyi: Excavation and Critique*. London: Pluto Press.
Danbom, David B. 1991. "Romantic Agrarianism in Twentieth-Century America." *Agricultural History* 65 (4): 1–12.
Daniel, Shepard. 2013. "Situating Private Equity Capital in the Land Grab Debate." In *The New Enclosures: Critical Perspectives on Corporate Land Deals*, edited by Ben White, Saturnino M. Borras Jr., Ruth Hall, Ian Scoones, and Wendy Wolford, 97–124. New York: Routledge.
Danish Church Aid. 2011. "Stolen Land, Stolen Future: A Report on Land Grabbing in Cambodia and Honduras." Danish Church Aid, Copenhagen.
Davis, Mike 2006. *Planet of Slums*. New York: Verso.
Day, Jared N. 1999. *Urban Castles: Tenement Housing and Landlord Activism in New York City, 1890–1943*. New York: Columbia University Press.
De Boeck, Filip. 2011. "Inhabiting Ocular Ground: Kinshasa's Future in the Light of Congo's Spectral Urban Politics." *Cultural Anthropology* 26 (2): 263–86.
Deininger, Klaus, and Derek Byerlee. 2011. *Rising Global Interest in Farmland: Can It Yield Sustainable and Equitable Benefits?* Washington, DC: The World Bank.
Deininger, Klaus, Selod Harris, and Anthony Burns. 2012. *The Land Governance Assistance Framework: Identifying and Monitoring Good Practice in the Land Sector*. The World Bank, Washington, DC.
Delhi Development Authority. 2007. *Delhi Master Plan 2021: People-Friendly Version*. New Delhi: Rupa.
Denizen, Seth. 2019. "Baroque Soil: Mexico City in the Aftermath." In *Political Geology: Active Stratigraphies and the Making of Life*, edited by Adam Bobette and Amy Donovan, 71–104. London: Springer.

Department for Communities and Local Government (DCLG). 2012. "Accelerating the Release of Surplus Public Sector Land: Progress Report One Year On." Accessed May 16, 2019. https://www.gov.uk/government/uploads/system/uploads/attachment_data/file/6251/2140164.pdf.

Deshpande, Satish. 2016. "Caste In and As Indian Democracy." *Seminar* #677, January. https://www.india-seminar.com/semframe.html.

De Soto, Hernando. 2000. *The Mystery of Capital: Why Capitalism Triumphs in the West and Fails Everywhere Else.* New York: Basic Books.

Deutsche Bank Research. 2012. *Real Assets: A Sought-After Investment Class in Times of Crisis.* Frankfurt Am Main: Deutsche Bank.

Djurfeldt, Goran. 1982. "Classical Discussions of Capital and Peasantry: A Critique." In *Rural Development: Theories of Peasant Economy and Agrarian Change*, edited by John Harriss, 129–59. London: Routledge.

Dunbar-Ortiz, Roxanne. 2014. *An Indigenous Peoples' History of the United States.* Boston, MA: Beacon Press.

Duncan, Gustavo. 2006. *Los señores de la guerra: De paramilitares, mafiosos y autodefensas en Colombia.* Bogotá: Editorial Planeta Colombiana.

Duncan, Gustavo. 2014. *Más que plata o plomo: El poder político del narcotráfico en Colombia y México.* Bogotá: Penguin Random House Grupo Editorial.

Durkheim, Emile. 1984. *The Division of Labor in Society.* New York: Free Press.

Dwoskin, E. 2010. "New York's Ten Worst Landlords." *Village Voice*, March 16. Retrieved from http://www.villagevoice.com/2010-03-16/news/new-york-s-ten-worst-landlords/full.

Dwyer, Michael. 2013. "Building the Politics Machine: Tools for 'Resolving' the Global Land Grab." *Development and Change* 44 (2): 309–33.

Dwyer, Michael. 2015. "The Formalization Fix? Land Titling, Land Concessions, and the Politics of Spatial Transparency in Cambodia." *Journal of Peasant Studies* 42 (5): 903–28.

Eagleton, Terry. 1979. "Ideology, Fiction, Narrative." *Social Text* 2 (summer): 62–80.

Edelman, Marc, and Wendy Wolford. 2017. "Introduction: Critical Agrarian Studies in Theory and Practice." *Antipode* 49 (3): 959–76.

Eichengreen, Barry, and Ngaire Woods. 2016. "The IMF's Unmet Challenges." *Journal of Economic Perspectives* 30 (1): 29–52.

Eilenberg, Michael. 2014. "Frontier Constellations: Agrarian Expansion and Sovereignty on the Indonesian-Malaysian border." *Journal of Peasant Studies* 41 (2): 157–82.

Elson, Diane, ed. 2015. *Value: The Representation of Labour in Capitalism.* London: Verso.

Emel, Jody, Matthew T. Huber, and Madoshi H. Makene. 2011. "Extracting Sovereignty: Capital, Territory, and Gold Mining in Tanzania." *Political Geography* 30 (2): 70–79.

Engels, Friedrich. 1997 [1872]. *The Housing Question.* Moscow: Progress Publishers.

Engels, Friedrich. 1894. "The Peasant Question in France and Germany." In *Selected Works.* Vol. 2. *Karl Marx and Friedrich Engels*, 381–99. Moscow: Foreign Languages Publishing House.

Epstein, Scarlett. 2007. "Back to the Village." *Seventh Annual M. N. Srinivas Memorial Lecture, NIAS Lecture L2–2007.* Bangalore: National Institute of Advanced Studies.

Ernst & Young. 2015. *Infrastructure Investments: An Attractive Option to Help Deliver a Prosperous and Sustainable Economy.* London: Ernst & Young.

Escobar, Arturo. 2008. *Territories of Difference: Place, Movements, Life*. Durham, NC: Duke University Press.
Fairbairn, Madeleine. 2013. "Indirect Dispossession: Domestic Power Imbalances and Foreign Access to Land in Mozambique." *Development and Change* 44 (2): 335–56.
Fairbairn, Madeleine. 2014. "'Like Gold with Yield': Evolving Intersections between Farmland and Finance." *Journal of Peasant Studies* 41 (5): 777–95.
FAO, IFAD, UNCTAD, and the World Bank Group. 2010. "Principles for Responsible Agricultural Investment that Respects Rights, Livelihoods and Resources (extended version)." A discussion note prepared by FAO, IFAD, UNCTAD and the World Bank Group to contribute to an ongoing global dialogue. January 3.
Ferguson, James. 2006. *Global Shadows: Africa in the Neoliberal World Order*. Durham, NC: Duke University Press.
Fernandez, Rodrigo, Annelore Hofman, and Manuel Aalbers. 2016. "London and New York as a Safe Deposit Box for the Transnational Wealth Elite." *Environment and Planning A* 48 (12): 2443–61.
Ferring, David, and Heidi Hausermann. 2019. "The Political Ecology of Landscape Change, Malaria, and Cumulative Vulnerability in Central Ghana's Gold Mining Country." *Annals of the American Association of Geographers* 109 (4): 1074–91.
Fields, Desiree. 2015. "Contesting the Financialization of Urban Space: Community Organizations and the Struggle to Preserve Affordable Rental Housing in New York City." *Journal of Urban Affairs* 372: 144–65.
Fields, Desiree, and Sabina Uffer. 2016. "The Financialisation of Rental Housing: A Comparative Analysis of New York City and Berlin." *Urban Studies* 53 (7): 1486–1502.
Fogelson, R. M. 2013. *The Great Rent Wars: New York, 1917–1929*. New Haven, CT: Yale University Press.
Foucault, M. 1990 [1976]. *The History of Sexuality*. New York: Vintage.
Foucault, Michel. 2003. *"Society Must Be Defended": Lectures at the Collège de France, 1975–1976*. New York: Picador.
Fox Gotham, Kevin. 2006. "The Secondary Circuit of Capital Reconsidered: Globalization and the U.S. Real Estate Sector." *American Journal of Sociology* 112 (1): 231–75.
Frankel, Francine. 1971. *India's Green Revolution: Economic Gains and Political Costs*. Bombay: Oxford University Press.
Fraser, Nancy. 2014. "Can Society Be Commodities all the Way Down? Post-Polanyian Reflections on Capitalist Crisis." *Economy and Society* 43 (4): 541–58.
Frehen, Rik, William N. Goetzmann, and K. Geert Rouwenhorst. 2014. "Dutch Securities for American Land Speculation in the Late Eighteenth Century." In *Housing and Mortgage Markets in Historical Perspective*, edited by Eugene N. White, Kenneth Snowden, and Price Fishback, 287–304. Chicago: University of Chicago Press.
Freund, David M. P. 2010. *Colored Property: State Policy and White Racial Politics in Suburban America*. Chicago: University of Chicago Press.
Friedman, Eli. 2014. *Insurgency Trap: Labor Politics in Postsocialist China*. Ithaca, NY: Cornell University Press.
Froud, Julie, Colin Haslam, Johal Sukhdev, Jean Shaoul, and Karel Williams. 1998. "Persuasion without Numbers? Public Policy and the Justification of Capital Charging in NHS Trust Hospitals." *Accounting, Auditing, and Accountability Journal* 1 (1): 99–125.

Furman Center for Real Estate and Urban Policy. 2014. "Profile of Rent Stabilized Units and Tenants in New York City." New York: New York University School of Law, Wagner School of Public Service. Retrieved from http://furmancenter.org/files/FurmanCenter_FactBrief_RentStabilization_June2014.pdf.

Gargan, Edward. 1981. "Camden Struggling to Live Day by Day: The Talk of Camden." *New York Times*, June 1.

Gebrekidan, Selam, Matt Apuzzo, and Benjamin Novak. 2019. "The Money Farmers: How Oligarchs and Populists Milk the E.U. for Millions." *New York Times*, November 3. https://www.nytimes.com/2019/11/03/world/europe/eu-farm-subsidy-hungary.html.

Gelman, E. 2007. "The Bronx Is Burning a Hole in My Pocket." Master's thesis, Massachusetts Institute of Technology, Cambridge, MA.

Ghertner, D. Asher. 2005. "Purani Yojana ki Kabr par, Nayi Yojana ki Buniyad: *Dilli Master Plan 2021* ki Chunauti aur Sambhavnae [Building the New Plan on the Grave of the Old: The Challenges and Possibilities of the *Delhi Master Plan 2021*]." *Yojana* 24 (7): 14–20.

Ghertner, D. Asher. 2014. "India's Urban Revolution: Geographies of Displacement Beyond Gentrification." *Environment and Planning A* 46 (7): 1554–71.

Ghertner, D. Asher. 2015a. *Rule by Aesthetics: World-Class City Making in Delhi*. New York: Oxford University Press.

Ghertner, D. Asher. 2015b. "Why Gentrification Theory Fails in 'Much of the World.'" *CITY* 19 (4): 552–63.

Ghertner, D. Asher. 2017. "When Is the State? Topology, Temporality, and the Navigation of Everyday State Space in Delhi." *Annals of the American Association of Geographers* 107 (3): 731–50.

Gidwani, Vinay. 1992. "Waste and the Permanent Settlement in Bengal." *Economic and Political Weekly* 27 (4): PE39—PE46.

Gidwani, Vinay. 2008. *Capital, Interrupted: Agrarian Development and the Politics of Work in India*. Minnesota: University of Minnesota Press.

Gillespie, John. 2012. "The Emerging Role of Property Rights in Land and Housing Disputes in Hanoi." In *State, Society, and the Market in Contemporary Vietnam: Property, Power and Values*, edited by H.-T. Ho-Tai and M. Sidel, 103–22. New York: Routledge.

Gillette, Howard. 2005. *Camden after the Fall: Decline and Renewal in a Post-Industrial City*. Philadelphia: University of Pennsylvania Press.

Goetzmann, William N., and Frank Newman. 2010. "Securitization in the 1920s." NBER Working Paper 15650. Cambridge, MA: National Bureau of Economic Research.

Goldman, Michael. 2011. "Speculative Urbanism and the Making of the Next World City." *International Journal of Urban and Regional Research* 35 (3): 555–81.

Goldstein, Jesse. 2013. "Terra economica: Waste and the Production of Enclosed Nature." *Antipode* 45: 357–75.

Goodman, David, Bernardo Sorj, and John Wilkinson. 1987. *From Farming to Biotechnology: A Theory of Agro-Industrial Development*. Oxford: Basil-Blackwell.

Gorton, Gary B. 2016. "The History and Economics of Safe Assets." NBER Working Paper 22210. Cambridge, MA: National Bureau of Economic Research.

Gorton, Gary, Stefan Lewellen, and Andrew Metrick. 2012. "The Safe Asset Share." *American Economic Review: Papers & Proceedings* 102 (3): 101–6.

Goswami, Manu. 2004. *Producing India: From Colonial Economy to National Space*. Chicago: University of Chicago Press.

Gottesman, E. 2003. *Cambodia After the Khmer Rouge: Inside the Politics of Nation Building*. New Haven: Yale University Press.
Gourinchas, Pierre-Olivier, and Olivier Jeanne. 2012. "Global Safe Assets." BIS Working Papers 399. Basel: Bank of International Settlements.
Government of Delhi (GNCTD). 2009. *Delhi Economic Survey 2008–09*. New Delhi: Department of Economic Affairs, Government of the National Capital Territory of Delhi.
Government of India. 1950. *The Rajasthan-Madhya Bharat Jagir Enquiry Committee*. New Delhi: Government of India Press.
Government of India. 2017. "Value Capture Finance Policy Framework." Ministry of Urban Development. https://amrut.gov.in/writereaddata/3-VCF%20Policy%20Book_FINAL.pdf.
Government of Rajasthan. 1959. *Report of the State Land Commission for Rajasthan*. Jaipur: Government of Rajasthan.
Government Property Unit (GPU). 2013. "Government's Estate Strategy: Delivering a Modern Estate." Accessed May 16, 2019. https://www.gov.uk/government/uploads/system/uploads/attachment_data/file/209484/Government_s_Estate_Strategy_-_June_2013_v1.pdf.
Gowan, Peter. 1999. *The Global Gamble: Washington's Faustian Bid for World Dominance*. New York: Verso.
Grandin, Greg. 2019. *The End of the Myth: From the Frontier to the Border Wall in the Mind of America*. New York: Metropolitan Books.
Granovetter, Mark. 1985. "Economic Action and Social Structure: The Problem of Embeddedness." *American Journal of Sociology* 91 (3): 481–510.
Grimsditch, M., and N. Henderson. 2009. "Untitled: Tenure Insecurity and Inequality in the Cambodian Land Sector." Bridges Across Borders Southeast Asia, Centre on Housing Rights and Evictions, and Jesuit Refugee Service, Phnom Penh and Geneva.
Grimsditch, M., and Schoenberger, L. 2015. "New Actions and Existing Policies: The Implementation and Impacts of Order 01." NGO Forum on Cambodia, Phnom Penh.
GTZ. 2006. "Overview of Major Legal Categories of Lands and Waters in Cambodia." GTZ, Phnom Penh.
Guangzhou Municipal Government. 2011. *Guangzhou City Monograph, 1991–2000*.
Guangzhou Social Science Planning Leadership Office. 2012. "Study of Land Questions in Rural Villages and Villagers' Land Revenues in Guangzhou" (in Chinese).
Guha, Sumit. 1985. *The Agrarian Economy of the Bombay Deccan, 1818–1941*. New Delhi: Oxford University Press.
Gunnoe, Andrew, and Paul Gellert. 2011. "Financialization, Shareholder Value, and the Transformation of Timberland Ownership in the US." *Critical Sociology* 37 (3): 265–84.
Gururani, Shubhra. 2013. "Flexible Planning: The Making of India's 'Millennium City,' Gurgaon," In *Ecologies of Urbanism in India: Metropolitan Civility and Sustainability*, edited by Anne M. Rademacher and K. Sivaramakrishnan, 119–44. Hong Kong University Press.
Guthrie, James. 1998. "Accrual Accounting in the Australian Public Sector." *Financial Accountability and Management* 14 (1): 1–19.
Hackworth, Jason. 2001. "Inner-City Real Estate Investment, Gentrification, and Economic Recession in New York City." *Environment and Planning A* 335: 863–80.
Hackworth, Jason. 2002. "Postrecession Gentrification in New York City." *Urban Affairs Review* 376: 815–43.

Hackworth, Jason, and Neil Smith. 2001. "The Changing State of Gentrification." *Tijdschrift voor Economische en Sociale Geografie* 92 (4): 464–77.
Hall, Derek, Philip Hirsch, and Tania Murray Li, eds. 2011. *Powers of Exclusion: Land Dilemmas in Southeast Asia*. Honolulu: University of Hawai'i Press.
Hall, Ruth. 2011. "Land Grabbing in Southern Africa: The Many Faces of the Investor Rush." *Review of African Political Economy* 38 (128): 193–214.
Hall, Ruth, Marc Edelman, Saturnino M. Borras Jr, Ian Scoones, Ben White, and Wendy Wolford. 2015. "Resistance, Acquiescence or Incorporation? An Introduction to Land Grabbing and Political Reactions 'from Below.'" *Journal of Peasant Studies* 42 (3–4): 467–88.
Hanchett, Thomas W. 2000. "Financing Suburbia: Prudential Insurance and the Post–World War II Transformation of the American City." *Journal of Urban History* 26 (3): 312–28.
Hanke, Steve, and Barney Dowdle. 1987. "Privatizing the Public Domain." *Proceedings of the Academy of Political Science* 36 (3): 114–23.
Haraway, Donna. 1989. *Primate Visions: Gender, Race, and Nature in the World of Modern Science*. New York: Routledge.
Haraway, Donna. 1991. *Simians, Cyborgs, and Women: The Reinvention of Nature*. New York: Routledge.
Haraway, Donna. 1997. *Modest_Witness@Second_Millennium.FemaleMan_Meets_OncoMouse: Feminism and Technoscience*. New York: Routledge.
Harms, Erik. 2011. *Saigon's Edge: On the Margins of Ho Chi Minh City*. Minneapolis: University of Minnesota Press.
Harms, Erik. 2016. *Luxury and Rubble: Civility and Dispossession in the New Saigon*. Berkeley: University of California Press.
Harriss-White, Barbara. 1996. *A Political Economy of Agricultural Markets in South India: Masters of the Countryside*. New Delhi: Sage.
Hart, Gillian. 2002. *Disabling Globalization: Places of Power in Post-Apartheid South Africa*. Berkeley: University of California Press.
Hart, Gillian. 2016. "Relational Comparison Revisited: Marxist Postcolonial Geographies in Practice." *Progress in Human Geography* 42 (3): 371–94.
Harvey, David. 1982. *The Limits to Capital*. New York: Verso.
Harvey, David. 2003. *The New Imperialism*. New York: Oxford University Press.
Harvey, David. 2005. *A Brief History of Neoliberalism*. Oxford: Oxford University Press.
Harvey, David. 2007 [1982]. *The Limits to Capital*. New York: Verso.
Harvey, David. 2013. *Companion to Marx's Capital*. New York: Verso.
Harvey, David. 2014. *Seventeen Contradictions and the End of Capitalism*. New York: Oxford University Press.
Hasty, Steven. T. 2012. "Protecting Tenants at Foreclosure by Funding Needed Repairs." *Journal of Law and Policy* 20 (2): 581.
Hausermann, Heidi. 2015. "'I Could Not Be Idle Any longer': Buruli Ulcer Treatment Assemblages in Rural Ghana." *Environment and Planning A* 47 (10): 2204–20.
Hausermann, Heidi. 2018. "'Ghana Must Progress but We Are Really Suffering': Bui Dam, Antipolitics Development and Implications for Rural People." *Society and Natural Resources* 31 (6): 633–48.
Hausermann, Heidi, David Ferring, Bernadette Atosona, Graciela Mentz, Richard Amankwah, Augustus Chang, Kyle Hartfield, Emmanuel Effah, Grace Yeboah Asuamah, Coryanne Mansell, and Natasha Sastri. 2018. "Land-Grabbing, Land-Use Transformation and Social Differentiation: Deconstructing 'Small-Scale' in Ghana's Recent Gold Rush." *World Development*, 108: 103–14.
Hayek, Friedrich. 1944. *The Road to Serfdom*. Chicago: University of Chicago Press.

Heinrich Bolle Foundation (HBF). 2011. "Negotiations about Development Cooperation with Cambodia: Land Crisis Requires a Political Solution," December 13 (German language only). http://www.boell.de/weltweit/asien/asien-landkrise-landgrabbing-kambodscha-13643.html.
Henely, Kalvin. 2010. "The Forgotten Space." *Slate*, February 12. https://www.slantmagazine.com/film/the-forgotten-space.
Herring, Chris, and Emily Rosenman. 2016. "Engels in the Crescent City: Revisiting the Housing Question in Post-Katrina New Orleans." *ACME: An International Journal for Critical Geographies* 15 (3): 616–38.
Heseltine, Michael. 2012. "No Stone Unturned." Accessed May 16, 2019. https://www.gov.uk/government/uploads/system/uploads/attachment_data/file/34648/12-1213-no-stone-unturned-in-pursuit-of-growth.pdf.
Hilson, Gavin, Abigail Hilson, and Eunice Adu-Darko. 2014. "Chinese Participation in Ghana's Informal Gold Mining Economy: Drivers, Implications and Clarifications." *Journal of Rural Studies* 34: 292–303.
Hilson, Gavin, and Sandra Pardie. 2006. "Mercury: An Agent of Poverty in Ghana's Small-Scale Gold-Mining Sector?" *Resources Policy* 31 (2): 106–16.
Hilton, Rodney Howard. 1975. *The Transition from Feudalism to Capitalism*. London: Verso.
The Hindu. 2011. "BJP Alleges Rs 15,000 Cr Land Scam in Pune." Mumbai, April 11.
The Hindu. 2018. "Construction Prohibited in Unauthorised Colonies: SC." New Delhi, April 25.
Hindustan Times. 2014. "FIR against 14 Developers Including Balwa, Goenka," Mumbai, July 23.
Hirsch, Philip. 2011. "Titling against Grabbing? Critiques and Conundrums around Land Formalisation in Southeast Asia." Paper presented at International Conference on Global Land Grabbing, April 2011.
HM Treasury. 2015. "Spending Review and Autumn Statement 2015." Accessed May 16, 2019. https://www.gov.uk/government/uploads/system/uploads/attachment_data/file/479749/52229_Blue_Book_PU1865_Web_Accessible.pdf.
Ho, Peter. 2001. "Who Owns China's land? Policies, Property Rights and Deliberate Institutional Ambiguity." *China Quarterly* 166: 394–421.
Hodge, Tony, Susan Holtz, Cameron Smith, and Kelly Hawke Baxter, eds. 1995. *Pathways to Sustainability: Assessing Our Progress*. Ottawa: National Roundtable on the Environment and the Economy. Accessed May 17, 2019. http://publications.gc.ca/collections/collection_2016/trnee-nrtee/En134-2-11-1995-eng.pdf.
Hoffman, Lisa. 2014. "The Urban, Politics and Subject Formation." *International Journal of Urban and Regional Research* 38 (5): 1576–88.
Hsing, You-tien. 2010. *The Great Urban Transformation: Political of Land and Property in China*. Oxford: Oxford University Press.
Huffington Post. 2016. "The Untold Tragedy of Camden, NJ," March 8.
Hughes, Caroline. 2007. "Transnational Networks, International Organizations and Political Participation in Cambodia: Human Rights, Labour Rights and Common Rights." *Democratization* 14: 834–52.
Hughes, Caroline. 2008. "Cambodia in 2007: Development and Dispossession." *Asian Survey* 48: 69–74.
Hull, Matthew. 2012. *Government of Paper: The Materiality of Bureaucracy in Urban Pakistan*. Berkeley: University of California Press.
Hydén, Goran. 2006. *African Politics in Comparative Perspective*. Cambridge: Cambridge University Press.

Imbroscio, David. 2006. "Shaming the Inside Game: A Critique of the Liberal Expansionist Approach to Addressing Urban Problems." *Urban Affairs Review* 42 (2): 224–48.
Imbroscio, David. 2012. "Beyond Mobility: The Limits to Liberal Urban Policy." *Journal of Urban Affairs* 31 (1): 1–20.
IMF. 2012. *Global Financial Stability Report: The Quest for Lasting Stability*. Washington, DC: International Monetary Fund.
Incoder. 2012. "Caracterización jurídica y saneamiento de los territorios colectivos de Curvaradó y Jiguamiandó." Informe técnico elaborado por el Incoder, en cumplimiento de los autos 045 y 112 del 2012, proferidos por la Corte Constitucional. Bogotá: Incoder.
Inderst, Georg. 2010. "Infrastructure as an Asset Class." *EIB Papers* 15 (1): 70–105.
Ingham, Geoffrey. 2004. *The Nature of Money*. Cambridge: Polity.
Internal Displacement Monitoring Centre (IMDC). 2016. Colombia. http://www.internal-displacement.org/countries/colombia.
Ircha, Michael C., and Robert Young. 2013. "Introduction." In *Federal Property Policy in Canadian Municipalities*, edited by Michael C. Ircha and Robert Young, 3–37. Montreal & Kingston: McGill-Queen's University Press.
Ironside, Jeremy. 2011. "The Competition for the Communal Lands of Indigenous Communities in Cambodia." Presentation at International Conference on Global Land Grabbing, April 2011.
Irzik, Gürol. 2007. "Commercialisation of Science in a Neoliberal World." In *Reading Karl Polanyi for the Twenty-First Century: Market Economy as a Political Project*, edited by A. Bugra and K. Agartan, 135–53. New York: Palgrave Macmillan.
Jackson, Kenneth. 1985. *Crabgrass Frontier: The Suburbanization of the United States*. New York: Oxford University Press.
Jaffrelot, Christophe. 2003. *India's Silent Revolution: The Rise of the Lower Castes in North India*. New Delhi: Orient Blackswan.
Jaleel, Syed Imtiaz. 2014. "2G Scam Accused, Top Builders Named in FIR in Pune Land Scam Case." *NDTV*, July 24.
Jessop, Bob. 2007. "Knowledge as a Fictitious Commodity: Insights and Limits of a Polanyian Perspective." In *Reading Karl Polanyi for the Twenty-First Century: Market Economy As a Political Project*, edited by A. Bugra and K. Agartan, 115–34. New York: Palgrave Macmillan.
Johnson, Leigh. 2014. "Geographies of Securitized Catastrophe Risk and the Implications of Climate Change." *Economic Geography* 90 (2): 155–85.
Joint Center for Housing Studies of Harvard University (JCHS). 2016. *The State of the Nation's Housing 2016*. Cambridge, MA: JCHS.
Joshi, Yogesh. 2014. "FIR in Pune Land Deal Involving Pawar Kin." *Hindustan Times*, Mumbai, July 24.
Kafka, Franz. 2012. *The Trial*. Mineola, NY: Dover.
Kautsky, Karl. 1988 [1899]. *The Agrarian Question*. London: Zwan.
Keating, W. Dennis. 1998. "Rent Regulation in New York City: A Protracted Saga." In *Rent Control: Regulation and the Rental Housing Market*, edited by W. Dennis Keating, Michael Teitz, and Andrejs Skaburskis, 151–68. New Brunswick, NJ: The Center for Urban Policy Research.
Kelly, Alice B. 2015. "The Crumbling Fortress: Territory, Access, and Subjectivity Production in Waza National Park, Northern Cameroon." *Antipode* 47 (3): 730–47.
Kelly, Mike. 2015. "N.J.'s Poorest City, Camden, 'Not a Shining Example Yet.'" NorthJersey.com, January 16.

Kenney-Lazar, Miles. 2011. "Dispossession, Semi-Proletarianization, and Enclosure: Primitive Accumulation and the Land Grab in Laos." Paper presented at the International Conference on Global Land Grabbing, Institute of Development Studies, Brighton, UK, April 6–8.

Kerkvliet, Benedict J. Tria. 2014. "Protests over Land in Vietnam: Rightful Resistance and More." *Journal of Vietnamese Studies* 9 (3): 19–54.

Khera, Reetika. 2013. "Democratic Politics and Legal Rights: Employment guarantee and Food Security in India." Working Paper No. 327. Delhi: Institute of Economic Growth.

Khetan, Ashish. 2011. "Land Grab. And How to Make Millions." *Tehelka* 8 (21): 28–36.

Khorakiwala, Ateya. 2017. "The Well-Fed Subject: Modern Architecture in the Quantitative State, India." PhD diss., Harvard University, Cambridge MA.

Kiker, B. F. 1966. "The Historical Roots of the Concept of Human Capital." *Journal of Political Economy* 74 (5): 481–99.

Kim, Annette M. 2011. "Talking Back: The Role of Narrative in Vietnam's Recent Land Compensation Changes." *Urban Studies* 48 (3): 493–508.

Kinder, Kimberley. 2016. *DIY Detroit: Making Do in a City without Services*. Minneapolis: University of Minnesota Press.

Kindleberger, Charles P. 1984. *A Financial History of Western Europe*. New York: Routledge.

Kirp, David, John Dwyer, and Larry Rosenthal. 1995. *Our Town: Race, Housing, and the Soul of Suburbia*. New Brunswick, NJ: Rutgers University Press.

Knuth, Sarah. 2015. "Global Finance and the Land Grab: Mapping 21st Century Strategies." *Canadian Journal of Development Studies* 36 (2): 163–78.

Knuth, Sarah. 2016. "Seeing Green in San Francisco: City as Resource Frontier." *Antipode* 48 (3): 626–44.

Knuth, Sarah. 2018. "'Breakthroughs' for a Green Economy? Financialization and Clean Energy Transition." *Energy Research and Social Science* 41: 220–29.

Korf, Benedikt, Tobias Hagmann, and Martin Doevenspeck. 2013. "Geographies of Violence and Sovereignty: The African Frontier Revisited." In *Violence on the Margins*, edited by Benedikt Korf and Timothy Raeymaekers, 29–54. New York: Palgrave Macmillan.

Krippner, Greta R. 2011. *Capitalizing on Crisis*. Cambridge, MA: Harvard University Press.

Krippner, Greta R., and Anthony S. Alvarez. 2007. "Embeddedness and the Intellectual Projects of Economic Sociology." *Annual Review of Sociology* 33: 219–40.

Krippner, Greta, et al. 2004. "Polanyi Symposium: A Conversation on Embeddedness." *Socio-Economic Review* 2 (1): 109–35.

Krishnan, Eesvan. 2014. "Land Acquisition in British India, c. 1894–1927." Doctoral thesis, University of Oxford.

Kromer, John. 2001. *Neighborhood Recovery: Reinvestment Policy for the New Hometown*. New Brunswick, NJ: Rutgers University Press.

Krueckeberg, Donald. 1995. "The Difficult Character of Property: To Whom Do Things Belong?" *Journal of the American Planning Association* 61 (3): 301–9.

Kumar, Aneesha Sareen. 2016. "Express Justice: When a Ludhiana Farmer became Owner of Swarna Shatabdi Train." *Hindustan Times*, March 16.

Kumar, Dharma. 1998. *Colonialism, Property, and the State*. New York: Oxford University Press.

Labbé, Danielle. 2015. "Media Dissent and Peri-Urban Land Struggles in Vietnam: The Case of the Văn Giang Incident." *Critical Asian Studies* 47 (4): 495–513.

Lachman, Hannes. 2007. "The Slight Transformation: Contesting the Legacy of Karl Polanyi." In *Reading Karl Polanyi for the Twenty-First Century: Market Economy as a Political Project,* edited by A. Bugra and K. Agartan, 49–64. New York: Palgrave Macmillan.

Lake, Robert. 2018. "Locating the Social in Social Justice." *Annals of the American Association of Geographers* 108 (2): 337–45.

Lake, Robert, Kathe Newman, Phillip Ashton, Richard Nisa, and Bradley Wilson. 2007. *Civic Engagement in Camden, New Jersey: A Baseline Portrait.* New York: MDRC.

Land Administration Sub-Sector Program (LASSP). n.d. *Land Is Life.* Ministry of Land Management, Urban Planning and Construction, Royal Government of Cambodia. English version.

Langley, Paul. 2010. "The Performance of Liquidity in the Subprime Mortgage Crisis." *New Political Economy* 15 (1): 71–89.

Latour, Bruno. 2004. "Why Has Critique Run Out of Steam? From Matters of Fact to Matters of Concern." *Critical Inquiry* 30 (winter): 225–48.

Latour, Bruno. 2005. *Reassembling the Social: An Introduction to Actor-Network Theory.* New York: Oxford University Press.

Latour, Bruno. 2008. "Where Are the Missing Masses? The Sociology of a Few Mundane Artifacts." In *Technology and Society, Building Our Sociotechnical Future*, edited by D. J. Johnson and J. M. Wetmore, 151–80. Cambridge, MA: MIT Press.

Laulajainen, Risto. 2003. *Financial Geography: A Banker's View.* New York: Routledge.

Law, Alex. 2016. "The Untold Tragedy of Camden, NJ." *HuffPost Politics,* March 8.

Lawson, Ronald, ed. 1986. *The Tenant Movement in New York City, 1904–1984.* New Brunswick, NJ: Rutgers University Press.

Leal, Claudia, and Eduardo Restrepo. 2003. "Unos bosques sembrados de aserríos: Historia de la extracción maderera en el Pacífico colombiano." Medellín: Universidad de Antioquia, Universidad Nacional sede Medellín, Instituto Colombiano de Antropología e Historia.

Le Billon, Philippe. 2000. "The Political Ecology of Transition in Cambodia 1989–1999: War, Peace and Forest Exploitation." *Development and Change* 31: 785–805.

Lees, Loretta, Hyun Bang Shin, and Ernesto Lopez-Morales, eds. 2015. *Global Gentrifications: Uneven Development and Displacement.* Bristol: Policy Press.

Levien, Michael. 2018. *Dispossession without Development: Land Grabs in Neoliberal India.* New York: Oxford University Press.

Levien, Michael, Micahel Watts, and Yan Hairong, eds. 2019. *Agrarian Marxism.* London: Routledge.

Levitin, Adam, and Susan Wachter. 2013. "Commercial Real Estate Bubble." *Harvard Business Law Review* 3: 83.

Li, John. 1991. "Embedding Polanyi's Market Society." *Sociological Perspectives* 34 (2): 219–35.

Li, Tania Murray. 2007. *The Will to Improve: Governmentality, Development, and the Practice of Politics.* Durham, NC: Duke University Press.

Li, Tania M. 2010. "Indigeneity, Capitalism, and the Management of Dispossession." *Current Anthropology* 51 (3): 385–414.

Li, Tania Murray. 2014a. "What Is Land? Assembling a Resource for Global Investment." *Transactions of the Institute of British Geographers* 39 (4): 589–602.

Li, Tania Murray. 2014b. *Land's End: Capitalist Relations on an Indigenous Frontier.* Durham, NC: Duke University Press.

LICADHO. 2009. "Land Grabbing and Poverty in Cambodia: The Myth of Development." LICADHO (Cambodian League for the Promotion and Defense of Human Rights), Phnom Penh.

LICADHO. 2012. "Carving up Cambodia: One Concession at a Time. LICADHO and the Cambodia Daily." http://www.licadho-cambodia.org/land2012.

Lima, Cristiano. 2016. "Ivanka Trump Sits in on Meeting with Japanese Prime Minister," *Politico*, November 11.
Lind, Diana. 2014. "What Will an NBA Team Bring to a Struggling City? 'Not Much.'" *Next City*, June 12. https://nextcity.org/daily/entry/philadelphia-sixers-practice-move-camden-new-jersey.
Local Government Association (LGA). 2016. "475,000 Homes with Planning Permission Still Waiting to Be Built." Accessed May 16, 2019. https://www.wired-gov.net/wg/news.nsf/articles/LGA+475000+homes+with+planning+permission+still+waiting+to+be+built+07012016124000?open.
Locke, John. 1980 [1690]. "Of Property." In *John Locke. Second Treatise of Government*, edited by C. B. Macpherson, chapter 5. Indianapolis: Hackett.
López, Claudia. 2007. "La ruta de la expansión paramilitar y la transformación política en Antioquia." In *Parapolítica: La ruta de la expansión paramilitar y los acuerdos políticos*, edited by Mauricio Romero Vidal, 123–232. Bogotá: Intermedio Editores.
Ludden, David. 1999. *An Agrarian History of South Asia*. Cambridge: Cambridge University Press.
Lund, Christian. 1998. "Struggles for Land and Political Power: On the Politicization of Land Tenure and Disputes in Niger." *The Journal of Legal Pluralism and Unofficial Law* 30 (40): 1–22.
Lund, Christian. 2008. *Local Politics and the Dynamics of Property in Africa*. London: Cambridge University Press.
Luxemburg, Rosa. 2003 [1913]. *The Accumulation of Capital*. London: Routledge.
Lyne, Jack. 2004. "$1.1B Redevelopment Targets Camden, N.J., One of Nation's Poorest Cities." Snapshot from the Field, *Site Selection Magazine*, January 5. Retrieved from https://siteselection.com/ssinsider/snapshot/sf040105.htm.
Lyons, Kristina Marie. 2014. "Soil Science, Development, and the "Elusive Nature" of Colombia's Amazonian Plains." *Journal of Latin American and Caribbean Anthropology* 19 (2): 212–36.
Lyons, Kristina Marie. 2016. "Decomposition As Life Politics: Soils, *Selva*, and Small Farmers under the Gun of the U.S.-Colombian War on Drugs." *Cultural Anthropology* 31 (1): 56–81.
Lyons, Kristina Marie. 2020. *Vital Decomposition: Soil Practitioners and Life Politics*. Durham, NC: Duke University Press.
MacIntyre, Alisdair. 2007. *After Virtue: A Study in Moral Theory*. 3rd ed. Notre Dame, IN: Notre Dame University Press.
MacKenzie, Donald, Fabian Muniesa, and Lucia Siu, Eds. 2007. *Do Economists Make Markets?* Princeton, NJ: Princeton University Press.
Mann, Susan. 1990. *Agrarian Capitalism in Theory and Practice*. Chapel Hill: University of North Carolina Press.
Mantena, Karuna. 2010. *Alibis of Empire: Henry Maine and the Ends of Liberal Imperialism*. Princeton, NJ: Princeton University Press.
Marston, Andrea. 2019. "Vertical Framing: Tin Mining and *Agro-Mineros* in Bolivia." *Journal of Peasant Studies*. doi.org/10.1080/03066150.2019.1604511.
Marx, Karl. 1973. *The Grundrisse*. London: Penguin.
Marx, Karl. 1981 [1894]. *Capital*. Vol. 3. New York: Penguin.
Marx, Karl. 1990 [1867]. *Capital: A Critique of Political Economy*. Vol. 1. London: Penguin Classics.
Massey, Doreen, and Alejandrina Catalano. 1978. *Capital and Land: Landownership by Capital in Great Britain*. London: Edward Arnold.

May, Charlotte. 2014. "Report: Camden Most Dangerous City in the U.S." NBCphiladelphia.com. https://www.nbcphiladelphia.com/news/local/local-city-named-most-dangerous-in-US-290907701.html.
McBride, Stephen. 2005. *Paradigm Shift*. 2d ed. Halifax: Fernwood.
McCarthy, James. 2015. "A Socioecological Fix to Capitalist Crisis and Climate Change? The Possibilities and Limits of Renewable Energy." *Environment and Planning A* 47 (12): 2485–2502.
McGillivray, Kate. 2017. "Contemplating the Future of the Iconic Dominion Public Building." *CBC News*, April 17. Accessed November 27, 2017. http://www.cbc.ca/news/canada/toronto/dominion-public-building-questions-1.4071120.
McKellar, James. 2006. "The Management Framework for Real Property–Government of Canada." In *Managing Government Property Assets: International Experiences*, edited by Olga Kaganova and James McKellar, 49–76. Washington, DC: Urban Institute Press.
McKinsey Global Institute. 2013. *Infrastructure Productivity: How to Save $1 Trillion a Year*. New York, NY: McKinsey Global Institute.
McMichael, Phillip. 1997. "Rethinking Globalization: The Agrarian Question Revisited." *Review of International Political Economy* 4 (4): 630–62.
McNally, David. 1990. *Political Economy and the Rise of Capitalism: A Reinterpretation*. Berkeley: University of California Press.
Meek, James. 2014. *Private Island: Why Britain Now Belongs to Someone Else*. London: Verso.
Mei, Todd. 2017. *Land and the Given Economy*. Evanston, IL: Northwestern University Press.
Menon, Nivedita, and Aditya Nigam. 2007. *Power and Contestation: India Since 1989*. London: Zed Books.
Messerli, Peter, Marcus Giger, Michael B. Dwyer, Thomas Breu, and Sandra Eckert. 2014. "The Geography of Large-Scale Land Acquisitions: Analysing Socio-Ecological Patterns of Target Contexts in the Global South." *Applied Geography* 53: 449–59.
Miescher, Stephan F. 2005. *Making Men in Ghana*. Bloomington: Indiana University Press.
Milbank Tenants Memorandum of Law. 2009. Tenant-Defendants Memorandum of Law, *Milbank*, No. 380454/09 N.Y. Sup. Ct. Bronx Cnty. Mar. 17, 2009.
Milne, Sarah. 2014. "Under the Leopard's Skin: Land Commodification and the Dilemmas of Indigenous Communal Title in Upland Cambodia." *Asia Pacific Viewpoint* 54 (3): 323–39.
Minerals Commission, Ministry of Lands and Natural Resources, Ghana. 2012. "Small-scale Mining Sector in Ghana and Mineral Commission's Role in Managing It." Paper presented at the Stakeholder Sensitization Workshop, University of Mines and Technology, Tarkwa, Ghana, October 4.
Ministry of Agriculture, Forestry and Fisheries (MAFF). n.d. Company profile. Accessed mid-2011. http://www.elc.maff.gov.kh/en/profile/17-kkg.html.
Ministry of Construction. 2007. *Research on Issues of Villages in the City Construction and Planning*. China Building Industry Press (in Chinese).
Ministry of Land and Resources. 2011. *Research Report on Landownership Problems in the Redevelopment of Villages in the City*. Accessed November 14, 2017 (in Chinese). http://www.mlr.gov.cn/wskt/flfg/201109/t20110906_938685.htm.
Ministry of Land Management, Urban Planning and Construction (MLMUPC). 2017. *Report of the General Assembly of the Ministry of Land Management, Urban Planning and Construction: Results of 2017 and Planning for 2018*. Phnom Penh.

Ministry of Planning and United Nations Development Program (UNDP). 2007. *Cambodia Human Development Report: Expanding Choices for Rural People.* Phnom Penh.

Miraftab, Faranak. 2009. "Insurgent Planning: Situating Radical Planning in the Global South." *Planning Theory* 8 (1): 32–50.

Mitchell, Timothy. 2002. *Rule of Experts: Egypt, Techno-Politics, Modernity.* Berkeley: University of California Press.

Mitchell, Timothy. 2005. "Economists and the Economy in the Twentieth Century." In George Steinmetz, ed. *The Politics of Method in the Human Sciences,* 126–41. Durham, NC: Duke University Press.

Mitchell, Timothy. 2007. "The Properties of Markets." In *Do Economists Make Markets? On the Performativity of Markets,* edited by Donald Mackenzie, Fabian Muniesa, and Lucia Siu, 244–75. Princeton, NJ: Princeton University Press.

Mitrany, David. 1951. *Marx against the Peasant.* London: Weidenfeld and Nicolson.

Morris, Meghan L. 2018. "Property in the Shadow of Post-Conflict Colombia." Ph.D. diss., University of Chicago.

Morris, Meghan L. 2019. "Speculative Fields: Property in the Shadow of Post-Conflict Colombia." *Cultural Anthropology* 34 (4): 580–606.

Muellerleile, Chris. 2013. "Turning Financial Markets Inside Out: Polanyi, Performativity, and Disembeddedness." *Environment and Planning A* 45: 1625–42.

Mukherjee, Sanjeeb. 2015. "Acquiring Irrigated Multi-Crop Land May Become More Difficult." *Business Standard*, March 9.

Müller, Franz-Volker. 2012. "Commune-Based Land Allocation for Poverty Reduction in Cambodia: Achievements and Lessons Learned from the Project: Land Allocation for Social and Economic Development (LASED)." Paper prepared for presentation at the Annual World Bank Conference on Land and Poverty, Washington DC, April 23–26.

"Municipal Rehabilitation and Economic Recovery Act (MRERA) Four Year Report." 2006. https://dspace.njstatelib.org/xmlui/handle/10929/16274.

Murugan, Perumal. 2017. "T. M. Krishna's Song in Solidarity with Chennai's Endangered Creek." *The Wire*, January 19.

NAREIT. 2019. "US REIT Industry Equity Market Cap." Accessed November 28, 2019. https://www.reit.com/data-research/reit-market-data/us-reit-industry-equity-market-cap.

Neef, Andreas, Siphat Touch, and Jamaree Chiengthong. 2013. "The Politics and Ethics of Land Concessions in Rural Cambodia." *Journal of Agricultural and Environmental Ethics* 26 (6): 1085–1103.

Neeson, J. M. 1993. *Commoners: Common Right, Enclosure, and Social Change in England, 1700–1820.* Cambridge: Cambridge University Press.

Neuwirth, Robert. 2006. *Shadow Cities: A Billion Squatters, A New Urban World.* New York: Routledge.

New Jersey, Office of the Governor. 2019. *Governor's Task Force on EDA Tax Incentives.* State of New Jersey, Office of the Governor, Trenton.

New York Governor Press Office. 2015. "Governor Cuomo, A.G. Schneiderman, Mayor Bill de Blasio Join Forces to Combat Landlord Harassment of Tenants," February 19. Retrieved January 5, 2018. https://www.governor.ny.gov/news/governor-cuomo-ag-schneiderman-mayor-bill-de-blasio-join-forces-combat-landlord-harassment.

New York State Attorney General. 2010. Settlement with "Vantage Properties." Retrieved from http://www.ag.ny.gov/press-release/new-york-state-attorney-general-andrew-m-cuomo-announces-1-million-settlement-new-york.

New York State Attorney General. 2014. Secures More Than $1 Million for Tenants. Retrieved from http://www.ag.ny.gov/press-release/ag-schneiderman-secures-more-1-million-relief-tenants-living-1700-nyc-apartments.

New York State Homes and Community Renewal. 2016. "Governor Cuomo Highlights Success of Tenant Protection Unit," April 5. Retrieved January 5, 2018. http://www.governor.ny.gov/news/governor-cuomo-highlights-success-tenant-protection-unit.

New York Times. 2006. "Federal Scrutiny of State Senator Shines Light on Connections in Trenton," April 14.

New York Times. 2007. "Lawmaker in New Jersey is Charged With Fraud," March 30.

New York Times. 2019. "The Tax Break Was $260 Million. Benefit to the State was Tiny: $155,520," May 3.

Newman, Kathe, and Elvin K. Wyly. 2006. "The Right to Stay Put, Revisited: Gentrification and Resistance to Displacement in New York City." *Urban Studies* 431: 23–57.

NGO Forum on Cambodia. 2008. "Statistical Analysis on Land Disputes in Cambodia." http://www.ngoforum.org.kh/eng/enallpublication.php.

NGO Forum on Cambodia. 2009. "Statistical Analysis on Land Dispute Occurring in Cambodia." http://www.ngoforum.org.kh/eng/enallpublication.php.

NGO Forum on Cambodia. 2010. "Statistical Analysis on Land Disputes in Cambodia." http://www.ngoforum.org.kh/eng/enallpublication.php.

Nielsen, Eric. 1986. *A Study Team Report to the Task Force on Program Review: Real Property*. Ottawa: Minister of Supply and Services Canada.

Nightingale, Andrea J. 2011. "Bounding Difference: Intersectionality and the Material Production of Gender, Caste, Class, and Environment in Nepal." *Geoforum* 42 (2): 153–62.

NJ.Com. 2014. "Camden-Bound Companies Set to Receive $630 Million in State Tax Breaks," December 15. https://www.nj.com/south/2014/12/camden-bound_companies_set_to_receive_630_million_in_state_tax_breaks.html.

Obeng-Odoom, Franklin. 2015. "Understanding Land Reform in Ghana: A Critical Postcolonial Institutional Approach." *Review of Radical Political Economics* 48 (4): 1–20.

O'Brien, Kevin J. 1996. "Rightful Resistance." *World Politics* 49 (1): 31–55.

O'Brien, Kevin J., and Lianjiang Li. 2006. *Rightful Resistance in Rural China*. New York: Cambridge University Press.

O'Connor, James. 1988. "Capitalism, Nature, Socialism: A Theoretical Introduction." *Capitalism, Nature, Socialism* 1 (1): 11–38.

OECD. 2015. *Fostering Investment in Infrastructure*. Paris: Organization for Economic Co-operation and Development.

Office of Government Commerce (OGC). 2005. "Guide for the Disposal of Surplus Property." Accessed May 17, 2019. http://webarchive.nationalarchives.gov.uk/20110822131357/http:/www.ogc.gov.uk/documents/Guide_for_disposal_of_surplus_property_PDF.pdf.

Office of the Mayor. 2015. "State of the City: Mayor Puts Affordable Housing at Center of 2015 Agenda to Fight Inequality," February 3. Retrieved January 5, 2018. http://www1.nyc.gov/office-of-the-mayor/news/088-15/state-the-city-mayor-de-blasio-puts-affordable-housing-center-2015-agenda-fight.

Ogden, Laura. 2011. *Swamplife: People, Gators, and Mangroves Entangled in the Everglades*. Minneapolis: University of Minnesota Press.

O'Keefe, K. 2009. "Land is Life: Land Conflict Interventions in Cambodia: A Review of Case Studies and NGO Perceptions." NGO Forum, Phnom Penh.

O'Leary, D. 2006. "Independent Review of Transparency and Accountability Issues in the Systematic Land Titling Field Systems and Procedures of the Land Management Administration Project (LMAP) Adjudication Areas," February. Washington, DC: World Bank.

Olson, Olov, James Guthrie, and Christopher Humphrey, eds. 1998. *Global Warning–Debating International Developments in New Public Financial Management.* Bergen, Norway: Cappelen Akademisk Forlag.

Open Development Cambodia. 2013. Company Profiles for "Koh Kong Plantation Company Limited" and "Koh Kong Sugar Company Limited." http://www.opendevelopmentcambodia.net/company-profiles.

Ouma, Stefan. 2014. "Situating Global Finance in the Land Rush Debate: A Critical Review." *Geoforum* 57: 162–66.

Oxfam. 2011. "Land and Power: The Growing Scandal Surrounding the New Wave of Investments in Land." Accessed December 15, 2017. https://www.oxfam.org/sites/www.oxfam.org/files/bp151-land-power-rights-acquisitions-220911-en.pdf.

Padova, Allison. 2005. *Federal Commercialization in Canada*. Ottawa: Parliament of Canada. Accessed November 27, 2017. http://www.lop.parl.gc.ca/content/lop/ResearchPublications/prb0545-e.html#appendix.

Painter, Joe. 2006. "Prosaic Geographies of Stateness." *Political Geography* 25: 752–74.

Parikh, Anokhi. 2015. *The Private City: Planning, Property, and Protest in the Making of Lavasa New Town, India*. PhD thesis, London School of Economics and Political Science.

Paschel, Tianna. 2016. *Becoming Black Political Subjects: Movements and Ethno-Racial Rights in Colombia and Brazil*. Princeton, NJ: Princeton University Press.

Peck, Jamie. 2013a. "For Polanyian Economic Geographies." *Environment and Planning A* 45: 1545–68.

Peck, Jamie. 2013b. "Disembedding Polanyi: Exploring Polanyian Economic Geographies." *Environment and Planning A* 45: 1536–44.

Pedersen, Rasmus Hundsbæk. 2016. "Access to Land Reconsidered: The Land Grab, Polycentric Governance and Tanzania's New Wave Land Reform." *Geoforum* 72: 104–13.

Peluso, Nancy Lee, and Christian Lund, eds. 2013. *New Frontiers of Land Control*. New York: Routledge.

Perry, Keisha-Khan Y. 2013. *Black Women against the Land Grab: The Fight for Racial Justice in Brazil*. Minneapolis: University of Minnesota Press.

Pew Research Center. 2013. *An Uneven Recovery, 2009–2011: A Rise in Wealth for the Wealthy; Declines for the Lower 93%*. Washington, DC: Pew Research Center.

Philadelphia Business Journal. 2006. "Camden, N.J., Redevelopment Plan Stalls in Court." January 24.

Philadelphia Inquirer. 2004. "Camden's Cramer Hill Plan Advances." May 19.

Philadelphia Inquirer. 2005. "Primas Aided Ex-cohort in Cramer Hill Deal," February 3.

Philadelphia Inquirer. 2007. "N.J. Sen. Bryant Charged With Corruption," March 30.

Philadelphia Inquirer. 2015. "Camden Is Calmer but Still N.J.'s Most Dangerous City," March 29.

Philly.com. 2014. "Economic Incentives Bill Brings Deals to S. Jersey." June 14.

Philly.com. 2015. "Moving to Camden." June 9. http://www.philly.com/philly/news/20150609_Moving_to_Camden.html.

Phuong, Tri. 2017. "Saint, Celebrity, and the Self(ie): Body Politics in Late Socialist Vietnam." *Positions: Asia Critique* 25 (4): 821–42.

Pickardt, T., C. Graefen, and Y. Müller. 2013. "Land Registration Supported by German Development Cooperation: Concepts and Practical Experiences." Paper prepared for presentation at the Annual World Bank Conference on Land and Poverty, Washington DC, April 8–11.

Podkul, Cezary. 2017. "Many 'Rent-Stabilized' NYC Apartments Are Not Really Stabilized," June 22. ProPublica. Accessed January 5, 2018. https://www.propublica.org/article/rent-stabilized-nyc-apartments-preferential-rent-mapped-zip-code.

Polanyi, Karl. 1977. "The Economistic Fallacy." *Review (The Fernand Braudel Center)* 1 (1): 9–18.

Polanyi, Karl. 2001 [1944]. *The Great Transformation: The Political and Economic Origins of Our Time*. Boston: Beacon Press.

Polanyi, Karl. 2002 [1947]. "Our Obsolete Market Mentality: Civilization Must Find a New Thought Pattern." *Commentary* 3: 109–17.

Pomar, Olga, David Podell, David Rammler, and South Jersey Legal Services. 2004. City of Camden Planning Board from South Jersey Legal Services, "Cramer Hill Redevelopment Study and Redevelopment Plan," May 11, typescript.

Portes, Richard. 2013. "The Safe Asset Meme." *Keynote Address, Federal Reserve Bank of Dallas*, June 11, 2013. https://www.dallasfed.org/assets/documents/institute/events/2013/526Portesslides.pdf.

Prashad, Vijay. 2007. *The Darker Nations: A People's History of the Third World*. London: The New Press.

Prequin. 2016. *2016 Preqin Global Alternatives Reports*. London: Prequin.

PricewaterhouseCoopers (PwC). 2014. *Asset Management 2020: A Brave New World*. London: PricewaterhouseCoopers.

PricewaterhouseCoopers (PwC). 2015a. *Compare and Contrast: Worldwide Real Estate Investment Trust (REIT) Regimes*. London: PricewaterhouseCoopers.

PricewaterhouseCoopers (PwC). 2015b. *Alternative Asset Management 2020: Fast Forward to Centre Stage*. London: PricewaterhouseCoopers.

Primas, Melvin. 2006. "Progress Report: Municipal Rehabilitation and Economy Recovery in Camden." City of Camden, Office of the Chief Operating Officer, December.

Puig de la Bellacasa, Maria. 2014. "Encountering Bioinfrastructure: Ecological Struggles and the Sciences of Soil." *Social Epistemology* 28 (1): 26–40.

Puig de la Bellacasa, Maria. 2019. "Re-animating Soils: Transforming Human-Soil Affections through Science, Culture, and Community." *Sociological Review* 67 (2): 391–407.

Pulido, Laura. 2016. "Flint, Environmental Racism, and Racial Capitalism." *Capitalism, Nature, Socialism* 27 (3): 1–16.

Purcell, Thomas, Alex Loftus, and Hug March. 2019. "Value-Rent-Finance." *Progress in Human Geography*. doi: 01.1177/0309132519838064.

Quesnay, François. 1963 [1767]. "General Maxims for the Economic Government of an Agricultural Kingdom." In *The Economics of Physiocracy: Essays and Translations*, edited by R. L. Meek, 231–62. Cambridge, MA: Harvard University Press.

Rabe, A. 2013. "Directive 01BB in Ratanakiri Province, Cambodia: Issues and Impacts of Private Land Titling in Indigenous Communities." Produced in collaboration with the Ratanakiri Communal Land Titling Working Group, with translation funding provided by Welthungerhilfe. SVC, NTFP, HA, CLEC and WHH, Phnom Penh.

Ramesh, Jairam, and Muhammad Ali Khan. 2015. *Legislating for Equity: The Making of the 2013 Land Acquisition Law*. New Delhi: Oxford University Press.

Ramey, Elizabeth A. 2017. "Agriculture and the Agrarian Question." In *Routledge Handbook of Marxian Economics*, edited by David M. Brennan, David Kristjanson-Gural, Catherine P. Mulder, and Erik K. Olsen, 300–309. London: Routledge.

Rancière, Jacques. 1995. "Politics, Identification, and Subjectivization." In *The Identity in Question*, edited by J. Rajchman, 63–70. New York: Routledge.

Ranganathan, Malini. 2014. "Paying for Pipes, Claiming Citizenship: Political Agency and Water Reforms at the Urban Periphery." *International Journal of Urban and Regional Research* 38 (2): 590–608.

Rappaport, Roy. 1963. *Pigs for the Ancestors: Ritual in the Ecology of a New Guinea People*. New Haven: Yale University Press.

Rasmussen, Mattias Borg, and Christian Lund. 2018. "Reconfiguring Frontier Spaces: The Territorialization of Resource Control." *World Development* 101: 388–99.

Redclift, Michael. 2006. *Frontiers: Histories of Civil Society and Nature*. Cambridge, MA: The MIT Press.

Reichel-Dolmatoff, Gerardo. 1971. *Amazonian Cosmos: The Sexual and Religious Symbolism of the Turkano Indians*. Chicago: University of Chicago Press.

Reno, William. 1995. "Reinvention of an African Patrimonial State: Charles Taylor's Liberia." *Third World Quarterly* 16 (1): 109–20.

Reno, William. 2001. "How Sovereignty Matters: International Markets and the Political Economy of Local Politics in Weak States." In *Intervention and Transnationalism in Africa: Global–Local Networks of Power*, edited by Thomas Callaghy, Ronald Kassimir and Robert Latham, 197–215. Cambridge: Cambridge University Press.

Rent Guidelines Board. 2014a. "Changes to the Rent Regulated Housing Stock in New York City in 2013." http://www.nycrgb.org/downloads/research/pdf_reports/changes2014.pdf.

Rent Guidelines Board. 2014b. "2014 Mortgage Survey Report." http://www.nycrgb.org/downloads/research/pdf_reports/14MSR.pdf.

Restrepo, Eduardo. 2013. *Etnización de la negridad: La invención de las "comunidades negras."* Popayán: Universidad del Cauca.

Richardson, Tanya, and Gisa Weszkalnys. 2014. "Introduction: Resource Materialities: New Anthropological Perspectives on Natural Resource Environments." *Anthropological Quarterly* 87 (1): 5–30.

Riles, Annelise. 2011. *Collateral Knowledge: Legal Reasoning in the Global Financial Markets*. Chicago: University of Chicago Press.

Riordan, Kevin. 2005. "Camden through the Years." *Courier-Post*, November 13.

Robbins, Paul, Kendra McSweeney, Anil K. Changani, and Jennifer L. Rice. 2009. "Conservation As It Is: Illicit Resource use in a Wildlife Reserve in India." *Human Ecology* 37 (5): 559–75.

Robertson, Morgan. 2012. "Measurement and Alienation: Making a World of Ecosystem Services." *Transactions of the Institute of British Geographers* 37 (3): 386–401.

Rodenbiker, Jesse. 2019. "Uneven Incorporation: Volumetric Transitions in Peri-Urban China's Conservation Zones." *Geoforum* 104: 234–43.

Rodgers, Scott, Clive Barnett, and Allan Cochrane. 2014. "Where Is Urban Politics?" *International Journal of Urban and Regional Research* 38 (5): 1551–60.

Rogan, Tim. 2017. *The Moral Economists: R.H. Tawney, Karl Polanyi, E.P. Thompson, and the Critique of Capitalism*. Princeton, NJ: Princeton University Press.

Romberg, Raquel. 2005. "Ritual Piracy: Or Creolization with an Attitude." *New West Indian Guide* 79 (3/4): 175–218.

Romero Vidal, Mauricio. 2007. *Para-política: La Ruta de la Expansión Paramilitar y los Acuerdos Políticos*. Edited by Mauricio Romero Vidal. Bogotá: Corporación Nuevo Arco Iris.

Romero Vidal, Mauricio. 2011. *La economía de los paramilitares: Redes de corrupción, negocios y política*. Edited by Mauricio Romero Vidal. Bogotá: Debate.

Ron, James. 2005. *Frontiers and Ghettoes*. Berkeley: University of California Press.

Rose, Carol M. 1994. *Property and Persuasion: Essays on the History, Theory, and Rhetoric of Ownership*. Boulder, CO: Westview Press.

Roy, Ananya. 2004. "The Gentleman's City: Urban Informality in the Calcutta of New Communism." In *Urban Informality*, edited by Nezar AlSayyad and Ananya Roy, 147–70. Lanham, MD: Lexington Books.

Roy, Ananya. 2005. "Urban Informality: Toward an Epistemology of Planning." *Journal of the American Planning Association* 71 (2): 147–58.

Roy, Ananya. 2009. "Why India Cannot Plan its Cities: Informality, Insurgence, and the Idiom of Urbanization." *Planning Theory* 8 (1): 76–87.

Rudolph, Lloyd I., and Susanne Hoeber Rudolph. 1984. *Essays on Rajputana*. New Delhi: Concept Publishing.

Saez, Emmanuel, and Gabriel Zucman. 2014. "Wealth Inequality in the United States since 1913: Evidence from Capitalized Income Tax Data." NBER Working Paper 20625. Cambridge, MA: National Bureau of Economic Research.

Sakolski, Aaron Morton. 1932. *The Great American Land Bubble*. New York: Harper & Brothers Publishers.

Salins, Peter. D. 1999. "Reviving New York City's Housing Market." In *Housing and Community Development in New York City: Facing the Future*, edited by M. Schill, 53–72. Albany: State University of New York Press.

Sar, Sovann. 2010. "Land Reform in Cambodia." FIG Congress Paper. http://www.fig.net/pub/fig2010/papers/ts07j%5Cts07j_sovann_4633.pdf.

Sartori, Andrew. 2014. *Liberalism in Empire: An Alternative History*. Berkeley, CA: University of California Press.

Schaffer, Richard, and Neil Smith. 1986. "The Gentrification of Harlem?" *Annals of the Association of American Geographers* 76 (3): 347–65.

Schuman, Michael. 2018. "China's Small Farms are Fading. The World May Benefit." *New York Times*, October 5. https://www.nytimes.com/2018/10/05/business/china-small-farms-urbanization.html.

Schmitt, Carl. 2006. *The Nomos of the Earth in the International Law of Jus Publicum Europaeum*. Translated by G. L. Ulmen. New York: Telos Press.

Schwartz, Alex. F. 2014. *Housing Policy in the United States*. New York: Routledge.

Schwenkel, Christina. 2015. "Reclaiming Rights to the Socialist City: Bureaucratic Artefacts and the Affective Appeal of Petitions." *South East Asia Research* 23 (2): 205–25.

Searle, Llerena Guiu. 2014. "Conflict and Commensuration: Contested Market Making in India's Private Real Estate Development Sector." *International Journal of Urban and Regional Research* 38 (1): 60–78.

Searle, Llerena Guiu. 2016. *Landscapes of Accumulation: Real Estate and the Neoliberal Imagination in Contemporary India*. Chicago: University of Chicago Press.

Searle, Llerena Guiu. 2018. "The Contradictions of Mediation: Intermediaries and the Financialization of Urban Production." *Economy and Society* 47 (4): 524–46.

SEC. 2014. "Demand and Supply of Safe Assets in the Economy." *Staff Memo, Division of Economic and Risk Analysis*. Washington, DC: U.S. Securities and Exchange Commission.

Secor, Anna J. 2007. "Between Longing and Despair: State, Space, and Subjectivity in Turkey." *Environment and Planning D: Society and Space* 25 (1): 33–52.

Sen, Amartya. 1981. *Poverty and Famines: An essay on Entitlement and Deprivation.* New Delhi: Oxford University Press.

Serres, Michel. 1995. *The Natural Contract.* Ann Arbor: University of Michigan Press.

Shatkin, Gavin. 2017. *Cities for Profit: The Real Estate Turn in Asia's Urban Politics.* Ithaca, NY: Cornell University Press.

Sheikh, Shahana, and Subhadra Banda. 2014. "The Thin Line between Legitimate and Illegal: Regularising Unauthorised Colonies in Delhi." A Report of the Cities of Delhi project. New Delhi: Centre for Policy Research.

Shih, Mi. 2017. "Rethinking Displacement in Peri-Urban Transformation in China." *Environment and Planning A* 29 (2): 389–406.

Shih, Mi. 2019. "Land and People: Governing Social Conflicts in China's State-Led Urbanisation." *International Development Planning Review* 41 (3): 293–310.

Shin, Hyun B., and Soo-Hyun Kim. 2016. "The Developmental State, Speculative Urbanisation, and the Politics of Displacement in Gentrifying Seoul." *Urban Studies* 53 (3): 540–59.

Sidorick, Daniel. 2009. *Condensed Capitalism: Campbell Soup and the Pursuit of Cheap Production in the Twentieth Century.* Ithaca, NY: Cornell University Press.

Siegel, James T. 1998. *A New Criminal Type in Jakarta: Counter-Revolution Today.* Durham, NC: Duke University Press.

Silver, Beverly, and Giovanni Arrighi. 2003. "Polanyi's 'Double Movement': The Belle Époques of British and U.S. Hegemony Compared." *Politics and Society* 31 (2): 325–55.

Silver, Jonathan. 2014. "Incremental Infrastructures: Material Improvisation and Social Collaboration Across Post-Colonial Accra." *Urban Geography* 35 (6): 788–804.

Singh, Dool. 1964. *Land Reform in Rajasthan: A Study of Evasion, Implementation, and Socio-Economic Effects.* New Delhi: Planning Commission, Government of India.

Siu, Helen. 2007. "Grounding Displacement: Uncivil Urban Spaces in Postreform South China." *American Ethnologist* 34 (2): 329–50.

Smallcombe, Mike. 2017. "Controversial Plans to Build 134 Homes on a Derelict Clifftop Training Camp near Newquay Are Given the Go-Ahead." Accessed May 16, 2019. http://www.cornwalllive.com/news/cornwall-news/controversial-plans-build-134-homes-554715.

Smith, Adam. 1990 [1776]. *The Wealth of Nations.* New York: P. F. Collier and Son.

Smith, Adrian. 2013. "Commentary." *Environment and Planning A* 45: 1656–61.

Smith, Neil. 1979. "Toward a Theory of Gentrification: A Back to the City Movement by Capital, not People." *Journal of the American Planning Association* 45 (4): 538–48.

Smith, Neil. 1982. "Gentrification and Uneven Development." *Economic Geography* 58 (20): 139–55.

Smith, Neil, Paul Caris, and Elvin Wyly. 2001. "The 'Camden Syndrome' and the Menace of Suburban Decline: Residential Disinvestment and its Discontents in Camden County, New Jersey." *Urban Affairs Review* 36: 491–531.

Smith, R. Nick. 2014. "Living on the Edge: Household Registration Reform and Peri-Urban Precarity in China." *Journal of Urban Affairs* 36 (1): 369–83.

Solomon, Nancy, and Jeff Pillets. 2019. "NJ Power Broker at Center of Tax-Break Controversy." WNYC.org and ProPublica, May 6. https://www.wnyc.org/story/nj-power-broker-center-tax-break-controversy.

Solomon, Steven Davidoff. 2016. "Rise of Institutional Investors Raises Questions of Collusion." *New York Times Dealbook,* April 12, 2016.
Speri, Alice. 2011. For Birthplace of Hip-Hop, New Life. *The New York Times*, November 7.
Srinivas, M.N. 1987. *The Dominant Caste and Other Essays*. New Delhi: Oxford University Press.
Star-Ledger. 2006. "AG Launches Inquiry into Bryant and Camden Redevelopment Aid." September 30.
Star-Ledger. 2008. "Once Powerful Lawmaker, Now a Convicted Felon," November 18.
State Council. 2014. "*The National New-Type Urbanization Plan 2014–2020.*" Accessed May 17, 2019. http://www.gov.cn/zhengce/2014-03/16/content_2640075.htm (in Chinese).
Steel, Griet, Femke van Noorloos, and Christien Klaufus. 2017. "The Urban Land Debate in the Global South: New Avenues for Research." *Geoforum* 83: 133–41.
Stegman, Michael. 1972. *Housing Investment in the Inner City: The Dynamics of Decline*. Cambridge, MA: MIT Press.
Stern, Robert. 1988. *The Cat and the Lion: Jaipur State in the British Raj*. Leiden: E.J. Brill.
Sternlieb, George. 1966. *The Tenement Landlord*. William and Byrd Press, Inc.
Sternlieb, George. 1975. *Housing Development and Municipal Costs*. New Brunswick: Center for Urban Policy Research.
Story, Louise, and Stephanie Saul. 2015. "Stream of Foreign Wealth Flows to Elite New York Real Estate." *New York Times*, February 7.
Sud, Nikita. 2012. *Liberalization, Hindu Nationalism and the State: A Biography of Gujarat*. New Delhi: Oxford University Press.
Sud, Nikita. 2014. "The Men in the Middle: A Missing Dimension in Global Land Deals." *Journal of Peasant Studies* 41 (4): 593–612.
Sud, Nikita. 2017. "State, Scale and Networks in the Liberalisation of India's Land." *Environment and Planning C: Politics and Space* 35 (1): 76–93.
Sulle, Emmanuel, and Fred Nelson. 2009. *Biofuels, Land Access, and Rural Livelihoods in Tanzania*. IIED. Accessed March 6, 2018. https://pubs.iied.org/12560IIED.
Sullivan, Sean. 2014. "Never Heard of George Norcross? Here's Why You Need To." *The Washington Post*, February 4.
Sundaresan, Jayaraj. 2017. "Urban Planning in Vernacular Governance: Land Use Planning and Violations in Bangalore, India." *Progress in Planning* 127: 1–23.
Suphal, Chan, Tep Saravy, and Sarthi Acharya. 2001. "Land Tenure in Cambodia: A Data Update." CDRI Working Paper 19. Phnom Penh.
Swyngedouw, Erik. 2011. "Interrogating Post-Democratization: Reclaiming Egalitarian Political Spaces." *Political Geography* 30 (7): 370–80.
Taibbi, Matt. 2013. "Apocalypse, New Jersey: A Dispatch from America's Most Desperate Town. No Jobs, No Hope—and Surveillance Cameras Everywhere. The Strange, Sad Story of Camden." *Rolling Stone*, December 11. https://www.rollingstone.com/culture/culture-news/apocalypse-new-jersey-a-dispatch-from-americas-most-desperate-town-56174.
Tarr, Alexander. 2015. *Have Your City and Eat It Too: Los Angeles and the Urban Food Renaissance*, PhD diss., University of California, Berkeley.
Taussig, Michael. 1993. *Mimesis and Alterity: A Particular History of the Senses*. New York: Routledge.
Taussig, Michael. 1997. *The Magic of the State*. New York: Routledge.
Teresa, Ben F. 2016. "Managing Fictitious Capital: The Legal Geography of Investment and Political Struggle in Rental Housing in New York City." *Environment and Planning A* 48 (3): 465–84.

Thien Thu, Truong, and Ranjith Perera. 2011. "Consequences of the Two-Price System for Land in the Land and Housing Market in Ho Chi Minh City, Vietnam." *Habitat International* 35 (1): 30–39.
Thompson, E. P. 1966. *The Making of the English Working Class*. New York: Vintage.
Thompson, E. P. 1975. *Whigs and Hunters: The Origin of the Black Act*. Oxford: Oxford University Press.
Thomson, Frances. 2014. "Why We Need the Concept of Land-Grab-Induced Displacement." *Journal of Internal Displacement*, 4 (2): 42–65.
TIAA-CREF. 2013. *The Case for Real Assets*. New York: TIAA-CREF.
Tilt, Bryan. 2010. *The Struggle for Sustainability in Rural China: Environmental Values and Civil Society*. New York: Columbia University Press.
Tiwari, Piyush, and Jyoti Rao. 2017. *Delhi's Changing Built Environment*. New York: Routledge.
Tôn Nữ Quỳnh Trân. 2010. *Thủ Thiêm–Quá khứ và tương lai* [Thu Thiem: Past and Future]. Thành phố Hồ Chí Minh, Nhà Xuất Bản Tổng Hợp.
Tönnies, Ferdinand. 2002 [1887]. *Community and Society*. Mineola: Dover Publications.
Toulmin, Stephen. 2001. *Cosmopolis: The Hidden Agenda of Modernity*. Chicago: University of Chicago Press.
Treasury Board of Canada. 2011. *Guide to the Management of Real Property*. Accessed November 26, 2017. https://www.tbs-sct.gc.ca/rpm-gbi/doc/gmrp-ggbi/gmrp-ggbitb-eng.asp.
Treasury Board of Canada. 2016. *Directory of Federal Real Property*. Accessed June 6, 2016. http://www.tbs-sct.gc.ca/dfrp-rbif/home-accueil-eng.aspx.
Tsing, Anna. 2005. *Friction: An Anthropology of Global Connection*. Princeton, NJ: Princeton University Press.
Turner, Frederick Jackson. 1893. "The Significance of the Frontier in American History." *Annual Report of the American Historical Association*, 199–207.
Twomey, Hannah. 2014. "Displacement and Dispossession Through Land Grabbing in Mozambique." Working Paper Series No. 101. Refugee Studies Centre, Oxford Department of International Development, University of Oxford. Accessed March 6, 2018. https://www.refworld.org/docid/55c9f0814.html.
Un, Kheang, and Sokbunthoeun So. 2009. "Politics of Natural Resource Use in Cambodia." *Asian Affairs* 36: 123–38.
Un, Kheang, and Sokbunthoeun So. 2011. "Land Rights in Cambodia: How Neopatrimonial Politics Restricts Land Policy Reform." *Pacific Affairs* 84: 289–308.
United Nations Cambodia Office of the High Commissioner for Human Rights (UNCOHCHR). 2007. "Economic Land Concessions in Cambodia: A Human Rights Perspective." UNCOHCHR, Phnom Penh.
United States Department of Justice. 2008. "Former State Senator Wayne Bryant Guilty of all Counts for Schemes to Obtain a Corrupt Low-show Job at UMDNJ and Fraudulently Pad State Pension." Press release of the U.S. Attorney, District of New Jersey, November 18. https://www.justice.gov/sites/default/files/usao-nj/legacy/2013/11/29/brya1118%20rel.pdf.
Universidad Nacional et al. 2009. "Amenaza, vulnerabilidad y riesgo por movimientos en masa, avenidas torrenciales e inundaciones en el Valle de Aburrá." Formulación de propuestas de gestión. Bogotá.
Urban Strategies, Inc. 2008. "Cooper Lanning Human Capital Plan for the Cooper Plaza Lanning Square Neighborhoods, Camden, New Jersey" (draft). St. Louis, MO: Urban Strategies, Inc.
USAID. 2011. "Property Rights and Resource Governance profile–Cambodia." http://usaidlandtenure.net/sites/default/files/country-profiles/full-reports/USAID_Land_Tenure_Cambodia_Profile.pdf.

Utas, Mats. 2012. "Introduction: Bigmanity and Network Governance in African Conflicts." In *African Conflicts and Informal Power: Big Men and Networks,* edited by Mats Utas, 1–31. London: Zed Books.
Van de Camp, Esther. 2016. "Artisanal Gold Mining in Kejetia (Tongo, Northern Ghana): A Three-Dimensional Perspective." *Third World Thematics: A TWQ Journal* 1 (2): 267–83.
Vanguard. 2014. *Learn About Alternative Investments.* Malvern, PA: Vanguard.
Vanguard. 2016. "Fast Facts About Vanguard." https://about.vanguard.com/who-we-are/fast-facts.
Varshney, Ashutosh. 1995. *Democracy, Development, and the Countryside.* Cambridge: Cambridge University Press.
Venkataraman, Ayeesha. 2016. "Indian Business Partners Hope to Exploit Their Ties with Trump." *New York Times,* November 20.
Verengo, Matías, and Kirsten Ford. 2014. "Everything Must Change So That the IMF Can Remain the Same: The World Economic Outlook and the Global Financial Stability Report." *Development and Change* 45 (5): 1193–204.
Verma, Gita Dewan. 2002. *Slumming India: A Chronicle of Slums and their Saviours.* Delhi: Penguin Books.
Vietnamese Ministry of Justice [Bộ Tư Pháp]. 2009. "Tranh chấp, khiếu nại, tố cáo về đất đai và giải quyết tranh chấp, khiếu nại, tố cáo về đất đai" [Disputes, petitions, and denunciations regarding land, and resolutions to disputes, petitions and denunciations regarding land]. *Đặc san tuyên truyền Pháp luật* [Special Issue on Legal Propaganda]. Hanoi, Hội đồng phối hợp công tác phổ biến, Giáo dục Pháp luật của Chính Phủ [Government Coordinating Committee for Publicizing Legal Education]: 1–61.
Visser, Oane. 2017. "Running Out of Farmland? Investment Discourses, Unstable Land Values, and the Sluggishness of Asset Making." *Agricultural Human Values* 34: 185–98.
Visvanathan, Shiv. 2003. *From the Green Revolution to the Evergreen Revolution: Studies in Discourse Analysis.* IDS Seminar on Agriculture, Biotechnology, and the Developing World.
Wallerstein, Immanuel. 2012. "Land, Space, and People: Constraints of the Capitalist World-Economy." *Journal of World Systems Research* 18: 6–14.
Walsh, Jeremy. 2008. "47 Haros Buildings May Soon Be Sold." *Times Ledger,* January 17. Retrieved from http://www.timesledger.com/stories/2008/3/20080117-archive38.html.
Watson, Vanessa. 2009. "'The Planned City Sweeps the Poor Away . . .' Urban Planning in 21st Century Urbanization." *Progress in Planning* 72 (3): 151–93.
Watson, Vanessa. 2014. "African Urban Fantasies: Dreams or Nightmares?" *Environment and Urbanization* 26 (1): 215–31.
Watson, Vanessa. 2015. "The Allure of 'Smart City' Rhetoric: India and Africa." *Dialogues in Human Geography* 5 (1): 36–39.
Watts, Michael. 1983. *Silent Violence: Food, Famine, and Peasantry in Northern Nigeria.* Berkeley: University of California Press.
Watts, Michael. 2014. "Oil Frontiers: The Niger Delta and the Gulf of Mexico." In *Oil Culture,* edited by Ross Barrett and Daniel Worden, 180–210. Minneapolis: University of Minnesota Press.
Wayne, Leslie. 1982. "The Return of the REIT's." *New York Times,* December 5, 1982.
Weber, Rachel. 2002. "Extracting Value from the City: Neoliberalism and Urban Redevelopment." *Antipode* 34: 519–40.
Weber, Rachel. 2015. *From Boom to Bubble: How Finance Built the New Chicago.* Chicago: University of Chicago Press.

Weber, Rachel. 2016. "Performing Property Cycles." *Journal of Cultural Economy* 9 (6): 587–603.

Weizman, Eyal. 2007. *Hollow Land: Israel's Architecture of Occupation*. London: Verso.

White, Ben, Saturnino M. Borras Jr., Ruth Hall, Ian Scoones, and Wendy Wolford, eds. 2013. *The New Enclosures: Critical Perspectives on Corporate Land Deals*. London: Routledge.

Whitehead, Judy. 2010. "John Locke and the Governance of India's Landscape: The Category of Wasteland in Colonial Revenue and Forest Legislation." *Economic and Political Weekly* 45 (50): 83–93.

Whiten, Jon. 2014. *New Jersey's Surge in Business Tax Subsidies Reaches New Heights*. Trenton, NJ: New Jersey Policy Perspectives, June.

Whiteside, Heather. 2017. "The State's Estate: Devaluing and Revaluing 'Surplus' Public Land in Canada." *Environment and Planning A* 51 (2): 505–26.

Whitford, Emma. 2015. "These Crown Heights Residents Saw Their Rents Double Last Fall." *Gothamist*, May 22.

Williams, Raymond. 1973. *The Country and the City*. London: Oxford University Press.

Wilson, Japhy. 2016. "The Village That Turned to Gold: A Parable of Philanthrocapitalism." *Development and Change* 47 (1): 3–28.

Wissoker, Peter. 2013. "From Insurance to Investments: Financialisation and the Supply Side of Life Insurance and Annuities in the USA (1970–2006)." *Cambridge Journal of Regions, Economy and Society* 6 (3): 401–18.

Wolford, Wendy, Saturnino M. Borras, Ruth Hall, Ian Scoones, and Ben White, eds. 2013. *Governing Global Land Deals: The Role of the State in the Rush for Land*. Oxford: Wiley-Blackwell.

Woodworth, Max, and Jeremy Wallace. 2017. "Seeing Ghosts: Parsing China's 'Ghost City' Controversy." *Urban Geography* 38 (8): 1270–81.

World Bank. 2002. "Project Appraisal Document, Land Management and Administration Project." Report No: 22869-KH, January 29.

World Bank. 2007a. *India: Land Policies for Growth and Poverty Reduction*. New Delhi: Oxford University Press.

World Bank. 2007b. *Land Policy Dialogues: Addressing Urban-Rural Synergies in World Bank Facilitated Dialogues in the Last Decade*. Washington, DC: World Bank.

World Bank. 2007c. *World Development Report 2008: Agriculture for Development*, Washington. DC: International Bank for Reconstruction and Development/The World Bank.

World Bank. 2009a. "Management Response to the Request for an Inspection Panel Review of the Cambodia Land Management and Administration Project," November 2. http://siteresources.worldbank.org/EXTINSPECTIONPANEL/Resources/LMAP_Final_Corrected_1DEC09.pdf.

World Bank. 2009b. *World Development Report 2009: Reshaping Economic Geography*. Washington, DC: World Bank.

World Bank. 2010. "Rising Global Interest in Farmland: Can It Yield Sustainable and Equitable Benefits?" Washington DC: World Bank.

World Bank. 2014. "Projects and Operations page, Land Titling Project, Lao PDR." https://projects.worldbank.org/en/projects-operations/project-detail/P004208?lang=en.

World Bank Inspection Panel (WBIP). 2010. "Investigation report: Cambodia: Land Management and Administration Project (Credit No. 3650—KH). Report No. 58016—KH," November 23. http://documents.worldbank.org/curated/en/839901468006013649/Cambodia-Land-Management-and-Administration-Project-Management-report-and-recommendation-in-response-to-the-Inspection-Panel-Investigation-Report.

World Bank Inspection Panel (WBIP). n.d. "Case tracker, Cambodia: Land Management and Administration Project." https://www.inspectionpanel.org/panel-cases/land-management-and-administration-project.

Yadav, Yogendra. 2000. "Understanding the Second Democratic Upsurge: Trends of Bahujan Participation in Electoral Politics in the 1990s." In *Transforming India: Social and Political Dynamics of Democracy*, edited by Francine Frankel, Zoya Hasan, Rajeeva Bhargava and Balveer Arora, 120–45. Delhi: Oxford University Press.

Yardley, Jim. 2013. "Illegal District Dot New Delhi as City Swells." *New York Times*, April 27.

Yaro, Joseph. 2013. "Neoliberal Globalization and Evolving Local Traditional Institutions: Implications for Access to Resources in Rural Northern Ghana." *Review of African Political Economy* 40 (137): 410–27.

Yeh, Anthony Gar-On, and Fulong Wu. 1996. "The New Land Development Process and Urban Development in Chinese Cities." *International Journal of Urban and Regional Research* 20 (2): 330–53.

Yeh, Emily. 2013. *Taming Tibet: Landscape Transformation and the Gift of Chinese Development*. Ithaca, NY: Cornell University Press.

Youssof, Kathryn. 2018. *A Billion Black Anthropocenes or None*. Minneapolis: University of Minnesota Press.

Zaloom, Caitlin. 2009. "How to Read the Future: The Yield Curve, Affect, and Financial Prediction." *Public Culture* 21 (2): 245–68.

Zanfi, Federico. 2013. "The Città Abusiva in Contemporary Southern Italy: Illegal Building and Prospects for Change." *Urban Studies* 50 (16): 3428–45.

Zeiderman, Austin. 2013. "Living Dangerously: Biopolitics and Urban Citizenship in Bogotá, Colombia." *American Ethnologist* 40 (1): 71–87.

Zeiderman, Austin. 2016. *Endangered City: The Politics of Security and Risk in Bogotá*. Durham, NC: Duke University Press.

Zhang, Li. 2006. "Contesting Spatial Modernity in Late-Socialist China." *Current Anthropology* 47 (3): 461–84.

Zhu, Yu. 2000. "In Situ Urbanization in Rural China: Case Studies from Fujian Province." *Development and Change* 31: 413–34.

Zimmer, Anna. 2012. "Enumerating the Semi-Visible: The Politics of Regularizing Delhi's Unauthorised Colonies." *Economic and Political Weekly* 47 (30): 89–97.

Zoomers, Annelies. 2010. "Globalisation and the Foreignisation of Space: Seven Processes Driving the Current Global Land Grab." *Journal of Peasant Studies* 37 (2): 429–47.

Zoomers, Anneleis, Femke van Noorloos, K. Otsuki, Greit Steel, and G. van Westen. 2017. "The Rush for Land in an Urbanizing World: From Land Grabbing Toward Developing Safe, Resilient, and Sustainable Cities and Landscapes." *World Development* 92: 242–52.

Contributors

Sai Balakrishnan is an assistant professor of global urban inequalities at the University of California, Berkeley, where she holds a joint appointment between the Department of City and Regional Planning and Global Metropolitan Studies. Through her research and teaching, Balakrishnan focuses on urbanization and planning institutions in the global south and the spatial politics of land use and property. She is the author of *Shareholder Cities: Land Transformations Along Urban Corridors in India* (University of Pennsylvania Press, 2019).

Brett Christophers is a professor in the Department of Social and Economic Geography at Uppsala University. His books include *The New Enclosure: The Appropriation of Public Land in Neoliberal Britain* (Verso, 2018) and *Rentier Capitalism: Who Owns the Economy, and Who Pays For It?* (Verso, 2020).

Michael B. Dwyer is a visiting assistant professor in the Department of Geography at Indiana University, Bloomington; and a senior associated research scientist with the University of Bern's Centre for Development and Environment. His research examines the intersection of agrarian change, environmental governance, and infrastructure development in Southeast Asia, with a focus on land, forest, and infrastructure politics in Laos and Cambodia.

David Ferring is a doctoral candidate in the Department of Geography at Rutgers University, whose dissertation explores the socioenvironmental outcomes of small-scale gold mining in rural Ghana. His research interests include critical health geographies, land-use change, and political ecology.

D. Asher Ghertner is an associate professor in the Department of Geography and director of the South Asian Studies Program at Rutgers University. His research focuses on displacement, environmental politics, and urban aesthetics in India. He is the author of *Rule by Aesthetics: World-Class City Making in Delhi* (Oxford University Press, 2015) and coeditor of *Futureproof: Security Aesthetics and the Management of Life* (Duke University Press, 2020).

Erik Harms is an associate professor of anthropology and international and area studies at Yale University with a focus on the social and cultural effects of rapid urbanization on the fringes of Ho Chi Minh City. He is the author of *Saigon's Edge: On the Margins of Ho Chi Minh City* (University of Minnesota Press, 2011) and *Luxury and Rubble: Civility and Dispossession in the New Saigon* (University of California Press, 2016), as well as coeditor of *Figures of Southeast Asian Modernity* (University of Hawai'i Press, 2013).

Heidi Hausermann is an associate professor in the Department of Anthropology and Geography at Colorado State University, with a research focus on land-use change, resource politics, and critical health geographies. She has carried out long-term fieldwork on agrarian change in Mexico and currently directs three projects focused on the political ecology of alluvial gold mining and disease dynamics in Ghana.

Sarah Knuth is an assistant professor in the Department of Geography at Durham University. Her research investigates the contemporary intersection of neoliberal urban and infrastructural development strategy, green economic development, clean energy transition and climate change resilience, and ongoing transformations in the global financial system.

Robert W. Lake is an emeritus professor in the Edward J. Bloustein School of Planning and Public Policy at Rutgers University. His research focuses on community-based planning, urban and environmental justice, and the uses of social theory in the production of knowledge in the social sciences. He is coeditor of *The Power of Pragmatism: Knowledge Production and Social Inquiry* (Manchester University Press, 2020).

Michael Levien is an associate professor of sociology at Johns Hopkins University. His research explores the relationship between dispossession and capitalism in comparative perspective. He is the author of *Dispossession After Development: Land Grabs in Neoliberal India* (Oxford University Press, 2018).

Meghan L. Morris is an assistant professor at the University of Cincinnati College of Law. Her research examines the role of law in war and peacemaking, with a particular focus on property and the ecologies of conflict.

Mi Shih is an associate professor in the Edward J. Bloustein School of Planning and Public Policy at Rutgers University. Her research focuses on the role of urban planning in shaping Chinese cities and the everyday lives of Chinese citizens in the postreform era.

Benjamin Teresa is an assistant professor in the L. Douglas Wilder School of Government and Public Affairs at Virginia Commonwealth University. His research examines how the increasing role of financial institutions, actors, and logics affects urban development and governance.

Michael John Watts is "Class of 1963" Emeritus Professor of Geography and Development Studies at the University of California, Berkeley. He is a leading critical intellectual figure of the academic left and has published widely on African development, political ecology, social movements, and oil politics. He has authored, coauthored, or coedited more than fifteen books, including *Silent Violence: Food, Famine, and Peasantry in Northern Nigeria* (University of California Press, 1983), *Liberation Ecologies* (Routledge, 1996, 2004), *Violent Environments* (Cornell University Press, 2001), *Curse of the Black Gold: 50 Years of Oil Struggle on the Niger Delta* (Powerhouse Books, 2008), and *Oil Talk: The Secret Lives of the Oil and Gas Industry* (Cornell University Press, 2015).

Heather Whiteside is an assistant professor of Political Science at the University of Waterloo and Fellow at the Balsillie School of International Affairs. Her research centers on the political economy of privatization, financialization, and fiscal austerity. Her books include *Capitalist Political* Economy (Routledge, 2020), *Canadian Political Economy* (University of Toronto Press, 2020), and *Purchase for Profit* (University of Toronto Press, 2015); and she has published in journals such as *Urban Studies, Economic Geography, Environment and Planning A, Review of International Political Economy,* and *Cambridge Journal of Regions, Economy and Society.*

Index

Aam Adani Party (India), 168
Abe, Shinzo, 1, 271n1
accrual accounting, public land valuation and, 56–57
Actor-Network Theory, 210, 222–23
Adivasi tribals (India), 22; agrarian propertied classes and, 122–23; dispossession of, 120; Khed SEZ land acquisition and, 117
agrarian capitalism, waste land and food scarcity and, 110–13
agrarian studies: land grabbing research, 19–20, 272n8; Polanyi's fictitious commodities concept and, 31–32
The Agrarian Question (Kautsky), 261
agricultural land: commodification of, 68–70, 260–69; formalization fiction in acquisition of, 146–48; Ghanaian appropriation for gold extraction, 246–47; Indian conversion to nonagricultural use of, 38–39; Indian land ceiling laws and, 113; Indian social and ecological dislocations linked to loss of, 42–43; Khed SEZ project and, 115–20; special economic zone creation and retention of, 40–42, 104–6; as tradable asset, 108–9; unauthorized buildings on, 173–75; unauthorized colonies on, 161–67; Yonghe villages support for urbanization of, 190–92
agricultural practices: commodification of land and, 32–34; Indian land reform and property ownership and, 35–37; land commodification and, 28–30; research on, 19–20, 272n8
Agricultural Price Commission, 112–13
alluvial accession, land titling practices and, 92–97
Alternative Enforcement Program (NYC), 139
Amazonian Cosmos (Reichel-Dolmatoff), 259
American Water Works, 240
Annie E. Casey Foundation, 235
Appadurai, Arjun, 15
Arctic exploration, 269
asset management: currencies and sovereign debt, 79; institutional investors and, 75–80; intangible property and, 73; land as asset in, 66–71; in low-vacancy, working-class neighborhoods, 135–38; private-label safe assets and, 80–85; real property investment and, 70–71; scarcity paradigm and, 82–85
asset-price Keynesianism, 64; property bubble collapse and, 73–74
Audit Commission (UK), 58

bagayat land (India), 109–10
Balakrishnan, Sai, 3, 22, 104–23
Ballard, B., 152
Ballvé, Teo, 94
banana industry, land titling in Colombia and, 94–97
bank leverage, 75–80
Bank of International Settlements (BIS), 63
bank runs, financial crisis of 2008 and, 75–76
Banner, Stuart, 266
Barker, Joshua, 267
Basel Committee regulatory framework (Basel III), 63, 80–81; private-label safe assets and, 80–81
Bear Stearns, 75
Becker, Gary, 235
Bengal Famine, 114
Benjamin, Walter, 107, 164, 258
Bhabha, Homi, 171–72
Bharat Forge, 115
Bhide, Amita, 168
Biddulph, R., 152
big men culture, Ghanaian power structure and, 250–52
biopolitics, land and money in welfare state and, 73–74
BIS Basel Committee, 80
BlackRock, 70–71, 76
Block, Fred, 29–30, 33, 226–27
Boeung Kak concession conflict (Cambodia), 149–54
Bombay Tenancy and Agricultural Lands Act, 272n6
Brenner, Robert, 64, 263
Bruno, Joseph, 130
Bryant, Wayne R., 4–6, 18
building construction: in Delhi unauthorized colonies, 173–75; in Yonghe village (Guangzhou, China), 191–92

319

Burawoy, Michael, 29
business process outsourcing (BPO), Indian land market liberalization and, 37–39
Butler, Judith, 7–8, 164–66, 172

cadastral surveys: Cambodian land titling and, 144–46; formalization of agricultural land acquisition and, 146–48; Indian land reforms and, 36–37
Çalışkan, Koray, 11–12
Callon, 11–12
Cambodia: economic land concessions in, 151–54; history and geography of, 150–61, 229, 242; land titling and dispossession in, 22–23; sugar concessions of agricultural land in, 154–60; World Bank titling conflicts in, 149–54
Cambodia Development Research Institute, 152
Cambodian Ministry of Land Management, 144–46
Camden, New Jersey: housing demolition in, 279n4; human capital planning in, 234–38; labor market and urban development in, 238–42; land acquisition fraud in, 3–5; land and housing values in, 279n3; land fiction in, 9–10, 24, 224–42; marketization of land in, 228–42; mismanaged assets rationalization and land appropriation in, 231–32; urban land marketization in, 229–34
Camden Churches Organized for People (COOP), 240
Camden Planning Board and City Council, 237–38
Camden Redevelopment Agency (CRA): human capital planning and, 234–38; urban land appropriation by, 230–34, 279n9
Cameron, David, 53
Campanile, Phillip, 8
Campbell, Jeremy, 13
Campbell Soup company, 9
Canada: accounting treatments of public land in, 56–57; life cycle of property narrative in, 52; privatization of public land in, 46–48; privileging of privatization over in-government land transfer in, 58–59; public land data in, 58; revenue sharing and public land disposal in, 57; surplus public land fiction in, 20–21, 52–55
Canada Land Company (CLC), 59–60
Canada Revenue Agency, 45

Canadian National Railways (CNR), land ownership by, 46–47
Capital (Marx), 16–17, 263
capitalism: Indian urbanization and, 120–23; Keynesianism and, 64–66; land as fictitious capital, 131–32, 140–43; land commodification under, 30; land fictions and influence of, 51; peasant cooperatives and, 261–62; real property investment and, 67–68; security assumptions and, 72–73
cash accounting, public land valuation and, 56–57
caste politics: food security and, 114–15; Indian land-based social power and, 112–13; Indian land investment and, 22; Indian land reform and property ownership and, 35–37; Indian urbanization and land acquisition and, 122–23; special economic zone development in India and, 41–42, 104–6
centralized assets, economic shocks and flight to, 77–80
Chamroon Chinthammit, 154–56
Chatterjee, Partha, 107–8
chengzongcun (villages in the city): Chinese collective ownership and, 182–84; Chinese land appropriation and, 185–88
Cherokee Investment Partners LLC, 232–34
China: agricultural land commodification in, 264–65; Arctic exploration by, 269; Ghanaian gold mining operations, 243–45, 254–56; peri-urban land commodification in, 268–69; regulatory fiction and land expropriation in, 184–88; social backwardness narrative and land appropriation in, 23–24
Chordia, Atul, 1–2
Chordia, Sagar, 1–2
Christophers, Brett, 20–21, 30, 44–61
Cinturón Verde (Green Belt) (Medellín, Colombia), 86–87, 97–103
City Development Corporation (CDC, Medellín, Colombia), 97–103
class politics: Delhi's incremental infrastructure and, 175–79; food security and, 114–15; Indian land investment and, 22; Indian unauthorized colonies and, 161–67; Indian urbanization and land acquisition and, 122–23; land revenue in India and, 109–10; mismanaged assets fiction in low-vacancy, working-class neighborhoods and, 135–38; reinvestment in NYC property markets and, 132–35

Cocobod (Ghana), 251–52
Code Napoleon, French land commodification and, 28–30
coefficient rate, Vietnamese land compensation, 202
collateralized debt obligations (CDOs), 68
collective land: Chinese state-led village development and, 182–84; legal fiction of Chinese state power and, 184–88; urban planning and ideology of, 188–89; in Yonghe village (Guangzhou, China), 191–92
collectively funded apartments (Yonghe village, Guangzhou, China), 191–92
collective titles, alluvial accession practices and, 93–97
Colombia: alluvial accession and titling practices in, 92–97; housing and property ownership in, 86–91; internal displaced population in, 86–91; land restitution processes in, 91–97; property reconfiguration in, 21
colonialism: Canadian land ownership and, 46; frontier social imaginaries and, 266–67; in India, post-independence land commodification and, 35–37, 39–40; Indian agricultural land during, 109–10; land as collateral in, 66–67; land fictions and influence of, 51; Polanyi's fictitious commodities concept and, 31–32; safety fiction and, 64; waste fictions and, 106
commercial mortgage-backed securities (CMBs): reinvestment in NYC property markets and, 133–35; underwriting based on, 136–38
commercial mortgages, insurance industry investment in, 67
commodification/decommodification politics: countermovements and, 226–28; Indian land conflicts and, 114–15
commodity fetishism: land acquisition and, 259–60; Vietnamese land documents and, 204–5, 210–11
commodity fiction: countermovements and, 258–59; food scarcity narrative and, 112–13; fuzziness in theory of, 28–30; in India, 8–9; land acquisition and, 5–10, 26–27; legal fictions and, 15–16
Commune Land Use Planning (CLUP) program (Cambodia), 157–59
Communist Party of India, 111
Comparo property development company, 44–45

compensation pricing: in Indian human rights laws, 108–9; land documentation and, 217–23; Vietnamese Thủ Thiêm New Urban Zone demolition and, 206–11
Congress Party (India), 168
Cornwall Council (UK), 44–45
corporate buyers, privatization of public land and, 50
countercyclicality, institutional investors and, 76–80
countermovements: commodity fictions and, 258–59; Indian agrarian land disputes and, 40–42, 105–6; Indian urbanization and land acquisition and, 121–23; Khed SEZ land acquisition and, 115–20; politics of, 226–27; rent-related NYC housing and rise of, 125–26, 138–40, 141–43
The Country and the City (Williams), 10–11
Cramer Hill redevelopment project (Camden, NJ), 4–5, 13, 18; legal challenges to, 230–34, 279nn11–12
credit-default swaps (CDSs), 68
credit-rating agencies: conflicts of interest with, 81–82; subprime mortgage investments and, 68
creditworthy debt, private-label safe assets and, 82–85
Crown corporations, Canadian divestiture of, 47–48, 53–55
Crown land: Canadian land designation as, 46–48; in United Kingdom, 48–50
Cuomo, Andrew, 139–40
currencies, as assets, 79
cyclicality, institutional investors and, 76–80

dairy farming (India), grazing land privatization and, 119–20
Dalit groups (India), 22; agrarian propertied classes and, 122–23; social and ecological dislocations for, 42–43
de Blasio, Bill, 124, 139–40
De Boeck, Filip, 13
debt accumulation, NYC rent-regulated housing speculation and, 124–26
defaulted loans, rent-regulated housing in NYC and, 137–38
defensive fictions, 71–85
deforestation, land titling in Colombia and, 94–97
Delhi, India: town planning in, 167–72; unauthorized colonies in, 161–67
democratization, land rights and, 211–12
Denizen, Seth, 268

deregulation: international financial volatility and, 78–80; mass deregulation of NYC rental units, 0
derivatives, security fiction and, 79–80
de Soto, Hernando, 55, 62–63, 145
Deutsche Bank Research, 71, 76
Dikshit, Sheila, 167
Directory of Federal Real Property (DFRP) (Canada), 48, 58
displacement: Cambodian land titling and, 22–23; Camden, NJ urban land appropriation and, 230–34; documentation in Vietnam of, 211–16; Ghanaian appropriation for gold extraction and, 246–47; mismanaged assets fiction in low-vacancy, working-class neighborhoods and, 136–38; reinvestment in NYC property markets and, 132–35; slum clearance and, 129; speculative real estate projects and, 13–14; Thủ Thiêm New Urban Zone demolition and, 206–11; titling practices in Colombia and, 100–103
dispossession: Cambodian land titling and, 22–23; Ghanaian appropriation for gold extraction and, 246–47; Ho Chi Minh City evictions and, 200–223; Indian land commodification and, 20, 26–43; Indian rural land reforms and, 39–40; land compensation policies and, 41–42; land documentation and probability of, 212–16; Marxian theories of, 27; rights-based laws in India as safety net, 108; social and ecological dislocation in India and, 42–43
Djurfeldt, Goran, 261
Dodd-Frank Wall Street Reform and Consumer Protection Act, 63, 80–81
Dollar Wall Street Regime (DWSR), 77–80, 83–85
Dominion Public Building (Toronto, Canada), privatization of, 44–45
double movement of capitalism: agrarian land politics and, 105–6; Camden, NJ land marketization and, 228–42; fictitious commodities sociology and, 32–34; land commodification and, 18, 26–30; politics of, 227–28; rent-regulated NYC housing speculation and, 125–26, 131, 137–40, 141–43
Dreze, Jean, 113–14
Durkheim, Emile, 273n8
Dwyer, Michael, 22–23, 144–60

Eagleton, 14
ecological destruction: fictitious commodities concept and, 33–34; land commodification and, 29–30
Economic Development Authority (NJ), 238–40
economic development zone (EDZ) (Yonghe village, Guangzhou, China): sanctuary of the collective in, 189–94; urbanization and pollution in, 180–84, 195–99
economic efficiency, commodification of land and, 20–21
economic land concessions (ELCs), in Cambodia, 151–54
Economic Recovery Board (ERB) (Camden, NJ), 3–4
economic shocks, capital flight and, 77–80
economic stimulus narrative, privatization of land and, 54–55
economic value, fictions about, public vs. private land and, 51–55
economic welfare, defensive narratives concerning, 72–85
economization, market making and, 11
Eilenberg, Michael, 266
electoral politics, Indian agrarian propertied classes and, 122–23
embeddedness: Indian land reforms and role of, 36–37; Polanyi's fictitious commodities theory and, 29–30
Emergency Rent Laws (1920) (New York State), 128–29
Emergency Repair Program (NYC), 139
Emergency Tenant Protection Act 1974 (New York State), 130
eminent domain: Indian land dispossession and, 28, 39–40; Vietnamese Thủ Thiêm New Urban Zone demolition and, 209–11
Enforcement Rules for the Land Administration Law (1999) (China), 185
Engels, Friedrich, 274n2
English enclosures: land fictions and, 51; Polanyi's research on, 28–30, 34, 224–27
Environmental Protection Agency (Ghana), 245, 253
environment pollution: Chinese villagers protests against, 183–84; sanctuary of the collective in Yonghe and, 194–99
Ernst & Young, 71
Ethiopia, foreign investment and land displacement in, 246
European financial crisis, IMF and, 80

evictions: documentation in Vietnam of, 211–16; in Ho Chi Minh city, 200–211; NYC housing shortage and, 126–27
exchange values: compensation for Thủ Thiêm New Urban Zone demolition and, 207–11; food scarcity and, 114; privileging of privatization and, 58–59; Vietnamese land documentation and, 217–23

Fairbairn, Madeleine, 63
famine, food scarcity and, 114
Fannie Mae, mass homeownership and, 73
Federal Housing Acts of 1949 and 1954, 129
federal jurisdiction in Canada, land management and, 46–48
federal price controls, housing shortages and, 129
Ferring, David, 17, 24–25, 243–56
feudal land tenure, 263–64; Indian land reform and private property and, 35–37
fiction, in human experience, 89–90
fictitious commodities. *See also* land fiction; planning fiction; regulatory fiction; rental fiction; safety fiction; surplus fiction: fuzziness of fictitiousness and, 28–30; historical phases of, 32–34; money as, 75–80; Polanyi's concept of, 5–8, 26–27; sociological meaning of, 30–34
financial sector: Chinese land appropriation and, 185–88; defensive fictions and, 71–85; energy infrastructure and rural land investment by, 68–70; institutional investors and, 74–80; intangible property and, 73; land as asset in, 66–71; legal fictions and, 15–16; private-label safe assets and, 80–85; real estate industry and, 62–66; real property and, 64–66; rental fiction and uneven development and, 131–32; rent-regulated NYC housing speculation and, 124–26, 138–40; surveillance of, 80; wealth extraction and reliance on, 74
Financial Stability Board, 81
financing gap narrative, investment promotion and, 71
first-mover advantage: real property investment and, 83–85; subprime mortgage market, 80
First Nations communities: Canadian government land management and, 274n1; private land transfer transactions with, 59–60
food availability decline thesis, 113–14
food security narrative: agricultural land politics and, 104–6; waste land in India and, 110–13

Ford Foundation, 235
foreign investment: frontmen in Ghana for, 252–53; Ghanaian gold mining and, 243–45; Ghanaian land deals and, 246–47; Ghanaian policies for, 248–50; US national debt and, 78
foreignization of space, 271n3
Forest Act (1878) (India), 110
Forest Rights Act (India), 108
formalization, fiction of: agricultural land acquisition and, 146–48; Cambodian land titling as, 144–46; just-in-time public land formalization, 156–60; sugar concessions of Cambodian agricultural land and, 154–60; uneven geography in Cambodia of, 148–54
Fraser, Nancy, 29–30
Friedman, Eli, 34
frontier perspective: colonialism in India and, 106, 109–10; Indian land commodification and, 2, 113, 115, 120–23; land commodification and, 12–13, 265–69; NYC housing investment and, 135–36; property financialization and, 63, 68–70, 80–84

general equilibrium theory, 235
gentrification: Camden, NJ land appropriation for, 231–34; mismanaged assets fiction in low-vacancy, working-class neighborhoods and, 135–38
George, Henry, 260
Ghana: business and government power structure in, 250–52; cross-border land deals and, 246–47; frontmen for foreign investment in, 252–53; land appropriation in gold mining sector of, 24–25, 243–56; secretaries for gold industry in, 253–56; state policies and procedures and gold extraction in, 247–50
Ghertner, D. Asher, 1–25, 161–79
Global Financial Stability Report (GFSR), 79, 80
global property investment: financial sector and, 62–66, 70; formalization of agricultural land acquisition and, 146–48; gold market and, 243–45; real estate investment trusts and, 68–69; safety fictions and, 62–85
global systemically important financial institutions (G-SIFIs), 81
Glorious Revolution of 1688, 272n4
gold mining: Ghanian land appropriation for, 24–25, 243–56; Ghanian policies and procedures for, 247–50

324 INDEX

Gold Standard, 75, 77
government bonds, institutional investment in, 82–85
Government Property Unit (UK), 58
The Great Transformation (Polanyi), 6–7, 26–27, 32–34, 51, 227
Green Revolution, Indian agrarian development and, 110–13, 119
Grimsditch, M., 152
ground fictions: alluvial accession and, 95–97; land fluidity and, 21; soil and, 90–91, 97–103
ground rent potential: in Camden, NJ, 230; Delhi's unauthorized colonies and, 163
Grow New Jersey program, 239
Guangzhou, China: collective land ownership and urbanization in, 188–89; state land appropriation and regulatory fiction in, 185–88; state-led land commodification in, 180–99
Guggenheim Investment Partners LLC, 269

Hackworth, Jason, 132
Hanchett, Thomas, 67
Haraway, Donna, 7–8, 89–90, 95
Harms, Eric, 24, 200–223
Harvey, David, 11, 16, 37, 43, 67–68, 77, 157
Hausermann, Heidi, 17, 24–25, 243–56
Hayek, Friedrich, 278n2
Heidegger, Martin, 260
Henderson, N., 152
Henley, Kalvin, 269
Heseltine, Michael, 52, 54
highest and best use (HABU) appraisals (Canada): First Nations land transfers and, 60; privileging of privatization and, 58–59
Hirsch, Philip, 147–48
Ho Chi Minh City (Vietnam), Thủ Thiêm New Urban Zone demolition and, 204–11
home equity, wealth generation and, 73
homeownership: financial crisis and collapse of, 73–74; New Deal-Keynesian welfare ideology and, 73
Homestead Act (US), 72–73
housing policies: commodification of housing and land and, 131; erosion of rent regulation in NYC and, 126–31; legislative reforms in New York State and, 128; in Medellín, Colombia, 87–88; mismanaged assets fiction in low-vacancy, working-class neighborhoods of, 135–38; in New York City, 124; reinvestment in property markets and, 132–35; Thủ Thiêm New Urban Zone demolition and, 206–11; under-maintenance of buildings and, 135–40; in Yonghe village (Guangzhou, China), 191–92, 195–99
Housing Preservation and Development Department (NYC), 139
hukou (household registration): Chinese state-led village development and, 181–84; in Yonghe village (Guangzhou, China), 191–92
Hull, Matthew, 210–11
human capital, Camden, NJ redevelopment and, 234–38
human vitality *(renqi)*, 183; Yonghe village urbanization and, 192–94
hydraulic engineering: fertile and waste land geographies and, 111–13; land revenue in India and, 110

illegal construction, in Delhi's unauthorized colonies, 173–75
immigrant housing, mismanaged assets fiction in low-vacancy, working-class neighborhoods and, 135–38
improvisational urbanism: Delhi's incremental infrastructure and, 175–79; Delhi's unauthorized colonies and, 163–64
inappropriate objects, Bhabha's concept of, 172
Incoder rural development agency (Colombia), alluvial accession practices and, 93–97
income, wealth extraction and, 74
Inderst, Georg, 77
India. *See also* Rajasthan (India): class and caste politics and land management in, 22; colonial enclosure advocacy in, 51; commodity fiction of land in, 8–9; countermovement and land wars in, 40–42; government-based land classification in, 23; Green Revolution in, 110–13; land acquisition fraud in, 1–3, 8–9; land commodification and dispossession in, 26, 35–43; land liberalization policies in, 37–40, 106, 113–15; land tenure system in, 107–15; Maharastra land commodification, 105–6; private property creation and land reform in, 35–37; social and ecological dislocations in, 42–43; special economic zones in, 20, 27–28, 37–38; unauthorized colonies in, 161–67; urbanization of land in, 120–23, 272n7
Indian real estate executives, Trump's meeting with, 1–3

indigenous dispossession, land commodification and, 265–67
Industrial Workers of the World (IWW), 242
informal urban settlements, in Colombia, 86–91
information technology sector, Indian land market liberalization and, 37–39
infrastructure development: incremental infrastructure in Delhi's unauthorized colonies, 175–79; Indian land market liberalization and, 37–38; investment in, 68–70
in-government public land transfer, privileging of privatization over, 59
Inquiry into the Nature and Causes of the Wealth of Nations (Smith), 235, 264
institutional investment: defensive fictions and, 71–85; insurance industry and, 74–80; land as asset in, 66–71; mismanaged assets fiction in low-vacancy, working-class neighborhoods and, 135–38; public land disposal and, 21; in rent-regulated NYC housing market, 124–26, 138–40; safe havens and, 82–85
insurance industry: institutional investors and, 74–80; real property investment in, 67; reliance on, 71–72
intangible property, assets as, 73
International Monetary Fund (IMF): currency and debt assets and, 79; financial system surveillance and, 80–85; Ghanian gold extraction and, 248; private-label safe assets and, 79–85; safety fiction and, 63, 79–80
international monetary system, institutional investors and, 75–80
international property investment, safe assets ideology and, 82–85

jagirdari tenure, Indian land reform and private property and, 35–37, 273n14
Jaipur Development Authority (JDA), 40
Jayaraman, Nityanand, 110
Jeffersonian ideology, safety fictions and, 64 72–73

Kanersar Gram Panchayta, Khed SEZ land acquisition and, 117
Kautsky, Karl, 261–62, 281n1
Keynesian economics, safety fiction and, 64–66
khalsa land tenure, 273n14
Khed region (India), ant-SEZ protests in, 41–42, 104–6, 115–20

kinship and patronage networks, Ghanian power structure and, 250–52
Knuth, Sarah, 21, 62–85
Kramer, Susan, 54
Krippner, Greta, 64
Krishna, T. M., 110

labor market: Camden, NJ land redevelopment and, 238–42; competition in Yonghe village (Guangzhou, China), 191–92; fictitious commodities and, 34
Lake, Robert W., 1–25, 224–42
land, commodity fiction of, 5–10
land acquisition: in Camden, NJ, 3–6, 224–42; comparative land fictions and, 18–25; fictitious commodity paradigm and, 5–10, 26–27, 260–69; as finance asset, 66–71; in Ghanian gold mining sector, 243–56; illicit acquisition in Colombia, 94–97; Kautsky's discussion of, 261–62; land fiction and, 260; mineral extraction and, 17–18; security assumptions about, 72–74; Trump Tower India project and, 2–3
Land Acquisition Act (1884) (India), 39–41, 110
Land Administration Law (1986) (China), 182–85
Land Allocation for Social and Economic Development (LASED) project, 153–54
Land and the Given Economy (Mei), 260
Land Ceiling Act (1961) (India), 8–9
land ceiling laws (India), food scarcity and, 113
Land Clearance and Compensation Committee (Vietnam), 217
land commodification, 5–10, 26–27; in Canada, 46–48; caste politics and, 119–20; comparative analysis of, 18–25; double movement politics and, 227–28; in Guangzhou, China, 180–99; Indian land market liberalization and, 37–39, 106, 113–15; Indian rural dispossession and, 26–27, 35–43; instrumentalization of, 55–61; Kautsky's discussion of, 261–62; legal fictions and, 15–16; *longue durée* of, 259–69; oil frontier and, 267–69; as primitive accumulation, 107–8; rent-regulated housing in NYC and, 22, 125–26, 131, 141–43; soil as part of, 89–91; wage subsidies and, 224–25
land compensation practices, in Ho Chi Minh city, 200–223

326   INDEX

land concessions: Boeung Kak concession conflict (Cambodia), 149–54; Cambodian expansion of, 148–54; economic land concessions, 151–54; foreign investment in Ghana and, 246–47; frontmen for foreign investment in, 252–53; Ghanian business and government power structure and, 250–52; Ghanian gold mining operations and, 243–45; Ghanian policies for, 248–50; global property investment and, 147–48; sugar concessions in Cambodia, 154–60
land consolidation, land titling in Colombia and, 94–97
land documentation: cultural importance of, 216–17; property values and, 217–23; record modernization and digitization, 38–39; rights-based perspective on displacement and, 211–16; value worksheets, 217–20; Vietnamese eviction and compensation practices and, 202–5, 209–11
land fiction: Cambodian land titling as, 144–46; Colombian urban development and, 102–3; comparative analysis of, 18–25; countermovements against, 19; defined, 6–10; frontier social imaginaries and, 265–69; in Guangzhou, China, 180–99; land documentation and compensation and, 211; marine and oceanic appropriation and, 269; Polanyi's fictitious commodities and, 258–59; rent regulation in NYC and, 125–26; social stories in support of, 10–18; surplus land fiction, 44–45, 50–55; Vietnamese land documents and, 202–5
land grabbing research: evolution of, 271n3; rural development and, 19–20
Land Is Life (Cambodian Land Management handbook), 144–46
land laundering, in Colombia, 94
Land Law (Cambodia), 151, 276n4
landlord organizations: mismanaged assets fiction in low-vacancy, working-class neighborhoods and, 135–38; rent-regulated housing and, 128–31
Land Management and Administration Project (LMAP) (Cambodia), 148–54, 157
land petitions, in Ho Chi Minh city, 200–223
land restitution, in Colombia, 91–97
Land Revenue Act (1956) (Rajasthan, India), 36–39
land revenue system (India), 109–10
Land's End (Li), 265–66
land's fictions: commodity fiction, 5–10; scholarship on, 10–18
landslide of Villatina (Colombia), 98–99

land tenure systems: in Cambodia, 151–54; Indian real estate market and, 107–15
Land Use Rights Reform (1989) (China), 185, 190
Lanning Square (Camden, NJ) development project, 237–38
Larco Investments, 44–45
Latour, Bruno, 205, 210, 220–23
legal fictions: Chinese land appropriation and, 184–88; commodity fiction of land and, 15–16; land titling in Colombia and, 96–97
Levien, Michael, 20, 26–43
Li, Tania, 11–12, 110, 258, 265–66
liberal capitalism, land fictions and influence of, 51
life cycle narrative of property, 52–53; public land disposal and, 57–58
Local Government Planning and Land Act (UK), 58
Locke, John, 51
Lund, Christian, 265
Luxemburg, Rosa, 31–32
Lyons, Kristina, 89–90, 102–3
Ly Yong Phat, 154–55

MacIntyre, Alisdair, 18
Maharashtra (India): land compensation in, 109–10; special economic zones in, 115–20
Maharashtra Industrial Development Corporation (MIDC), 115, 118
Mahindra & Mahindra Group, 40
Mahindra World City, 40
Maratha-Kunbis caste: Indian land-based social power and, 104–6, 112–13; Khed SEZ and, 115–16
market forces: Camden, NJ land marketization and, 228–42; Chinese collective land ownership and urbanization, 188–89; commodity production and, 30–34; economization and, 11–13; food scarcity and, 114–15; Indian land market liberalization and, 37–39, 113–15; land commodification and, 27, 224–25; privileging of, over in-government public land transfers, 59; Vietnamese Thủ Thiêm New Urban Zone compensation pricing and, 209–11; Yonghe village market activities and, 192–94
Marston, Andrea, 268
Marx, Karl, 16–17, 272nn3–4, 273nn5–7; on commodity fetishism, 204–5, 259–60; dispossession theories of, 30–32; land commodification and theories of, 260–64; primitive accumulation theory of, 31–32

masculinity paradigm: Ghanian business and government power structure and, 250–52; Ghanian frontmen for foreign investment and, 252–53
material existence, appropriation of, 8
material instability, soil risk zones and, 97–103
McGreevey, James, 4
McKinsey Global Institute, 71
Medellín, Colombia: housing and property ownership in, 86–91; soil risk zones in, 97–103
Mehta, Kalpesh, 1
Mei, Todd, 260
MetLife, 67
Miescher, Stephan, 250
mimetic faculty: Indian urban planning and, 164; symbolic piracy and, 178
mimicry: Bhabha's discussion of, 171; in Delhi's illegal housing construction, 173–75; Delhi's incremental infrastructure and, 175–79; Delhi's regulatory fiction as, 161–67; state-administrative planning and, 23; as urban planning practice, 161–67
mineral extraction: land acquisition fraud and, 17–18, 24–25; land grabbing research and, 271n3
Minerals Act 1962 (Ghana), 247–50
Minerals Commission (Ghana), 247–50, 253–56
mining concessions, land acquisition in Ghana through, 24–25, 250–56
mismanaged assets fiction: Camden, NJ urban land appropriation and, 230–34; rent-regulated housing in NYC and, 22, 135–38
Mitchell, Timothy, 115, 123
Modi, Narendra, 1
money and moneylike assets, institutional investors and, 74–80
Morris, Meghan L., 21, 86–103
mortgage-backed securities (MBSs), 79–80; land as assets and, 76–78; US property bubble and, 73–74
mortgage credit and securitization: collateralized debt obligations and, 68; mass homeownership and, 73; real property investment and, 67; reinvestment in NYC property markets and, 132–35; rent-regulated housing speculation and, 131–32; safety fiction and, 65–66
multilateral institutions, agricultural land acquisition and, 146–48

Municipal Rehabilitation and Economic Recovery Act (MRERA) (Camden, NJ), 3–4, 9–10, 230–34, 279n9
The Mystery of Capital (de Soto), 55

Narmada Bachao Andolan, 108–9
narrative: fictions of surplus and, 50–55; in land fictions, 10–18; of waste, 106–15
National Audit Office (UK), 58
National Bureau of Economic Research, 67
National Food Security Bill (NFSB) (India), 108
National Health Service (UK), public land sales by, 49–50
Nationalist Congress Party (NCP), 3
National Rural Employment Guarantee Act (NREGA) (India), 108
natural law, land fictions and influence of, 51
The Natural Contract (Serres), 88–89
negative value, public land portrayed as, 52–55
Nehru, Jawaharlal, 35
neoclassical econoic theory, surplus land commodification and, 55–61
neoliberalism: financialization of real property and, 67–68; Ghanian gold extraction policies and, 248–50; Indian land development and, 37–39; privatization and, 45; property management reforms and, 64–66
A New and Comprehensive Vocabulary of the Flash Language (Vaux), 257–58
New Jersey Economic Opportunity Act (EOA), 238, 240–41
New York City: erosion of rent regulation in, 126–31; financial investment in rent-regulated housing in, 131–32; mismanaged assets fiction in low-vacancy, working-class neighborhoods of, 135–38; property reinvestment in, 132–35; speculation on rent-regulated housing in, 22, 124–43; wartime housing shortage in, 126–27
New York State Homes and Community Renewal (NYSHCR), 140
Nielsen, Erik, 52–55
nonmarket institutions, land commodification and, 26–27, 31–34
Norcross, Donald, 240
Norcross, George, 240
Norcross, Philip, 240

O'Brien, Kevin J., 202
occupancy claims of nonpropertied groups, Indian rights laws and, 108–9
occupancy fiction, in Delhi's unauthorized colonies, 173–75

oil frontier, land commodification and, 267–69
Orban, Victor, 264
Organisation for Economic Co-operation and Development (OECD), 71
overleveraging, safe assets management and, 81–85

Pakistan, land documentation and compensation in, 210–11
Panchshil Realty, 2–3
paramilitary violence: land titling in Colombia and, 94–97; urban development in Colombia and, 99–103
paramountcy (India), land reform and, 35–37
Patil, Shyam, 117
Pawar, Sharad, 2–3
Pearl River Delta, Chinese rural industrialization in, 187
Peck, Jaimie, 19–20
pension funds: institutional investors and, 75–80; real estate investment by, 67; reliance on, 71–74; safe assets ideology and, 82–85
performative narrative: Ghanian gold extraction policies and, 249–50; institutional investors and, 76–80; regularization in Indian urban development and, 164–67
peri-urban development: agricultural land acquisition and, 120–23; caste politics and, 119–20; Chinese land appropriation and, 185–88; collective land fiction and, 188–89; Delhi's unauthorized colonies and, 163–67; Indian land commodification and, 8–9, 26–30; Indian post-independence land dispossession and, 39–40; land grabbing research, 19–20; neoliberal economic policies and, 37–39; post-independence Indian land reform and, 37
personal security, land and real property linked to, 71–85
Philadelphia 76ers, Camden, NJ training facility for, 239–40
Physiocrats, 55
Pigs for the Ancestors (Rappoport), 259
PL-480 agreement (India), 111–12
planned illegality, unauthorized colonies as, 172
planning fiction: Chinese peri-urban development and, 188–89; Delhi's unauthorized colonies and, 161–67
Polanyi, Karl, 5–8, 14; on countermovements, 105, 121–22, 227–28, 258–59; double movement theory of, 18, 28–30, 125–26, 131; fictitious commodity theory of, 26–30, 51–52, 258–59, 274n1; Kautsky and, 261; on land commodification, 42–43, 89–91; on land tenure and security, 65; on market liberalism, 278n2; on money, 75; on security assumptions, 72; sociological perspective in fictitious commodities and, 30–34; on Speenhamland scale, 224–25
political parties: Delhi's unauthorized colonies and, 168–72; food security and, 114–15
Popular Liberation Army (EPL) (Colombia), 94
Portes, Richard, 78, 81–82
portfolio management discourse, surplus land fiction and, 56–57
postcolonial land markets, Indian urbanization and land acquisition and, 121–23
power of attorney contractors (India), 40–42
precapitalist economic systems: fictitious commodities in, 28–30, 32; land dispossession and, 43
preferential rents, NYC rent regulation and, 130–31
PricewaterhouseCoopers (PwC), 71
Primate Visions (Haraway), 89–90
primatology, storytelling and, 89–90
primitive accumulation theory (Marx), 31–32, 272n3, 273n5; Cambodian sugar concessions and, 154–55; Indian land tenure and, 107–8
"Principles of Responsible Agricultural Investment" (PRAI) (UN FAO), 146–48
private equity, reinvestment in NYC property markets and, 133–35
private-label safe assets, 78; real property as, 79–80; scarcity of, 82–85
private land: compensation in India for, 108; economic power of, 55; surplus land fictions and, 50–55
private sector, idealization of, in surplus fiction narrative, 54–55
privatization of land: in Canada, 46; fictional narrative concerning, 16–17; Indian land reform and, 35–37; portfolio management discourse and, 56–57; as privileged disposal strategy, 58–59; surplus fictions and, 44–45; transfer of authority concerning, 59–60; in UK, 48–50; in Yonghe village (Guangzhou, China), 191–92

property bubble collapse: financial architecture of, 68–70; small property owners and, 73–74
property formalization, Cambodian land titling and, 145–46
property regime rhetoric, 12–13; Indian land liberalization and, 38–39
protected land reserves, market making and, 21
Prudential Insurance Company, 67
public housing, introduction of, 129–31
public land: accounting treatments in valuation of, 56–57; Cambodian land titling conflict and, 149–54; Cambodian sugar concessions and, 155–60; in Canada, 46; Canadian Crown corporations' use of, 47–48; Canadian privatization of, 47–48; disincentivization of, 56–57; formalization of property rights to, 157–60; management narratives for, 53–54; routinization and normalization of disposal of, 57–58; surplus land fictions and, 50–55; transfer of authority for disposal of, 59–60; UK privatization of, 48–50
public-private partnerships: Camden, NJ redevelopment and, 240–42; Indian land market liberalization and, 37–38; public land transfers and, 59–60
public sector: demonization of, 53–55; portfolio management discourse in, 56–57; reconfiguration of, in surplus fiction narrative, 55–61; routinization and normalization of disposal of, 57–58
public space, in Yonghe village (Guangzhou, China), 192–94
Puig de la Bellacasa, Maria, 90

racism: fiscal subordination and, 279n11; home equity and, 73; mismanaged assets fiction in low-vacancy, working-class neighborhoods and, 135–38; reinvestment in NYC property markets and, 132–35; wealth extraction and, 74
Rajasthan (India): as land broker state, 39–40; land commodification in, 35–43; land reform and private property creation in, 35–37; special economic zone creation in, 40–42
Rajasthan State Industrial Development and Investment Corporation (RIICO), 39–40
Rajasthan Tenancy (Fixation of Ceiling on Land) Rules (1963), 36

Rajput clan structure, Indian land reform and private property and, 35–37
Rappaport, Roy, 259
real assets investment, financial sector promotion of, 76–77
Real Estate Board of New York (REBNY), 128–29
real estate industry: in Delhi's unauthorized colonies and, 175; Indian liberalization of, 37–39; Khed SEZ land acquisition and, 118–20; NYC rent-regulated housing and, 130–31; post-financial crisis boom in, 62–66; in rural India, 106; speculative projects in India and, 2–3, 8–9, 13–14, 272n7; transnational development in India of, 106–7; Yonghe village housing development and, 195–99
real estate investment trusts (REITs), 62, 65–70
real property: defensive fictions concerning, 71–85; defined, 274n1; as financial sector investment in, 66–71; global increase in investment in, 68–70; ground fictions and, 90–91; institutional investment in, 76–80, 83–85; as mainstream asset, 70–71; safety fiction and, 64–66; security assumptions about, 72–74
reembedding, Polanyi's assumptions concerning, 29–30
regulatory fiction: Chinese land expropriation and, 184–88; Chinese state-led village development and, 182–84; Delhi's incremental infrastructure and, 175–79; Delhi town planning department and, 167–72; Delhi urban planning and, 161–79; Ghanian gold mining operations, 254–56; Haraway's concept of, 7–8, 16; mineral extraction and land acquisition and, 24–25; state-administrative planning and, 23; theory of, 164–65
Reichel-Dolmatoff, Gerardo, 259
renewal energy infrastructure, investment in, 69–70
rental fiction: land commodification and, 141–43; uneven development and, 131–32
Rent Guidelines Board (New York State), 130, 133–34, 136
rentiership, financial crisis and growth of, 74
rent-regulated NYC housing: countermovement in protection of, 138–40; erosion in twentieth-century NYC of, 126–31; fictitious capital ideology and, 141–43; financial investors and, 131–32; housing commodification and, 22, 125–26;

rent-regulated NYC housing (*Continued*)
legislative enforcement of, 128–29; luxury decontrol process, 130; mass deregulation of rental units and, 130–31; mismanaged assets fiction in low-vacancy, working-class neighborhoods and, 136–38; reinvestment in NYC property markets and, 132–35; rent stabilization system (NYC), 129–31; speculation in NYC housing market and, 125–43
resource land, investment in, 69–70
revaluation scenario, privatization of land and, 54
revenue sharing, public land disposal and, 57
Revolutionary Armed Forces of Colombia (FARC), 94
rhetoric, in land fictions, 10–18
rights-based laws: conflicting clauses in Indian laws, 108–109; Vietnamese land documentation and, 209–11; Western liberal perspective on, 211–12
Right to Fair Compensation and Transparency in Land Acquisition and Resettlement and Rehabilitation Act (LARRA) (India), 41–42, 104–7; compensation clause in, 108–9; food security clause in, 109, 113–15, 119
Right to Food campaign, 113–14
Riles, Annelise, 15, 50
Rising Global Interest in Farmland (World Bank), 17
risky soil, urban development in Colombia and, 97–103
Riverton Houses complex, 133–35
Rockefeller, Nelson, 129
Rockpoint Group, 133–34
Rodenbiker, Jesse, 268–69
Rogan, Tim, 225
Rose, Carol M., 13
Roy, Ananya, 164
rural development: Chinese land appropriation and, 184–88; Chinese rurality (*suzhi*) coding and, 189; financialization of, 68–70; Indian land commodification and, 8–9, 26–30; Indian neoliberal economic policies and, 37–39; Indian post-independence land dispossession and, 39–40; land grabbing research, 19–20; post-independence Indian land reform and, 37
rural governments, Khed SEZ project and, 117–20

safe assets: collapse of, 78–80; failures of surveillance and, 81–85; financial sector search for, 64–66; paradoxical search for, 80–85

safety fictions. *See also* defensive fictions: global property investment and, 62–85
sanctuary of the collective (*jiti de bihu*): Chinese state-led village development and, 183–84; environmental pollution *vs.*, 194–99; in Yonghe village (Guangzhou, China), 189–94
Scheduled Caste, land ownership and, 36
Scheduled Tribes, land ownership and, 36
Schmitt, Carl, 265
science-studies scholarship, land fiction and, 11–12
Searle, Llerena Guiu, 107, 120
security, assumptions about, 72–74
self-determination (*zizhu*), Chinese pollution problem and, 183–84
self-regulating market: institutional investors and, 75–80; Polanyi's fictitious commodities theory and, 6–7, 33–34
Sen, Amartya, 113–14
Serres, Michael, 88–89
Shih, Mi, 23–24, 180–99
Shiromani Akali Dal party, 114–15
Shiv Ram Park Extension (Delhi unauthorized colony), 169–72
Shree Renuka Sugar Ltd, 272n7
slum clearance, displacement linked to, 129
small property owners, wealth extraction from, 73–74
Smith, Adam, 235, 262–64
Social Land Concession (SLC) program (Cambodia), 153–54
social order: fictitious commodities concept and, 30–34; Indian land-based social power and, 112–13
social violence, land fictions and, 14
social welfare laws (India), land dispossession and, 108
soil: at conflict sites, 90–91; material fixity of land and, 21; political ecology of, 87–91; risk zones and, 97–103; vertical land fiction and, 268–69
soil grant entitlement (India), 2, 16
Somers, Margaret, 29–30
Southeast Asia, agricultural land acquisition in, 147–48
South Jersey Legal Services, 234
sovereign debt: as assets, 79; institutional investment in, 82–85; safe assets ideology and, 82–85
sovereign wealth funds, real property investment by, 67

spatial relegation and justice: agrarian studies, 19–20, 272n8; land grabbing research, 19–20
Special Economic Zone Act (2005) (India), 37–38
Special Economic Zone Policy (India), 37–38
special economic zones (SEZs): agricultural land appropriation for, 104–6; avoidance of resistance to, 40–42; creation in India of, 22, 27–28, 37–38; Indian social and ecological dislocations linked to loss of, 42–43; market movement and countermovement and, 115–20
speculative real estate projects, approval process for, 13–14
Speenhamland scale, 224–25, 227
squatter settlements (Delhi, India), regulatory fiction concerning, 165–67
state-collective landownership, Chinese rural industrialization and, 187–88
state power: Chinese land appropriation and, 23–24, 184–88; Delhi's incremental infrastructure and, 175–79; frontier social imaginaries and, 266–67; Ghanian gold extraction policies and, 248–50, 255–56; Ghanian land appropriation and, 247; housing in Medellín, Colombia and, 88–91; Indian government and land dispossession by, 39–40, 43; Indian land classification and, 23; land appropriation in Guangzhou, China, 180–84; land commodification through, 26–27; neoliberal land reforms in India and, 38–39; regulatory fiction and, 168–72; safe assets policies and, 82–85; UK land privatization and, 48–50; urban land takeover in Camden, NJ and, 230–34; Vietnamese urban zones and, 24
Steen, Anthony, 53
Stein, Andrew, 130
Stellar Properties, 133–34
Subaru of America, 240
subprime mortgage market: collapse of, 68–70; first-mover advantage narrative, 80; return of, 62; safety fiction and, 64
Subramaniam, C., 110
subsea mining, 269
Sud, Nikita, 38
sugar industry: Cambodian agricultural land grabbing and, 154–60; Indian real estate and, 2–3, 8–9, 272n7
surplus fiction: Canadian military bases designation as, 47–48; Chinese land appropriation and, 187–88; economic stimulus narrative for privatization of, 54; financial dynamics of, 21; (dis)incentivization techniques and, 56–57; Indian urbanization and land acquisition and, 121–23; instrumentalization of, 55–61; narrative of, 20–21; privatization of public land and, 44–45, 50–55; privileging of privatization in, 58–59; transfer of authority and, 59–60
Swabhiman Paksh party, 114–15
Swaminathan, M. S., 113

Taussig, Michael, 171–72, 179
tax credits for housing construction, 128; Camden, NJ redevelopment and, 239–42
tenant activism: formation of, 126–29; housing code enforcement and, 139–40; reinvestment in NYC property markets and, 135
Tenant Harassment Prevention Taskforce, 140
tenant-landlord relationship: erosion of rent regulation in NYC and, 126–31, 138–40; NYC rent-regulated housing speculation and, 124–26
Tenant Protection Unit, 139–40
tenement landlord mythology: mismanaged assets fiction in low-vacancy, working-class neighborhoods and, 135–38; NYC rent-regulated housing and, 128–31
Teresa, Benjamin F., 22, 124–43
Thakkars, Khed SEZ land acquisition and, 117–20
Thatcher, Margaret, 49
Thompson, Evan, 263
Thủ Thiêm Investment and Construction Authority (ICA), 209–11, 217–18
Thủ Thiêm New Urban Zone (Ho Chi Minh City): demolition of, 204–11; evictions and compensation payments controversy in, 200–205; rights-based perspective on displacement in, 211–16
TIAA-CREF, 71, 76
titling practices: alluvial accession and, 92–97; in Cambodia, 22–23, 144–46, 149–54; communal title procedures, 153–54; global property investment and, 146–48; Indian land reforms and, 36–37; land restitution process in Urabá, Colombia and, 91–97; land tenure in India and, 107; large landholders consolidation and, 94–97; market making and, 21; soil ecology and, 90–91; soil risk zones in Colombia and, 100–103; World Bank procedures in Cambodia and, 148–54

Tönnies, Ferdinand, 32, 273n9
too big to fail ideology: private-label safe assets and, 80–85; real property investment and, 70–71
Town and Village Enterprises (TVEs) (China), 187
trade deficits, foreign investment and, 78
Trump, Donald J., Indian real estate executives meeting with, 1–3
Trump Organization: India market for, 1; international projects of, 1–2
Trump Tower Pune (India), 1–3, 8–9, 16, 18
Turner, Frederick Jackson, 266–67

unauthorized colonies (Delhi, India): evolution of, 277n1; illegal building construction in, 173–75; incremental infrastructure in, 175–79; regulatory fiction and, 161–67; town planning and, 167
undervalued assets fiction: NYC property reinvestment and, 132–35; rent-regulated housing in NYC and, 22, 126, 135–38
underwriting of mortgages, reinvestment in NYC property markets and, 133–35
UN Food and Agricultural Organization (FAO), 146
United Electrical Workers Union, 242
United Kingdom: accounting treatments of public land in, 56–57; Glorious Revolution in, 272n4; land release strategies in, 53; land scarcity narrative in, 52–53; privatization of public land in, 48–50; privileging of privatization over in-government land transfer in, 59; public land data in, 58; surplus public land narrative in, 20–21, 52–55; wage subsidies and land commodification in, 224–25
United Progressive Alliance (UPA) (India), 108
United States: frontier social imaginaries in, 266–67; Indian land development and aid from, 111–12; New Deal-Keynesian welfare state and, 73; property bubble collapse in, 68–70; reliance on financial sector in, 84–85; security assumptions about property in, 72–74; urban blight and obsolescence in land fictions of, 51
Urabá, Colombia: alluvial accession practices in, 92–97; land restitution process in, 91–97; paramilitary control of, 94–95

urban communities *(shequ):* Chinese village reclassification as, 181–84; Yonghe villages admiration for, 190
urbanization of the people, Chinese national development plan and, 181–84
urban land: Camden, NJ contested fiction of, 224–42; ceilings, Indian abolition of, 38–39; Chinese state appropriation of, 184–88; marketization in Camden, NJ of, 229–34; soil stability and, 90–91; surplus fiction in UK about, 53
urban planning: Chinese state-led process for, 181–84; Indian unauthorized colonies and, 161–67
Urstadt Law 1971 (New York State), 130
US Federal Reserve: financial system surveillance and, 80; safety fiction and, 63
US Treasury Bonds, institutional investment in, 82–85
utilities, privatization of, public land transfer and, 49–50

vacancy decontrol, rent-regulation and, 129–30
value practices: land as fictitious commodity and, 26–27; land development and, 16–17, 55; public *vs.* private land and, 51–55; reinvestment in NYC property markets and, 134–35; Vietnamese land documentation and, 217–23; Vietnamese Thủ Thiêm New Urban Zone compensation pricing and, 209–11
Vanguard, 71
Van Klinken, Gerry, 267
Vaux, James Hardy, 257
Vietnam, land petitions and compensation in, 200–223
village development, Chinese state-led process for, 181–84
The Village Voice, 136
Visser, Oane, 11–12
Visvanathan, Sri, 111, 113

wage subsidies, land commodification and, 224–25
Walras, Leon, 235
waste land: colonial India definitions of, 109–10; fiction narrative of, 106–15
wasteland, fiction of surplus land as, 51, 53–55
waste land: food scarcity and, 110–15; Indian urban expansion and, 120–23; Khed SEZ project commodification of, 115–20; as revenue waste, 109–10; subsistence land designated as, 106

"waste" lands narrative, Indian land investment and, 22
water infrastructure, Delhi's unauthorized colonies and lack of, 175–79
Watts, Michael John, 12, 25, 257–69
wealth: Ghanian power structure and commitment to, 250–52; land as, 66–71
Weber, Rachel, 63
well drilling, by Delhi's unauthorized colonies, 175–79
Whiteside, Heather, 20–21, 44–61
Williams, Raymond, 10–11
Wilson, Lewis, 4
Wolford, Wendy, 246
World Bank, 71; Cambodian land titling and, 148–54; Ghanian gold extraction and, 248; Inspection Panel of, 149–54, 160; land projects of, 17; land titling projects of, 148

yield gap ideology, global real estate market and, 62–63
Yonghe village (Guangzhou, China): economic development zone (EDZ) in, 180–84; environmental pollution *vs.* sanctuary of the collective in, 194–99; livelihoods protection in, 190–92; public space in, 192–94; sanctuary of the collective in, 189–94

Zeiderman, Austin, 98–99
Zhang, Li, 183, 192–93
Zhujiang New Town (China), 187–88

Lightning Source UK Ltd.
Milton Keynes UK
UKHW010748080221
378223UK00014B/204